VICTORIAN
SENSATION

VICTORIAN

SENSATION

Or, the Spectacular, the
Shocking and the Scandalous in
Nineteenth-Century Britain

Michael Diamond

Anthem Press

This edition first published by Anthem Press 2003

Anthem Press is an imprint of
Wimbledon Publishing Company
75–76 Blackfriars Road
London SE1 8HA

British Library Cataloguing in Publication Data
Data available

Library of Congress in Publication Data
A catalog record has been applied for

Typeset by M Rules

ISBN 1 84331 076 7 (hbk)

1 3 5 7 9 10 8 6 4 2

For Bell with my love.

CONTENTS

Introduction

Up and down the blessed town I run for information;
Trying to discover if there's any new sensation.
Politics and accidents and scandalizing too, Sir,
Either's all the same to me, as long as it is new, Sir.[1]

As so often happened, a music hall song perfectly expressed popular feeling, in this case, the Victorian public's delight in 'sensation', which dictionaries define as 'a condition of excited feeling produced in a community by some occurrence',[2] as well as the occurrence itself. However, by the early 1860s, when this song was being sung, sensation-seekers did not have to run around town: they had only to pick up a newspaper.

The Victorians enjoyed sensations as much as we do. It is true that restraint and decorum were highly valued, that many sensational subjects were taboo, and that the misdemeanours of the high and mighty were covered up where possible to maintain the social hierarchy. However, the effort exerted in keeping the lid on a scandal, or an unpleasant subject under wraps often meant that in the end the explosion was all the greater.

The Victorians had more opportunity than any of their predecessors to enjoy sensations, due principally to the unprecedented development of the press. National sensations were comparatively few until the middle of the nineteenth century, when the removal of 'taxes on knowledge' made newspapers affordable for the first time to the less privileged – who were particularly sensation-hungry. In 1853 the tax on newspaper advertising was abolished; 1855 saw the repeal of stamp duty on newspapers, which had hindered their distribution, and in 1861 paper duty was dropped. At about the same time the development of railway transport meant that national newspapers could reach an infinitely wider public. When a male heir was born to Queen Victoria in 1841, the *Manchester Guardian*, which appeared only on Wednesdays and Saturdays, declared, 'This intelligence was brought by an express train to Birmingham yesterday, and forwarded by the last train from thence to this town. Although it has reached us indirectly we have no doubt as to its truth.'[3] Even twenty years later this would have seemed quaint.

With the most important papers concentrated in London, it was easier to create a sensation there than elsewhere. *The Annual Register for 1849* reported that a murder in Norfolk had generated huge excitement, but another in Bermondsey even more, largely because 'the latter deed was perpetrated in the metropolis, the daily press of which was thus enabled to record [developments] with all the skill of practised journalists'.[4]

Victorians were well aware of the importance of the press. As early as 1850, at an anti-Catholic meeting in Liverpool, a riot was in progress when the Reverend Hugh M'Neile rose to speak. When he found he could not be heard, 'he drew up a chair, and sitting down, leisurely began to make a speech to the reporters'.[5] In later years Gladstone did the same.

Of the newspapers most often quoted in this book, *The Times* was the leading journal of record, and reflected establishment attitudes; the *Era* offered the fullest coverage of the world of entertainment; and the radical and republican *Reynolds's Newspaper* expanded the limits of what could be reported to a large Victorian readership. It also showed how a newspaper can sensationalize news with the use of intemperate and abusive language. In contrast, the *Pall Mall Gazette* was conventionally decorous until W T Stead took over as editor in the 1880s. Then it became a pioneer of the New Journalism. This involved, on the one hand, discussion of formerly taboo subjects, interviews with important people and noisy journalistic campaigns; on the other, making the paper more reader-friendly, with smaller pages and clearer, larger print, broken up by cross-headings. Until then, Victorian newspapers, however sensational their content, offered a mass of small type which the modern reader would find exceptionally off-putting.

Stead was influenced by the press in the United States, where sensational journalism is thought to have originated. The American showman Phineas T Barnum had taught the British how to create a sensation as early as 1844, and in 1851 the country was plunged into a craze for Bloomers: Mrs Bloomer was an American, whose revolutionary championing of a short skirt and long loose trousers fascinated British women, to the bemusement, and often derision, of British men. The following year an American novel, *Uncle Tom's Cabin*, created an unprecedented publishing sensation. However, the idea that 'sensation' itself was an American import was advanced most frequently during the 1860s, when the word itself enjoyed a particular vogue. To quote *Punch*:

> Some would have it an age of Sensation,
> If the age one of Sense may not be –
> The word's not *Old* England's creation,
> But New England's over the sea.[6]

Punch and other comic magazines loved to ridicule sensation, and so did the writers of music-hall songs.

The 1860s were the decade of the 'sensation novel' and the 'sensation play'. They aroused fierce hostility as well as enthusiasm, and the idea of 'sensation' as disreputable was strong at this period. An article in the weekly *All The Year Round*, argued that the public had always had a taste for sensation, even though the word had not always been used. It complained that the 'universal customer' was being unfairly accused of having an unnatural appetite for it, 'a diseased craving, an unwholesome fancy', 'something novel and of significant degeneration'.[7] It is no coincidence that several of the most important sensation novels were published in *All The Year Round*, whose editor, Charles Dickens, had long filled his own work with sensational elements, and was fascinated by murder. So was his friend Wilkie Collins, whose source material included press reports of contemporary murder cases. At a key moment in Collins's *No Name*, the heroine reads a newspaper account of a murderer's confession, which takes a 'fearful hold on her mind'.[8]

The plethora of Victorian sensations, particularly those involving murder and sex scandals, makes selection an arbitrary business. There has been no room in this book for an account of the Great Exhibition, which drew vast crowds in the summer of 1851. Reasons of space also make it necessary to exclude two whole categories of sensation. The first is disasters. By modern standards, Victorian Britain was a dangerous place. Apart from waves of diseases, of which cholera was the most sensational, life was beset with accidents of every kind. A single mining disaster could claim hundreds of victims, and deaths in railway accidents seemed to happen every week. There was a significant difference in scale between Victorian disasters and our own: the loss of 51 lives in the sinking of the *Marchioness* on the Thames in 1989 was a terrible tragedy, but when the *Princess Alice*, another Thames pleasure boat, sank in 1878 more than 640 people died.

The second excluded category is sport, in which there were few sensations anyway. Only horse racing, cricket and pugilism can really be considered as national sports throughout the period. Where the last was concerned, bare-knuckle fighting increasingly ran into trouble with the law, and when it was replaced by boxing under the Queensberry rules, no single fight equalled the sensation of 1860 when the bare-knuckle champion of England, Tom Sayers, fought in a bloody and spectacular draw with the American J C Heenan, an early example of an international contest. It was only gradually during the Victorian period that better travel facilities made international sport possible. Also, the Victorians were not as conscious of sporting records as we are. In 1895, when W G Grace scored 1,000 runs in May, *The Times* did not know whether it had been done before: 'It must be something of a record, even for Dr Grace.'[9]

Sporting crowds were not truly vast unless the spectacle was free, as at the Derby and the University Boat Race. Perhaps the greatest surprise is football's low profile. The FA Cup was launched in 1871, and the Football League in 1888. As late as the 1895/6 season average gates were still under eight thousand. Even in 1892, a bemused writer tried to explain to his south of England readers a new development: in most towns north of Birmingham, 'Saturday is consecrated to football . . . There is no mistake about it; the exercise is a passion nowadays and not a recreation.'[10]

If women were scarcely involved in Victorian sport, their importance as members of the sensation-seeking public was often remarked upon in print, usually with disapproval. Women read avidly of sensational trials in the newspapers, and were even buyers of the broadside accounts of murder cases. One seller of these ill-printed single sheets of paper is quoted as saying, 'Mostly all our customers is females.'[11] They also attended the courts in person, whether the trial involved murder or, from 1858, divorce. At the Courvoisier murder trial in 1840, the court 'was crowded with ladies dressed to the eyes, and furnished with lorgnettes, fans and bouquets'.[12] Women were particularly fascinated by cases that centred on a woman, who usually wanted a divorce or was accused of murder. In a letter to *The Times* a correspondent complained that when the death sentence was being passed on Maria Manning 'others of her sex were, by the aid of double opera-glasses, watching the misery of mind of the wretched criminal at the bar'. They had shaken off 'all the delicacy of the female'.[13] The *Pall Mall Gazette* attacked the female spectators at the much later trial of an alleged murderess: 'Hour after hour did these ghoulish women, armed with opera glasses, sherry flasks and sandwich boxes, hang with eager curiosity upon every movement and look of their miserable sister.'[14]

The male journalists who wrote these attacks could not come to terms with the new female assertiveness. Sometimes their vituperation passed all bounds: 'Those brazen hussies who thronged the court', when the resorts of prostitutes were open to them, 'have no right to intrude their loathsome presence upon the Halls of Justice. If the adultery they practise at home is not sufficient, let them promenade the streets while their husbands are away at the House or in the country.'[15]

The much deplored female taste for sensation also extended to fiction. Women more than men were novel readers and the sensation novel, often written by women, was innovative in its portrayal of strong-minded females. Even when these protagonists were wicked, many women readers seem to have identified with them. Women were at last beginning to rebel against their subservient position in society and, above all, in marriage. The sensation novel provided an outlet for resentments that were expressed more openly in the 'New Woman' novels of the 1890s.

There were strong-minded females in real life too – passionate, idealistic women like Josephine Butler and Annie Besant. They were thought to have disgraced themselves by the very act of addressing an audience. Harriet Beecher Stowe refused to do it, when she visited Britain in the wake of the *Uncle Tom's Cabin* sensation. If a woman spoke publicly on such an indelicate subject as venereal disease or birth control a furore was the result, but these brave women were showing the way to their twentieth-century successors.

The confrontational arena of the courtroom provided an ideal setting for sensation. Not all cases involved murder or divorce. For example, the two Tichborne trials caused unique nationwide agitation, and the drama of Irish Home Rule was played out before the judges of the Special Commission investigating the accusations against the Irish leaders. Time and again the courtroom, like the pulpit, was compared with the theatre, at a time when melodrama was the popular form of entertainment. At the time of the Manning trial, *Punch* featured the 'Old Bailey ladies'. One tells the other, 'You *can't* think what a fluster I'm in. Dear me! If it isn't more exciting than the Opera; and then you know, love, what makes it more delightful, it's all true.'[16] The magazine even accused Madame Tussaud's of advertising its figures of murderers as a theatre manager advertised his stars. During her trial for murder Madeleine Smith was described as stepping into the dock 'with all the buoyancy with which she might have entered the box of a theatre',[17] and examining the court 'with all the curiosity of a mere spectator'.[18] As defendants accused of murder were not allowed to give evidence Madeleine was a spectator at her own trial – but also, because all eyes were on her, part of the spectacle.

The rigid social hierarchy of the Victorian age meant that a sensation was all the greater if the protagonist enjoyed high rank. In life, in fiction and on the stage, even a wicked baronet always seemed wickeder than a villain without a title. A duke exercised power as well as prestige, as, to an appropriately decreasing extent, did other lords and their relations. At the top of the steep social pyramid was the Royal Family. Before the expansion of the press in mid-century, the poor, great seekers after sensation, were less likely to read a newspaper than a broadside, whose most popular subjects were royalty and murder. Both continued to feature strongly in the press long after the broadside had been consigned to history.

Between the Victorian era and our own day, everything has changed, and nothing has changed. We need to study Victorian social conditions to understand why particular events became sensational, but the answer to why the Victorians loved sensation lies ultimately in human nature. Curiosity, the inclination to idolize and demonize prominent figures, the tendency to wallow in emotion – the Victorians suffered from these weaknesses just as we do. The royal family and murder still sell newspapers; so does sexual scandal. Once defendants appeared in open court, they were as vulnerable to the press as their modern contemporaries. Sexual delinquents had a far better chance than now of escaping public attention, but once they were found out, the treatment they received from the press was not so very different from what it would be today. Attitudes toward the royal family have changed greatly; even here, however, the tales the Victorians told represent the origins of modern reporting.

CHAPTER 1:

Royalty

'There was an immense crowd of people outside the Palace, and which I must say never ceased until we reached Windsor Castle. Our reception was most enthusiastic and gratifying in every way; the people quite deafening us': *Queen Victoria on her wedding day*[1]

'When our present Prince Consort came among us, the people bawled out songs in the streets, indicative of the absurdity of Germany in general. The sausage-shops produced enormous sausages which we might suppose were the daily food and delight of German princes': *W M Thackeray*[2]

Who more likely than the monarch and her heir to cause a sensation – 'a condition of excited feeling produced in a community'? It was natural that births, marriages and deaths in the Royal Family should inspire strong emotion in the Queen's subjects: these were the milestones which marked their own lives. However, it was not until the Queen's Golden and Diamond Jubilees of 1887 and 1897 that royal occasions attained a new magnificence, and produced the propaganda triumphs that became routine for Britain's twentieth-century monarchs. Despite her brief periods of unpopularity, the jubilees inspired enthusiasm and love for the Queen that was infinitely more intense and widespread than could have been imagined at the time of her wedding in 1840. Perhaps the most important factor in this was the rise in imperialist and nationalist feelings, which came to centre on the monarchy. In a sense, the rapturous jubilee crowds were celebrating themselves.

The great royal occasions showed clearly the link between royalty and showbusiness. Most sensations, whether involving crime, scandal, politics or religious conflict, are unwelcome to those involved. The Queen, as the target of would-be assassins, and the Prince of Wales, with his embarrassing appearances in court, certainly suffered from them, but the devisers of royal entertainments came to rival showbusiness impresarios in the deliberate manufacture of sensations from which they and their clients benefited. Of course, they could not entirely control the public response, notably in the commercialization of the events, and the satirists, for whom official sensations were attractive targets.

It is well known that the Queen was revered at the end of her reign for her great age, but often forgotten that when she came to the throne in 1837 her youth was the great attraction. Of her two immediate predecessors, William IV had become king at over sixty and George IV had been nearly as old. There had not been a young monarch since the twenty-two-year-old George III came to the throne in 1760, scarcely within living memory.

In 1838, the government splashed out four times as much on the coronation of the nineteen-year-old Victoria as had been spent on that of William IV. A new crown was made, and in London public excitement was evident from the size of the crowds that descended on the jeweller's shop on Ludgate Hill where it was put on show shortly before the big day. According to the diarist Charles Greville,

> There never was anything seen like the state of the town. It is as if the population had been on a sudden quintupled; the uproar, the confusion, the crowd, the noise are indescribable. Horsemen, footmen, carriages squeezed, jammed, intermingled, the pavement blocked up with timbers, hammering and knocking, and fallen fragments stunning the ears and threatening the head; not a mob here or there, but the town all mob, thronging, bustling, gaping and gazing at everything, at anything, or at nothing; the Park one vast encampment, with banners floating on the tops of the tents, and still the roads are covered, the railroads loaded with arriving multitudes.[3]

The tents in Hyde Park were being put up by the cream of the nation's showmen, out to make a killing from the visitors to London. The fair was opened, on 28 June 1838, by a gong struck in the park just as the first gun boomed to announce that the Queen was leaving Buckingham Palace for the Abbey. Of the hundreds of booths and stalls many offered food – those selling gingerbread were the most numerous, but the most prominent was the huge stall of Williams, the celebrated boiled-beef seller of the Old Bailey. The crowds were exploited so successfully that penny loaves were sold for sixpence, while a pot of beer fetched the unheard of price of a shilling.

The organisers of the fair were the proprietors of the famous Richardson travelling theatre show, but there were also menageries, wax-works, marionettes, conjurors, acrobats, jugglers and other circus acts, not to mention peep-shows, roundabouts and a display of giants, dwarfs, the woman with two heads, the living skeleton and the pig-faced lady.[4] Viewing 'freaks' was a popular form of entertainment throughout the Victorian era, a cruel caricature of the taste for sensation.[5]

Huge crowds lined the Coronation route, and outside the Abbey they applauded the arrival of those they could identify. The Duke of Wellington, widely regarded as the greatest living Englishman, received the warmest welcome and Marshal Soult, who had fought – and lost – against him in Spain as one of Napoleon's commanders.[6] After the ceremony when the Queen drove back to the Palace she was still wearing the new crown, and holding the orb and sceptre, a bonus for the crowds, which were reported to be even bigger and more vociferous than before.[7]

Two years later, in 1840, the Queen married Prince Albert. The year had begun inauspiciously when three Welsh Chartists[8] were tried for treason against Her Majesty. Perhaps this made the authorities cautious for although paupers in parts of London and other towns were supplied with beef, plum pudding and beer,[9] the ceremony, on 10 February, was conducted in the small Chapel Royal of St James's Palace, rather than at Westminster Abbey or St Paul's. This not only limited the number of spectators, but greatly shortened the drive from the Palace, and thereby restricted the size of the crowd.

Charles Dickens wrote to a friend that 'Society is unhinged here by her majesty's marriage', and added, 'I am sorry to add that I have fallen hope-lessly in love with the Queen.'[10] He was joking, of course, and street ballads were even less reverent:

A hundred thousand a year he may get,
For taking the Queen, which is something to whit;
I myself had 'proposed', had I known it, that's flat,
For I'd willingly take her for much less than that.[11]

A satire on Prince Albert's good financial deal was published in the *Sunday Times*:

> Yes, love, I hasten back to thee,
> My fervent passion never doubt;
> Ah! I am sick of Germany,
> Of slender purse and sharp sour krout!
> With you, my dear, I'd fain be dining -
> Than German fare there can't be worse,
> I long to see a *sov'reign* shining
> I'll hold thee in my heart and purse.[12]

Dickens was aware of this strand of public opinion, as his reference to two street performers shows:

> *Question.* Vell, Mr Bull Sir, what is your private opinions vith respectin' to German Sassages – fresh as imported Sir from Saxe Humbug and Go-to-her?
> *Answer.* My opinion is Sir as they comes wery dear.
> *Question.* Supposin' Mr Bull as these here foreign sassages wos to cost the country a matter o' thirty thousand pounds per annewum, who do you think ought to stand that 'ere wast and enormous expenditer?
> *Answer.* Them as awails themseves o' the sassages aforesaid.[13]

For the rest of Victoria's reign German princes were associated with sausages, and the assertion that they came to Britain to marry money.

Reaction in the country to the wedding varied: In Liverpool it was 'impossible to convey an adequate description of the universal joyous manifestations', but in Leeds, although a holiday had been declared, 'the badness of trade prevented any public festivity from taking place'.[14]

The greatest sensations tend to be unexpected, and the biggest royal sensation of the year was not the wedding but the attempt on the Queen's life. By then, Victoria was not only a young bride but also pregnant. 'ATROCIOUS ATTEMPT TO ASSASSINATE THE QUEEN AND PRINCE ALBERT' trumpeted *The Times*, which announced that 'the name of the ruffian' was Edward Oxford, and that 'the sensation produced by this diabolical attempt upon the lives of Her Majesty and her illustrious consort among

*During the Victorian era Germans never shook off the accusation that they
came here to marry for money, and were the butt of many popular jokes
about German sausages.*

the crowd in the vicinity of the palace may well be imagined'.[15] The
Sunday Times reported, 'The excitement continues to absorb all other
topics of public interest . . . every hour unfolds more horror in the catas-
trophe.'[16] Oxford had fired twice at the royal couple, from only a few
yards away, as they drove up Constitution Hill in a small carriage in the
early evening of 10 June. The father of the painter John Everett Millais
helped in the arrest, and the young Millais and his brother saw it all. Years
later Millais' brother told his story: 'When we were the only people on the
footpath, and had just taken off our caps as the Royal procession
passed . . . a sudden explosion was heard, and then another. My father,
who had seen what had caused them, immediately rushed away from us
and seized a man who was just inside the railings of the park, and held
him till some of the mounted escort came to his assistance.'[17]

Oxford was a seventeen-year-old unemployed pot-boy. Evidence was
reportedly found at his home that he belonged to a secret society, but this
was never confirmed, and it was argued that public agitation increased
because of the secrecy in which he was questioned and 'the refusal to

*The widespread prejudice against German princes marrying into
prominent English families, evident in the case of Prince Albert, increased
throughout the century with each marriage that took place.*

afford the public authentic information on the subject'[18]. Oxford was
eventually detained in an asylum. If there had been a plot, it was unclear
who was behind it, but the public were shocked to be reminded that the
heir to the throne was the autocratic King Ernst of Hanover. Had Oxford
been a better shot, 'the oppressor would have been abroad, and close on his
track the insurgents whom the oppressor makes and infuriates.'[19] In an age
of Chartist agitation these were ominous words.

The Queen and her husband were much admired for their coolness in
the face of danger. Their demeanour was 'precisely such as a high-spirited
and noble-minded nation would desire to witness, on such an occasion, in
the occupant of the throne'.[20] The *Observer* claimed that Her Majesty's
life had been preserved 'by the interposition of Providence, never, perhaps,
more strikingly manifested before in the history of princes'. It referred to
the 'true heroism' and 'the moral courage, the coolness, the spirit' of 'our
young, our lovely, our beloved Sovereign' who was 'in a most delicate
state of health'. When the royal couple had concluded their visit to the
Queen's mother, they returned in their open carriage along the same
route. 'Who else would have ridden bravely back past the same spot?' the
Observer asked.[21] *The Times* reported one moment of weakness, which set
the royal courage in even sharper relief: 'On reaching her private
apartments she burst into floods of tears.'[22] It would be interesting to

know by what journalistic methods the paper came by the information.

For days afterwards, whenever she appeared in public, Queen Victoria was cheered, and when she visited the opera for the first time after her ordeal the audience rose to her and the national anthem was sung. The *Sunday Times* used the opportunity to denounce her wildest critics and their outrageous language of the previous summer. Then the Queen's unmarried lady-in-waiting, Lady Flora Hastings, died of liver disease. The Queen had wrongly supposed that her illness was in fact pregnancy. 'When they call to mind the descriptions of the alleged orgies and vices of the Palace, their allusions to the constrained abdication of King James, their incautious application of that accursed woman 'Jezabel', they must feel the rebuke of Providence and take warning.'[23] This was more a court scandal than a national sensation, but it had aversely affected the Queen's popularity.

Before 1840 was out, another royal sensation hit the headlines. At the beginning of December a young intruder was found under a sofa in Buckingham Palace, in the room next to the Queen's bedroom. He became known as 'the boy Jones' although Edmund Jones was seventeen. He was 'very short for his age, and has a most repulsive appearance'. He told the police that he had got in by climbing over the garden wall, then slipping through a window. He had heard so many people moving about that he had soon left by the way he came. However, he returned, and stayed in the Palace on a Tuesday night and for the whole of Wednesday, only discovered early on the Thursday morning.[24] He had entered the building two years before, but, in the words of *The Times*, 'the sensation appears to be even greater than he produced by his apprehension in the same place in December 1838'.[25] Now the Queen was married and had a baby whom Jones heard 'squall', he said. Apparently 'He wanted to see what was going forward in the Palace, that he might write about it', and he said that, if he was found, 'he should be as well off as Oxford, who fared better in Bedlam than he did out of it'.[26]

Jones's escapade was celebrated in the song 'The Boy Wot Visits the Palace':

> How he gets in most puzzles all,
> Through window is't? or over wall?
> But down the Chimney *I* should state,
> As that's the best way to the Great! (*Grate*)[27]

'How he gets in most puzzles all,/Through window is't? or over wall?'
Bruton's popular song was one of many reworkings of Edmund Jones's
dramatic intrusion into Buckingham Palace in December 1840.

Four years later, in G W M Reynolds's immensely popular serial novel *The Mysteries of London* a boy 'of about sixteen or seventeen, and very short of stature' is helped over the palace wall by two villains who want him to commit a robbery. This he fails to do, but he hides under a sofa on which Victoria and Albert sit to talk – and achieves a sort of scoop: he discovers that the two are in love and intend to marry. Reynolds notes characteristically of Victoria that 'her bust is magnificent'.[28]

The infant whom the boy Jones claimed to have heard 'squall', was a girl, destined to become Empress of Germany. However, a male heir was born on 9 November 1841 to general delight. Crowds collected around the Palace, and Prince Albert was cheered all the way from there to the Privy Council offices in Whitehall. However, the applause for the Duke of Wellington was just as effusive. When the national hero walked with a friend into Green Park the police had to form a circle to keep the crowd at bay and a police cordon was thrown over Constitution Hill. When the Duke reached his home at Apsley House, there was a final enthusiastic cheer.[29]

In this period sensational news was often transmitted to large numbers of people by an announcement in the theatres. At the Adelphi in London, proclamation of the royal birth was greeted by shouts of 'God save the Queen'. However, the 'the vocalists of the establishment' had not arrived, and the audience had to wait until the end of the performance, when the entire company collected on stage, and even sang an extempore extra verse of the National Anthem: 'O Lord, in bounty shed/ Joys round the infant's head . . .' The next day, a journalist wrote, 'Nothing could exceed the enthusiastic acclamation with which the last verse was received, and the manifestations of loyalty and joy displayed by the audience in all parts of the house exceeded anything we have ever witnessed.'[30] There were similar reports elsewhere. In Liverpool, 'brilliant audiences received the news with loud hurrahs', and 'God Save The Queen' was played 'amid the shouts and congratulations of loyal hearts'.[31]

Out on the streets, the event meant a big boost to trade for the ballad singers and writers:

> There's a pretty fuss and bother both in country and in town,
> Since we have got a present, and an heir unto the Crown . . .

It went on to mention the toys and other essentials the child would need, and the consequence to the nation:

> Now to get these little niceties the taxes must be rose,
> For the little Prince of Wales wants so many suits of clothes,
> So they must tax the frying pan, the windows and the doors,
> The bedsteads and the tables, kitchen pokers, and the floors.[32]

There was a darker side to the story. Political unrest was still rife, and at one of the many meetings called to congratulate the Queen, chaired by William Sherrat Ellis, a young potter, an alternative to the original reso-lution was passed: it offered congratulations, but pointed, too, to the poverty and suffering in the country. Less than eighteen months later Ellis was sentenced to twenty-one years' transportation for arson on perjured evidence. It was claimed that he had been a marked man from the time of the meeting.[33]

It was surely a result of the general excitement that, a few days after the birth, a madman rang the bell at the equerry's entrance at Buckingham Palace announcing that he was the Prince of Wales and that he wanted to see the Queen as he had a box of diamonds for her.[34] At least he was not dangerous: Victoria was attacked seven times during her reign. In 1842, John Francis was acquitted of firing a pistol loaded with a bullet at her, but convicted of using 'gunpowder and other destructive material'. He was sentenced to death for treason. Then, two days after the sentence was commuted to life imprisonment, John William Bean fired at her with a pistol loaded with paper, tobacco and just a little gunpowder. The news of Bean's outrageous act 'flew like wildfire through the metropolis' and was 'the all engrossing topic of conversation among all classes'. When the Queen entered the Park the next day, the appearance of the royal carriage 'was the signal for one long, loud and continued shout of hurrahs, accom-panied by wavings of handkerchiefs and hats'; not a head was left uncovered. Once again 'the news was communicated to the lessees of the various theatres' and attracted the same loyal response. At Her Majesty's Opera House in the Haymarket the opera had started when the Queen entered her box that same evening. The performance was halted by 'every possible demonstration of the liveliest joy'.[35] In the early years of her reign, the Queen experienced several periods of unpopularity, but each assassination attempt reversed that. She was certainly courageous in persisting with her rides along Constitution Hill and in Green Park. However, those responsible for her security were grossly incompetent by modern standards in allowing these rides to continue.

There was no bullet in William Hamilton's pistol when he fired at the Queen on 19 May 1849, again as she drove down Constitution Hill, but a year later she was hurt for the only time. A retired lieutenant of hussars called Robert Pate struck her over the eye with a stick as she was taking a ride in Green Park, this time with her children. Only the broad brim of her bonnet saved her from serious injury. Had the police not intervened the crowd would probably have torn Pate limb from limb. *The Times* declared that the attack would be received 'with burning indignation in every portion of the world where an Englishman is to be found'. The Queen insisted on going to the opera that evening – this time to Covent Garden – although the bruise was visible on her face. She did not arrive until the second act of Meyerbeer's *The Prophet*, when two or three voices from the pit began to shout, 'The Queen, God save the Queen.' The performance was stopped, and in seconds the whole company was on stage. At first, few in the audience knew of the attack, but news sped round the house and, according to *The Times* reporter, 'We have witnessed many exhibitions of loyalty, but never were present at one more spontaneous and generous than this.'[36] The sensation would probably have lasted longer, had not Sir Robert Peel fallen from his horse two days later and died.

On 29 February 1872 Queen Victoria had another fright. This time her attacker was politically motivated. The seventeen-year-old Irishman Arthur O'Connor pointed an unloaded pistol at her as she was about to alight from her carriage in front of Buckingham Palace. He was trying to force her into accepting the petition he held in his other hand, which demanded the release of 'the Irishmen known and celebrated as the Fenian prisoners'. He set his demands rather high: the prisoners were not only to be freed for the rest of their lives but to be as exempt from police supervision as any other of Her Majesty's subjects, and to be allowed to go back to Ireland or go wherever else they might choose. The Queen had been confronted not by a madman but by a boy who did not understand the hopelessness of his actions. According to O'Connor, the Fenian who had shot a policeman had been justified in doing so, and he would have done the same. He himself was ready to die, he said, but he demanded that he should receive the death due to him 'as a Christian and a republican': in other words he should not be 'strangled' but shot, and his body given to his friends. In the event, he was sentenced to a year's hard labour and twenty strokes of the birch. Even after he had pleaded guilty, the defence persisted in using insanity as mitigation: a number of his relations had been declared insane, including Feargus O'Connor, the Chartist leader.[37]

On the day Roderick Maclean fired on the Queen in March 1882, the Prince of Wales was due at the Royal Court Theatre. He decided to carry on with his visit 'to allay public anxiety'. When he realised that on hearing the news, some of the audience had begun to leave he authorised an announcement to be made saying that his mother had suffered no ill effects. This was received 'with great cheering by a crowded audience who rose to the Prince in a body'. Neither did the Queen's daughter, Princess Louise, put off her visit to the opera that night. *The Times* struck a modern note when it declared the next day, 'There is a kind of infamous notoriety, much coveted by some disorderly minds, which can be easily and certainly earned by such deeds.' To have fired on the Queen of England 'confers on the culprit a most unenviable distinction, but a distinction none the less'.[38] Queen Victoria was the ultimate celebrity target.

The Prince of Wales, who had created a sensation by being born, brought off another coup in getting married. It helped that his bride, Princess Alexandra of Denmark, was very beautiful. But the ceremony on 10 March 1863 was held at St George's Chapel, Windsor. The Queen did not use her family's marriages for publicity purposes as ruthlessly as General Booth used his to glorify the Salvation Army. However, Alexandra's journey from the coast, by royal yacht, train and carriage, up the Thames and through London to Paddington station, was a triumph. The Prince was waiting for her at Gravesend, and earned rapturous applause by dashing up the ship's gangway to kiss her. As the young couple stepped on to Gravesend pier, they were greeted by girls dressed in the Danish national colours of white and red, who scattered spring flowers at their feet. The royal couple's special train to Southwark had to crawl along as so many people spilled on to the line, and it took four hours to travel from Southwark to Paddington – the police could not prevent their cordons being breached. They crossed London Bridge into the City and from there drove along the Strand, Pall Mall, St James's Street and Piccadilly.[39] 'It is curious to see London gone mad,' Dickens wrote. 'Down in the Strand here, the monomaniacal tricks it is playing are grievous to behold, but along Fleet Street and Cheapside it gradually becomes frenzied . . . At London Bridge it raves.'[40]

In a novel of the same year, *John Marchmont's Legacy*, Mary Braddon, the author of *Lady Audley's Secret*, referred to 'that triumphant journey of last March, when the Royal bridegroom led his Northern bride through a surging sea of eager, smiling faces, to the musical jangling of a thousand bells'.[41] The crowds were more sensational than the procession, which many thought should have been more splendid. According to Edward VII's biographer, Sir Sidney Lee, 'Everywhere in the British Isles and the colonies the wedding was celebrated with a barely paralleled ardour. Bonfires on the highest hills and illuminations of all the cities of the United Kingdom (save Dublin) testified to the national good will.' Forty years later the Bishop of Ripon told the Prince of Wales how, as an undergraduate, he had been nearly crushed to death by the crowd in Cambridge. So many people wanted to read about all this that newspaper sales rocketed – *The Times* nearly doubled its circulation.[42]

However, as is well known, the Prince of Wales was not a faithful husband. On 16 February 1870, a case opened that provided one of the two embarrassing occasions when he was questioned in a court of law. The so-called Mordaunt divorce case was not about divorce as much, but had to determine whether Lady Mordaunt had been sane enough for a divorce suit to be brought against her at the time the writ was served. When the trial opened it was generally agreed that she had gone off her head. The Prince's appearance in the witness box made the case the sensation it became.[43] In his evidence Sir Charles Mordaunt said: 'I was also aware that the Prince of Wales had an acquaintance with my wife . . . He never came to my house at my invitation. I warned my wife against continuing the acquaintance with his Royal Highness for reasons which governed my own mind. I did not enter into particulars. I told her I had heard in various quarters circumstances connected with the Prince's character which caused me to make that remark.'

Then Sir Charles spoke of the confession his wife had made to him soon after she had given birth to a daughter: 'She said, "Charlie, you are not the father of that child; Lord Cole is the father of it, and I am the cause of its blindness." She was silent a quarter of an hour, and then burst into tears, and said "Charlie, I have been very wicked; I have done very wrong." I said, "Who with?" She said, "With Lord Cole, Sir Francis Johnstone, the Prince of Wales and others, often in open day".'[44]

Lady Mordaunt's confession came about after she had expressed surprise that Lord Cole, later the 4th Earl of Enniskillen, was still a bachelor. Sir

GEORGE LEWIS.

H.R.H
THE PRINCE
OF WALES

OCCUPIED A
SEAT

ON THE LEFT OF
THE LORD
CHIEF
JUSTICE

MRS
LYCETT
GREEN

The Mordaunt divorce suit involved investigation of an alleged liaison between Lady Mordaunt and the Prince of Wales: his appearance in the witness box turned the case into a sensation.

Charles had told her that he was thought to suffer from a disease which prevented him marrying. In a guilty panic, Lady Mordaunt decided that her daughter's eye problem was the result of syphilis, and confessed. Sir Charles came reluctantly to believe her and, according to him, there was never any doubt of her guilt until her father intervened: her family insisted that she was suffering from a form of dementia caused by childbirth. Sir Charles was convinced that Lady Mordaunt had been persuaded by her father to feign madness. For the family to be saved from disgrace, and perhaps for the Prince's guilt to be covered up, the admission of adultery had to have been made by a mad woman. Lady Mordaunt's father, Sir Thomas Moncreiffe, it seemed, preferred his daughter to be thought mad than adulterous.

However, it was not Lady Mordaunt's reputation that the public cared about, and the excitement in court can be imagined when the Prince was called. Sir Thomas's counsel questioned him:

'Were you acquainted with Lady Mordaunt before her marriage?'
'I was.'
'On her marriage did your Royal Highness write to her and make some wedding present?'
'I did.'. . .
'And has she gone to the theatre with both your Royal Highnesses?'
'She has.'. . .
'I have only one more question to trouble your Royal Highness with. Has there ever been any improper familiarity or criminal act between yourself and Lady Mordaunt?'
'There has not.'[45]

There was a burst of applause which was at once repressed.

At the end of this exchange it was expected that Sir Charles's counsel would cross-examine the Prince. However, he did no such thing. The Prince was cheered as he left the court, but Sir Charles was furious. Had his counsel been got at? Had eminent doctors, with royal connections, been got at? The latter had convinced the jury that, when divorce proceedings were started, Lady Mordaunt had not been sane enough to instruct counsel, even though local doctors who knew her better had said the opposite. Sir Charles also wondered if pressure had been put on the judge to stress the evidence which indicated an early onset of madness over that which did not.

More suspicions arose over who would pay for Lady Mordaunt's upkeep and Sir Charles and his father-in-law had a mighty row about it. Matters were resolved eventually when an unknown person agreed to contribute. A few years later Sir Charles was granted his divorce when his wife's wits returned long enough for the case to proceed: Lord Cole pleaded guilty, so the divorce was given on the grounds of Lady Mordaunt's adultery with him alone; the culpability of her other alleged partners was not investigated further. Had somebody got at Lord Cole to make him renege on his previous denials? Had he been bribed to ensure that the Prince did not appear in court again, when he might have been cross-examined?

Nothing could be more sensational than the heir to the throne being asked in public whether he had committed adultery. Although in this case he might well not have done so – his letters to Lady Mordaunt were innocuous – the trial gave the public an inkling of what was already known to the privileged few: that the Prince and his friends had a lot to hide. *The Times* was certainly over-generous in its comment: 'It is evident that the Prince's error was simply this – that he had been too careless of his reputation. He had acted as a young man who did not understand the passion too many have for scandal, and he had given occasion to misconstruction through simple heedlessness.'[46] However, two months later a Sheffield paper dared to report that the Prince was likely to be cited as a co-respondent in the divorce between the Earl and Countess of Sefton. At the end of the year, when Sir Edward Hamilton was debating whether to accept the post of tutor to the Prince's eldest son, Prince Eddy, his mother told him, 'I have heard things said about the Prince of Wales that make me afraid that he himself and those about him are not what they ought to be, and it is a very grave question, whether it is right to place oneself in an atmosphere of evil for any consideration on the other side.'[47] 'Evil' was a remarkable word to choose.

The Prince's siblings were far less important than he, of course, and their best chance of causing a sensation was through marriage. The wedding that most nearly rivalled that of the heir to the throne took place on 21 March 1871 between the Queen's fourth daughter, Princess Louise, and the Marquess of Lorne. It was wildly popular: Louise's three older sisters had all married Germans, and the prejudice against German marriages, so evident in the case of Prince Albert, had increased with each one that took place. The Marquess was the eldest son of the 8th Duke of

Argyll, whose lineage was thought in Scotland to be quite as good as the Royal Family's. It was the first time that the daughter of a reigning sovereign had wed a commoner since 1515. Argyll was a member of Gladstone's cabinet, and Lorne himself a Liberal MP, but fears that the Crown might be dragged into politics were not borne out. More people worried instead about the thirty thousand pounds voted to Louise by Parliament, although at least it would be spent at home. *Punch's* description of the engagement as 'A Real German Defeat'[48] was much quoted. Henry Parker, composer of the Louise–Lorne quadrilles, also wrote 'The Louise-Lorne Wedding Day Grand Matrimonial Fantasia arranged on united Scotch and English melodies. A REAL GERMAN DEFEAT'. The music halls, too, loved to cock a snook at German princes:

> But talking of 'marriage' reminds me,
> We've given the Germans a shake,
> They fancied Louise and her cash was for them,
> That's where they made their mistake.[49]

A broadside ballad, sold in the streets, took the same line:

> They may leave off fishing for England's crown
> For oatmeal's gone up, German sausages down.

However, it also comments on Louise's dowry:

> But as times they are hard & money is scarce,
> It's rather a long pull for Johnny Bull's purse,
> Don't think I joke, but as the job must be done,
> Why I'd take her myself for just half of the sum.[50]

This was the old joke which had been told at the Queen's wedding thirty years earlier. The ballad 'Came the Lord of Lorne a Wooing' evinces a more elevated tone:

> Foreign princes would have sought her,
> Noble suitors, sons of kings,
> But the heart of England's daughter
> To her mother country clings.[51]

THE WEDDING OF
Louise and Johnny of Lorne.

They say I'm too young, but I am not I'm sure
For my dear mammy she did it before,
Or I should not have been here, it's the truth
    I am speaking,
And if Johnny's no tin I've enough to keep him
For kind Johnny Bull will bawbees dub down,
With nice yellow boys, 30,000 bright pounds
And 6000 a-year, and I'm cheap at the price
You'll say it is naughty, but I'm sure it is nice

Now there's my German cousins think it too bad
That their combs should be cut by this braw
    Highland lad,
They may leave off fishing for England s crown
For oatmeal's gone up, German sausages down
I am glad said John Bull, their hopes are up
    the flue,
We had Cobugs & Wertenbugs,& humbugs too
Let 'em put it in their pipes & smoke it at home
If we want any bugs we've some of our own.

As thro' life this young couple jog on together
O'er the hills far away, in the blooming heather
The rose and the thistle will then be combined
But I hope that no thorn in their path they
    will find,
But good luck to them both, is what I now say
If they've children a score we the piper will pay
What's the odds, if you're happy, don't give
    way to sorrow,
If I had Johnny Lorn's chance I would
    marry to-morrow.

You that are fond of fun just listen awhile,
    ditty I'll sing that will cause you to smile,
For the lines I have pen'd is sure for to please
It's concerning the wedning of charming Louise
She'll be married at last, oh, is it not fun,
To a bave highland lad, one of Scotia's sons,
They'll be married in March, and that in
    paime style,
And Louise will sing bless the Duke of Argyle.
CHORUS.
All Scotland will dance, while bagpipes do play
For the 21st of March is Louise wedding day,
at the castle at Windson the trick will be done
With Johnny of Lorne, Argyle's eldest son.

Now little Louise without any mistake.
Fell in love with a lad from the land of cakes,
For she said my dear sisters have husbands
    you see,
and dear little babies to dance on their knees.
So I taink to live single it is a great shame,
and I'm sure that the lasses cannot me blame
Don't I love my Johnny, the brave lord of Lorn
He'll be useful in winter to keep my back warm

Now I've one thing to say 'ere I finish my song
And I think you'll say, I'm not in the wrong,
I think it is rather stiff to go begging round
Tho' it's just the old style to raise a few pound
But as times they are hard & money is scarce,
It is rather a long pull for Johnny Bull's purs
Don't think I joke, but as the job must b
    done,
Why I'd take her myself just for half of the
    sum.

Disley, Printer, High Street, St. Giles.

The wedding between Princess Louise, the queen's fourth daughter, and the Marquis of Lorne was wildly popular. Contemporary media billed the match as 'A Real German Defeat'.

The marriage also inspired digs at the French: the wedding at Windsor coincided almost to the day with the arrival at Dover of the deposed Emperor of France, Napoleon III, to begin his exile in England. It was also the time of the Paris Commune: headlines like 'The Reds Hold Paris' were accompanied in the illustrated journals by artists' impressions of the carnage.[52] The press made much of the merits of the British monarchy, and compared the tranquil state of Britain with the turmoil across the Channel.

The wedding ceremony provided the newspapers with colourful copy. It was a beautiful spring day, and Queen Victoria herself gave away the bride. Apart from the bride and groom, the Queen and the Prince of Wales, the star attractions were two men in remarkable but contrasting tribal dress. One was the groom's father, who wore a kilt in the Campbell tartan, complete with sporran and claymore, with a green scarf over his shoulder, and his Order of the Thistle. The other was Maharajah Duleep Singh, in the traditional silk turban of the Punjab and yellow pyjamas, with his Indian sword. Like his wife, who was resplendent in red and gold, the Maharajah sparkled with diamonds and emeralds.[53] The picturesque Highland dress inspired a London music hall entertainment in which Scottish songs were sung against a backdrop of Scottish castle and Highland scenery and young ladies performed the Highland Fling and the Sword Dance.

Before 1871 ended, there was a sensation of a darker kind: the Prince of Wales contracted typhoid and was at death's door. It was exactly ten years since his father, Prince Albert, had died of the same disease. The Earl of Chesterfield, a friend of the Prince, and the Prince's groom, who had fallen ill at the same time, died, but the Prince recovered. The spontaneous outburst of national joy was widely credited with stifling an upsurge of republican sentiment and making the throne safe for the rest of Victoria's reign.

The republican's most effective advocate was Sir Charles Dilke, MP for Chelsea, and reaction to his speaking campaign at the end of the year is a significant reflection of public opinion. In a speech at Newcastle on 6 November 1871, which caused quite a stir, Dilke stressed the unfairness and extravagance of the Royal Family's privileges, and referred to the Prince of Wales, 'who would never be allowed a command in time of war', having been 'put to head the Cavalry Division in the Autumn Manoeuvres, thus robbing working officers

of the position and of the training they had a title to expect'.[54] Reaction
to the speech was overwhelmingly hostile, and even more so when the
nature of the Prince's illness was made public on 23 November. That
evening Dilke, who had already had a hard time in Bristol, spoke at
Leeds town hall. A vast crowd turned up to sing the National Anthem
and give three cheers for the Queen, so Dilke backtracked, saying he
wanted reform of the monarchy rather than abolition.[55] At his meeting
in Bolton on 30 November rioting erupted and a man was killed. Dilke
was finally defeated in January 1872 when a vestry meeting in Chelsea
voted by a majority of two to allow him the use of a hall to address his
constituents, but advised him to postpone the event for a month 'in consequence of the illness of the Prince of Wales and the present disturbed
state of public feeling'.[56]

27 February, 1872, was declared National Thanksgiving Day and the
Queen accompanied her son through dense, cheering crowds to a service
at St Paul's; onlookers hung from the branches of trees and the tops of
iron palings. *The Times* referred to 'an event for ever remarkable in the history of England', and claimed that 'no monarch ever saw such a spectacle
as Queen Victoria did yesterday'. However, as in the case of the Prince's
wedding procession, this was attributed to the size and enthusiasm of the
crowd rather than to the spectacle provided by officialdom: 'Almost any
minor state of Europe would have made a more imposing military display.' The paper provided three pages of detailed description of the
London celebrations, street by street.[57] The *Illustrated London News*
showed, among many other pictures, the extraordinary Gothic arch built
at Ludgate Circus.[58] Commercial interests, of course, took full advantage:
in houses along the route five guineas was the going rate for a seat and
fifty for the hire of a room. Private speculators built stands at many of the
best vantage points, the most prominent on the area where the new Law
Courts were to be built, overlooking the spot where the royal procession
met up with the Lord Mayor's.[59]

The provinces joined in the celebrations. In York, most shops closed
and there were special church services. In the evening the Mansion House
was lit up by gas, the façade bearing a large wreath with the monogram
AE (Albert Edward) on each side and the Prince of Wales' feathers on
top. In Liverpool the theatres and music halls rang to the sound of 'God
Save the Queen', and 'God Bless the Prince of Wales'.[60] The latter had
been written in 1862 in the Prince's honour by the Welsh composer

Brinsley Richards and almost rivalled the national anthem, but new compositions celebrated his recovery:

> England greets thee Prince of Wales,
> Rising from thy couch of pain,
> Through the land resounds the cry,
> 'Welcome to our hearts again'.[61]

Even Tennyson joined the loyal outpourings: he added an epilogue to his 'Idylls of the King', addressed to Queen Victoria:

> When, pale as yet, and fever-worn, the Prince
> Who scarce had pluck'd his flickering life again
> From halfway down the shadow of the grave,
> Past with thee through thy people and their love,
> And London roll'd one tide of joy thro' all
> Her trebled millions . . .

According to the *Manchester Guardian*, 'An extraordinary reversion of feeling towards the Prince has taken place during the last few months, and he has suddenly come to be one of the most popular men in the country . . . If ever there was a display of popular feeling it was seen yesterday.' It concluded that 'timid and bigoted people' should have more faith in the monarchy, and stop hurling brickbats at republicans. 'Surely we can afford to let Sir Charles Dilke alone.' However, it also alluded to the responsibilities of the future monarch: 'At the top of all stands the sovereign, who by the mere force of his example may without exaggeration be said to set the tone of morals and of manners for the whole nation.'[62]

If some people still suspected that the Prince was ill-suited to give such a lead, the unsavoury side of his reputation, to which the Mordaunt case had drawn attention, was now brushed aside. In any case, there was a positive angle to his love of pleasure. While, to the public's dismay, his mother shut herself away at Osborne, the Prince's appearance at theatres, music halls, racecourses and regattas maintained the popularity of the Crown. He identified himself with popular causes such as the campaign to open museums on Sundays and was at is best when entertaining royal visitors, of whom the most prestigious was the Sultan of Turkey.

Although the Ottoman Empire was in decline, no one with any

historical sense could fail to see the visit in July 1867 as sensational, and
The Times rose to the occasion: 'Yesterday, for the first time in England's
history, the great chief of the Mussulman race, the representative of the
last line of Caliphs and Sultans, whose power, a little more than a century
ago, was the dread of Western Europe, landed on our shores.'[63] However,
what historians might have found sensational the general public did not.
The Sultan rarely kept to schedule: even his departure time from
Boulogne for the voyage to Dover was not known until the last minute. In
fact, the whole programme for the day, 12 July, was uncertain until the
previous evening and even when it was fixed it was not always followed.
A scheduled stop of five minutes at Tunbridge Wells station on the journey from Dover to Charing Cross brought a crowd of ladies and
gentlemen and a guard of honour of Volunteers on to the platform, but
the train steamed past at top speed.[64] On the eve of the Sultan's visit to
the Horticultural Gardens he said he could not come until two days later,
and on the day of the postponed visit he stayed so long at the Duke of
Sutherland's banquet that he was three hours late.[65]

However, his arrival at Dover was splendid indeed. He was accompanied by varied representatives of his still considerable empire – 'Arab
chiefs, Circassians, and, above all, Albanian magnates in their exquisitely
embroidered velvet jackets' – who appeared armed to the teeth. The Royal
Navy, then at the height of its power, made a notable contribution to the
display: two wooden frigates – 'the beauty of their form and exquisite "sit"
upon the water' – contrasted favourably with the new ironclads.[66]

The spectacle was kept up throughout the visit. When the Sultan
attended the opera at Covent Garden, 12,000 plants decorated the Floral
Hall, which he passed through on the way to his seat, and his retinue was
'in accordance with the pomp and splendour that traditionally attaches
to an oriental potentate'. The auditorium was decked out with a magnificence that could only be compared to that provided for Napoleon III
in 1854, when France was fighting alongside Britain in the Crimean
War.[67] Also, the Guildhall was decorated so magnificently for a reception
that over the next three days 40,000 people went in to look at it. The ball
at the Foreign Office could only be compared with the fête given by the
City of London to the Prince and Princess of Wales after their marriage,
although it was pointed out that 'Eastern monarchs do not dance, and
are said to wonder why other people should, when men and women
could be hired to undergo this fatigue'.[68] The Foreign Office building

was new and what became known as the Durbar Court was used for the first time.[69]

However, these grand indoor occasions could be enjoyed only by the privileged few. The weather ruined the Sultan's visit for the general public. When he went to Spithead for the naval review, rain pelted down and it was almost impossible to see anything. There was heavy rain on the day of the Guildhall visit, too. When the Sultan, accompanied by the Prince of Wales, reviewed the volunteer troops on Wimbledon Common, with a Household Cavalry brigade and four battalions of Foot Guards, the downpour cut the ceremony short.[70]

Six years later, the Shah of Persia presented the public with such an alluring mixture of Oriental splendour and comedy that they took him to their hearts. The Shah disembarked at Dover with his luggage – 'a multitude of boxes and packages, of swords in velvet cases, of silver jugs and a golden teapot, which caused much tittering and gossip'. The Sultan had worn a general's uniform, which scarcely distinguished him from some of his entourage, but the Shah's coat was 'faced with broad rows of diamonds, with rubies between them. The scabbard of his scimitar was crusted with diamonds, and seemed to burn and blaze in the sun.' The rubies 'seemed, as they neared the collar of his uniform, to be about the diameter of the buttons of a great coat'. The crowds were mesmerised.

He was welcomed at Charing Cross station by the Prince of Wales and taken to Buckingham Palace. (Queen Victoria remained in Windsor as she had for the Sultan's visit.)[71] Sir Henry Ponsonby wrote:

'Had the Shah arrived in Western dress and worn a frock-coat and tall hat, nobody would have been vastly interested, but he fulfilled their highest expectations by being dressed in an astrakhan cap and a long coat embroidered with gold, while he wore as many diamonds and precious stones as his apparel would bear. His total inability to make himself understood and his undisguised admiration for childish pleasures all fitted in with the preconceived notions people had formed of an Eastern potentate.'

He added that the popular catchphrase was 'Have you seen the Shah?': it was particularly apt, as 'there had rarely in history been so much cause for surprise and wonder'.[72] 'Have You Seen the Shah' became the title of a song, sung both on the music halls and in a burlesque at a West End theatre:

> Behold a man from Teheran,
> Come out on the rampage,
> Determined quite, that's *if* he can,
> To race and beat the age;
> So when the small boys stare and cry,
> 'We wonder what you are,
> So like a Guy Faux in the sky,'
> I say, 'Well, I'm the Shah.'

> *Chorus*   Have you seen the Shah, boys, have you seen the Shah?
> With five-pound notes, he lines his coats, which is pecu*liah*!
> From head to waist, with Paris paste , he twinkles like a St*ah*!
> You don't know what it is to be the Shah'.[73]

He was celebrated in music halls all over London, although, it was pointed out, he was bad for business because he took the audiences elsewhere.[74] Even two and a half months after he left the country he was a popular subject for a song.[75] The Lord Chamberlain had stepped in to force an actor to alter his makeup so that he did not resemble the Shah so closely – but the music halls could get away with what theatres could not; one performer was reproached for not wearing enough jewels on his costume.[76]

When the Shah journeyed to Windsor to visit the Queen, his epaulettes were reported to be of diamonds with a great emerald in the middle of each. On arrival at Windsor station, he was cheered by 800 schoolboys from the nearby Eton college, with the heartiness 'for which the cheering of the boys of our public schools is renowned'.[77] Perhaps his greatest public triumph was on the longer journey to Spithead to view the fleet, and especially on the journey back: 'All the way to London the stations were crowded, people had come across the country to gates and fences to see the royal train pass, and quite a frenzy of sight-seeing was written in the faces that strained vainly to decipher the Shah as the train shot by . . . Through the London outskirts the windows and housetops were crowded, and men, women and children cheered, and raced and ran and waved hats and handkerchiefs as if for their lives.' For the drive to

HAVE YOU SEEN THE SHAH?

WRITTEN AND COMPOSED BY

BRACEY VANE,

IN THE BURLESQUE AT THE CHARING CROSS THEATRE,

AND ALSO BY

V A N C E .

Price 3/-

LONDON: HOPWOOD & CREW, 42, NEW BOND ST.

The Shah of Persia, with his alluring mixture of oriental splendour and comedy, was an instant hit. In the opinion of a courtier, 'there had rarely in history been so much cause for surprise and wonder'.

Buckingham Palace there was 'clamorous rapture' and a 'delirium of delight'. Vast crowds had assembled on Wandsworth Road and Vauxhall Bridge. *The Times* found it romantic that 'a Shah of Persia should inspect the ironclads of England' and referred to 'the impression and measurement of national strength, which was the real meaning of the solid thunder of those holiday salutations'.[78] This was an important aspect of the public's enjoyment of the Shah's visit. While people marvelled at his splendour, they knew that he in turn was dazzled by the might of the British Empire.

According to *The Times*, the most impressive spectacle to confront the royal visitor was on the Thames. When the Shah was taken by boat from Tower stairs to Greenwich, 'the scene on our noble river was such as it had never presented even to our own Princes', and would not take place a second time in the same generation. 'It would have been impossible for any display of commercial greatness to have exceeded that presented in the West India Dock.' The vast basin was crammed with ships, just a single channel left open in the centre so that the Shah's vessel could pass through it. Each ship was dressed with flags, the decks were packed with people, and seamen swarmed like ants up the rigging. There was also an extraordinary display by the London Fire Brigade. The men in full uniform, led, in silver helmet, by their chief, Captain Shaw, stood on five river fire engines locked together in line. To huge cheers, they discharged several hundred jets of water.[79]

However, the Shah seemed to enjoy nothing as much as his visit to Madame Tussaud's, then in Baker Street:

> I've seen your Lord Mayor, Prince, your Queen,
> Your Leicester Square, your fleet,
> But I liked most of all I've seen,
> Your show in Baker Street.
> Yet there a little boy cried, 'Look,
> Oh! Here's a swell, Papa!'
> Though he's not numbered in the book
> Stuffed wax he thought the Shah![80]

The British public delighted in the Shah's love of pleasure, and did not mind his lack of dignity.

The Prince of Wales was at his best during his mother's jubilee processions of 1887 and 1897. However, between the two he made a second highly embarrassing appearance in court. By June 1891, the Prince could no longer be excused as inexperienced. He was a 50-year-old grandfather aged fifty. What became known as the Tranby Croft Affair took place at a house he had been visiting near Doncaster so that he could attend the St Leger race meeting. It emerged that he liked to gamble at night as well as by day, and that his chosen game was baccarat, which, as a game of chance, was illegal. The scandal erupted after one of the players at Tranby Croft was accused of cheating. He was Sir William Gordon Cumming, who belonged to an old Scottish family. The accusation was a disaster for a man who prided himself above all else on being an officer and a gentleman, and his reputation as a brave soldier, particularly during the Zulu war, was unquestioned. He was also, like the Prince, a tireless womaniser.[81]

Two others at Tranby Croft, General Owen Williams and Lord Coventry, confronted Cumming with the news that five members of the house party had accused him of adding to or subtracting from the baccarat counters, indicating the size of his stake, according to whether he had won or lost. He denied it but was told that the evidence of five witnesses was conclusive, and he must sign a promise never to play cards again. In return his disgrace would be kept secret. Still protesting his innocence, he agreed, perhaps because he saw the need for the Prince's participation in an illegal activity to be kept quiet. It emerged eventually that the Prince had played the important role of banker, that he had brought along his own baccarat counters, bearing the Prince of Wales's feathers in gold on the back, and that the game had been played only at his insistence.

Too many people were in the know for the scandal to be kept secret. When it got out, Gordon Cumming sued his accusers for slander. General Owen Williams and Lord Coventry had informed the Prince that he was guilty before they had heard his side of the story. In obtaining the Prince's approval for the forced confession, they had led him to break army regulations: as a field marshal it was his duty, as it was the General's, to inform Gordon Cumming's commanding officer, who should have dealt with the case.

When it reached the Law Courts in the Strand, in June 1891, the heir to the throne was in the witness box, and in court for every day of the trial except the last, when he went to Ascot races. Although his testimony contained nothing so dramatic as in the Mordaunt case, excitement swelled as he was stepping down because a plucky juryman intervened to ask him two pertinent questions that counsel had failed to put. The Prince answered good-humouredly.

However, Sir Edward Clarke, the leading counsel for Gordon Cumming, stirred things up properly. The Prince had been treated with kid gloves by the prosecution lawyers, but Sir Edward, who was Solicitor-General, told the jury, 'If you find that Sir William Gordon Cumming was not guilty of that which is charged against him, and if, as I trust he may, he goes forth from this court justified by your verdict, I am bound to say that I think it is impossible that Sir William Gordon Cumming's name should be removed from the Army list, and that the names of Field-Marshal the Prince of Wales and Major-General Owen Williams should remain there.' As the *Daily Chronicle* commented, 'This was warm.' The paper reported that the missile had hit its mark, and the *Star* added that 'There was an extraordinary sensation at this very bold alternative thus suggested.'[82]

Clarke's closing speech to the jury was so eloquent that it seemed Gordon Cumming might win. However, he was refuted point by point by the aged Lord Chief Justice Coleridge. As a result of Coleridge's biased summing-up, as many saw it, Gordon Cumming lost the case, and was socially ruined. The cheers that greeted the Prince at Ascot were mingled with boos, and he was subjected to shouts of 'Have you brought your counters?' and 'If you can't back a horse you can baccarat [back a rat].' The press also weighed in. *The Times* said it was a pity that the Prince had not signed a pledge never to play cards again, and the *Daily Chronicle* argued that until the Prince swore that it was not he who had broken 'the solemn pledge of secrecy', he was as dishonoured as Gordon Cumming was supposed to be. The *Nottingham Express* asserted that the British Empire was humiliated.[83]

The Nonconformists were very critical of the Prince, but although the Bishops of Carlisle and Durham preached against his way of life the Church of England was otherwise muted in speaking out against its future head. The music halls, however, were entirely loyal to the man whose love of pleasure they shared, and they treated Gordon Cumming as a joke:

> Said Coventry to Albert E – 'Such doings must be barred –
> We'll make him sign a paper that no more he'll touch a card!'

Then they got him in a corner, and they kicked up such a row,
Sweet William signed the paper, and he lives with Mother now . . .

They say he put a fiver on, but if he saw a *coup*
He'd quickly double it, to make a 'score or two',
Well if he did all that they say, to try and win their pelf,
I really cannot blame him, for I've done the same myself.[84]

To the tune of 'The Campbells are Coming' they sang the 'The Scandals are "Cumming"',[85] but on one occasion it was soon switched to 'God Bless the Prince of Wales' and 'For He's a Jolly Good Fellow', sentiments which, it was reported, 'are greeted with the most loyal demonstrations'. At another London hall 'an allusion to the Prince of Wales was greeted with applause, proving that the loyalty of the [audience] had not been shaken in the slightest degree by recent events'.[86]

Some of the most hostile comments came from *Reynolds's Newspaper*, which had been fiercely republican throughout the 40 years of its existence. It published front page leaders on two successive Sundays, the first of which was entitled 'The Heir Apparent and His Gambling Gang'. The Prince was compared unfavourably with Charles II, 'the vilest spawn of the Stuarts', and 'the no less contemptible' George IV. The reference to 'the adulterers Charles and George' was a rare hint that the Prince's loose living was not confined to gambling.[87]

The paper suggested that the judge had wanted a verdict for the defence. The Prince would have been badly damaged had the jury decided that the man to whom he had denied the proper army proceedings had been falsely accused. The Lord Chief Justice had also treated the playing of baccarat as though it was legal, again presumably to protect the Prince's reputation, and he had shown little knowledge of the Gaming Acts – 'Poor men's clubs are invaded by the police every week, the men playing for a few shillings arrested and imprisoned or fined. While the Prince of Wales, the Lord High Gambler of the time, and his friends are honoured as if they were paragons of all the virtues.' To add insult to injury, Coleridge had excluded the public from the court by issuing tickets to his friends, 'Duchesses, Countesses and the like'[88]. This was certainly true. The courtroom had at times been like a salon for the upper classes, with the ladies to the fore, particularly Coleridge's pretty young wife. As the *Echo* had commented, 'For each day that the case has been going on,

Lady Coleridge has been giving delightful little luncheon parties in the private room of the Master of the Rolls, while Lord Coleridge himself has entertained the Prince of Wales and Sir Francis Knollys to a similar necessary repast in his own room.'[89] For the judge to lunch with a witness was extraordinary.

Reynolds's Newspaper claimed that the monarchy was tolerated 'because the reigning sovereign is, with all her weaknesses, a well-intentioned and good-living woman' has echoes in the twenty-first century. It was fair comment that the Prince was so intoxicated with gaming that 'he seldom travels without carrying amongst his luggage all the implements of the gamester', but not true that 'his passion for this so-called sport amounts to madness'. It showed little sense of history to claim that 'never has a royal house been thrown into such convulsions by the depravity of its future head. Never has a country with the slightest pretence to civilization been covered with such incredible shame as England.' Nor was it true that 'from the universal howl of execration that went up in all countries', 'the Prince of Wales is held in abhorrence as one whose character is damned, and who has brought the monarchy of England to the verge of destruction'.[90]

In 1891, the monarchy was a long way from destruction. The Queen's seclusion after the death of Albert caused resentment, but had ensured that she was not involved in unpleasant incidents. A rare exception from August 1875 stands out. The Queen had been on the deck of the royal yacht *Alberta* when it had run down a sailing vessel in the Solent, and killed three people. The yacht had been travelling too fast, and the captain was eventually reprimanded by the Admiralty. However, there was confusion over whether he or the Queen's nephew, Prince Ernst Leiningen, was responsible. Leiningen was the superior officer on board, but was expected to attend Her Majesty whenever she required him.[91] Various investigations failed to reach a verdict, and a cover-up was suspected. It was widely believed that the jury would have reached a decision at the original inquest at Gosport, had influence not been used to appoint two jurymen who were close to the royal household. The crowd turned on the *Alberta*'s officers, including Leiningen.[92] Feelings continued to run high and the following April an MP claimed in the House that 'public justice had been perverted and the nation's money used as hush money [a reference to compensation pay-outs]'.[93]

By 1891, the atmosphere was very different. Imperialism dominated the British mood and sealed the popularity of the Queen Empress. The turning point had been the Golden Jubilee of 1887. If royal occasions earlier in the reign could have been more spectacular, the lessons had been learned. The procession on 21 June 1887, from Buckingham Palace to Westminster Abbey and back, was all that could be desired. Moreover, the weather was magnificent – 'Queen's weather'.

Here are a few vignettes from the mass of reporting, first of the view looking up Waterloo Place and Regent Street:

> Overhead and at the sides was a rich blaze of varied colour, and down the roadway there seemed to flow a majestic river whose surface glittered incessantly in the powerful rays of the noonday sun. All knew that the glitter came from sabres and decorations, from the rich trappings and dazzling weapons of the Indian escort, not the least impressive accompaniment of the procession, from helmets and cuirasses. Nevertheless the likeness to a river of gold, flowing between banks of extraordinary richness and splendour, was too strong to be resisted, and was mentioned by many persons as the procession vanished out of sight down the eastern portion of Pall-mall'.

By contrast Trafalgar Square was a mass of onlookers, mostly the poor who could not afford seats in the huge stands that lined most of the route. They stood on benches and boxes, on costermongers' barrows, on Landseer's lions and on one another's shoulders. 'Here she is; I have seen her, she is alive' roared a sturdy patriot from the East End.'[94]

The popularity of the Indian contingent arose partly from the public's delight in Oriental splendour and partly from pride in the most glamorous country of the British Empire. There were loud cheers for a maharajah, 'whose shoulders were covered with bullion woven into his tunic', but even more for the turban of the Rao of Kutch, 'which, when the sun flashed upon it, really blazed with the scintillating light of diamonds, rubies, and emeralds'. By contrast, 'a little Hindoo woman stood on the edge of the crowd over by the Mall anxious to see her Queen'. She was discomfited by the pushing and shoving and hemmed in by some of the mounted troops; to the cheers of her fellow spectators officers of the Scots Guards beckoned her to cross to the other side of the road where she got a better view.[95]

In the evening one reporter was taken up to the gallery of St Paul's to see the lights. Mr Green, the dean's verger, told him, 'The last time I saw anything like this was when I took Dickens up here to view the illuminations at the close of the Crimean War.' From that splendid vantage point, 'Primrose Hill, or what is conjectured to be such, displays a huge beacon, and to judge by the glow in the sky, the bonfires on Highgate-hill and on Hampstead Heath must be of enormous dimensions.' The illuminations in central London depended less on electric light, which was still quite new, than on thousands of coloured gas and oil lamps massed together. The Bank of England, the Royal Exchange and the Mansion House were the most magnificently lit buildings of the capital, but in New Oxford Street the crowds gazed with special wonder at the display offered by the Pears Soap Company, in which a large portrait of the Queen was accompanied by words Shakespeare had used of Elizabeth I, 'A pattern to all princes living with her, and all that shall succeed'.[96] In 1887, there were still many private mansions in central London, owned by the nobility, who vied with one another in decorating and lighting up the facades. They were imitated all over the capital by humbler citizens, which inspired a rare outburst of dissent from the sensational novelist Wilkie Collins: 'Has anybody told you that "The Jubilee" was an outburst of Loyalty? I tell you that it was an outburst of Fear and Cant. In my neighbourhood there was a report that we should have our windows broken if we did not illuminate.'[97]

Another object of criticism was the inevitable commercialisation of the event:

> Our Gracious Queen's Great Jubilee has now become a craze
> Amongst her loyal subjects, and to illustrate their praise,
> They've Jubilee this, they've Jubilee that, they've made it quite a
> fad,
> In fact this Jubilee has nearly sent the people mad.
>
> My wife's gone quite cracked about the Jubilee . . .
> She's got the house chock full of ornaments and crockeree,
> And every blessed article she's christened Jubilee,
> We've a Jubilee kettle and dishes too, and as true as I'm a man,
> We've got a Jubilee Tom Cat, and a Jubilee frying pan.[98]

However, all over the country there was plenty of free food for the poor, and children were well provided for, most spectacularly at the fête in Hyde Park the day after the procession. The Prince and Princess of Wales came to see them, and so did the Queen, although she did not stay long or get out of her carriage. To make sure no one got lost, each child wore a ticket with their name and the number of the tent allocated to their school. As well as a silver-plated memorial medal, the 26,000 children were each given a paper bag containing a meat pie, a piece of cake, a bun and an orange. The entertainment included a score of Punch and Judy shows, eight marionette theatres, 85 peep shows and cosmoramic views, nine troupes of performing dogs, ponies and monkeys, and several hundred Aunt Sallies and 'Knock-'em-downs'. There were also 100 lucky-dip barrels and 42,000 presents: skipping-ropes, dolls, money-boxes, pencil-cases, whistles, popguns and – curiously – walking sticks.[99]

The Times commented on the Jubilee that: 'Its mere spectacular magnificence was unrivalled; its moral significance was absolutely unique.'[100]

It was much the same at the Diamond Jubilee of 1897. The Queen did not look ten years older. Her eldest daughter, the dowager Empress of Germany, seemed the same age as her mother, perhaps because her husband the Emperor had died since the earlier jubilee. There was less illumination this time, although electricity played a bigger part. The service was held outside St Paul's instead of in the Abbey. The procession took in the south side of the river, which provided many of the biggest crowds. Whereas in 1887 there had been much emphasis on visiting European royalty, 1897 included troops from every part of the Empire. They wore 'colours that are rarely seen to such perfection in this hemisphere, least of all in the grey atmosphere of these islands'. Once again, none outshone the Indians: 'Her Majesty's Indian escort, a stalwart body of native officers, whose dignified and martial mien sent a murmur of involuntary admiration along the lines of the people.' According to the *Manchester Guardian*, the most moving moment for those lucky enough to be near St Paul's came after the Archbishop of Canterbury gave his blessing, when all present sang the Old Hundredth (an old setting of the hundredth psalm) 'The good simple old hymn poured forth in unison and the enormous crowd of princes, soldiers and spectators adding their voices swelled the moving volume of sound. It was a strange and wonderful experience. Many were moved to tears, and the old Queen, who had been affected by the whole service, was moved to agitation.'[101]

The Jubilee inspired the same enthusiasm nationwide. One of the most sensational sights was at Liverpool, then the greatest port in the world. It was possible 'without special effort – simply taking ships which happened to be in port – to parade a fleet that afforded special evidence of the greatness of England on the sea'. There was a double line of ships two and a half miles long, dressed 'from stem to stern'; those in dock were as beflagged as those out on the river, which was crowded with busy little steamers taking spectators up and down. The great liners were the most imposing, but scarcely less so the merchant ships 'that carry our flag to the Pacific, South America, our Indian Empire and the shining seas of the Orient'.[102]

The sight on the Mersey bore comparison with what the Thames had offered the Shah of Persia a quarter of a century earlier. Here was the substance of the greatness of Victorian England, and, despite the vicissitudes she and her family had undergone during her reign, its symbol was the Queen herself.

CHAPTER 2:

Political Movements

We look at other nations, and we pity them because
They're not a little patch on dear old England.[1]

In democracy and freedom, Victorian Britain was highly defective by modern western standards and a world leader by the standards of the day – *the* world leader, in the view of most British people. Hence this paradox: large numbers of Britons believed that the political system failed to further their interests but that they belonged to the greatest nation on earth, not only in power but in virtue. Both nationalism and the drive for reform were powerful ingredients in political sensations, although the latter became less of a factor as advances in democracy were introduced. That reform, not revolution, was the goal is a sign that, particularly after the European revolutions of 1848, what was seen as sensational in a British context would usually not have been so considered on the continent.

The years 1867 and 1884 saw significant increases in the number of men allowed to vote at parliamentary elections. Nevertheless reports of parliamentary debates, available in the papers in mind-numbing detail, rarely excited the masses. Most political sensations involved large crowds coming together to support or oppose an idea or a person. The Victorian taste for melodrama, where characters were either gloriously heroic or deeply villainous, certainly extended to political figures, whose public appearances could inspire tumultuous demonstrations of love or hate. However, up to and including 1848, class conflicts led to sensations in which the main emotion generated was fear.

What a row and a rumpus there is I declare,
Ten thousands are flocking from every where,
To petition the Parliament onward they steer,
The Chartists are coming, oh dear, oh dear.[2]

Those lines from a street ballad sound breezy enough, but the Chartists frightened the upper and middle classes. Theirs was, after all, 'the greatest movement of popular protest in British history',[3] which, in the ten years from 1838, 'came nearer to being a mass rebellion than any other movement in modern times'.[4]

The Chartist march on Newport in November 1839 was sensational. Thousands of men gathered in the hills and arrived at the town in military formation. At their head were three prominent Chartists, the best known being John Frost, who had been a magistrate and Mayor of Newport. The attack, which had been carefully planned, centred on the Westgate Hotel, where known local Chartists were under military guard. A Chartist column, armed with firearms and long sticks tipped with iron, was cheered when it stopped in front of the building. Windows were smashed and the Chartists burst in to be met with a volley of bullets from the troops stationed inside. Within twenty minutes they were running in all directions, leaving behind several hundred weapons and nine corpses. The final death toll was more than twenty.[5] The Mayor of Newport, who had called out the troops, was wounded when he tried to put up a shutter at one of the broken windows. No one seemed to know for certain why the raid was carried out, and rumours spread of a nation-wide insurrection. Many believed that widespread violence would indeed take place.

The six points of the Charter, promulgated the previous year – universal male suffrage, no property qualification for MPs, payment for MPs, annual elections, equal constituencies and secret ballots – represented the aspirations of working people all over the country. Whole communities were involved, and many employers discovered that their entire workforce supported the Charter. The Great Reform Bill of 1832 had left those without property or wealth outside the political process, and the Chartists wanted this changed.

The press reports of Newport are, of course, one-sided. The most important Chartist paper, the *Northern Star*, based in Leeds, had no reporters on the spot, and had to rely on 'the biased London press'.[6] It was particularly bitter against *The Times*, which it accused of being taken in by 'an anonymous and hired slanderer . . . sent down to Wales to fabricate testimony'.[7] Middle class papers were by their nature anti-Chartist. One writer portrayed a journalist, not altogether unfairly, as someone who believed that Chartists were people who could not pay fivepence for a newspaper and who 'either affects contempt for them, or abuses them heartily for the benefit of those who can'.[8] Certainly, the mainstream local press was no more sympathetic to Chartism than *The Times*. The main difference between the *Monmouthshire Beacon* and the *Monmouthshire Merlin* was that the former blamed the Whig government for the uprising, while the latter defended it. The *Beacon* said that it was sad to have to fight one's own countrymen, but 'When men arm themselves with pikes and muskets, and proceed to deeds of turbulence and insurrection . . . they must be dealt with as enemies and aliens.' 'The enemy of mankind' could not devise a more ingenious plan 'than by advising them to seek redress 'by the horrid instrumentality of the pike and the sabre'. The paper conjured up the horrors of the French Revolution, which were still within living memory.[9] The *Merlin* referred to 'the charter of rapine', 'the privilege to destroy', 'the right to kill' and 'immunity to plunder and riot'.

The *Northern Star* claimed that most of the Chartist guns in Newport had not worked, and argued that the violence had started only when a young boy had let off a shot, and the Chartists had supposed that they were being fired on.[10] The paper claimed not to know the motives of Frost and his associates, but pointed out how hard it was to protest peacefully. Peaceful meetings had been declared illegal and broken up by force; the best, most intelligent and often most moderate Chartist leaders had been locked up. The paper concluded that it would be no thanks to the Whig government if the events in Wales were not repeated in other parts of the country 'and on a more fearful scale'.[11] The thought of being faced with the sinister menace of the 'men in the hills' was enough to produce a shudder anywhere. The announcement at the end of November of Queen Victoria's engagement to Prince Albert might have seemed irrelevant to the issue but the *Northern Star* pointed out that if the trial of the three Welsh leaders were delayed until near the time of the marriage pardons might be available.[12]

However, the three were convicted and sentenced to death. Tension mounted. By the time the sentence was commuted, less than three weeks later, to transportation for life there had been an attempted rising in Bradford. Even then, the anger did not die away and the release of the men of Newport became one of the most insistent Chartist demands until they were pardoned in 1854.

Throughout the 1840s outbreaks of violence became local sensations, but the Chartists caused a nationwide scare in April 1848, when, having massed in London for a march on Parliament, they seemed poised to precipitate a revolution. Just across the Channel, Louis Philippe, King of the French, had been deposed only two months earlier.

There was indeed talk of revolution at the Chartist convention, which opened in London on 3 April. A mass petition, demanding the six points of the Charter except the ballot, had been drawn up for presentation to Parliament, and the plan was that on Monday the tenth, the Chartists would mass on Kennington Common then march to Westminster. The government banned both the mass meeting and the march, but the Chartists declared that they would go ahead. One radical, who was not a Chartist, wrote to his wife on 7 April, 'London is in a state of panic from the contemplated meeting of the Chartists, two hundred thousand strong, on Monday; for myself, nothing that happened would in the least degree surprise me: I expect a Revolution within two years: there may be one within three days. *The Times* is alarmed beyond measure.'[13]

The Times certainly was. It had written on the third that 'There is not a being who has an eye to see and a heart to feel but regards the present state of things with other sentiments than those of curiosity and fear.' It increased the stakes by claiming that 'the destiny of all races' centred on England. 'If she fall, who shall stand? If she perish, who shall live?'

Charles Greville, the famous diarist and a senior civil servant, wrote on the ninth,

All London is making preparations to encounter a Chartist row tomorrow: so much so that it is either very sublime or very ridiculous. All the clerks and others in different officers are ordered to be sworn in special constables, and to constitute themselves into garrisons. I went to the police office with all my clerks, messengers etc., and we were all sworn ... Colonel Harness, of the Railway department, is our commander in chief; every gentleman in London is become a constable, and there is an organisation of some sort in every district.[14]

The windows of the Treasury and other public offices were barricaded. Piles of government publications were used in the defences, and someone remarked that this was the best use ever found for them.[15] The aged Duke of Wellington was in charge of the thorough military preparations. Riflemen were stationed on top of the Houses of Parliament, and three guns and a howitzer at Buckingham Palace, although the Queen and Prince Albert had been sent away for safety.

The 150,000 special constables ranged from Charles Dickens to the future Napoleon III, still in exile but the ultimate beneficiary of the fall of Louis Philippe. The former had written unkindly about the Chartists, so the Chartist newspaperman and sensation novelist, G W M Reynolds, later sneered at Dickens, 'swaggering about the vicinage of Regent's park with the staff in his hand, while he knew perfectly well that the Chartists were over at Kennington – five miles distant'.[16] In fact, Dickens had written on the tenth to a friend, 'I have not been special constable-ing myself today. Thinking there was rather an epidemic in that wise abroad, I walked out and looked out at the preparations, without any luggage of staff, warrant, or affidavit.'[17]

The weather started fine on the tenth and, just after ten, a procession set off from near the south east corner of Regent's Park, for Kennington Common. The first carriage had a platform specially built for the petition, which was rolled up into five huge bales, like cotton, and a banner in the Chartist colours of red, white and green, with the six points of the Charter inscribed on it. In the next carriage rode Feargus O'Connor, the dominant figure in the movement, and other Chartist leaders. Mottoes like 'The voice of knowledge will silence the cannon's roar' and 'We are a million and claim to live by the fruits of our industry' decorated the sides of the vehicles. The carriage horses from the Chartist Land Company's farm, also decked out in red, white and green, were much admired. Chartists followed on foot, eight abreast, about two hundred to start with, but the numbers gradually swelled. They crossed Blackfriars Bridge without interference. Most of the shops on the way were closed, and although the windows were mostly filled with spectators there was little cheering.

From the Elephant and Castle to Kennington there was a moving mass of more than ten thousand people. When the main procession reached the Common, it passed through the lines of trade and society representatives, already drawn up in military array with flags and banners. The police and the troops had taken over a nearby tavern from which a messenger was seen to approach O'Connor. He and the chairman of the convention got down from their carriage, thereby providing one of the most dramatic moments of the day.[18]

As a participant described it,

> I heard a cry of 'They have got him'. And a wild rush was made towards the western side of the Common. Looking in that direction, I saw the giant form of Feargus O'Connor . . . towering above the throng, as he moved towards the road, accompanied by a courageous inspector of police. There was a cry repeated through the vast throng that O'Connor was arrested; a moment of breathless excitement, and then a partial rolling back of the mass of human forms that had suddenly impelled itself towards the road.'[19]

O'Connor was not arrested. He had been sent for to hear from the police commissioner that the authorities were determined to enforce the ban on the procession returning north to Westminster but would let the meeting continue, provided it was orderly. O'Connor sold this compromise to the crowd, with the help of some exuberant oratory: 'I would rather be stabbed to the heart than resign my proper place at the head of my children.' They responded with cheers, and at least one shout of 'Go it, old fellow'. He also declared that he would not forget Ireland.[20] O'Connor was, of course, an Irishman, and the close links between Chartism and the Irish alarmed the government. Not all of the crowd could hear the main speakers, but there were others on different parts of the common, including Reynolds. When the crowd dispersed, only the carriages carrying the petition and the Chartist leaders were allowed back over the Thames straight away. The rest were allowed to cross the bridges in small groups. There was no revolution.

The government had won by a display of overwhelming force, but O'Connor was a moderating influence and few Chartists wanted violence. Large though the crowd on the common had been, it was smaller than predicted, and the petition was eventually found to have attracted no more than two million signatures instead of the five million which had been claimed. There were many forgeries and joke names; the Duke of Wellington's appeared several times. Chartism did not disappear immediately, but 10 April 1848 was its high water mark, and it did not frighten governments again. Working-class movements made little political progress in the next few years, which may help to explain why during this period three sensations were inspired by Continental freedom struggles. It was as though the masses were projecting on to visiting foreigners their deeply felt emotions about oppression and liberty.

———

No doubt you've heard of General Haynau so famed in Hungarian
    story,
How by flogging the Ladies, and hanging the men he arrived at
    this high pitch of glory.[21]

Haynau became a hate figure in the aftermath of the 1848 revolutions against Austrian rule in northern Italy and Hungary for his brutal suppression of the revolutionaries. In September 1850 he visited London and was shown round the Barclay and Perkins brewery in Southwark, which claimed to be the largest in the world. When he signed the visitor's book, word soon spread that a hated symbol of tyranny was at hand. In the words of *Reynolds's Weekly Newspaper*:

This ruffian, miscreant and butcher has dared to show his hateful face in our country; but, thank God! The brave hearts of our noble-minded countrymen and countrywomen, inflamed with indignation at the sight of his villainous countenance, and at the recollection of his blood-thirsty and demoniac deeds, hooted, hissed, pelted and kicked the flagellator of women . . . until he was obliged to seek shelter and save himself in a dusthole! We are informed on good authority that a large portion of females took part in this glorious manifestation, and tore the fellow's grisly moustachios until he roared again with pain and fury.[22]

Haynau's long moustache was a tempting target. The brewery workers attacked him with whips and brooms, and almost tore the clothes off his back. When his companions bundled him out of the building, he was chased down the street with shouts of 'He's a murderer; give it to him!' 'Down with the Austrian butcher!' and 'Shove him in the river!' He sought shelter in the George Inn on Bankside where, according to some reports, he was found cowering in a dustbin. Eventually he was locked into a bedroom for his own safety until the police arrived. A meeting in the City to support the brewery workers declared that they had expressed the feelings of 'all true Englishmen', and Friedrich Engels was among the

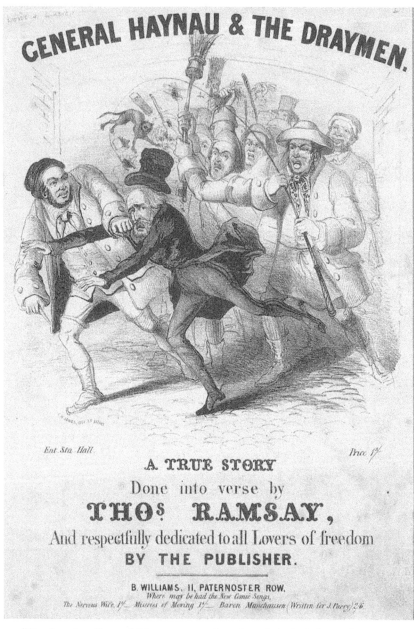

The Austrian General Haynau was a hated symbol of continental tyranny:
on a visit to the Barclay and Perkins brewery in Southwark, the workers
attacked him with whips and brooms.

speakers. The chairman declared that if the brewery, which had apologised to Haynau, took action against his attackers, every man in the land would pledge himself never to drink their beer again, although this might have been a promise too far. Henry Mayhew, chronicler of the London poor, mentions the popularity with costermongers of songs ridiculing Haynau and praising the draymen.[23] One song, dedicated to 'all lovers of freedom' stressed the moral of the story:

> Some people say it serves him well right, some others do excuse
> him,
> As being a stranger on our shores, we'd no right to ill use him;
> This may all be very good, to strive ill deeds to smother;
> But may Tyrants all be served the same, as they would serve
> another.[24]

A year later, working people again showed their support for the oppressed Hungarians when the defeated hero of their revolution, Lajos Kossuth, paid a three-week visit to England. Never before had a foreign leader been so rapturously received. As his ship entered the Solent on 23 October 1851, the Mayor of Southampton went out in a boat to greet him and the streets were packed as he drove to the town hall. As the bells rang out, a group of working men lifted him out of his carriage and carried him inside. After the defeat of the Hungarian revolution, Kossuth had fled to Turkey, which, with British support, had refused to extradite him. He told his delighted listeners in Southampton, 'I am free because England willed it so . . . It is a glorious sight to see a queen upon the throne that represents the principle of freedom.'[25] Kossuth was a famous orator, and his English was extraordinarily good, considering that he had learnt it in an Austrian prison.

The journey to London was carried out in short stages so that the hero could be entertained at a series of banquets along the way. Kossuth mania took over the whole country, although the *Spectator* commented that 'The close of the Great Exhibition has left the English public at a loss for some means of excitement . . . The arrival of a genuine foreign lion at such a moment was a godsend; and when it was found that instead of inarticulate roaring the lion was expressing itself eloquently in good idiomatic English, public delight knew no bounds.'[26] Kossuth paid triumphant visits to Birmingham and Manchester, although their mayors played no official role in the proceedings for fear of offending the Austrian government.

They were not the only ones to worry. Lord Ponsonby begged Disraeli, then in opposition, not to submit to 'the nonsense about Kossuth', alluding to the Hungarian's 'deification', and, unfairly in view of his favourable reference to the Queen, 'the attack upon the monarchy'. Disraeli replied that he saw what was going on with 'apprehension and disgust'. Kossuth should never have been allowed to land. In the present state of Britain, 'with a new reform bill agitating the public mind, it is really tempting our fate'[27]. Even the Foreign Secretary, Lord Palmerston, had to withdraw an invitation to Kossuth to visit his home, but still found himself embroiled in controversy when a deputation of working men, thanking him for his sympathy for the Hungarians and Poles, used violent language about the Austrian and Russian despots. Continental newspapers reported that Palmerston had written to the Austrians denying that his government had taken any part in the 'Kossuth mania', and promising to take steps to damp it down.

The Times, too, was terrified of Kossuth's possible influence on the masses. It attacked him so fiercely that copies were burnt 'in public houses, coffee rooms and other places of general resort'.[28] Feargus O'Connor denounced the 'bloody old *Times*' for its hostility to both the Hungarian hero and the brewery workers who had attacked Hungary's oppressor.[29] Immense crowds continued to turn out all over Britain to see Kossuth, and 300 towns begged him to be their guest, but his departure for the United States had been fixed for 19 November. When he got back, he settled in England for eight years.

In 1864 history repeated itself with the sensational visit of Giuseppe Garibaldi, who, even more than Kossuth, inspired love in the masses and, it was claimed, fear among Britain's rulers. While Kossuth had been defeated by his country's oppressors, Garibaldi was a liberator. The hyperbole of *Reynolds's Newspaper* tells its own story. Garibaldi supposedly represented 'all the valour of a Homeric hero, combined with all the chivalry of a Christian knight'. He was 'a glory to the whole human race' and 'in him and through him we obtain a glimpse of the godlike capacities and divine origin of human nature'[30]. Garibaldi's battles on behalf of a united Italy against the Roman Catholic powers, most importantly the Pope, chimed with the deep-rooted anti-Catholicism of Victorian Britain. He was a living symbol of liberty and national independence. His dignity and simplicity were greatly admired, and his humble origins increased his popular appeal.

Everyone knew his romantic life story, from his time as a cowboy hero in South America to his latest wound suffered in the cause of freedom.

He arrived, to a tumultuous reception, at Southampton on 3 April to thank the British nation for their support, and to be treated for his leg wound. Many in the crowd wore ribands in the Italian colours, and several ladies wore red jackets, the colour associated with Garibaldi.[31] But this was nothing to his triumphal entry into London on 11 April. The London and South West Railway Company provided a train of ten carriages for the journey from the coast. Between Clapham and Nine Elms, where the formal welcome took place in the company's great goods shed, the crowd stood shoulder to shoulder along the line. From there the great man's carriage proceeded over Westminster Bridge via Trafalgar Square to Stafford House – now Lancaster House – where he was to stay with the Duke of Sutherland. Half a million people, mostly working class, were estimated to be in the crowd, which was so dense that the three-mile journey took five hours. 'The population took the thing into their own hands,' John Morley, Gladstone's friend and biographer, wrote. 'London has seldom beheld a spectacle more extraordinary or more moving'.[32]

The diarist Arthur Munby, who stood waiting for three hours, recorded that 'this coarse mob behaved with the utmost good humour and peacefulness, though their patience must have been taxed to the utmost'. When Garibaldi came into view,

> that vast multitude rose as one man ... They leapt into the air, they waved their arms and hats aloft, they surged and struggled round the carriage, they shouted with a mighty shout of enthusiasm that took one's breath away to hear it: and above them on both sides thousands of white kerchiefs were waving from every window and housetop ... One would have known that heroic face among a thousand: and in his bearing and looks there was combination utterly new and most impressive, of dignity and homeliness, of grace and tenderness with the severest majesty ... This of today has been the greatest demonstration by far that I have beheld or, probably, shall behold. No soldier was there, no official person: no King nor government nor public body got it up or managed it: it was devised and carried out by men and women simply as such; and they often of the lowest grade ... How rare and how beautiful, to see hundreds of thousands of common folks brought together by motives absolutely pure, to do homage to one who is transcendentally worthy.[33]

Munby thought that the previous year's sensation, when Princess Alexandra had arrived to marry the Prince of Wales, had not produced the same 'ardour and deep pathetic force' expressed by Garibaldi's admirers. Less convincingly *Reynolds's Newspaper* claimed that 'compared with Garibaldi's English welcome, that experienced last year by the Princess Alexandra is as the glimmer of some thousands of rushlights to the full effulgence of the meridian sun'.[34]

The excitement never slackened. The Stafford House courtyard was repeatedly invaded, and Garibaldi was rapturously received, whether at the Guildhall to receive the freedom of the City of London, at mass meetings in the Crystal Palace, or receiving a stream of deputations wanting to honour him. Like Haynau, Garibaldi visited Barclay and Perkins's brewery, but was received very differently.

The elegant audience at the Covent Garden opera welcomed him, and when he passed through the crowded Floral Hall his sex appeal caused a furore. According to the *Scotsman*, 'Women, more or less in full dress, flew upon him, seized his hands, touched his beard, his poncho, his trousers, any part of him that they could reach . . . They were delirious with excitement and behaved in the proverbially barbaric manner that Englishwomen of the middle class always do when they are unduly excited and bewildered by anything that they consider splendour.'[35] Gladstone, who was in the auditorium, wrote in his diary of the audience's welcome that 'it was good but not like the *people*'.[36]

Although Garibaldi was the darling of the masses, his stay was firmly in the hands of the Duke of Sutherland and other members of high society. He even met the Prince of Wales, to Queen Victoria's fury. Controversy exploded when what would have been a triumphant tour of the provinces was suddenly cancelled, even though Garibaldi had specifically said that he was in Britain to thank the people for their support. Despite the testimony of an eminent doctor, many refused to believe the official explanation that his health would not stand the strain. Palmerston, now prime minister, and his cabinet paid homage, but it was widely believed that they did not want the popular enthusiasm in London replicated across the country. Pressure was thought to have been exerted by Louis Napoleon, now Napoleon III, and Victor Emmanuel, King of Italy, that Garibaldi had helped to create was reportedly scandalised that the whole British nation should have gone mad at the sight of a red shirt. Other factors supposedly contributing to the decision included danger from Irish Catholics, outraged by Garibaldi's defiance of the Pope.

———

Continental despotisms have the means of preventing political debate, but in England the people are free to meet and deliberate over their national interests, provided they do nothing to endanger the public peace.[37] *Daily Telegraph*, 3 July 1876

Garibaldi's British supporters provided a link between the fight for liberty on the Continent and reform at home. The following year, the Reform League was founded with Edmund Beales as its president. In June the Liberal/Whig government put forward a Reform Bill to widen the franchise and distribute seats more fairly, but was defeated by the Conservatives and a minority of its own supporters. Shortly afterwards the Conservatives took power and their attempts to stop the Reform League holding open air meetings, supposedly to prevent breaches of the peace, were attributed to their dislike of reform. The League held a number of mass meetings in Trafalgar Square, despite government opposition. When one was banned in early July, Beales declared that if there were a breach of the peace the government would be responsible. In the event, an estimated 69,000 attended and the meeting passed off peacefully.

However, all this was just a prelude to 23 July 1866, the most sensational day in the Reform League's history. The League was determined to hold a mass meeting that evening in Hyde Park, and the government was equally determined to put a stop to it. League members were recommended to have pencil and paper with them so that they could take the numbers of any violent policemen. The park gates were closed at five o'clock, and the huge crowd trying to get in was confronted by police drawn up in front of the railings. Deafening cheers greeted Beales and other leaders of the Reform movement when they appeared near Marble Arch. They got out of their carriages and walked towards the park, but were stopped, and in the mêlée, Beales' coat was badly torn. He returned to his carriage, from which he led between ten and fifteen thousand people to Trafalgar Square. On the way Conservative institutions like the Carlton Club were hissed and booed, and there were cheers for Gladstone and Bright, who had championed the Reform Bill and whose faces adorned banners. When the procession reached Marlborough House, the

Prince of Wales's home, Beales stopped his carriage and called for three cheers for the Prince. 'These were given with an enthusiasm which proved that his Royal Highness is a thorough favourite with the people'.[38] The unrevolutionary theme was resumed in Trafalgar Square with three cheers for the Queen. In his speech, Beales did not fail to denounce the anti-reform *Times*, 'that slanderous and incorrigible bully of Printing-house Square'.[39]

However, the real drama was enacted back at the park where the railings began to sway backwards and forwards under pressure from the crowd. Those who had climbed to the top hurried down, and everyone within range grabbed a rail to increase the motion. Eventually 50 yards of railing toppled into the park. Immediately hundreds of young men and boys clambered through the gap, although some were captured by police, who used the inside of Marble Arch as a lock-up. There was a charge of mounted police, and several people were badly beaten. This made the crowd more aggressive, and they singled out policemen who had been particularly free with their truncheons. One was pummelled until he apparently lost consciousness. Blood flowed from truncheon wounds, and eventually more sections of the railing were forced in. Some of the prisoners were rescued and, with the police under tremendous pressure, troops were called in. For some reason, the Guardsmen were cheered as warmly as the police had been hooted. They eventually restored order, but not before 400 yards of railing had been forced to the ground.

Of the many printed notices in shop windows or stuck on posts or walls along the processional route, one announced that things in general and opinions in particular were banned. Another called for 10,000 costermongers to parade Rotten Row on their donkeys to test whether 'this or any other portion of Hyde Park belongs to a class or the entire people'. According to one speaker along the way, the park was being kept for 'those who rode in their carriages and had courtesans instead of wives, and prostitutes for their companions – who rode with them in Rotten Row, and especially on Sundays'.[40] It was certainly true that many of the elegant ladies who rode in the Row were looking for clients.

The comparison with the Chartist day of 10 April 1848 was not overlooked. The authorities were accused of making a provocative show of strength, and it was pointed out that on 10 April the Duke of Wellington had kept his force tactfully in the background. Although hundreds got into the park, the Reform League failed to hold its meeting there, just as the Chartists had failed to march to Parliament. Beales, like Feargus O'Connor before him, had retreated rather than risk violence. However, the day was a victory for the demonstrators. In the words of one historian 'it convinced conservative opinion that electoral reform could not be delayed'.[41] The following year the Conservative government passed a Reform Bill, which was more far-reaching than the one that had been defeated. Despite the disturbances, Britain was again shown to be comparatively stable. The destruction of 400 yards of railing, although sensational in British terms, was trivial compared with the wars going on in Italian- and German-speaking Europe.

———

Until yesterday we could not have believed that there lived among us men capable of such a deed.[42]

If Britain was stable, however, Ireland was not. The end of the American Civil War in 1865 had released the energies of some formidable Irish Americans, members of the Fenian Brotherhood, to work for rebellion in Ireland. When Habeas Corpus was suspended there, the Fenians changed tack, and in 1867 Irish violence hit the British mainland.

After a failed Fenian attempt in February to seize the arms stored at Chester Castle, the first of the year's two sensational incidents took place in Manchester. Two men with Irish American accents were arrested for loitering suspiciously, and one turned out to be a big fish: 'Colonel' Kelly, the so-called 'Chief Executive of the Irish Republic'. On 18 September the two men and other prisoners were being taken in a van, guarded by seven policemen, from a cell in the police court to Bellevue prison outside the city. They had been handcuffed after two suspected Fenians had been seen outside the courtroom, and one had drawn a knife before he was arrested. The van, which had just passed a railway arch, was shot at on the road. The police could not see where the shots came from, and fanned out. Thirty or more Fenians attacked the van. To break it open they tried hammers, hatchets and stones, and eventually ordered the police sergeant inside with the prisoners to hand over his keys. He refused. A revolver was put to the keyhole and he was shot dead. A bystander was also killed, and two other policemen wounded. The Fenian prisoners were freed and got away after a tremendous chase, never to be recaptured, although 29 arrests were made.

The Times commented that 'there is no other class of criminals which would have had the audacity to effect such a rescue. The outrage is characteristic of Irish Americans . . . It is startling thus to find ourselves face to face with an armed enemy in one of the most important cities of the kingdom. The Fenians have declared war on our institutions, and have carried it to the very heart of the country'.[43] The Manchester police had been warned by their counterparts in Dublin that an attempt to spring the prisoners would be made, but had failed to take the rigorous precautions that were usual in Ireland.

Feelings ran high. The funeral of the police sergeant was 'one of the most imposing police funerals ever witnessed'. The streets were thronged for two miles from the dead man's house to the cemetery.[44] In Barnsley, when a young warehouseman confessed his Fenian sympathies to his workmates, they set up a jury and sentenced him to be hanged. A rope was put round his neck and he was suspended in mid-air. Although he was quickly cut down, he was black in the face. The participants were each fined ten shillings.[45]

The emotion lasted longer on the Irish side. Four of the men who took part in the attack on the van were sentenced to death. Although the accused in murder trials were not allowed to give evidence, they could speak after the sentence was passed. William Allen made a stirring speech accusing the witnesses of perjury, but said he wanted no mercy. He was prepared to die for Ireland. The last words in court of all of the prisoners were 'God save Ireland.' One of the condemned men was reprieved, but Allen, Michael Larkin and William Gould, alias O'Brien, became known to Irish nationalists as the Manchester Martyrs. To the English they were terrorists.

The public hanging took place in Manchester on 24 November 1867. It was 'an event which of its kind has excited more public interest than any execution within the memory of living man'[46]. The crowd of eight to ten thousand was smaller than at most public executions, but the police had warned people to keep away and erected barriers well away from the gaol. The fear of Fenian vengeance and of a last-minute rescue attempt was so great that 2,500 special constables were sworn in.

That same day in London 2,000 people marched from Clerkenwell Green to Hyde Park to express solidarity with the three men. Ironically it was in Clerkenwell that the second sensation occurred. Richard O'Sullivan Burke, who had instigated the escape of Kelly and his companion, was awaiting trial in Clerkenwell gaol along with another Fenian prisoner. On 12 December an explosion, which was heard for miles around, wrecked both the prison wall separating the exercise yard from the street and the houses opposite. The hole at the top of the wall was 60 feet wide, narrowing towards the ground. 12 people were killed and 30 were injured; some, including children, were horribly mutilated.

Despite the carnage, the rescue attempt failed. The authorities had known that something was up and had exercised the prisoners earlier in the day. Nevertheless, the country had been severely shocked by a new and dreadful experience – the first bombing on the mainland – for the second time in less than three months. As Gladstone put it, the Fenians had conditioned the British people 'to embrace in a manner foreign to their habits in other times the vast importance of the Irish controversy',[47] and he realised now that drastic measures were needed to conciliate the Irish. In that sense the two outrages of 1867 marked the beginning of an era.

They also marked the end of one. After six men had been put on trial for the Clerkenwell bombing, the number was reduced to four, of whom three were acquitted. Then, on 26 May 1868, the only man to be found guilty, Michael Barrett, became the last person to be hanged in public in Britain.

The Tichborne case forms an epoch in the moral and legal history of England. It has weighed upon the public mind like an incubus. Nobody could make out head or tail of it in its inception and in its progress. It was either a great wrong suffered, or a portentous fraud concocted.'[48]

Meanwhile the longest-running sensation of the Victorian age was gathering momentum. It was politically significant but transcended politics. As the lost heir returning to claim his fortune and a mystery figure with a disputed identity, the protagonist was a stock character of melodrama twice over. In 1854 the young Sir Roger Tichborne, heir to great estates in Hampshire, had disappeared. He was presumed drowned when the ship on which he was travelling capsized off the coast of Brazil. However, his mother offered a reward for the discovery of her son. Eventually a man surfaced in Australia, and at Christmas 1866 he came to England to claim the inheritance. He became known as 'the Claimant'. His knowledge *and* his ignorance were extraordinary: if he was Sir Roger, it was amazing what he did not know; if he was an impostor, it was amazing what he did. However, an old Tichborne family servant had retired to Australia, and perhaps the Claimant had learnt a lot from him.[49]

Lady Tichborne had recognised the Claimant but she died, and the rest of the family argued that she had been so desperate to have her son restored to her that she could not bring herself to reject the man. They stood firm against the Claimant, who brought his claim to court in May 1871. At 103 days, the trial became the longest civil action on record. When interest in it flagged periodically, a sensational incident gave it new life, notably the Claimant's assertion that, before sailing to South America, he had seduced his cousin and been told by her that she was pregnant. There was no supporting evidence for this, and even if it were true no gentleman, let alone an English baronet, should have revealed such a thing about a lady. She was now married and sitting in court: her honour had been impugned, but she had no opportunity to defend herself in the witness box until months later.

The Claimant's case collapsed suddenly in March 1872 because he could not show the tattoos that witnesses said Sir Roger had worn. For the *Standard*, the Claimant 'may certainly plume himself on having for months past engrossed a greater amount of attention of a certain kind than all the rest of the world put together. He may boast that he divided society into two hostile camps.' The *Daily News* referred to 'the most extraordinary trial which has taken place in our time'.

Everyone took sides. For the masses it was a class issue. Sir Roger's family had disowned him because he had come down in the world. Yes, he had his rough edges and did not know French, which Roger Tichborne had spoken fluently. But why should someone who had lived as a common working man not inherit a fortune? Why should he speak French? What did it matter that Sir Roger had been thin, and the Claimant was enormously fat? He had put on weight; he was a big-eating, hard-drinking man of the people. As the Tichbornes were an old Roman Catholic family, they had surely hatched a papist plot against the rightful heir because he would not follow the family tradition of giving largesse to the Church. (Many radicals backed the Claimant, but his few supporters in Parliament were aggressive anti-Catholic Protestants.)

On the other hand, a society paper sneered that 'an English crowd is almost always ready to cheer anybody from Garibaldi to the Claimant.'[50] Disraeli called him an 'infamous impostor', and wrote of another politician, 'I always remember, when he is expressing absurd opinions about

PORTRAIT OF THE CLAIMANT
FROM A PHOTOGRAPH

The case of the Tichborne Claimant, which combined farce and melodrama, sex and class politics, was described by the Daily News as 'the most extraordinary trial which has taken place in our time'.

politics, that he believes in the Claimant.'[51] This disdain was widely shared throughout the educated classes. For them the Claimant was Arthur Orton, son of a Wapping butcher, who had practised his father's trade in Australia under the name of Thomas Castro.

Then there were the Tichborne bonds. The Claimant had been declared bankrupt in 1869. He was hopeless with money and had big legal fees to pay. The bonds promised the holders £100 within a month of his taking possession of the estates, on condition that he could not be sued if he lost, and were sold at a huge discount, often for as little as twenty or thirty pounds. The £40,000 raised was less than hoped, and had been spent within eighteen months. Many small investors put their money on the Claimant, and, if he were not checked, other doubtful claims might be financed in this way.

When the Claimant lost his case he was immediately arrested, thrown into prison, and charged with perjury, and forgery for signing the bonds 'Roger Tichborne'. Most of the press heartily approved, but there was a wave of public revulsion. It was believed that the state was trying to crush a folk hero, and that the forgery charge was an extra piece of spite: in forgery cases the defendant had no right to bail.

The criminal trial opened on St George's Day 1873. At 188 days, it was the longest ever – the Claimant had notched up a second record for the length of time he kept a court in business. This time he could not afford top lawyers, and his chief counsel was the eccentric Edward Vaughan Kenealy, whose wild language introduced more and more sensational aspects to the case. He told the jury that they were 'the only representatives of decency and honour in the low and crooked world of law in which they now found themselves; that all force and fraud had been massed to crush the defendant'.[52] The Lord Chief Justice, Sir Alexander Cockburn, was presiding for a second time, although his conducting of the first trial and his out of court comments thereafter had angered the Claimant's supporters. Kenealy proclaimed that Cockburn was the paid servant of a corrupt government and aristocracy, trying to give a semblance of fairness to a punishment that had been predetermined. This did not amuse his lordship. Kenealy, who had turned against the Catholicism of his boyhood, also argued that if his client was extremely stupid and had seduced his cousin, it could only have been because of the education that he, Sir Roger, had received at the Jesuit public school, Stonyhurst. He was about to enlarge on the alleged immoral activities of the Jesuits, and their private theatricals in which boys took women's parts, when Cockburn interrupted: 'The nature of the insinuations you are now making is perfectly fearful. I see no foundation for them.'[53] Like many of Kenealy's remarks they were not especially relevant.

Cockburn's summing up began on 29 January 1874. It was said that he never forgave Gladstone for calling a general election three days earlier and depriving him of the limelight.[54] He spoke for 20 days, and on 28 February, the Claimant was sentenced to seven years on each of two counts of perjury, to be served consecutively. This, too, was seen as vindictive, and, by some lawyers, illegal. It was argued that every crime of perjury involved more than one untruth; on that basis a sentence could go on for ever.

Kenealy's abusive language lost him his livelihood: his patent as a Queen's Counsel was revoked, and he was disbarred by the benchers of Gray's Inn – yet more examples of establishment vindictiveness, in the view of the Claimant's supporters.

Kenealy did not give up. He was certain that the Claimant was Sir Roger Tichborne. He addressed meetings, gave lectures and, most effectively, founded a weekly newspaper, the *Englishman*, with himself as its editor. It presented the Claimant as a martyr, whose ill-treatment was a symptom of how much was wrong with the country. It also continued Kenealy's vendetta against the Lord Chief Justice, referring to the number of times he had been arrested for debt in his youth, and to his three illegitimate children by a greengrocer's wife. It was even hinted that he had committed murder.

Not surprisingly, The *Englishman* wanted lawyers excluded from Parliament and attacked their drunkenness, debauchery and swindling. It declared its opposition to 'the full march of Romanism and Jesuitry'. This was sensation journalism, and the *Englishman*, which cost twopence, sold more than a hundred thousand copies in the first week when, according to Kenealy's daughter, some were bought for a shilling and even half a crown. After seven weeks, sales of half a million were claimed. True or not, the paper sold well for some years, although not all its causes took off. It advocated the vote for married women, 'which would help to stem the wave of atheism and communism which is beginning to flow' as 'all women are naturally religious, honest and good'.[55]

Kenealy's crusade for the Claimant made him so popular that, in 1875, he won a by-election at Stoke-on-Trent with a majority of more than

three thousand. When he came to take his seat he hung his umbrella on
the mace, which caused great mirth, but he soon got down to the serious
matter of proposing a motion for a Royal Commission on the Claimant's
case. Its defeat, by 302 to 1, showed how far the Tichborne story divided
all the political parties from mass opinion. As Kenealy was a teller, the one
vote against was cast by an Irish Nationalist, Major O'Gorman, perhaps
because, like the Claimant, he was immensely fat.

The music halls were solidly pro-Claimant. Between the two trials he
had visited a number to whip up support, and been enthusiastically
received.[56] They took up the favourite expression of the Tichborne
family's leading counsel in the first trial, 'Would you be surprised to
hear?', and it became a catchphrase.

> Now would you be surprised to hear,
> You'll never get your claim,
> And would you be surprised to hear,
> That Tichborne's not your name;
> Now would you be surprised to hear
> (Deny it if you can)
> Your weight alone would make you out
> To be a *Wapping* man.[57]

As a music-hall subject, the Claimant was milked so hard that a letter
to the *Era* complained. 'Surely we are sufficiently tortured with the case in
the papers . . .' and pointed out that one song was in contempt of court:
it had libelled the judge, slandered the jury, 'declared there to be a huge
conspiracy against the 'Claimant' and beslobbered him with all that was
sweet, to the insane delight of the groundlings'.[58]

No wonder that the halls made a hero of Kenealy too. One imperson-
ation was so effective that 'in a little time people will be saying, "Have you
seen Harry Jackson's Dr Kenealy?"'as they used to say "Have you seen the
Shah?" . . . How the audience shrieks with delight, especially when he
says, "I'm an *Englishman*, you can buy me for twopence per copy at any
street corner".'[59] However, the harping on Kenealy also led to complaints:
'It is absolutely sickening to find a man who has made a certain reputation
by scurrility being metaphorically patted on the back by topical vocalists,
and cheered by the undiscriminating gods night after night and week after
week.'[60]

Kenealy kept the pot boiling so effectively that even when the Claimant had been in gaol for more than a year his name was still better known than that of 'anybody who has existed since the days of the divine Nazarene'. The uneducated ploughman, miner, or 'navvy' knew nothing of Shakespeare, Milton or Cromwell, but speak to them of the Tichborne Claimant, and 'to a man, they would be familiar with his career, and perhaps express a sorrow for his present position . . . After all there is nothing very unreasonable about it, for no other man was half so well advertised.'[61]

At the 1880 general election Kenealy, by then a dying man, lost his seat. After his death the *Englishman* declined. The Claimant's release in October 1884 was an anticlimax. Perhaps his loss of weight in prison detracted from his appeal:

> The Claimant is free, and he lives once again,
> On pheasant, beef pudding and jelly;
> His hair has turned grey, and they've taken away
> A lump of his fine derby kelly.[62]

He had no money for such fine fare, and his appearances on the halls did not earn him much. In 1898 he died in poverty and out of the public eye, although never forgotten by those who had lived through the 1870s. In 1892 Robert Louis Stevenson wrote, in a letter from Samoa, '(in the old Tichborne trial phrase) would you be surprised to learn?'[63]

> There's a cry from the East that is heard through the land
> That causes John Bull's fist to double;
> And with instinct to stretch forth a strong helping hand,
> To assist the oppress't in their trouble.[64]

The Tichborne furore had passed its peak when, in June 1876, the *Daily News* published a report beginning 'Dark rumours have been whispered about Constantinople during the last month of horrible atrocities committed in Bulgaria.' This was an unlikely subject to change the course of British domestic politics, but it did. The paper's correspondent was reporting from the capital of the Ottoman Empire on the latest unrest in the Sultan's European dominions. In 1876 Gladstone had resigned from the Liberal leadership, and had supposedly retired from politics. This report in the *Daily*

News, and a second two weeks later, started a mass movement which swept the country, and a chain of events which brought him back to power.[65]

Painstakingly sifting fact from rumour, the *Daily News* correspondent gave the lowest estimate of Bulgarians killed as 12,000. He reported that their savage treatment seemed to derive from the view of Turkish officials that all Christians were revolutionaries who should be hunted down and massacred. This was what had happened. To begin with, the Christian Bulgarians who, like the Jews elsewhere, were envied for their economic success, were attacked by their Muslim neighbours, with Ottoman officialdom standing idly by, or worse. Then the Turkish irregular troops, known as Bashi Bazouks, joined in and whole villages were burned; men, women and children slaughtered.

The Victorians knew nothing of Bulgaria but 'at this era of their history, the British masses were susceptible to gusts of outward-looking moral indignation unparalleled before or since, or in any other country'.[66] Their lofty view of foreign oppression angered many Irishmen, but was consistent with a world view in which Britain was the home of liberty. The rule of Christians by Muslims was an emotive issue at the best of times. Passions were inflamed further because the Turks appeared to think, according to the *Daily News*, that 'England will defend us against Russia while we look after our rebels.'[67] Disraeli's government protested ignorance but was not widely believed. It did not want to know about, let alone publicise, Turkish crimes because Russia was Britain's great rival in the East and Turkey had to be supported against her.

Meetings were held all over the country to protest against 'the Turkish atrocities' or 'the Bulgarian atrocities', as they were often called, and against the government's inaction. His part in the campaign made W T Stead, the editor of the *Northern Echo* in Darlington, nationally known for the first time. Meetings in support of the government also raised the temperature.

At the beginning of September Gladstone joined in – 'It was less a case of Gladstone exciting popular passion than of popular passion exciting Gladstone'.[68] He published the best selling of all his many writings, a pamphlet called *Bulgarian Horrors and the Question of the East*. By the end of the month 200,000 copies had been sold, not counting pirate editions and long summaries in the newspapers. Anthony Trollope read it aloud to his family.[69] Disraeli described it as 'not so ill-written as his custom'.[70] But the impact was not due to its style, although the phrase adjuring the Turks to carry themselves off 'bag and baggage' became

Men of London attend the
PEACE MEETING
IN
HYDE PARK
AT
Three o'clock on Sunday
FEBRUARY 24th, 1878,

COUNTRYMEN,

Can you who love your own liberty, hinder the Subject Races of Turkey from getting full liberty?

You will, if you let the English Government stand in the way of their Emancipation.

Russia has done wrong to Poland.

We still hope to see Poland rise once more as a Nation.

But for the sake of Russia's wrong-doing to Poland, will you oppose her right-doing to the Eastern Christians?

It is not the Russian Government, but the Russian people who have made this war.

They have long felt burning sympathy for the suffering of their brothers in race and religion.

Who is perfect? Is any country perfect?

Has not every country committed some national crimes?

Russia has been cruel, so has England; but Russia is now breaking the yoke of the most oppressive Government in Europe.

So don't stop her present good deeds because of her past bad deeds.

Englishmen, remember the traditions of your own hard-won liberties!

Irishmen, remember the eloquent appeal in Parliament of your countrymen P. Smyth and A. M. Sullivan on behalf of these subject races, against the tyranny of Turkey, against the war-policy of the English Government!

Do not be led by Dizzie & Co. for their own purposes!
War means High Prices, Suffering and Future Bad Trade!
Peace means Plenty, Reform and Better Laws.

Attend and Vote for PEACE.

WORKMEN'S HYDE PARK DEMONSTRATION
COMMITTEE IN FAVOUR OF PEACE.
Committee sits every night at 8-30 p.m. at the "Occidental Rooms," Fountain Court, Strand.

This bill urges people not to be 'led by Dizzie & Co. for their own purposes': the issue of British intervention against Russia became a duel between Disraeli (anti-Russian) and the pro-peace Gladstone.

famous. The sensation was that this mighty champion of Liberal values, an ex-prime minister, had returned to the fray.

Gladstone understood news management. As soon as he launched his campaign, he saw the editor of *The Times*, which reported on Tuesday 5 September that 'Mr Gladstone arrived in London on Saturday night. He will complete his pamphlet on Bulgarian atrocities and put it in the hands of his publishers on Wednesday, and he expressed his willingness to place himself after that day at the command of his constituents.' The result of this gesture to the electors of Greenwich was a speech on Blackheath the following Saturday. The crowd was estimated at about ten thousand, despite heavy rain that lasted for an hour before the start of the meeting. Gladstone was not worried that ten thousand people could not hear everything he said in the open air. He knew that his most important audience were the readers of the next morning's newspapers. *The Times* gave him nearly four columns. For the crowd, whether or not they could hear, it was a great event to *see* a celebrity in the flesh, particularly Gladstone who was known for his commanding presence and eloquent gestures. Many came from outside the constituency, judging by the rush for the railway station at the end.[71]

The speech was short by Gladstone's standards: he spoke for only an hour. He said that he would not mention details of the atrocities from 'a desire not to shock the natural feelings of both women and of men'. His pamphlet referred to 'unbridled and bestial lust', which was more blunt than the circumlocutions of the *Daily News*, such as 'women exposed to the last insults' and 'while life and property suffered in this terrible way, honour fared no better'.

However, for many the Tsar was as great a tyrant as the Sultan, and Gladstone's opponents tried to show that Russian atrocities, for example in Poland and Lithuania, were as bad as Turkish ones. Thomas Carlyle sided with Gladstone; Algernon Swinburne attacked Carlyle. When, at a great meeting in December, Gladstone denounced Disraeli, Thomas Hardy was in the audience and Anthony Trollope spoke, unfortunately overrunning his time.[72] This was the climax of the Bulgarian episode. When Russia declared war on Turkey in April 1877, Britain was in a quandary as to whether she should support and even fight alongside the Turks, as she had in the Crimea 20 years earlier. The new war sustained the frenzy about events in places nobody had ever heard of, until the crisis was resolved at the Congress of Berlin in July 1878. At this period Victorian politics can be seen most plausibly as a duel between Disraeli and Gladstone.

In February 1878, when Russian troops were a few miles from Constantinople and Turkey was near to defeat, both the war party, who wanted Britain to intervene against Russia, and the supporters of peace and British neutrality held meetings simultaneously in Hyde Park. The peace demonstration was broken up by thugs on the other side, whose Polish and Turkish banners were torn from their poles. Some anti-Russian groups processed from Hyde Park Corner to Downing Street, which was already full of onlookers, demonstrators and police. Disraeli, or Lord Beaconsfield as he had become, spoke only a few words before he swept into No. 10. That same day windows in Gladstone's house were smashed. Among the prominent anti-Russian organisations were the Chelsea Tichborne Release Association and the Ladies of West Brompton Tichborne Society.[73]

The Times referred to the Reform League demonstrations in 1866, and pointed out that 'the political protests of huge mobs' were now directed at different targets because the country's institutions had since become more democratic and therfore direct action by huge mobs was now a less effective means of political protest.[74] They continued, nevertheless. The pro-Disraeli anti-Russian demonstrations had a carnival atmosphere and attracted young people more interested in excitement than politics. There was 'a liberal allowance of torchlight processions, brass bands, bonfires, beer and "Rule Britannia"'.[75] The violence and rowdiness was mainly on this side, and many peace meetings were broken up.

The anti-Russians were strongest in London, the North West and the West Midlands. They were known as 'Jingoes' from the chorus of one of the most popular music hall songs of the century:

> We don't want to fight but by jingo if we do
> We've got the ships, we've got the men, and got the money too!
> We've fought the Bear before and while we're Britons true
> The Russians shall not have Constantinople.

The verses' theme was that:

> The misdeeds of the Turks have been 'spouted' thro' all lands,
> But how about the Russians, can they show spotless hands?

And examples were included:

They butchered the Circassians, man, woman, yes, and child,
With cruelties their Generals their murderous hours beguiled,
And poor unhappy Poland their cruel yoke must bear,
Whilst prayers for 'Freedom and Revenge' go up into the air.[76]

As one journalist put it, 'Popular sentiment is delightfully handled in this effusion, and the audience go into ecstatics over it.'[77] That was in May 1877, at the outbreak of the Russo-Turkish war, and the song retained its popularity until the crisis ended over a year later. A later commentator was only a little harsh in writing, 'In ordinary times politics plays no important part in these feasts of sensationalism, but the glorification of brute force and an ignorant contempt for foreigners are ever-present factors which at great political crises make the music-hall a very serviceable engine for generating military passion.'[78]

The singer and writer of 'the Jingo song', G H Macdermott, and G W Hunt, both typical music hall Tories, were entirely sincere. Years later, Macdermott told an interviewer, 'I swear I never sang that song without feeling every word of it. How it went! I let 'em have it every time, and they returned the chorus as earnestly . . . Did it sell? I should think so. They could hardly print it fast enough.'[79] The last point mattered because many purchasers of music-hall songs would never have condescended to enter a music hall. Some songs were more warmongering even than 'The Jingo Song':

We shall have to fight the Russians, boys, and what say you?
We may have to go ourselves, my boys, and what say you?
Your verdict now will help to guide the Government you know;
I hear your Patriotic cry – 'All right! We'll go!'[80]

The illusion that music hall audiences stiffened the Prime Minister's resolve to face down Russia was widespread, but there is no evidence for it. *Punch* got it right when it confronted the Great Ben – Disraeli – with the Great Bounce, an imaginary writer of jingoistic music-hall songs. In addressing his hero, Bounce somewhat overrates his own patriotic work: 'Yes, our lines are a little different; yours is prose, though topping of its kind; mine, poetry, which of course fetches 'em smarter'. Alone, the Great Ben describes Bounce as 'this swelling ape', and adds, 'I feel as feels the traveller at a country inn, who gazes on his own features, hideously yet recognisably reflected in the distorted medium of a rustic mirror.'[81]

However, Disraeli continued to be cast as the hero and Gladstone as the villain on the London music halls, where performers often made up as the two men. In the East End, one visitor complained, 'As much 'Jingoism' and blustering language is indulged in, I with some others ventured to show my disapprobation of this in the usual legitimate way, and was also guilty of applauding the impersonator of Mr Gladstone. An individual sitting near me, whose business it appeared was to take the money for the reserve seats . . . suddenly turned on myself and a brother who was with me, and let fly at us a volley of abusive language.'[82]

Britain acquired Cyprus at the Berlin Congress, and Disraeli came back proclaiming 'peace with honour'. These developments were celebrated not only in song but in elaborate spectacles, described rather generously as 'ballets'. *Aphrodite*, named after the Greek goddess who supposedly rose from the sea off the Cyprus coast, opened with Lord Beaconsfield asleep in his study. A shapely young woman representing 'Mischief' told the audience he was dreaming of Cyprus. There was a distant chorus of 'We Don't Want to Fight . . .', which died away amid the laughter of the audience. Beaconsfield danced with Aphrodite and visited Cyprus, riding in triumph on an elephant.[83]

The jingoism of London music halls was so extreme that parody became irresistible. The 'Jingo' song became 'I don't want to fight, I'll be slaughtered if I do', and some lines have a distinctly modern ring:

> Newspapers talk of Russian hate, of its ambition tell,
> Of course they want a war because it makes the papers sell,
> But when the army's fighting for the honour of the flag,
> They sit in Fleet Street offices and let the papers brag,
> Let all those politicians who desire to help the Turk,
> Put on the uniform themselves and go and do the work.[84]

If the music hall did not influence policy, it certainly raised the political temperature.

Disraeli triumphed in 1878, but the resurgence of Gladstone was still under way. In 1879 he decided to give up his seat at Greenwich and stand for Midlothian. On 24 November he set off from Liverpool to launch the first 'Midlothian campaign'. In a sensational two weeks, he initiated a new form of political activism.

Gladstone commented that 'the journey from Liverpool was really more like a triumphal procession', and his biographer, John Morley added: 'Nothing like it had ever been seen before in England . . . On this journey of a bleak winter day, it seemed as if the whole countryside were up. The stations where the train stopped were crowded, thousands flocked from neighbouring towns and villages to main centres on the line of route, and even at wayside spots hundreds assembled, merely to catch a glimpse of the express as it dashed through.' Gladstone addressed big crowds at Carlisle, Hawick and Galashiels, and 'When he reached Edinburgh after nine hours of it, the night had fallen upon the most picturesque street in all our islands, but its whole length was crowded as it has never been crowded before or since by a dense multitude transported with delight that their hero was at last among them.'[85] As he drove from Waverley station, Gladstone stood in his carriage for a good mile, acknowledging the crowd.[86]

The next day, in Edinburgh, he made his first speech of the campaign, with more than seventy reporters from newspapers all over the country in the crowded hall. According to the chairman of the meeting, 'The whole empire was waiting for the words of the great statesman now seated upon the platform.' Scottish airs played on the organ warmed up the audience while they waited for Gladstone to arrive. When at last he rose to speak, he castigated the government's policies for an hour and three quarters. To loud, prolonged cheering, he ended 'And I say from the bottom of my soul, 'God speed the right.'[87] The pattern had been set.

Dalkeith, a market town and Gladstone's first stop, had never known such excitement. Nearly every business was shut and many people were left outside the packed hall where he spoke. When he drove back to the station, the road was lined with torchbearers. Back in Edinburgh, university students provided another torch-lit procession. *The Times* described the atmosphere:

> If Mr Gladstone's journey to Edinburgh was a triumphal procession, his appearance in Midlothian, beginning with his reception on Monday night, has been a continued ovation. The Gladstone fever has fairly taken hold of the people – of high and low, of old and young, of women no less firmly than of men. Gladstone, like the east wind, is in the air, and the former seems to make the latter tolerable. Delicate ladies equally with robust men defy the elements in their devotion to the hero of the hour. They stand literally for hours in the muddy streets and

at gusty corners, in the dim light of gas lamps as cheerfully as in the broad light of day, on the chance or in the hope of catching a passing glimpse of the sharp features and white locks of the popular favourite.'[88]

During those two weeks, Gladstone made several speeches every day. Understandably Morley stressed his closely reasoned demolition of the government's financial record, in front of 4,500 people at the Edinburgh Corn Exchange. However, he was nearer to the essence of Gladstone's success when he wrote,

Physical resources had much to do with the effect; his overflowing vivacity, the fine voice and flashing eye and a whole frame in free, ceaseless, natural and spontaneous motion. So he bore his hearers through long chains of strenuous periods, calling up by the marvellous transformation of his mien a strange succession of images – as if he were now a keen hunter, now some eager bird of prey, now a charioteer of fiery steeds kept well in hand, and now and again we seemed to hear the pity or dark wrath of a prophet, with the mighty rushing wind and the fire running along the ground.'[91]

This was a man only a month short of seventy. Gladstone's performance was easily parodied by those who dismissed him as a demagogue, stirring up the masses and endangering the right order of society. Take, for example, the music hall song 'When We Were Young':

Our statesmen always held aloof
Nor pandered to the rabble rout.
They did not climb a carriage roof
And from it fume and foam and spout.[90]

The *Saturday Review* said that for statesmen to make more than occasional speeches to public meetings weakened the constitution, 'accelerates the prevalence of democracy and aggravates its evil tendencies'.[91] *The Times* agreed. Only a few days into the campaign, it claimed that, with 'no sign of any diminution in the torrent of Mr Gladstone's words', the public would tire before he did. What was wanted was not 'a mere brilliant display of rhetoric; not a succession of Herculean feats of continuous speaking' but 'some reserve of language and deliberation in argument'. A more passionate temper may be popular for a while, but 'it sacrifices the confidence of the more thoughtful classes'.[92]

This was whistling in the wind. The franchise had been extended in 1867, and Gladstone was to extend it again in 1884. By bringing his message directly to the voters he was modernising politics, which his detractors hated. When the general election was called the following year, Gladstone returned to Midlothian, this time from London, enabling crowds to mass around the railway stations along a different route. He not only became MP for Midlothian, but prime minister for the second time.

> Some thousands of workmen are starving, so they say,
> And the loafers take advantage of the fact,
> With a bit of coloured bunting they gaily march away,
> To show the working people how to act.
> Sir Charley won't allow them to act upon 'the Square',
> And obey his orders everybody must,
> Oh! a sight it is to see all the roughs and Bobbies there,
> All dotting one another on the crust![93]

The electric telegraph made it possible for what happened in a small Midlothian town to be printed in the next day's newspapers but it could not entirely correct the imbalance caused by London's status as the capital of the news media and the Empire. In 1886 rioters attacked almost every hosiery factory in Leicester, where 3,500 men were on strike. This received negligible coverage compared with the rioting in London's West End.

What frightened people above all was that socialists were on the move. 'Socialist' was then as frightening a word as 'Communist' was to become. In the winter of 1885–6, the Social Democratic Federation, founded less than five years before, organised meetings and demonstrations of the unemployed. On 8 February 1886, it held a mass meeting in Trafalgar Square in which its leader, H M Hyndman, expounded his left-wing views. Precautions had been taken against disturbances, with a hundred policemen guarding Buckingham Palace and nearly as many in the middle of the square. However, they were not much use when the demonstrators streamed down Piccadilly to fashionable Pall Mall and St James's street.

The police in Trafalgar Square stayed put, with their backs against Nelson's monument – 'propping it up apparently lest it should topple over, or keeping watch upon the lions for fear they should run away'.[94] The rioters smashed windows and looted as they went. In Oxford Street, a jeweller's shop was cleaned out, and the windows of Marshall and Snellgrove's department store were broken. Carriages were stopped in Hyde Park, and the ladies inside had their jewels torn from them.

A socialist meeting and an attack on a fashionable area of London were seen as cause and effect. Hyndman and three other prominent members of the Federation were prosecuted, including John Burns, who three years later became a leader of the great London dock strike. Argument raged as to whether the event was political or criminal. The *Morning Advertiser* declared that 'In no other capital of the world could fellows like Burns and Hyndman have been permitted to preach the detestable doctrines they did.' *The Times*, which referred to 'the most destructive riot in living memory', was quick to call for their arrest. On the other hand, the *Morning Post* thought that the destruction was the work of 'a few fanatics, a great amount of loafers and idlers, and a huge contingent of professional thieves'.[95] The *Pall Mall Gazette* agreed that the West End had been looted by 'the thieves of Seven Dials and Whitechapel', but was mainly concerned with the failure of the police force, which it described as 'the dodo of Scotland Yard'.[96] Britain had become a peaceful country since the days of the Chartists, and the police had lost their ability to meet a challenge. The events of February 1886 would have been routine elsewhere in Europe, and would hardly have been a sensation if they had taken place elsewhere in Britain. Eventually the leaders of the Social Democratic Federation were acquitted.

The following year Trafalgar Square was the scene of something more serious – the events that became known as the 'Bloody Sunday' riots. Once again, left-wing protest was linked to Ireland, which was in turmoil over a campaign to reduce farm rents. One of the leaders, William O'Brien, a Nationalist MP and influential newspaper editor, had been imprisoned and, to attract Irish support, the Social Democratic Federation called a meeting for Sunday 13 November, demanding his release and endorsing his refusal to wear prison clothes. Only two months earlier in Ireland the police had shot dead three men in a crowd of O'Brien supporters.

The Social Democratic Federation had called a number of meetings in

Trafalgar Square since the riot the previous year. Some had been allowed, some not. The Commissioner of Police, Sir Charles Warren, was determined to put a stop to this one and – even more so than at Kennington Common in 1848 and Hyde Park in 1866 – the issue was whether the authorities had the right to ban peaceful protest in a large public space. Even the great advocate Sir Charles Russell, a Liberal and an Irishman, thought they did, as the square was Crown property. However, Warren also banned organised processions from approaching it; in addition to 1,500 police in the square, another 2,500 were engaged in breaking up processions or waiting in reserve.[97]

A procession from Clerkenwell was nearing the square when it was charged by police, mounted and on foot, lashing out with their truncheons in all directions. According to one reporter, the spectacle of blood flowing from the head wounds was 'sickening'. When a procession from South London suffered a similar fate a woman was knocked down and trampled by a police horse. Liberal papers gave many examples of police brutality – young boys beaten, fallen men attacked, women struck across the breast. There were more than a hundred casualties and two deaths. Notwithstanding all of this, a large crowd reached the side of the square, which, according to the *Pall Mall Gazette*, was filled with 'one long continuous indignant roar, the inarticulate anathema of the masses of London upon the usurpers who, in the name of the Crown, were trampling under foot one of the most cherished liberties of the people'.

The Times saw things differently. It congratulated Warren on crushing an attempt to 'terrorize London by placing the control of the streets in the hands of the criminal classes'. It exulted in the failure of 'the agitators', and claimed that bricks, iron bars and knives had been used against the police. The *Pall Mall Gazette* replied that police casualties were trivial, and that the crowd had not wanted to touch a single policeman unless he had attacked them. Once again, John Burns was heavily involved. He was arrested along with a radical MP, Cunningham Graham, who had headed a rush of about four hundred men to get into Trafalgar Square. After his arrest Grahame was beaten about the head. At the Old Bailey he and Burns were eventually sentenced to six months imprisonment, but the next day a Bow Street magistrate despatched less eminent demonstrators to prison on police evidence alone. This, too, aroused Liberal indignation, and much talk of 'Tory terror'.

'Are we in London or Saint Petersburg?' asked *Reynolds's Newspaper*. It claimed that 'an insolent oligarchy' was riding roughshod over the liberties of the people on both sides of St George's Channel. The paper attacked Gladstone who 'never removes an abuse until it is rotten-ripe', and the Prince of Wales, who had supposedly paid for food and drink to be sent to the police from nearby public houses 'at his own expense'. 'That fat podgy German' and 'do-nothing and eat-all Prince' had never done a day's work in his life, so how could he have paid for anything 'at his own expense'? John Burns, who had asked for shorter hours and more pay for the police, had been mercilessly bludgeoned by them for his pains.[98]

Hero to some, Sir Charles Warren was villain to others. At the music halls, a policeman was either a villain or a comic figure. 'Who Killed Cock Warren?' was set to the tune of 'Who Killed Cock Robin?' and ''Twas in Trafalgar Square' parodied 'The Death of Nelson':

> They cried, as down the Strand we ran,
> Warren expects that every man
> Will much exceed his duty,
> Will spoil some fellow's beauty.

> The 'Times' throughout the nation has made a big sensation –
> Hibernian indignation by its articles is stirred;
> It says Parnell wrote letters to plot against his betters,
> And if he did he well deserves their censure, on my word! [99]

The Times unleashed its sensation on 18 April 1887, seven months before Bloody Sunday. As part of a series of articles entitled 'Parnellism and Crime', a letter from Charles Stuart Parnell, the leader of the Irish Home Rule Party, was published in facsimile. It condoned the murder in 1882 of Lord Frederick Cavendish, the newly appointed chief secretary for Ireland, and his under-secretary, T H Burke. They had been stabbed to death in Phoenix Park, Dublin. The letter said that 'to denounce the murders was the only course open to us' but 'though I regret the accident of Lord F. Cavendish's death I cannot refuse to admit that Burke got no more than his deserts'. Argument raged for more than two years over whether the letter was genuine.

If it was, it was the 'smoking gun' Parnell's enemies wanted. In their view, Home Rule for Ireland would begin the break-up of the British Empire. If they could discredit Parnell, the whole cause was discredited,

PARNELLISM AND CRIME.

REPRINTED FROM

The Times.

———o———

SECOND SERIES,

INCLUDING THE FACSIMILE OF MR. PARNELL'S LETTER.

SECOND EDITION.

PRICE ONE PENNY.

LONDON :
PRINTED AND PUBLISHED BY GEORGE EDWARD WRIGHT, AT THE TIMES OFFICE,
PRINTING HOUSE SQUARE.

1887.

Controversy raged for two years over The Times' *publication of a letter by Charles Stuart Parnell. Richard Pigott's confession of forgery in February 1889 humbled* The Times *and marked the high point of Parnell's reputation.*

and so, too, were Gladstone and the Liberal Party, who were now his allies. Parnell denounced the letter in the House of Commons as 'a villainous and bare-faced forgery', but he did not sue, which allowed the affair to drag on. In June the Queen's Golden Jubilee celebrations distracted attention even from this sensation, and it was not until another Irish Nationalist decided that 'Parnellism and Crime' had libelled *him* that events moved forward. His case against *The Times* failed, but during the court proceedings of July 1888 more letters, allegedly from Parnell, were read out. Parnell now asked for a Select Committee of the House of Commons to investigate the matter. The Conservative government refused, but set up a special commission of three judges to examine the range of accusations *The Times* had made against the Home Rulers, notably that they had committed and abetted crimes in pursuit of political ends. In effect, the government had put them on trial.

Although law officers of the Crown routinely appeared for private clients, by 1888 the practice had fallen into disrepute. The Attorney-General's appearance for *The Times* in this case confirmed that the paper and the government had a common interest. Parnell was represented by two prominent Liberals – Sir Charles Russell, an Ulster Catholic and a future Lord Chief Justice, and Herbert Asquith, a future prime minister. Russell's speech attacking the whole record of British rule in Ireland was published as a 600-page book, but his sensational contribution to the proceedings was his cross-examination of Richard Pigott, a shady Irish journalist through whom *The Times* had acquired the notorious letters. By this stage, a government agent had already told of how he had penetrated a secret Irish organisation in the United States and discovered their lurid secrets, but he had failed to make a link with Parnell and his colleagues. Everyone was waiting for the authenticity of the letters to be examined. They remained in suspense until the commission had been sitting for more than four months.

On 20 February 1889 Pigott arrived in court. When Russell rose to cross-examine, he asked him to write some words on a piece of paper, but there was no immediate reference to this. A few minutes later, he asked Pigott whether he had known about *The Times*'s accusations against Parnell before they were published. Pigott swore that he had not. Russell drew some papers from a shelf in front of him – 'There was not a breath, not a movement. I think it was the most dramatic scene in the whole cross-examination, abounding as it did in dramatic scenes.'[100] He drew out a letter, handed it to Pigott, and asked him if he had written it. Pigott admitted that he had. Russell read it aloud. Three days before the publication of the first of the *Times* articles, Pigott had disclosed a plan to destroy Parnell and his party. Shown up as a liar from the outset, he spent the next two hours squirming, sweat pouring down his face, as Russell exposed the inconsistencies in his evidence. The next day, he was back in the box, listening to Russell's revelations of his career as a blackmailer and writer of begging letters. One spectator wrote, 'It was the most exciting time I ever spent. In the end we came away astonished that a fellow-creature could be such a liar as Pigott. It was very funny too; but I could not help thinking of Becky Sharp's "It's so easy to be virtuous on £5000 a year"; and to see that old man standing there, with everybody's hand against him, driven into a corner, after all his twists and turns, was somewhat pathetic.'[101]

Pigott had been asked to write down words that occurred in the letters, one of which was 'hesitancy', which he spelt 'hesitency', as it appeared in the most notorious letter. They were fakes, and Pigott had forged them. That was on a Friday. The following Tuesday Pigott was due back in court, but he did not appear: he had fled to the Continent. Russell announced that over the weekend Pigott had signed a full confession in the presence of two prominent journalists, one of them the radical MP, Henry Labouchere. On Thursday 28 February Pigott reached Madrid, where, as police burst into his hotel room, he placed the muzzle of a revolver in his mouth and pulled the trigger.[102] The 'smoking gun' had been turned on its inventor.

This was the high point of Parnell's reputation. He emerged as an innocent man traduced by his enemies. The mighty *Times* had been humbled and, to an extent, the Conservative government too. On the Friday night, when Parnell appeared in the House of Commons, Gladstone led the opposition, the Liberals and Irish Nationalists, in a spontaneous ovation.

Although *The Times* withdrew the letters, it persisted with the rest of its case. When the Commission report was published a year later, not all the Irish Nationalists emerged unscathed, but Parnell did. It was a reminder of his triumph.

Who says England's star is setting?
Echo answers firmly, No.
We are stronger, more united
Than we were twelve months ago.

To the Union Jack of England
We will all the firmer cling,
When we think of Baden-Powell
And the siege of Mafeking.[103]

With the eclipse of Parnell, Ireland no longer dominated British politics. The 1890s were the decade of imperialism, as manifested most spectacularly at the Queen's Diamond Jubilee. In South Africa, Imperialism led to the Boer War, which began in October 1899. Ironically the greatest sensation of the war was not a British victory: the British Empire versus the Boers was supposed to be an unequal contest and the victories, when at last they came, were no more than the public felt was its due. However, in the first months of the war the Boers had won a string of battles, and had encircled British-held towns, notably Ladysmith and Kimberley. The small town of Mafeking in Cape Province, near the borders with Bechuanaland and the Transvaal, was less important but after Ladysmith and Kimberley had been relieved within about four months the siege of Mafeking dragged on.

After seven months, on 17 May 1900, persistent rumours were circulating in London that Mafeking had been relieved.[104] They continued to build throughout the next day until at 9.20 in the evening a placard appeared outside the Mansion House confirming the end of the siege. The Lord Mayor had trusted Reuter's news agency, whose message had arrived three minutes earlier and was being sent around the world. When the leader of the House of Commons, Arthur Balfour, was questioned at midnight, he could neither confirm nor deny the Reuters report. The placard at the War Office in Pall Mall, where the crowds were naive enough to expect reliable information, said merely 'No News'. Inside enquirers were told, 'The resident clerks had retired, and if any news did come, it would not be posted.'[105]

Nevertheless, the Lord Mayor was not alone in trusting Reuters, and it was from 9.20 that evening the 'Mafficking' began. A large coloured picture of Colonel Baden-Powell, the commander at Mafeking and the future founder of the Boy Scouts, was fixed over the Mansion House balcony, where the Lord Mayor appeared to tremendous cheers from the vast crowd below. He told them, 'We never doubted what the end would be,' and that 'British pluck and valour when used in a right cause must triumph.' At the end of his speech there was a deafening outburst of shouting, cheering and singing, with blasts from tin whistles and cornets, and pounding drumbeats.

By ten o'clock, long processions were marching from the City to the West End. From the Mansion House to Pall Mall there was a continuous roar. Many people waved the Union Flag – those on foot were acknowledged by others brandishing flags from cabs and the tops of omnibuses. Cyclists carried them on long poles. Where flags had run out, over a shop in Regent Street, people waved blankets, tea cloths, towels and 'various feminine garments which are usually displayed only on a clothes line'.

The theatres were still important centres for the spread of news, and the glad tidings were announced from the stage, usually by the actor-manager, who was keen to bathe in reflected glory. Although the crowds were noisy, they were good-humoured and well-behaved. Strangers smiled at each other, even shook hands. A reporter noted, somewhat equivocally, that 'ladies in evening dress were squeezed in the crowd, but only smiled happily'. Anyone wearing a uniform was cheered, even postmen. Delighted newsboys were seen throwing late editions into passing cabs free of charge, but others charged twopence for a halfpenny paper.

There was little let-up during the night. Night workers at Smithfield and Covent Garden shouted the news to early risers. In the Home Counties, engine drivers blew their whistles to announce the news to villages on their line. The celebrations continued from Friday right through the next day. From ten in the morning until late, the Mansion House was the focus for a huge crowd. In the City an elderly bald-headed clerk balanced on an office-window sill marking time with a silk umbrella to the singing crowd below. Urchins beat out tunes on biscuit tins, and cab drivers competed to see who could stick the most flags into a horse's harness. Young women burst into song, as they walked arm in arm and six abreast. At Euston station, the entire clerical staff of the London and North Western Railway appeared on the gallery, then descended into the hall to sing the National Anthem. It was the same in the East End. Working men with flags and banners walked along the Bow Road singing patriotic songs and hundreds of cyclists, bearing photographs of Baden-Powell, paraded through Poplar and Stepney. A number of Jewish boys were wearing khaki and South African-style slouch hats.[106]

Of course the old Queen was nowhere to be seen, but an estimated two thousand people were outside Marlborough House to cheer the Prince and Princess of Wales as they left for the theatre. Anyone with the remotest connection to Baden-Powell or Mafeking was granted heroic status. The Colonel's mother's house at Hyde Park Corner was another centre of attention. A long strip of coloured cloth had been put in front of the balcony with 'Mafeking' in big letters, surrounded by flags. On the Saturday evening, Mrs Baden-Powell, and two sons not in South Africa, sat in a box at the Alhambra music-hall, which had been decorated with flags and flowers.

The provinces went wild too. Rudyard Kipling wrote from Sussex, 'You've seen something that I never suspected lay in the national character – the nation letting itself go.' He added, 'We had a merry little riot down here – turned out *en masse* and formed processions and shouted ourselves hoarse,' although, according to his wife's diary, Kipling himself had instigated the celebrations.[107] In Liverpool, the noise was so great that the Lord Mayor gave up trying to address the crowd and settled for leading the National Anthem. In Newcastle, on a clear night, masses of people saw rockets fired from the offices of a local newspaper. In Brighton, church bells were rung, electric light blazed from municipal buildings and ships sounded their whistles. In Bradford factories sounded their buzzers. Nearly all demonstrations were good-humoured, but in Leeds, where one firm was reported to have sold 25,000 flags, 3,000 people turned up outside the house of a prominent pro-Boer and smashed the windows. In some towns effigies of President Kruger were burned.

The rejoicing was all unofficial. There were no flags on government buildings in Whitehall. So why had such a minor military development inspired these 'demonstrations unparalleled in recent times'?. Within three weeks British troops had occupied both Johannesburg and Pretoria without anything like so much fuss.

According to *The Times*, the man in the street knew that he was not celebrating a military victory, but was overjoyed that a small handful of his countrymen had been succoured by British troops. He also thought of Mafeking as an affair of the people rather than of the army, that the garrison was largely made up of civilians like himself, called upon to do their best. The paper gathered together all the clichés about stiff upper lips and underdogs in its attempted explanation: 'Throughout the Empire it is instinctively felt that at Mafeking we have the common man of the Empire, the fundamental stuff of which it is built, with his back to the wall, fighting an apparently hopeless battle without ever losing hope, facing overwhelming odds without a thought of surrender . . . The story of Mafeking has all the elements of romance.'.[108] And there was 'relief' in two senses: the end of the siege, *and* deliverance from the nightmare of national humiliation.[109]

In the Mafeking celebrations, the nationalism that had been but one ingredient in so many political sensations of the Victorian age took over, and hero-worship knew no bounds. Before this, Baden-Powell had been unknown. The tendency to laugh at sensations and satirize them was scarcely visible – it was as though the Victorians had lost their sense of humour in the fervour. It was the last great popular outburst of the Victorian era; the next, occasioned by the Queen's death, occurred, of course, in the reign of Edward VII.

CHAPTER 3:

Religion and Morality

The men who have awakened slumbering generations, who have begun mighty movements, shaken idols or Popes, or huge vices from their thrones, have not been uniformly characterized for severity of language, sobriety of illustration or chasteness of style.[1]

In the nineteenth century, Christianity aroused strong passions, and few non-believers were as brave as Charles Bradlaugh, who professed his atheism in public. Protestantism was seen as an essential element of the national identity, and an inspiration behind Britain's emergence as the most powerful country in the world. Roman Catholicism, however, was the religion of Britain's historic enemies, Spain and France. The Pope was seen by many as another continental tyrant, and the Catholic–Protestant divide was an important factor in the estrangement of the Irish from the Crown. In England, the Anglican Church held a commanding position in national life, and among the Anglican establishment even other Protestant denominations were suspect. Now that the Victorian pride in Protestantism and hatred of the Roman Catholic Church have largely evaporated, and the link between religion and nationalism has been broken, it comes as a surprise to discover that many sensations were bound up with religious issues, and how passionately the Victorians could be stirred by them.

In July 1848, an apparently innocuous ceremony took place: a new Roman Catholic cathedral was consecrated in Southwark, the first since the Reformation of the sixteenth century. *The Times* wrote of Dr Nicholas Wiseman, 'his huge form towering over every one around him, and dilated beyond its usual dimensions by the dress and insignia of an archbishop'. As Wiseman was not yet archbishop, the newspaper had made a slip, which turned out to be curiously prophetic – although less significant than its description of him as 'the last of a line of prelates and priests sufficiently long to frighten the isle from its Protestant propriety'.[2]

A little over two years later Wiseman frightened the isle from 'its Protestant propriety' with a vengeance. In the autumn of 1850 he became the first post-Renaissance English cardinal, and Pope Pius IX also named him Archbishop of Westminster, one of a dozen new sees in England and Wales. This caused a furore. By giving the bishoprics 'territorial' titles, like Westminster, the Pope seemed to English Protestants to be trying to exercise power and authority over the places named– if not over the whole country. Wiseman, who was in Rome, made matters worse by the language of pastoral letter which he sent to his flock: 'Till the Holy See shall think fit otherwise to provide, we govern, and shall continue to govern, the counties of Middlesex, Hertford and Essex, as Ordinary thereof, and those of Surrey, Sussex, Kent, Berkshire, and Hampshire, with the islands annexed, as Administrator with Ordinary jurisdiction.'[3] It was easy to interpret these words in a temporal sense because the Pope still ruled as a monarch over a significant part of Italy.

A month after it had outraged popular opinion over General Haynau, whose cruelty had been exercised on behalf of Roman Catholic Austria, *The Times* now became the voice of unrestrained Protestant nationalism: 'We can never forget the part which Papal power has at different times played, or endeavoured to play, in presumptuous hostility to the independence and liberties of this realm.' Wiseman had thought fit 'to enter the service of a foreign Power, and to accept its spurious dignities'. The Pope had shown his 'unambiguous intention to insult the Church and Crown of England'.[4] A few days later the paper referred to 'the Church which has maintained so dark a superstition and bred so constant a disaffection amongst a large part of the Irish people'.[5] An Irish dimension to any problem was always thought to make it worse. Apart from the deplorable fact that the inhabitants of Ireland were mainly Catholics, Irish immigration had accounted for most of the rise in the Catholic population of Britain from 30,000 at the turn of the century to 750,000 in 1850. *The Times* was expressing a common view when it described these immigrants as 'men who have imbibed superstition from their cradle', and declared that innocent Protestants 'may easily become a prey to teachers so subtle, so skilful, so insinuating as Romish emissaries are known to be'.[6]

Protestantism was seen as an essential element in the national identity, and an inspiration behind Britain's emergence as a world power, but the Anglican Establishment was outraged by the influence of other religious denominations.

All but two Anglican bishops sent an address to Queen Victoria asking her to 'discountenance by all constitutional means the claims and usurpations of the Church of Rome'. She replied that she was determined 'to uphold alike the rights of my crown and the independence of my people against all aggressions and encroachments of any foreign Power'.[7]

The papal brief establishing the new hierarchy had been dated 29 September 1850, which gave a tremendous boost to Guy Fawkes Day. The Fifth of November 'was no longer a mere amusement for the street rabble; but many displays evidently emanated from a class having larger means at their disposal'.[8] Effigies of the Pope and Wiseman were burned all over the country: as Roman Catholic conspirators against the Protestant order, they were perceived as worse than Guy Fawkes himself. In Ware, an effigy of His Holiness, dressed in full pontificals, with not only the triple crown on its head but also a large pair of ram's horns, and a figure of a donkey representing the Cardinal Archbishop were paraded through the streets to a hill overlooking the town. There they were hanged on a gallows placed over a huge pile of faggots and tar-barrels, then set ablaze amid the roars and curses of the crowd.

Much the same happened in Salisbury, but with more pomp. The figure of His Holiness was brought out amid cheering, at about half past six, then paraded with effigies of Wiseman and the new bishops in a procession of torch-bearers and a brass band. The figures were placed on a great wooden platform, and a volley of rockets was sent into the air. As the fire under the platform was lit, hundreds of fireworks were hurled at the effigies. Then came the National Anthem.[9] Exeter, another cathedral town, also put on a splendid display. Thirty bare-headed 'friars' preceded two hundred other representatives of popish orders and dignitaries bearing gigantic effigies of the Inquisitor-General as well as Wiseman and the Pope. Masked men carried gridirons, shackles and other torture instruments. Ten thousand spectators gazed in astonishment at the fireworks and coloured lights as the effigies were burned in the cathedral yard.[10]

In central London the figures of Wiseman 'were built up of enormous proportions, the red hat of the cardinal having a brim as large as a loo-table, and his scarlet cape being as long as a tent'. Guy Fawkes was there, too, on a barrel marked 'Gunpowder', with lantern and matches in his 'radishy and gouty fingers', but much smaller, showing his relative insignificance.[11] Pope and cardinal continued to star in the Guy Fawkes parades until the outbreak of the Crimean War four years later, when the Tsar of Russia became the main hate figure.[12] Shortly after Guy Fawkes night an explosive letter from the Prime Minister, Lord John Russell, to the Bishop of Durham was released. He wrote that 'there is an assumption of power in all the documents which have come from Rome – a pretension to supremacy over the realm of England, and a claim to sole and undivided sway, which is inconsistent with the Queen's supremacy, with the rights of our bishops and clergy, and with the spiritual independence of the nation, as asserted even in Roman Catholic times'.[13]

In his investigation of *London Labour and the London Poor*, Henry Mayhew heard from a street entertainer how 'the Papal Aggression', as it was called, made Wiseman and the Pope popular subjects for street singers and 'patterers'; they were worth a sixpenny tip in the City and a shilling in the West End. His informant said that the entertainers bore the Pope no ill will; they merely gave the public what it wanted. 'And for the first time in their innocent lives, the parsons came out as stunning patrons of the patter'. One of the most popular songs went:

Now Lord John Russell did so bright,
To the Bishop of Durham a letter write,
Saying while I've a hand, I'll fight
The Pope and Cardinal Wiseman . . .

Now we don't care a fig for Rome,
Why can't they leave the girls alone,
And mind their business at home,
The Pope and Cardinal Wiseman?
With their monastical red cardinal's hat,
And lots of wafers in a sack,
If they come here with all their clack,
We'll wound them fil fal la ra whack.[14]

Protests against 'papal aggression' continued into the following year, when a law was passed banning the assumption of ecclesiastical titles already taken by Anglican clergy – even though the titles of the Catholic bishoprics did not clash with Anglican ones. Twenty years later it was repealed.

If the villains of religious sensations were Catholic, the heroes had to be Protestant. However, those looking for a preacher to inspire great crowds had to look outside the established Church. The Baptists provided Charles Spurgeon.

He began as a boy wonder. As *The Times* put it, looking back from his fiftieth birthday, 'This mere boy, still in his teens, came into this dark and dreary region [of South London], and never for the moment had the least doubt that he would win a good harvest of souls. So he won them.' On the lack of learning often alleged by Spurgeon's critics, the paper continued, 'The boy who began to convert souls whilst our future rectors and curates are deep in criticism, history, and examination subjects, and who never had time to go to school or university since, is not impeccable in the matter of taste.'[15] Even this comparison with Anglican parsons was not entirely in the latter's favour. Having begun as a Baptist preacher, Spurgeon transcended sects and denominations, but he was clearly not an Anglican. Neither did he endear himself to the Church of England by referring to it as 'this very powerful sect'.

He preached so successfully at Waterbeach in Cambridgeshire that some South London Baptists invited him to their chapel in New Park

Street, and he began his ministry there when he was only 19 years old. This was in March 1854, the month Britain entered the Crimean War. Both admirers and detractors saw his preaching as essentially theatrical. The playwright James Sheridan Knowles was quoted as saying, 'I was once lessee of Drury Lane theatre; were I still in that position I would offer him a fortune to play for a season on the boards of that house. Why, boys, he can do anything he pleases with his audience! He can make them laugh and cry and laugh again in five minutes. His power was never equalled.' The *Sheffield and Rotherham Independent* described the same phenomenon more harshly: 'He is nothing unless he is an actor, unless exhibiting that matchless impudence which is his great characteristic, indulging in coarse familiarity with holy things, declaiming in a ranting and colloquial style, strutting up and down the platform, as though he were at the Surrey Theatre, and boasting of his own intimacy with Heaven with nauseating frequency.'[16]

Spurgeon sounded like an Old Testament prophet: 'Woe to thee, Oh land, when the great ones love the harlot's house . . . Oh, God, have mercy upon the land whose justice seats and palaces are defiled with vice.' Or 'Our souls have recoiled within us because of the wickedness in which we dwell; it has sometimes made us feel as if we could borrow God's thunderbolts with which to smite iniquity. Even they that love men best and love God most cry, "How long, how long, how long, great God, wilt thou endure all this?"[17] As one newspaper put it, 'When pronouncing the doom of those who live and die in a state of impenitence, he makes the vast congregation quake and quail in their seats. He places their awful destiny in such vivid colours before their eyes that they almost imagine they are already in the regions of darkness and despair.'.[18] *Punch* was less respectful:

> May his tonsils and windpipe ne'er call for a surgeon,
> Be tough as bull-leather, O lungs of my Spurgeon.[18]

Very soon the chapel in New Park Street was far too small so it was enlarged. Even then it was still not big enough, and, two and a half years after his ministry began, Spurgeon hired a vast new building, which had just opened, and could take 10,000 people. This was the Surrey music-hall in Surrey Gardens, intended for secular entertainment but free for hire on Sundays .

On the first Sunday, 19 October 1856, an estimated twelve to fourteen thousand overflowed the hall, with more thousands in the gardens and the surrounding streets. As Spurgeon launched into his sermon, there were cries of 'Fire!' and 'The galleries are giving way, the place is falling.' There was a rush down the stairs from the galleries. Although Spurgeon shouted that there was no fire, that thieves and pickpockets were trying to create a diversion, the stampede continued. An iron balustrade on a stone stair-case from the first gallery gave way; crowds piled on top of one another; people were trampled on. In the panic some threw themselves through thick plate glass windows. Seven died, and 28 were badly hurt, many less so.[20]

Spurgeon, who was carried fainting from the pulpit, was convinced, probably rightly, that the shouts had been prearranged by enemies of his ministry. Unfortunately the text of his sermon had been 'The curse of the Lord is upon the house of the wicked, but He blesseth the habitation of the just'. Unfortunately, too, when Covent Garden Theatre had burned down earlier in the year, Spurgeon had said that the fire was the judgement of God on the wicked theatre-goers.[21]

Only about fifty pounds' worth of damage resulted, and seven dead did not constitute a major disaster – in the 1850s, large halls and theatres often burned down. However, the fiasco of the first service conducted by a controversial religious superstar in a vast new building was a sensation. In the words of one of Spurgeon's supporters,

At the most solemn moment of the occasion, the wicked rose in their strength, like a whirlwind sin entered, followed by terror, flight, disorder and death. From the cellar to the palace, the events of that dreadful night have been the theme of eager discourse. In the squares, the streets, the lanes and alleys, as well as in the workshops and counting-houses, and the chief places of concourse, it has been, through each successive day, the one great object of thought and converse.

The writer added that many people had believed preposterous rumours – that the building had been reduced to ashes, and that 10,000 people had been buried under the rubble. The rumours added to the sensation, whether or not, as was alleged, the press had 'lied as well as exaggerated most fearfully'.[22]

The twenty-two-year-old Spurgeon seems to have suffered a minor nervous breakdown, but he soon recovered and his sermons continued to delight his admirers and infuriate his critics. At a fundraising bazaar Spurgeon spoke on the legitimate pleasures of a Christian. He included dancing, but men and women should dance apart, as the their dancing together produced unholy thoughts. *Reynolds's Newspaper* claimed that the poor were strikingly absent from the congregation. 'Smug faces and well-shaven faces, and faces round and fat, and smirking, are here – the self-same faces, smiling from the same places as the audience of yesterday's comic songs and brass band.'

An indignant correspondent to the paper described Spurgeon as a friend of the poor, and asked why 10,000 people would congregate on Sunday after Sunday if he were a mountebank. The paper backtracked: it was only ridiculing some of Spurgeon's 'absurd and priggish' opinions, like the one about dancing, and his comparison between the doors of theatres and the gates of hell. It also criticised his habit of addressing the deity 'as though He were sitting in a corner of the Surrey Music Hall, and had paid a shilling to hear Mr Spurgeon'.[23]

Music hall singers poked fun with 'The Great Sensation Song':

> Mr Spurgeon asked me if
> I'd like to be his mate, Sir,
> He would preach and I would have
> To go round with the plate, Sir,
> To sing a comic song or two
> To please the congregation.
> 'Any dodge is fair,' says he,
> To raise a good sensation.[24]

The song dates from 1861, the year when the new preaching house opened. The Metropolitan Tabernacle in Newington Butts, Southwark, where Spurgeon preached for 30 years, was 184 feet long, 81 feet wide and 62 feet high, with two galleries. Six massive Corinthian columns held up the pediment of the façade. *The Times* called it 'one of the ornaments of the metropolis, and of a region wanting ornament', and probably the 'largest and best edifice for congregational worship in this country'.[25] Gladstone visited it, much to the delight of Spurgeon, who wrote, 'I feel like a boy who is to preach with his father to listen to him.'[26]

Spurgeon also had a public who never heard him. Every Thursday from August 1854, his Sunday sermon, suitably revised, was published and sent to all parts of the kingdom. He often preached ten or twelve times a week, and many sermons were first published long after his death, up to 5,000 with a total world sale, it was claimed, of 100 million copies.[27] He had no physical advantages apart from his voice: he was only five foot six, and stout after the first flush of youth had gone, but he maintained his huge following until his death in January 1892.

Spurgeon's heyday as a preacher was the 1850s and 1860s, and anti-Catholic outbursts persisted throughout this period. The latter decade was remarkable for the rabble-rousing of the extreme Protestant 'lecturer against Romanism', William Murphy. The battles between his supporters and working class Irish Catholics were known as the Murphy Riots, and were particularly brutal in Birmingham in 1867 and Ashton-under-Lyme in 1868. Murphy, a renegade Irish Catholic, tried to prove that 'every Popish priest was a murderer, a cannibal, a liar and a pickpocket', that the Virgin Mary was a Protestant, and that she did not believe in nunneries, which should, he thought, be subjected to government inspection.[28]

This was the background to a sensational court case that gripped the public for nearly the whole of February 1869, when a Roman Catholic nun sued her mother superior for libel, and conspiracy to expel her from her convent. Gothic novels about Catholic nuns immured in convents against their will were still familiar, if no longer fashionable. For those with different literary tastes, there were pamphlets like the anonymous *The Appalling Record of Popish Convents and the Awful Disclosures of Tortured Nuns*, which castigated 'the revolting crimes of Monks, and the horrible fate of Females inveigled into Nunneries by Catholic Priests and their tools, the Puseyite parsons of the Church of England'. However, a nun determined to stay, in the face of her mother superior's determination to get rid of her, was new.

In the course of the 20-day trial, the jury were presented with so many examples of petty persecution that they begged the judge to move on, but there was also enough sensational material to transfix a public eager to know what went on behind convent walls, and only too keen to believe the worst. The lead counsel for the plaintiff was the Solicitor-General, Sir John Coleridge, who as counsel for the Tichborne family two years later was to coin the catchphrase 'Are you surprised to hear?'. To him, the case showed 'what women were capable of when they shut themselves up from their kind, and did violence to the instincts of their nature'. The

jury, all male and Protestant at least nominally, would have been reminded
of the frustrated nuns of Gothic fiction. Nor would they have missed the
Solicitor-General's reference to the Inquisition when he said that 'though
bodily torture had ceased, the same spirit remained'.[29]

While Coleridge was at pains to point out that this was no 'ultra-
Protestant or indiscriminate attack on the largest body of Christians in the
world', the leading defence counsel warned against anti-Catholic bias. He
told the jury that 'it would be natural if you were in some degrees preju-
diced' against the defendants, who had 'secluded themselves from the
world – as you and I may think unwisely, but still sincerely and reli-
giously'. He warned them not to be influenced by popular prejudice.
Coleridge replied that neither should they be afraid of doing what was
right, just because it happened to be popular, and added that the case
destroyed any veil of sanctity or unreal halo with which 'the devout imag-
inings of good people' had invested the religious life. The Lord Chief
Justice, in his summing-up, believed that he was addressing 'twelve gentlemen who belong to our great Protestant community, and, as such,
perhaps also as thinking men, you may think that convent life is an object
of dislike and suspicion', that making it impossible for women to be wives
and mothers was 'contrary to the laws of nature and the ordinance of
God'. However, he pointed out that the plaintiff and her family, as well as
the defendants, were Roman Catholics.

It would be hard to find a more staunchly Roman Catholic family
than that of Susan Saurin, otherwise known as Sister Mary Scholastica.
(Her convent name belied her atrocious spelling.) Her two sisters were
nuns, her brother was a Jesuit, and her uncle a parish priest. She and her
main antagonist, the mother superior, known in the case as Mrs Starr, had
both come from Ireland. Miss Saurin accused Mrs Starr and another
senior nun of conspiring to drive her out of a convent near Hull by ill-
treatment and by slandering her to the Bishop of Beverley. She claimed
that the persecution had begun when she had refused to tell the Mother
Superior what had passed between her and her priest in the confessional.
She was supposed to have shown her unsuitability to be a nun by breaking the rule against communicating with the outside world without the
mother superior's permission. She had clandestinely written to her uncle,
the parish priest in Ireland, and her letters to her relatives were 'too tender
and affectionate'. The term 'my ever dearest uncle' was considered exces-
sive. All correspondence was seen by the mother superior, and letters to

POLICE NEWS EDITION.

THE EXTRAORDINARY
DISCLOSURES ^{OF}A NUNNERY

ACTION BY A SISTER OF MERCY.

(SAURIN v. STARR AND KENNEDY.)

LIFE OF THE PLAINTIFF.
MYSTERIES OF CONVENT LIFE.
EXAMINATION OF THE WITNESSES.
SUMMING UP AND VERDICT, &c., &c.

MISS SAURIN

MRS. KENNEDY

ONE PENNY.

G. PURKESS, 286, STRAND, AND ALL NEWSAGENTS.

In February 1869 'the great convent scandal' gripped a public hungry for details about 'the horrible fate of Females inveigled into Nunneries by Catholic Priests and their tools, the Puseyite parsons of the Church of England'.

Sister Scholastica were held back, even when her father was seriously ill; her family had been greatly distressed when she did not answer. Other letters had passages blotted out, because 'they contained reflections on the community'; others were destroyed 'lest they might lead to distraction'. She claimed that the death of a brother had been concealed from her for months. The defence pointed out that the essence of the religious life was obedience to rules which might seem trivial to the outside world, and that the case must turn on the obligations the plaintiff had undertaken when she joined the order. Nevertheless, the ban on expressions of affection to family members shocked many people.

In her letters to the Bishop, the mother superior implied accusations she could not sustain. While teaching small children, the plaintiff was supposed to have stolen dinners they had brought with them, although when she was partially strip-searched nothing was found. The children and their parents gave evidence that no meals had been stolen. More sensationally, Sister Scholastica was said to have been in 'a state of excitement' when a certain priest visited the convent. Those who were convinced that, sooner or later, sex would rear its ugly head were not disappointed, although the Mother Superior denied in court that her words implied what they were generally believed to imply. Sister Scholastica, who was prevented from speaking to other nuns or to the children when she was not teaching them, was accused behind her back of stealing clothing from the body of a nun who had just died and wearing it in chapel.

Neither did the Bishop of Beverley emerge unscathed. He had set up a commission of inquiry at which the written evidence of the other nuns against Sister Scholastica was never presented to her. A summary was read out, but it did not contain all the accusations. Any defence involving her accusing *them* was disallowed. It is true that the rest of the small community were unanimously against Sister Scholastica, who seems to have been a difficult woman, but this was allegedly due to their unquestioning obedience to their mother superior. The Bishop did not help his case when he was reproached for supplying documents to the defence, which he denied to the prosecution. 'Do you think it was fair to us?' 'Yes; I acted under the advice of their counsel . . . [Much laughter].'

Several newspapers considered that the summing up favoured the defence, but the jury found for Sister Scholastica on the main counts. She did not get anything like the five thousand pounds she had asked for, but as she had taken a vow of poverty perhaps that was just as well. The huge

PEOPLE OF THE DAY, No. 1.
" I felt very uncomfortable."

In the Sister Scholastica case, Mrs Starr, the Mother Superior, was accused of bullying, cruelty and slander.

crowd outside the small Queen's Bench courtroom were delighted. 'They wanted justice to be done, but they were quite satisfied that the Catholics were in the wrong. Subtleties of evidence, nice questions of propriety were but slightly canvassed. "We don't like priests and nuns, and we don't want them and their ways encouraged here." . . . The throng outside rejoiced as much as if they or their relations had suffered from Catholic oppression.'[30]

In the courtroom, a Catholic contingent had reserved seats for the last few days of the trial. 'The galleries were filled with ladies; while in the body of the court, if you except the barristers, there were at least four ladies to one gentleman.' But they 'were of a very different class from the women who are wont to be seen in courts of law'. Many wore crucifixes or necklaces of black beads like rosaries. Every comment of the Lord Chief Justice in favour of the defendants was greeted with 'smiles and sparkling glances'.[31] The verdict was received in silence.

The partisanship in – and outside – the court was reflected in the press. For *The Times* 'an investigation of a matter alien from the whole spirit of English national feeling, conducted so patiently and dispassionately' was 'honourable to our legal machinery'. The defendants had accused the plaintiff of being mean, cunning, gluttonous, miserly, a liar and a thief. 'If she be, it is Convent life which has made her such. If she be not, the Conventual discipline again must bear the reproach of having trained up a society of false witnesses.'[32]

According to the *Tablet*, on the Roman Catholic side, Miss Saurin had 'preferred to appeal to twelve Protestant tradesmen' instead of Cardinal Manning or the Pope. Perhaps she thought they were better qualified to decide a question of convent discipline. The paper referred to 'the odious chorus of blind exultation' with which the verdict had been received in the press. The case had been said to reveal 'the failure and astounding pettiness of the Catholic religious system', but really showed 'the astounding unfairness, and shallow meanness, and jaundiced prejudice of what is too pretentiously assumed to be the British public'.[33]

The British public did not care about the views of the *Tablet*. Neither did it excite itself unduly about the law, enacted six months later, that disestablished the Anglican Church in Ireland. This was one of the measures by which Gladstone hoped to conciliate Ireland's overwhelmingly Catholic population. But 'the great convent scandal' was more interesting – and certainly more fun.

In 1873, almost twenty years after Spurgeon's first appearance in London, the Americans Dwight Moody and Ira Sankey began their first great revivalist tour of Britain. Moody preached the gospel and Sankey sang it. Moody had preached in England before, but both men were unknown when they arrived in Liverpool on 17 June. When they returned to Chicago over two years later, they were being compared favourably with John Wesley. Spurgeon attended one or two of their meetings in London, and invited Moody to speak at his Tabernacle.

Moody charmed his audience rather than battered them. 'He was a folksy story teller, described by *The Times* as friendly and full of American humour, 'often, it must be owned, a little vulgar'. He told Bible narratives, 'as if they were good American stories picked up in Chicago'.[34] As *Punch* put it,

> They proclaim Gospel truths, in spite of grave prepossessions,
> In colloquial slang and commercial expressions,
> State scriptural facts in American phrases,
> And interpolate jokes 'twixt their prayers and their praises.[35]

Another paper called Moody 'diffuse, unconnected, rambling and given to repetition' but 'earnest and full of pith'. He said 'quaint racy things such as we are quite unaccustomed to hear from a pulpit'. His Americanisms fell fresh on English ears, and often raised an audible laugh.[36]

Sankey's organ playing and hymn singing were equally important. He accompanied himself on the harmonium in a clear and strong, deep, rich and sonorous voice; each word was articulated with great distinctness. Sometimes he almost spoke the words, to which the music was always subservient, although the congregation were humming the best tunes as they left. *Sacred Songs and Solos*, better known as *The Moody and Sankey Hymn Book* contributed to the fame of the pair.

They began in the north of England, and were soon holding two huge meetings a day, complemented by discussions in the 'inquiry room' for those who wanted to commit themselves to Christ. When they moved to Scotland, they hired the Corn Exchange in Edinburgh, which held 6,000. An Edinburgh divine expressed the general amazement: 'If anyone had told us six months ago that our still and decorous city would be stirred to its depth by two strangers, we would hardly have believed the tale.'[37]

Had Calvinism not lost ground in Scotland, their impact would have been less. Moody proclaimed that Christ died for *all* men, and an important element in his success was that he reached out to all sects and branches of Christianity. Even so, there was criticism. Moody was said to undermine the authority of the local minister, and the organ playing was not always liked. And when the campaign was over? A plaintive letter to the *Glasgow Herald* asked, 'How are we to be let down from the fever heat of these meetings to the quiet old-fashioned manifestations of the Christian life?'[38]

Moody and Sankey crossed to Dublin in October 1874, where they aroused the hostility of the young Bernard Shaw. According to him, their success was down to publicity, curiosity, novelty and excitement, and they tended to turn their converts into highly objectionable members of society. However, Shaw's attack, his first appearance in print, was published in an unimportant newspaper.[39] Then the evangelists visited Liverpool, where they could not find a big enough building, and had one built of iron sheeting to hold 7,000. In Birmingham, verses sold in the streets told the story:

> Oh, the town's upside down, everybody seems mad,
> When they come to their senses we shall all feel glad,
> For the rich and the poor, the good and the bad,
> Are gone mad over Moody and Sankey.[40]

At last, in February 1875, they arrived in London. Their venues, always the largest buildings available and always packed out, included the Agricultural Hall in Islington, which held 15,000, and Exeter Hall in the Strand, the gigantic preaching house, where Spurgeon, too, had held forth in the days before the Metropolitan Tabernacle. Not only the pious were drawn to them: outside the venues where they preached there were 'multitudes of young men full of fun and joking; multitudes also of evil women and girls, gaily dressed, joining in the ribaldry; the two together forming a mass of well-dressed but disreputable blackguardism,' showing, it was said, that the revivalists had come where they were badly needed.[41] Photographs of the pair on sale in bookshops, and penny editions of Sankey's songs hawked on the streets, testified to their impact. As with Spurgeon, it is impossible to know how many went to witness the sensation rather than to be saved, but there were huge numbers in the latter category. Gladstone attended three times in a month, and wrote that 'The sight was wonderful and touching in a high degree; also the earnestness of Mr Moody.'[42]

As *The Times* reported, even midday prayer meetings were well attended. They opened with the chairman reading out long lists of requests for prayers from people needing help. A young woman wanted her parents directed in the right way, a clerk his employer, and so on. The phrase used repeatedly was 'a great outpouring of God's spirit on this great city'. There was much talk of London being given up to sin and needing God's help to save it from destruction.[43] For the many who saw it as the wickedest city in the world, London was the 'New Babylon'.

Who made up the audience? The godless poor whom Church and Chapel had failed to reach? Or religious people like Gladstone? In the latter group the Americans were preaching to the converted, and there is some evidence to suggest that they worried about this.[44] The argument hotted up when they established themselves in the East End, building in Bow the kind of structure they had put up in Liverpool. It was gas-lit, with a galvanised iron roof and sawdust floor, and held 8,000. A writer to *The Times* claimed that he had attended a service when it was only a fifth full, and that few in the congregation had been from the working class but were clergymen, dissenting ministers and country visitors attracted by the novelty. However, as the local Anglican vicar he was a rival, and he revealed his prejudices by referring to 'this religion of mere emotionalism and sensationalism' and 'its arbitrary divisions of the converted and the unconverted, its preaching of terror and damnation, its test question "Are you saved?" and its confessional in its guise of the inquiry room.'[45]

He was answered by a resident of Bow, who claimed to have visited the hall thirty or forty times and never seen it so sparsely attended as the vicar claimed. He had seen large numbers of men and women, 'ragged, dirty and degraded, listening intently to the earnest appeals of the preacher, who exhorted them to give up sinful habits and companions'. Of course, as well as costermongers, fallen women and street arabs, many thousands of 'respectable sinners' had been present.[46]

The Bow vicar admitted grudgingly that Moody and Sankey were better than no religion at all, although too dangerous for respectable Christians. This idea provoked an extraordinary furore when the revivalist

*The sensational methods which brought success to the Salvation Army
also aroused virulent opposition, as the cover to this contemporary
songsheet demonstrates.*

mission was taken to Eton. The college was at the heart of a powerful
Anglican establishment, whose members were outraged by the idea of the
boys coming under an extraneous religious influence.

In June 1875 a large tent appeared just outside the college's grounds,
and the news got round that Moody and Sankey were to hold a meeting
there with the approval of the college authorities. According to E H
Knatchbull-Huguessen, an old Etonian and Conservative MP, whose son
was at the college, this cast doubt on whether the religious teaching on
offer was satisfactory. He expostulated to *The Times* that parents had a
right to have their sons protected from 'the semi-dramatic performances
which have lately caused so much excitement in London'. Such performances were excusable in the case of the masses of people whom Church
and Dissent had failed to reach, but 'this cannot be applicable to Eton
boys'. What was more, if the College let in revivalists, would they stop at
Roman Catholics?[47]

Seventy-four MPs, either Old Etonians or parents or both, wrote a
letter hoping that the meeting would not go ahead. In the House of
Lords, the Marquess of Bath wondered how many of 'these performances'

would be given. A *Times* leader said that many would see the service as 'a sensational and impudent demonstration, made to give something to talk about and boast of in the lower ranks of the religious world'. (*The Times* did not define 'the lower ranks'.) On the other hand, it was better, on the whole, to let the service take place. The boys would come away 'with their emotions in their normal state and their attachment to the Church of England unimpaired'.[48]

The Eton authorities made clear that, although the boys were not banned from visiting Moody and Sankey – any more than they were banned from Windsor races – they were not encouraged either. Then it was announced that the meeting could not be held as planned: the Buckinghamshire police would not undertake to keep order. Windsor town hall was hired but, just before the meeting was due to start, the Windsor authorities cancelled it. In the end, it was held in a nearby private garden. Attended by between 150 and 200 Eton boys and three or four hundred others, it passed off uneventfully.[49] The hullabaloo, not the occasion, was significant.

Moody and Sankey were repeatedly accused of putting on 'performances', despite Sankey's undeclamatory style. Even Queen Victoria referred to 'this sensational style of excitement, like the Revivals'. In her view, this religion could not last, 'and it is not wholesome for the mind or heart, though there may be instances where it does good'.[50] It was even suggested that the American master of sensation, Phineas T Barnum, was using Moody and Sankey as a money-making venture.[51]

They eventually left for home in August 1875. It was claimed that during their four months in London two and a half million people attended their meetings. They returned in the autumn of 1881 for another successful, but inevitably less sensational, three-year campaign. Even if the people they attracted were mainly Christians already, their faith was refreshed: a leading Congregationalist said that they were transformed by new joy and elasticity of spirit.[52]

If faith could cause a sensation, so could unbelief. Charles Bradlaugh was worse than a Roman Catholic: he was an avowed atheist. This in itself made his views on moral issues suspect, but he was also a republican and a radical, who supported Home Rule for Ireland and votes for women. In his courageous battle against the tide of opinion in all those areas he was a titan of the age. So was his colleague, Annie Besant.

Religion and morality were inevitably intertwined, but morality was also bound up with decorum. Among respectable people, if one discussed an immoral subject – which usually meant sex – one was besmirched by it. This meant that the reform of sexual mores could only be effected by breaking taboos. Moral campaigners were associated with sensation, whether they liked it or not – especially if they were women. As decorum was conventionally thought especially important for women, those who did not stay at home with their families but campaigned on 'immoral' subjects were assailed with abuse and ridicule. They had to be very brave to do so.

Together Bradlaugh and Besant set up the Freethought Publishing Company and worked closely on the newspaper the *National Reformer*, which Bradlaugh edited. They lectured tirelessly to spread their views. Bradlaugh was a good speaker with a fine presence, but Annie Besant's beautiful voice, good looks and the fact that she was a woman made her even more remarkable. Their collaboration was so close that assumptions were made about other aspects of their relationship, which were probably untrue but added piquancy to any sensation in which they might be involved, especially one involving sex.

Such a sensation broke out in 1877, even though most newspapers did not want to report it. They knew that most of their readers thought public discussion of the sexual act disgraceful, and were loath to read about a case involving the advocacy of contraception. Yet the repulsive nature of the subject had its own attraction, and this dichotomy was an essential part of the sensation. The trial of Bradlaugh and Besant, presided over by the Lord Chief Justice, led to 'a great agitation throughout the country'. Annie Besant wrote that 'Some huge demonstrations were held in favour of free discussion; on one occasion the Free Trade Hall, Manchester, was crowded to the doors; on another the Star Music Hall, Bradford, was crammed in every corner; on another the Town Hall, Birmingham, had not a seat or a bit of standing-room unoccupied. Wherever we went, separately or together, it was the same story.' The huge interest in the case extended to the whole of Bradlaugh and Besant's radical agenda.[53]

It all began in December 1876 when a Bristol bookseller was summonsed for selling an allegedly indecent book. This was *The Fruits of Philosophy*, a pamphlet on birth control by an American doctor, Charles Knowlton. It had been in print for 40 years without spectacular sales. The publishing rights in it were held by a close associate of Bradlaugh, who did not know that it was being sold in Bristol, pepped up by a couple of shocking illustrations to suggesting a spicy text, at three times the usual price. The pamphlet's subtitle 'The Private Companion of Young Married Couples' reinforced this impression. Bradlaugh's friend decided not to fight the case and withdrew the pamphlet, whereupon Bradlaugh and Besant published it, with a new subtitle and without the doubtful pictures. In the name of freedom of expression, they invited the authorities to prosecute them.

Even the *Lancet* had denounced 'beastly contrivances' and 'filthy expedients for the prevention of conception', so it was brave to take a stand on artificial birth control, and especially so of Annie Besant, the first woman in Britain to do so. As a young mother separated from her husband, she was particularly vulnerable. Her association with Bradlaugh and the case cost her the custody of her daughter.[54]

At the trial, which began on 18 June 1877, the two defendants represented themselves. Bradlaugh, who was an effective if self-trained lawyer, was the legal brains for both. However, for a woman to represent herself, especially on such a subject, was extraordinary. The pair had already been accused at the magistrate's court of 'corrupting the morals of youth', of inciting them and others to 'indecent, obscene, unnatural and immoral practices', and of bringing them to a state of 'wickedness and debauchery'. The pamphlet was described as 'indecent, lewd, filthy, bawdy and obscene'.

Knowlton had pointed out that married couples were being impoverished by the birth of children they could not afford to maintain, fear of which induced men to delay marriage and end up in the arms of prostitutes . However, leading for the prosecution, Sir Hardinge Giffard – a successor as Solicitor-General to Coleridge, who had opposed him on the Claimant's behalf – asked a key question: would *The Fruits of Philosophy* not suggest 'to the unmarried as well as to the married, and any persons into whose hands the book might come – the boy of seventeen and the girl of the same age – that they might gratify their passions without the mischief and the inconvenience and the destruction of character which would be involved if they gratified them and conception followed'?[55] In other words, did not contraception encourage extra-marital sex? Annie Besant replied that it was a calumny on English women for it to be thought that they kept chaste only from fear of motherhood, and that as women who had sex outside marriage were already depraved they could not be corrupted by Dr Knowlton.

When Lord Chief Justice Cockburn declared that there never was a more ill-advised and malicious prosecution, an acquittal seemed likely. In fact, the jury decided that although *The Fruits of Philosophy* was calculated to deprave the public, the defendants had no corrupt motive in publishing it. Cockburn told them that this amounted to a verdict of guilty. Sentencing, which was expected to be lenient, was delayed for a week.

In the meantime, Bradlaugh and Besant addressed a packed meeting, it was estimated that about a third of the audience were women, many of whom were very young. There was a great deal of cheering, and Bradlaugh announced that Garibaldi had sent a message of support, another link between him and English radicals. *The Fruits of Philosophy* sold large numbers, and Annie Besant asserted that there was sure to be a retrial because the verdict was inconsistent, and the judge had been on their side.[56]

The Lord Chief Justice was furious. He insisted that he had not taken sides in his summing-up, and that the sale of a condemned publication was a grave offence. The defendants were sentenced to six months in prison, fined £200, and were to enter into a recognizance of another £500 to be of good behaviour. This was hard. However, at the beginning of the trial Bradlaugh had argued that the indictment should be quashed because it did not set out which passages in the pamphlet were supposed to be obscene. When the Solicitor-General had replied that the whole thing was, Cockburn had reserved judgement. After the sentence was passed, Bradlaugh asked for it to be suspended until this point had been decided. He was turned down. The prisoners had left the dock, and the wardress's hand was on Annie Besant's arm when the judge changed his mind. If they would promise not to sell the pamphlet in the meantime, he would suspend the gaol sentence until the Court of Error had examined Bradlaugh's argument. (It examined matters of law only; there was no Court of Appeal until 1907.) They were released on their own recognizance of £100, but Bradlaugh paid for them both: as a married woman, Besant could not enter into her own recognizance. In January 1878 the Court of Error granted Bradlaugh's point and quashed the sentence. However, for his many enemies he had only escaped on a technicality. He was still a notorious atheist and pornographer who deserved to be locked up, if, indeed, prison was not too good for him.

It is worth digressing briefly to consider one of the few truly sensational parliamentary events. Samuel Plimsoll, Liberal MP for Derby, had been waging a campaign against 'coffin ships', overloaded and unsafe vessels sent to sea, regardless of seamen's lives, by unscrupulous owners out to cash in on insurance money. Under pressure from Plimsoll, Disraeli's government had brought in a Merchant Shipping Bill which Plimsoll supported although he did not think it went far enough. However, on 22 July 1875 Disraeli told the House that the Bill would not proceed for the time being, so raising suspicions that the shipowners had got at him. Plimsoll dashed into the gangway, gesticulating and shouting. He looked at one point as though he was about to assassinate Disraeli. He claimed that no ship of the past 30 years had been broken up because it was worn out, and some shipowners never built a ship or bought a new one but were simply 'ship's knackers'. When he dared to say that MPs were among the guilty men, supporters of the shipowners of 'murderous tendencies', and named the member for Plymouth, there was uproar. Plimsoll was ordered out of the House, and left in a state of great emotion, shouting, 'Scoundrels, scoundrels, scoundrels!'.[57] He soon published a protest, 'laying upon the head of the Prime Minister and his fellows the blood of all the men who shall perish next winter from perishable causes'. The following year a new law *was* passed, giving the Board of Trade the necessary powers of inspection, and confirming Plimsoll's status as a people's hero.

Three factors were behind Plimsoll's ability to create a scene in the House that became a sensation in the country: he personified a cause with mass support; his explosion of temper humanised the formalities of parliamentary debate; and the occasion precipitated the dramatic involvement of the Prime Minister. Only Bradlaugh offered as much in the five years after 1880, when he shared in the great Liberal victory by winning a Northampton seat at the third attempt. In a bitter campaign against him, posters were addressed to 'the Christian electors of Northampton' calling him 'The Greatest Enemy of God and of His Truth Now Living Among Men'.[58]

On 24 June 1880 *The Times* reported, 'When the doors of the House were thrown open, the scene which presented itself at once indicated that proceedings far surpassing in interest the usual Wednesday business were about to take place. The benches on both sides of the House were fully occupied, the Stranger's Gallery soon became crowded and both within and without the House there were unwonted evidences of expectancy and excitement.' Bradlaugh was determined to take the oath as a Member of Parliament, although the House had just decided that he should not be allowed to. A constituency's right to elect anyone they chose had yielded to the belief that an atheist had no place in the House of Commons.

Bradlaugh had asked that he should be allowed to affirm rather than swear on the Bible. Although a law passed 14 years earlier had allowed a few religious groups to dispense with this practice, it did not apply to atheists, and the Speaker, Sir Henry Brand, had turned him down. Bradlaugh had then declared that he was ready to take the oath, but was refused on the grounds that he had shown he would not be bound by it.

He was allowed to address the House on that Wednesday in June 1880, but the decision against him had been taken and all his eloquence could not change it. He was ordered to withdraw, and when he refused he was briefly imprisoned in the Clock Tower of the Palace of Westminster, the last man to suffer this penalty.

The Conservative Member who moved the motion that he 'be not permitted to take the Oath or make the Affirmation' was Sir Hardinge Gifford, who had led for the prosecution in the Knowlton trial three years earlier. Another Conservative described Bradlaugh as 'a man whose livelihood, whose profession for a series of years had been to disseminate cheap and pernicious literature among the mass of the people'.[59] However, the most important of his enemies was Lord Randolph Churchill, father of Winston, who cynically used the case to embarrass a Liberal Party torn between love of free speech and hatred of atheism.

The Liberals had a comfortable majority so without the divisions on their side there would have been no crisis. All seemed set fair for Bradlaugh, when a motion was passed that he be allowed to affirm after all. He took his seat on 2 July, and earned respect as an assiduous MP over the next eight months. His most cherished cause was to put an end to 'perpetual pensions', annual payments the state had originally awarded to national heroes but which were now pocketed by their descendants. A beneficiary of the system, by the huge sum of £4,000 a year, was the Duke of Marlborough, father of Lord Randolph Churchill.

However, as soon as Bradlaugh had taken his seat, his enemies had mounted a legal challenge to his right to do so without having taken the oath. In March 1881, he lost the case. On 7 April he was returned again at the resulting by-election. Again he tried to take his seat, was turned down and asked to withdraw, refused and was expelled. With the

Liberals divided, the hostility of most Irish MPs was repeatedly decisive. The Catholics, like the Jews, indignantly denied that the fight to allow an atheist into Parliament had anything to do with the battles fought earlier in the century on their behalf. Ironically, many Protestants considered an atheist MP only marginally more dangerous than Lord Ripon, the new Viceroy of India. He was the first Roman Catholic in the post.

Gladstone's government announced a bill allowing atheists to affirm, but withdrew it after fierce resistance. However, Bradlaugh did not give up. On 2 August 1881 an estimated fifteen to twenty thousand people met in Trafalgar Square to protest against his exclusion from Parliament. Bradlaugh spoke to them, claiming to have addressed meetings in the provinces of 200,000 people. In the rush to see him leave, two of the granite pillars at the base of Nelson's column were knocked down. Wrongly believing that Bradlaugh would go straight to the House, five thousand of his rougher supporters stormed down Whitehall and Parliament Street. A few got into Palace Yard but were expelled by police, so, after three cheers for Bradlaugh, there was a surge towards Westminster Abbey and back down Parliament Street. The crowd was not completely dispersed for another couple of hours.

The next day tension was high when Bradlaugh tried again to take his seat. A special train had been chartered from Northampton to bring a deputation of 300 people, bearing a petition to Parliament. Four or five thousand spectators cheered them when they arrived at the House at eleven thirty in the morning. Ten minutes later Bradlaugh drew up in a gleaming hansom cab decorated with his Northampton colours, and went inside. Annie Besant was in the crowd, and in her autobiography described what happened next:

Angry murmurs were heard, for no news came from the House, and they loved 'Charlie', and were mostly north country men, sturdy and independent. They thought they had a right to go into the lobby, and suddenly with the impulse that will sway a crowd to a single action there was a roar, 'Petition, petition, justice, justice,' and they surged up the steps, charging at the policemen who held the door. Flashed into my mind my chief's charge, his words 'I trust to you to keep them quiet', and as the police sprang forward to meet the crowd I threw myself between them, with all the advantage of the position on the top of the steps that I had chosen, so that every man in the charging crowd saw me, and as they checked themselves in surprise I bade them stop for his sake.

An invasion of the House would have been disaster for Bradlaugh. According to Besant, 'many a man said to me afterwards in northern towns, "Oh! If you had let us go we would have carried him into the House up to the Speaker's chair.'". She went on, 'We heard a crash inside, and listened, and there was sound of breaking glass and splintering wood, and in a few minutes a messenger came to me: "He is in Palace Yard." And we went thither and saw him standing, still and white, face set like marble, coat torn, motionless, as though carved in stone, facing the members' door.'[60]

Besant claimed that fourteen men, police and ushers, had thrown themselves on Bradlaugh to get him out of the building. They 'pushed and pulled him down the stairs, smashing in their violence the glass and wood of the passage door'. Nevertheless, *The Times* reported that the police did their best not to use more force than was needed, and Besant agreed: she blamed the ushers.

> The strong, broad, heavy, powerful frame of Mr Bradlaugh was hard to move, with its every nerve and muscle strained to resist the coercion. Bending and straining against the overpowering numbers, he held every inch with surprising tenacity, and only surrendered it after almost superhuman exertions to retain it. The sight – little of it as was seen from the outside – soon became sickening. The overborne man appeared almost at his last gasp. The face, in spite of the warmth of the struggle, had an ominous pallor.

When Palace-yard was reached Mr Bradlaugh, who was physically a powerful man, seemed to be quite exhausted. The heat and excitement made him feel faint, and he called for a glass of water, which he was given.[61] *Punch* joked about it:

> They fought and they tussled away down the stairs,
> With many a gasp and a gurgle,
> And poor Daddy Longlegs, who won't say his prayers,
> Lost his collars and tails in the struggle . . .

Who profits by this? The reply's not remote,
Not the Rough, nor the Bobby nor gaoler,
But as Mr Bradlaugh must have a new coat,
'Tis a capital thing for his tailor.[62]

For Bradlaugh, though, it was serious. Although big and strong, he did not enjoy good health. It was said that he was never the same man, mentally or physically, after his rough treatment at the hands of a parliament he revered.[63]

However, he did not give up. In those days Parliament was usually in recess from August until February, and the following February there was a repeat of what had happened: a big meeting in Trafalgar Square, and another attempt by Bradlaugh to take his seat. However, after another vote to ban him, he tried a new tactic. Before anyone could stop him he had administered the oath to himself on a New Testament he had brought with him. The next day the House voted on Lord Randolph Churchill's motion that Bradlaugh be expelled. He had to leave. This time, he had antagonised some of his fellow non-believers, one of whom referred to 'the comic spectacle of an atheist, smitten with devotion and remorse, fighting his way to kiss the Bible'.[64]

Another by-election, but this time Bradlaugh shared the limelight. As crowds gathered in front of newspaper offices all over the country, the report came through that Roderick Maclean had fired on Queen Victoria outside Windsor railway station. Half an hour later the news arrived that Bradlaugh had yet again been re-elected for Northampton.

He did not try to take his seat immediately, because this time the government put forward an Affirmation Bill. Even in his absence he was responsible for a great parliamentary occasion, for some thought that Gladstone made the speech of his life. He had wrestled with his Christian conscience, and decided to put all his strength on the side of tolerance to the atheist. 'I have no fear of Atheism in this House,' he thundered, but he lost the Bill by three votes. Had he spoken less well, and insisted more firmly on party unity, in the modern manner, he would have won.

The drama continued. Bradlaugh was tried for blasphemy: his enemies knew that a man convicted twice of that offence was disqualified from being a Member of Parliament. He was acquitted. Then he took the oath, before the Speaker could stop him, but this time in collusion with

Gladstone as a way of referring the issue to the courts. He lost again, appealed, and lost again.

He was returned for Northampton for the fourth time in the 1885 general election. When Parliament met the following January it re-elected Speaker Peel, who had replaced Brand. Amid breathless excitement, before other Members had been sworn in, and before therefore they had the right to intervene, the Speaker said that his predecessor had followed the House's instructions but now there was a new House. He had no right to prevent a Member taking the oath, and it was not for him to ask a Member's views when he did so. Public opinion had swung towards Bradlaugh by now. There was no more trouble. Home Rule for Ireland had Gladstone's support, and was to be the dominant parliamentary issue for the next five years.

By the time Bradlaugh died five years later, he and Annie Besant had parted company. She had been become a socialist, and not only took part in the march from Clerkenwell to Trafalgar Square on 'Bloody Sunday' when the famous anti-government riot of 1887 occurred, but stood bail for many of the men who were subsequently charged. Bradlaugh, although he admired her actions, always opposed socialism.

Like Besant, Josephine Butler, the tireless champion of the rights of prostitutes, was an effective speaker with a lovely voice. She, too, was good looking, but her appearance only added to the bile expressed by her male opponents. Although she was motivated by her Christian faith, she was accused of being more wicked than the women for whom she campaigned.

No subject was more repellent to most Victorians than the compulsory examination of women for venereal disease. Like birth control, it drew attention to the physical aspects of sex. There was no debate in either House when the first of the Contagious Diseases Acts was passed in 1864. Because venereal disease was making so many servicemen unfit for combat, the Act forced regular internal examinations, and hospital treatment if necessary, on prostitutes, who were suspected of being carriers, in 11 towns near military and naval bases. Two more Acts followed, extending the number of towns to 18, and increasing police powers. After the third was passed in 1869, Josephine Butler began her long fight to have them repealed.[65]

Throughout her campaign respectable newspapers rarely covered her speeches, because their content was so sensational. In 1870, the House of

Commons even barred reporting of its debate on the Acts. The *Pall Mall Gazette* hoped that the lesson would not be lost on 'these passionate female orators', who had been thrusting unsavoury details on the public, which they dressed up 'for the edification of the uneducated masses in inflammatory harangues'. It was 'the lowest and most obscene newspapers' who had shown their approval 'by printing them in full alongside of the police-court abominations of the week'.[66]

Josephine Butler had founded a home for prostitutes in Liverpool, after her husband had become principal of Liverpool College in 1866. She was convinced that they were decent women, desperate to earn money to live. Her investigations took her to Maidstone and Dover, two towns where the Acts applied. She found little girls playing a game of arrest and inspection on the pavement, and men with venereal disease roaming the streets looking for sex. Many married men passed on the disease to their wives. According to the Victorians' double standard of morality, women should pay dearly for their sexual transgressions but not men. The report of the Royal Commission on the Contagious Diseases Acts, which sat in 1871 as a result of Butler's campaign, expressed this view: 'There is no comparison to be drawn between prostitutes and the men who consort with them. With one sex the offence is committed as a matter of gain, with the other it is an irregular indulgence of a natural impulse.'[67]

The protestors disputed whether the Contagious Diseases Acts reduced the incidence of venereal disease in the armed forces. If they did not, there was no case to keep them; if they did, the interests of men and women were shown to be irreconcilable, as they enabled men to indulge themselves safely at women's expense. Any working-class woman might be forced to undergo an inspection if she had been going out with a soldier, been falsely informed on, mistaken for a prostitute or seen waiting at a street corner. Examination was a horrific experience, and a woman who resisted might be strapped to a bed for days until she gave in, her legs braced apart by clamps,[68] and the tray of instruments was a terrifying sight in itself. Josephine Butler fought the Acts *and* an influential body of opinion that wanted them extended to the whole country.

Following the Royal Commission's report, the first Gladstone government brought forward a Bill to do precisely that. Moreover, if a woman imprisoned for prostitution was found at the end of her sentence to have a contagious disease, she would be detained for a further nine months. If a Justice of the Peace was satisfied that she would give up prostitution, she could be immediately discharged, whether or not she were infected.

To Josephine Butler, this was another Bill to protect men at women's expense, and she campaigned against it. However, many abolitionists were sorry when it was withdrawn. It would also have raised the age of consent for girls from 13 to 14, and brought in measures to protect the under 16s.

The opponents of the Contagious Diseases Acts, like the suffragettes in their day, made the Liberal Party their main target. Both groups had more Liberal than Conservative supporters, but were thwarted by Liberal governments. Among the anti-abolition Liberals, Sir Henry Storks, nicknamed 'The Bird', was a prominent victim of the Butler campaign. He had implemented the Acts as High Commissioner in Malta, and wanted them to apply to servicemen's wives. At a stormy by-election in October 1870, he stood for Colchester where an abolitionist candidate split the Liberal vote and let in the Conservative. During the campaign, Butler was driven from her hotel by hooligans threatening to burn it down – an event scarcely reported in the press.

The abolitionists also claimed credit for reducing the Liberal majority at the Pontefract by-election of 1872, the first British parliamentary election to use the secret ballot. The press scarcely mentioned them or the mob organised by brothel-keepers and supporters of the Liberal candidate to wreck their meetings. The *Saturday Review* reported only that 'Those dreadful women who appear on the eve of every election to foul the ears and minds of simple people on the Contagious Diseases Acts flitted through Pontefract, and did not disappear without some hooting.'[69]

In 1875, a case emerged that showed what could happen in towns where the Acts applied. Mrs Percy, a poor widow and a music hall performer in Aldershot, was so concerned about her 16-year-old daughter that she always took her with her to her dressing room, and arranged for two soldiers to escort them home. One night the police stopped them, sent the soldiers back to their regiment, and ordered mother and daughter to present themselves for examination. Mrs Percy refused and wrote to the *Daily Telegraph*. The authorities had her blacklisted throughout Aldershot, and when she found work in Windsor, the proprietor of the hall was told that, if he engaged her, he would be prosecuted for keeping a disorderly house. With nowhere to live or work, mother and daughter were driven on to the streets, and Mrs Percy committed suicide in the Basingstoke canal. Josephine Butler gave the daughter a home. At the inquest no character witnesses for either mother or daughter were allowed, and Mrs Percy's name was noted in the court record as that of a known prostitute.[70]

A letter from her daughter was read at a protest meeting: 'Since this law was made it is not considered respectable to speak to a soldier, nor have one in your house; but I can tell you, that though I have lived among soldiers ever since I was born, I never had a rough word or an insult from one in my life.'[71] The Percy case broke the taboo on reporting events connected with the Contagious Diseases Acts.

By this time, the Liberals had lost power, and the abolitionists were focusing on Parliament. A former Liberal cabinet minister, James Stansfeld, had become leader of the movement. Year after year he tried to get the Acts repealed, year after year he failed, until 1883, when the Liberals were back in power. A motion was passed that 'This House disapproves of the compulsory examination of women under the Contagious Diseases Acts', which made the Acts a dead letter. They were repealed three years later.

However, the wider evils of prostitution remained untouched – in particular, child prostitution. In 1882, a commission of the House of Lords published a damning report. As soon as a girl reached her 13th birthday, she might be found in bed with an old man, and the police could not rescue her unless they had a writ in her name for *Habeas Corpus* against the brothel-keeper. Even when the child was under 13, the prosecution often failed because she had to prove that when she took the oath she understood it. The next year, a Criminal Law Amendment Bill to remedy these evils passed the Lords but was shelved in the Commons. Neither party cared enough to push it through, and a small band of MPs, some with notorious private lives, opposed it.

Mrs Butler had been concentrating her energies on fighting the sale of young girls to brothels abroad, 'the white slave trade'. When she was at last brought to believe that this evil was as common in London as it was in Brussels and Paris, she discovered it was another issue considered too disgusting for public attention. However, this time she found an ally in a sensation-monger of the highest class, W T Stead, editor of the *Pall Mall Gazette*. He ensured that, while it took 16 years to repeal the Contagious Diseases Acts, the campaign to pass the Criminal Law

Amendment Bill succeeded in under two. He did this by creating the biggest newspaper sensation of the Victorian era.

As editor of the *Northern Echo*, Stead had been ahead of Gladstone in agitating for the oppressed Bulgarians. As editor of the *Pall Mall Gazette* from 1883, he acquired a unique reputation for making things happen. He had demanded that more money be spent on the Royal Navy, and more money was spent. He had campaigned for General Gordon to be sent back to the Sudan, and Gordon was sent (to his death). Now when Stead asked a former head of the CID why the thought of screaming children forced into prostitution did not raise hell, he was told that it did not even raise the neighbours. 'Then I will raise hell,' said Stead, and he did.[72]

Stead was a journalist of verve and courage. His four articles on child prostitution in London were called 'The Maiden Tribute of Modern Babylon', and ran from 6 to 10 July 1885. They were trailed on the Saturday before with the warning 'All those who are squeamish, and all those who are prudish, and all those who prefer to live in a fool's paradise of imaginary innocence and purity, selfishly oblivious of the horrible realities which torment those whose lives are passed in the London inferno, will do well not to read the *Pall Mall Gazette* of Monday and the three following days.'[73] Stead was not the last popular journalist to advertise his wares by warning his readers against them. The first article claimed that the series would be read 'with a shuddering horror that will thrill throughout the world'. It was.

The predators Stead attacked followed an age-old tradition of the rich sexually exploiting the poor. He referred to 'princes and dukes, and ministers and judges' purchasing for damnation 'the as yet uncorrupted daughters of the poor', and claimed that 'we might subpoena half the legislature' to prove the accuracy of his account.[74] He did not name names, but the belief that he could weighed heavily. However, not only the guilty were alarmed to read that 'the future belongs to the combined forces of Democracy and Socialism, which when united are irresistible'.[75] Even in 1885, democracy was not universally loved, let alone socialism. If socialism could benefit from the revelations, surely they should not be made.

Stead and his 'Secret Commission' of investigation, which included Josephine Butler, had interviewed prostitutes and brothel-keepers. They told of how some prostitutes kept their children only because 'when they get to be twelve or thirteen they become merchantable'. The East End was 'the great market for children who are imported into West-end houses, or taken abroad wholesale when trade is brisk'. Some men insisted that the girls should be virgins – 'The shriek of torture is the essence of their delight, and they would not silence by a single note the cry of agony over which they gloat.' Half the money for the girl was paid down, and half when her virginity had been certified by a doctor.[76]

The tricks of the ghastly trade were exposed in detail: how a child of 13 might be bought for five pounds; how when girls stepped off the boat from Ireland their boxes were seized and whisked off to supposedly respectable lodging houses, how brothel keepers paid some policemen three pounds a week to turn a blind eye.

In the third article Stead boasted of 'an effect unsurpassed in the history of journalism' and that 'the excitement in London yesterday was intense'. The stationers W H Smith banned the *Pall Mall Gazette* from its railway bookstalls. Stead replied that he could not meet the demand for copies anyway.[77] The paper was sold on the streets at anything from two pence to a shilling instead of a penny, its true price. In the City, an attempt was made to suppress it by arresting the newsboys. The paper's offices were besieged. The crowd 'raged and wrestled, fought with fist and feet, with tooth and nail, clamouring for sheets wet from the press, a sea of human faces tossed hither and thither by the resistless tide which swept from the Strand above, gesticulating unceasingly, hooting, groaning, climbing on the window-sill, taking refuge on doorsteps'. It was 'unprecedented in the history of a newspaper office' and the police were called. That evening the paper was out of print by eight o'clock. The last article had to be postponed a day.[78]

Suddenly the Criminal Law Amendment Bill was a top priority. The Commons rushed through its second reading while the last article was coming out. Stead, aware that the *Pall Mall Gazette* hardly circulated outside London, addressed huge meetings in a triumphant tour of the north of England. Many religious leaders sent letters of support, including Charles Spurgeon. The provincial papers supported Stead too, but his London rivals denounced him as a sensation-monger interested only in boosting sales. The *Standard* thundered, 'So far as ordinary people can judge from the flaunting posters, the roaring newsboys, the successive editions, the elaborate advertisements, which characterize sales of this sort of literature at the present day, the philanthropic crusade of the agitators has been worked on a strictly commercial basis. The sewer that runs underground may need cleaning; but the zeal that makes a handsome profit by turning it into the street will hardly be appreciated.'[79] Stead replied that the country was afire, as it had been nine years before over the Bulgarian horrors, and the blaze would not be put out because of 'a few old women in Shoe-lane or Fleet-Street'.[80]

The Bill became law on 10 August, raising the age of consent to 16, and introducing harsh penalties for intercourse with minors. However, Stead's opponents had their revenge. His account of 'A Child of Thirteen Bought for £5' was based on his own experience of posing as a customer. To buy the girl from her mother, he had employed a reformed brothel keeper called Rebecca Jarrett, who had come under the wing of Josephine Butler. A certificate of virginity was obtained, the girl was taken to a brothel, and Stead entered the room, so that all stages of the transaction were carried out except the last. The account ends, 'There arose a wild and piteous cry – not a loud shriek, but a helpless, startled scream, like the bleat of a frightened lamb. And the child's voice was heard crying in accents of terror, 'There's a man in the room. Take me home; oh, take me home!'' Afterwards, Eliza Armstrong, whose real name had not been used in the article, was well cared for, but her mother, taunted by the neighbours about the sale, wanted her back. Stead was tried for abduction, ironically in one of the first cases under the Criminal Law Amendment Act. He conducted his own defence – Charles Russell represented Jarrett – but accepted that, as the law stood, he was guilty because the father had not agreed to his daughter being taken away. He was sentenced to three months in gaol.

The revelation that one of the terrible episodes in 'The Maiden Tribute' had been a put-up job was a godsend to Stead's rivals. In a typical attack, the *Morning Post* said there was not 'one tittle of evidence in support of the loathsome narratives and the foul allegations'. The *Observer* showed how starkly it differed from Stead and the journalistic school he inspired by proclaiming that 'Journalism is not a mission, and editors are neither missionaries nor evangelists.' However, referring to Stead's alliance with Josephine Butler, a provincial paper, the *Western Morning News*, said that he was a good man spurred on by the 'shrieking sisterhood' who had done so much harm in another direction by the best of motives.[81]

Although the *Pall Mall Gazette* enjoyed a huge short-term rise in its readership, many regular readers, including the Prince of Wales, cancelled their subscriptions and circulation fell. Stead was unrepentant: two years later he launched a slashing attack on the government over Bloody

Sunday called 'Remember Trafalgar Square'.[82] He also acknowledged the debt his campaign owed to 'the intrepid soldiers' of the Salvation Army, and in particular Bramwell Booth, son of the founder. Bramwell was so heavily involved in the Eliza Armstrong transaction that he was also charged, but acquitted. Rebecca Jarrett was a Salvationist too: the Army considered reformed sinners like her the best people to convert others – their past crimes were good publicity. Jarrett was sentenced to six months, but at Bow Street the Hallelujah lasses supported her in force. These young women were known for interspersing with whoops of joy the hymns they accompanied on the banjo, concertina and tambourine. The Armstrong case brought them a lot of publicity, and thrust the Army's rescue work to the forefront of its mission.

In 1885, the Salvation Army was only seven years old. It thrived on sensation, so its alliance with Stead was appropriate. No method of publicity was thought illegitimate in the war against sin and it was hard to embarrass a Salvationist. One marched at the head of processions with a stiff leg, opening and shutting his umbrella as he went. If a crowd had not gathered, he opened the umbrella and raced around in a circle. He would tear up his songbook to show how the devil attacks sinners, and dive off the platform with swimming motions to indicate the sea of God's love. Another would lie down in a snow-covered market square to attract a crowd.[83] A woman Salvationist let down her hair, put ribbons in it and hung a sign around her neck that read, 'I am Happy Eliza.' She became so notorious that she featured in a music hall song:

> They call one Happy Eliza and one Converted Jane,
> They've been most wicked in their time, but will ne'er do so
>   again.[84]

Two other women paraded the streets in their nightgowns to announce a meeting 'to the immense sensation of the whole population'.[85] In the year of 'The Maiden Tribute' and the Armstrong trial, a clergyman published a book about how the Salvation Army had alienated his daughter from him. Its long title began, *Sensational Religion as Resorted to in the System Called the 'Salvation Army'*.[86] When Bramwell Booth had married in 1882, there was a shilling admission charge to the service, which was turned into an Army rally. At the wedding of his sister Emma in 1888, ticket prices ranged from sixpence to five shillings. Because they were to go to India afterwards, the pillars in the hall were decorated to look like palm trees, and members of the band wore coloured turbans, as did the groom who appeared barefoot in a calico robe carrying a begging bowl.[87]

For the conventionally pious, this was worse than Spurgeon and Moody; the Salvation Army was destroying reverence for the sacred. The Bishop of Oxford declared a holy life impossible 'when young persons of both sexes were called together in excited meetings, held up to a late hour at night, and permitted to go away without control'.[88]

As the Salvationists took their bands, ecstatic services and cavorting women into the street, there was no avoiding them:

> Fanatics at the corner of the street are heard to spout,
> If you want to be a Christian you must sing and dance and shout,
> I object to being taught by men whose piety is shammed,
> And have shoddy second hand religion down my throttle
>   crammed,
> It makes me feel so nervous to be told I must be—[89]

Music-hall songs about the Salvation Army were all hostile. Above all, the halls, close allies of the brewers, hated the Salvationists for their campaign against drink, and portrayed them, particularly General Booth, as drinkers on the sly, and dishonest in money matters:

> The way to make money is easy to see, why not, eh, why not?
> Only start something like the Salvation Army, why not, eh, why
>   not?
> Sing songs to brass bands, make religion grotesque,
> And cash will pour into your pious burlesque, why not, eh, why
>   not?
> Ask Booth how much money he's got, why not?[90]

The brewers were competing with the Salvationists for the pennies of the poor, and joined forces against them with the bishops. The innuendo of their allies on the halls was coarse:

> [She] was so young and beautiful
> But oh! our Army journals tell
> She was pious, brave and good,

But she came from St John's Wood,
The one we loved so well.[91]

St John's Wood was notorious for high-class whores.

The Salvationists replied by setting their own words to music-hall tunes, and even held their meetings in music-halls and theatres. They damned popular entertainment, but adopted its methods to attract audiences. What looked from a distance like a circus or theatre poster might turn out to advertise the Salvation Army. A poster of the early 1880s advertised 'A Yankee Lass, a Wonder! Dressed in American Costume! With a Turban on her Head! Splendid Singer, Good Talker, and Proper Tambourine Player!' Preachers were advertised as 'The Salvation Midget', 'The Saved Drunkard' and 'The Converted Sweep', who told how he had heard 'The Salvation Fiddler' and had the Devil fiddled out of him.[92]

General Booth's latest biographer has called him 'the greatest publicist of his age and generation',[93] and others might have awarded that title to Stead, but both men brilliantly exploited the Victorian taste for sensation to serve a crusade. Both were moralists lacking in self-doubt, and had imbibed their Christianity outside the respectable embrace of the Church of England. Stead's father had been a Congregationalist minister, and the young William Booth left the Anglicans for Methodism, before finding it too over-conformist for his taste. Stead involved himself in fierce battles to establish that what had been considered too sensational to publish could and should be printed. General Booth, although less enthusiastic than Bramwell over 'The Maiden Tribute', rejected the squeamishness that decreed sensation had no place in the fight to save souls – he made even Spurgeon and Moody seem shrinking violets. Unafraid to be damned as sensation-mongers, Stead and Booth were both men of the future.

CHAPTER 4:

Sex Scandal

'I hope and trust that we have not become so corrupt that we cannot bear to look in the face or name the vices around us. That is a state of things that has been described as the greatest curse that can befall a country, and I hope we have not yet arrived at it.' *Mr Henley, MP for Oxfordshire.*[1]

As the campaigns of Josephine Butler and W T Stead show, public revulsion made discussion of sexual morality difficult, which contrasts with the widespread interest in sex scandals. Most emanated from the courts, which had a unique obligation to get at the truth. In court, private diaries and letters could be read out, which would have been impermissible in any other context. Embarrassing personal questions were put, and had to be answered. As a result, respectable newspapers sometimes offered far spicier copy than novels. The criminal courts had always provided such material, but from 1858 the new Divorce Court offered a rich new source. However, reporting was not without constraint: a fierce debate ensued in the press on what could be published.

One of the most heated debates concerned a homosexual scandal, the Boulton and Parke case. It was not so much that the Victorians were homophobic, but that respectable opinion did not even want to acknowledge the existence of homosexuality. It was by flaunting their sexuality in public that Boulton and Parke provoked a determined police campaign against them. Until 1861 sodomy was a capital offence, although the law had fallen into disuse. Nine years later it still carried a sentence of life imprisonment.

On 28 April 1870, Ernest Boulton and William Park were arrested as they left the Strand Theatre in London, wearing women's clothes padded at the breast. When they were charged at Bow Street magistrate's court, the evidence showed that, even when dressed as men, their makeup caused confusion as to their orientation. However, they had made their intentions clear to men in the stalls at the Alhambra music-hall in Leicester Square by leering at them from their box, and had been turned out more than once for being dressed as women. On one occasion 'a number of gentlemen' had followed them out.[2] They had also been ejected from the Burlington Arcade.

Evidence was given about men with whom they had shared a bedroom, one of whom was Lord Arthur Clinton, a son of the Duke of Newcastle, but Clinton died before he could be brought to court – officially of scarlet fever, but he was rumoured to have committed suicide. It was established, however, that 'Stella' Boulton had been posing as Clinton's wife, even having visiting cards printed to that effect, and that 'Fanny' Park saw himself as Clinton's sister-in-law. That Boulton was christened Ernest may shed light on the controversy over whether the name has a homosexual meaning in Oscar Wilde's most famous play. Wilde must have known about the case.[3]

One of the most sensational aspects of the hearing was the letters read out in court. 'What a wonderful child it is. I have three minds to come up to London, and see your magnificence with my own eyes. Would you welcome me? Probably it is better that I should stay at home and dream of you.' Another letter, which the magistrate would not allow to be read in court, persuaded him not to grant bail.[4]

However, none of this was proof of sodomy, and it was the methods used to obtain proof that precipitated the fiercest debate over what was too disgusting to report. The *Pall Mall Gazette*, as squeamish a paper as any in its pre-Stead days, stated only that a surgeon had 'given evidence of a medical character which it is impossible to print'.[5] An article entitled 'Indecent Publications', said, 'Apart from the case of *Reynolds's Newspaper*, where the revolting details are fully given, the particulars published in several daily papers have been so broadly stated that it has been impossible to leave copies of these papers within reach of young people or anyone having the faintest pretension to be considered an honest woman.' The writer was particularly critical of the *Daily Telegraph*, which gave a hint of the kind of medical inspections that had taken place.[6]

Reynolds's left no room for doubt. One doctor who had treated Park 'found two syphilitic sores in the anus – a primary chancre, which had been created by an unnatural intercourse with another person . . . the anus gaped sufficiently to expose the mucous membrane and the sore on it.' Another who had examined both men at the police station found Boulton's anus 'much dilated, and the muscles readily opened. These appearances . . . were, he thought, attributable to the fact of his having had frequent unnatural connections – one insertion would not have caused them.'[7] Astounding stuff to discover in any Victorian paper. It appeared under the sub-heading 'The Men in Petticoats – Horrible and Revolting Disclosures'. The paper defended itself on the grounds that everything that transpired in a court of justice should be reported. It pointed out that the nature of the evidence did not drive away the crowd, which was prepared to stand for five hours in the oppressive atmosphere of a badly ventilated courtroom. Boulton and Park were from middle-class families, and *Reynolds's Newspaper* angrily rejected *The Times* view that homosexual behaviour was, 'with rare exceptions', associated with the lower classes. 'If called upon to give an opinion as to the particular grade of society most given to the perpetration of unnatural offences, we should at once point to the episcopacy.'[8]

As in the *Telegraph*, the reports in *The Times* were detailed but without the medical evidence. The paper's emphasis on class was essential to its justification for reporting the case: 'In the present day it is impossible to prevent such a case from being discussed by the public at large, and particularly by people who unite to a strong appetite for the morbid and the sensational a credulity beyond bounds concerning the malpractices of the classes above them.' The (fairly) full facts had to be published to prevent millions of people believing untrue rumours about their betters.[9]

The *Daily Telegraph* pointed out defiantly that its reports had been carefully edited to exclude all objectionable details, and the magistrate had the power to ban reporting, if he wished. Rumour, gossip and calumny might hit the innocent if the facts were not published. In pointing out that gossip, 'even we must admit', had 'the largest circulation in the world', the *Telegraph* was referring slyly to its own world-record sales.[10] All this was too much for the *Pall Mall Gazette*, which declared that the *Telegraph* printed these indecent stories because it paid to do so. It rebutted the argument that some details were needed to understand the case by asking 'In the name of all that is pure and good, why should we fairly understand the case at all?'

There were other things the *Pall Mall Gazette* did not understand. It declared, 'Scandals will always be with us, but the present condition of our atmosphere breeds fouler specimens than we ever recollect.' The Boulton and Park affair was one such. A number of papers made comparison with the Mordaunt divorce case, the other great sexual scandal of the year, and still in the news because of Sir Charles's appeal to the House of Lords. However, the other 'foul specimen' of scandal singled out by the *Pall Mall Gazette* was Josephine Butler's campaign against the Contagious Diseases Acts. The writer was not held back by the admission that 'When we find men sitting in the stifling air of a crowded court to fill their minds with obscenity, we can scarcely venture to throw stones at women of any kind.' He condemned women 'who can in honest principle shock the modesty of other people; who can so far get the better of nature as to expatiate with unembarrassed speeches on contagious diseases and the train of obscene explanation and illustration the subject involves'. As long as men were able to act for them, he could not believe that women who did not shrink from such a false position were not moved by pleasure as well as duty. They had, he wrote, sacrificed the gentle graces of womanhood on the altar of false ambition. The filthy details of the Boulton and Park case had been published alongside 'a full report of a woman's speech on contagious diseases, a report meant to interest the same readers'.[11]

When the full trial opened a year later, it competed for public attention with the opening of the first Tichborne trial, and with the bloodshed and burning in Paris during the Commune, but 'for twelve months [the case] has been a topic of general conversation, and has never been lost sight of by the general public'.[12] The prosecution brought a charge of conspiracy to commit sodomy, even though it could not prove that sodomy had been committed, so earning itself a severe reprimand from the Lord Chief Justice. He also censured the medical inspections that had been ordered by the police without reference to a magistrate. Boulton, Park and two other men were acquitted, despite the appearance for the prosecution of the Attorney-General and the Solicitor-General. 'Not even the mighty Tichborne case' could boast a more brilliant array of lawyers.[13] As at Bow Street, every shred of evidence in favour of the accused received an enthusiastic response, and the acquittals were greeted with cheers. Despite society's homophobia, enough homosexuals attended the trial to give their side solid support.[14]

By 1870, the newspaper-reading public, unused to being confronted with homosexuality, had been feasting on the scandals of the Divorce

Court for a dozen years. Moralists deplored that the papers should report
the court's salacious proceedings in such detail and at such length, but few
refrained from doing so. They knew what their readers wanted. Gladstone
had fought tooth and nail against Parliament's decision to set up the
court, and wrote in 1889 that 'unquestionably' over the intervening period
of more than thirty years 'the standard of conjugal morality has percepti-
bly declined among the higher classes of this country, and scandals in
respect to it have become more frequent'. He did admit, though, that the
Divorce Act was not the only cause.[15]

Until 1858, divorce had been impossible for a woman, and both very
difficult and very expensive, for a man. Although the 1857 Divorce Act
was a great advance, it retained the age-old double standard with respect to
the sexual behaviour of men and women. A husband could divorce his wife
by proving that she had committed adultery; his wife could only divorce
him if, in addition to adultery, she could prove cruelty, desertion, bigamy or
incest. In the first year of the new Act there were 253 petitions for divorce,
97 filed by wives. Horror! The figures would surely fall when there was no
longer a backlog of cases based on marriage breakdowns many years in the
past. Needless to say, they did not.[16] However, although divorce became
cheaper and easier, it was still neither cheap nor easy, hence the high pro-
portion of litigants from high society. When the sensation-novelist Charles
Reade listed the subjects he thought the public were interested in, 'an aristocratic divorce suit' was at the top of his list, followed by 'the last great
social scandal [often the same thing], a sensational suicide from Waterloo
Bridge, a woman murdered in Seven Dials, or a baby found strangled in a
bonnet-box at Piccadilly Circus'.[17] One unfortunate consequence of the
seemingly endless first Tichborne trial, according to a writer in the society
magazine *Vanity Fair*, was that 'people have come to believe that it is
standing in the way of many other trials of an exciting and sensational
nature, and feel themselves much aggrieved thereat'. He added, '"I have
seen only one really good divorce trial this year," writes a lady to us, "and I
know there are a great many interesting cases ready to come on."'[18]

In January 1865, the judge in the Chetwynd v. Chetwynd divorce case
described it as 'remarkable for revealing a condition of things existing in
the home of a gentleman of high position and honourable family such as
probably no one could have believed or imagined who had not heard the
evidence'.[19] This described exactly what the public most wanted to read
about.

William Henry Chetwynd was the second son of a baronet, and had married his 18-year-old bride, the niece of an earl, when he was 42. It was a remarkable household in that the servants were all women, and the husband did all the hiring. In 1864, he was accused of persistent adultery with several of them. The letters he had written to a discarded servant-mistress were damning evidence against him, but under the Act adultery was not enough for divorce so Mrs Chetwynd accused him of cruelty too:

'Five or six months after our marriage, his manner became very cross to me, I felt it keenly. He used to call me a damned infernal bitch.' (The witness mentioned some other language which he had used to her too disgusting for repetition.) 'On one occasion when there were guests in the house, and I was unintentionally late for breakfast, he called me a damned lazy sow, and said he would kick me out of bed, to teach me not to be late again. This was said in the presence of other people. On various occasions, he threatened to kick me out of bed. He had locked me out of my bedroom, and I had to sleep on the stairs . . . I have often had to wait for him in the carriage outside public houses. He would ask me to wait for half a minute, and would keep me waiting till 12 or 1 or 2 o'clock in the morning, and then I have had to drive him home drunk. I have waited in that way four or five hours at a time. In March or April 1861 we were invited to dine at Beaudesert. My friends objected to my going, and I begged to be released from the engagement. He said I had two courses open to me: I might either leave his house and become a prostitute in the streets, or I must go wherever he went, even if it was into a brothel.'[20]

Mrs Chetwynd also alleged that her husband had forced their daughter to spit at her, and their son to kick her and spell out the word 'whore' in her face letter by letter. There were juries in divorce cases then, and the jury in the Chetwynd case accepted the cruelty charge. The wife got her divorce, and was also cleared of the husband's allegations that *she* had committed adultery – with a lawyer and a theology student. The lawyer, Henry Matthews, was a Roman Catholic, and Mrs Chetwynd had become friendly with him when she converted despite, or perhaps because of, her husband's virulent anti-Catholicism. Her diary was produced in court, from which it was clear that she had passionate feelings for

Matthews. However, it was equally clear that they were not reciprocated, and that, far from yielding, she had repressed them: 'And yet in me to love is sin. Holy virgin, look down and intercede for my troubled soul. Quench these earthly, unhallowed thoughts.'[21]

However, Mrs Chetwynd's reputation was badly damaged. Not only had she got heavily into debt, but her husband made a revelation that aroused the indignation of opposing counsel: 'Before entering on an examination of the evidence, he remarked upon the conduct of the respondent in instructing his counsel to drag before the public the irrelevant fact that his wife was delivered of a child soon after the marriage. His unspeakable baseness in taking such a course had covered him with everlasting disgrace, especially as no-one knew better than he whether his marriage, instead of being an act of generosity, as he had represented it, was not an act of simple justice.'[22]

'Unspeakable baseness' of another kind was alleged against Colonel Valentine Baker, although the sensational trial which brought about his fall was not held in the divorce court. The verdict, at Croydon Assizes on 2 August 1875, ended Baker's career in the British army.[23] *The Times* commented that since he had first been brought before magistrates in June, 'a large part of the public have taken more interest in his case than in any political event of the day'.[24] He was cleared of rape, but convicted of having indecently assaulted a young woman in a railway carriage. The sentence was a year's imprisonment and a £500 fine. Although the first murder on a British train had been committed when a German tailor had obtruded into a first-class carriage 11 years earlier, the indignation at Baker's behaviour was all the greater because he had been travelling first class. If a young woman was not safe in first class, where was she safe? It was only because Miss Kate Dickinson, at 21 less than half Baker's age, was a self-confident middle-class woman, with a lawyer brother, that she had had the courage to bring the case. As was pointed out at the time, if Baker had behaved in the same way in third class he would probably have got away with it. Even if a poor woman had dared to start legal proceedings, she could probably have been bribed to give them up. For example, back in 1861, a 33-year-old man, John Moriarty, had assaulted a Miss Miller in a third class carriage. Moriarty was not charged with rape. He was fined six pounds for having been drunk on a train and for having annoyed a passenger. The case was hardly noticed.[25]

The class of the carriage supposedly reflected the class of its passengers. It was Baker's high position in society that caused the sensation. He was a friend of the Prince of Wales and, had he not been disgraced, would have accompanied the Prince to India. He was thought to share the way of life of the 'Marlborough House set', and the Prince always stayed loyal to him. Baker had raised the class issue by asking, in vain, to be tried by a special jury, arguing that it would be a terrible humiliation to be tried by an ordinary one. *The Times* was careful to explain that although the jury was not 'special' in the sense of being chosen from a prepared list of particularly qualified men, it was made up of jurors of 'the better class', all substantial tradesmen or men of independent means.[26]

The evidence was sensational in itself. Miss Dickinson alleged that Baker had tried to raise her skirt, and kissed her many times on the lips. 'His body was on me at the time.' There were no communicating doors between carriages, so once she had struggled free of her attacker, she travelled for some miles crying for help on the outside step of the moving train. Her screams were heard three or four carriages back. She had risked her life to save her virtue and shown that she believed that there was indeed a fate worse than death. Charles Reade, who thought that Baker had received too severe a sentence, stressed that eventually she had to ask him to hang on to her to prevent her falling on to the rail.[27] Having got herself out backwards on to the step, she held on to him with one hand while she grasped the door handle with the other. He tried to persuade her to get back into the carriage by telling her that he would get out of the door on the other side. This was not convincing, given the speed of the train and, in any case, she knew that that door was locked. When the train got to the station, one witness said that he had seen Colonel Baker with most of his fly buttons undone.[28]

Like many Victorian sex scandals, the case raised the issue of how much sexual licence men should be allowed. The arguments raged for years, and Baker had many supporters in high society who agreed with the Prince of Wales that his distinguished record as a soldier far outweighed what they considered a peccadillo. Baker also enjoyed the support of that bastion of Victorian machismo, the music-halls. Ten years later when he had long been serving under the Sultan of Turkey, whom some considered a highly suitable employer for him, a music-hall song called 'In the Days of Auld Lang Syne' included this verse:

A soldier did offend the laws,
In the days of Auld Lang Syne.
He had to leave Old England's shores,
In the days of Auld Lang Syne.
An exile from his native land,
He's suffered much, I understand,
Let's take poor Baker by the hand,
For the sake of Auld Lang Syne.[29]

Audiences cheered when Baker's name was mentioned.

Three years after the case, an indignant reviewer protested that a comedian should leave out his allusion to Baker: 'I was much distressed to hear him sing of this person as "that naughty naughty man" and then ask the audience to say he was a very fine fellow. "Mamma," said a little girl who sat by me, "who was Colonel Baker, and what did he do that was very naughty?" It is hardly worth while, when so many topical allusions are at hand, for a comedian to rake up this foul and infamous transaction, and fling it in the face of innocent boys and girls.'[30]

Baker's enemies thought the sentence too lenient, that his social connections had got him off the rape charge, and that his conditions of confinement were too luxurious. An anonymous pamphleteer brushed aside the judge's argument that hard labour was a worse punishment to an educated man of social position than to a working man.

> The greater the social opportunities and advantages of such a man, the more heinous his offence. We had far better have tigers and crocodiles let loose amongst us than such men, decked in gorgeous trappings . . . prowling loose in our midst seeking whom they may destroy – be it an annual tribute of virgins, or the victims of a neat little drawing-room series of violated hearths and dishonoured homes . . . It was known that this man was what was known as a 'pal' of the Prince of Wales, and is, or was, in the 10th Hussars, which is the Prince's Own; and so attached was His Royal Highness to this precious specimen of the military, that he was about, it is said, to take him to India, in order, we suppose, that the defenceless women of Hindustan might have an opportunity of knowing what brawny old ravishers the army of England can boast among its General Officers.

This pamphlet continues its invective for 16 pages:

This cowardly ruffian, it appears, is the son of a clergyman of the Church of England. Clergymen's children are, in general, a set of licensed scoundrels or rogues, swindlers or common cheats, going about the country defrauding or despoiling the unwary or unprotected men and women of England. The man whose doings we are about to give to the world, took to the gallant exploit of ravishing as many of his countrywomen as he could entice or compel to comply with his filthy desires.[31]

This was strong stuff, but one of the stock villains of Victorian melodrama was the army officer of loose morals, much older than his young and beautiful intended victim.

Baker fought with distinction for Turkey in the 1877–8 war with Russia, then took command of the Egyptian police. His supporters never gave up their attempts to have him reinstated in the British army. They failed in his lifetime, but the British garrison in Cairo buried him with full military honours.

Apart from the Baker case, the greatest sex scandals continued to surface in the Divorce Court. The most exciting year in its juicy history was 1886, when two cases caused more excitement than the two changes of government or Gladstone's conversion to Home Rule for Ireland. The first involved an important politician. It had come to light in August of the previous year. The furore over 'The Maiden Tribute of Modern Babylon' had far from run its course when the *Pall Mall Gazette* ran the headline 'GREAT SOCIAL SCANDAL/AN EX-CABINET MINISTER IN THE DIVORCE COURT/PETITION FILED AGAINST SIR CHARLES DILKE', and went on, 'For some days past the air of London has been thick with rumours as to a scandal affecting one of the most prominent leaders in English politics. Down to the last moment it was believed that the efforts made to hush the affair up would be successful, and that the scandal would not find its way into the public prints.'[32]

The case opened in February 1886 and formed 'the chief topic of public discussion throughout the United Kingdom'.[33] Dilke had lived down his reputation for fierce republicanism, which had marked him out 15 years earlier, and it was thought that he would become foreign secretary in Gladstone's third government, formed that month, until Mrs

Mrs Crawford's lurid account of her affair with Sir Charles Dilke led to sensational reporting in the popular press, and Dilke's fall from political grace.

Crawford, the wife of the Liberal MP for North East Lanarkshire, made her sensational confession to her husband.

The confession was described in court by Crawford himself, as his wife – extraordinarily – was not asked to appear. She had told him that Dilke, who had been her mother's lover, had seduced her a few months after her marriage, when she was still under twenty, and that she had been his mistress for two and a half years. Dilke, a widower, denied it. He was advised not to appear as a witness, as this would lead to exposure of his lurid past. It was bad advice. The judge ruled that Mrs Crawford's uncorroborated word could not prove the case against Dilke, but that her confession of adultery with him was enough for a divorce. People joked that she had committed adultery with him but he had not committed adultery with her.

Dilke had promised his constituents in Chelsea to resign or clear his name. His name had not been cleared, but he had not resigned either. Having been given a chance to assert his innocence on oath, he had not taken it. His opponents seized on this. One of the most persistent and aggressive was Stead, who had recently emerged from prison. His *Pall Mall Gazette* approved of Dilke's Liberal imperialism, but denounced the *Daily Telegraph* for supporting him now.[34] It commented that although 'in the low morality of high life ordinary intrigues are regarded as but venial offences', seduction was much worse. The accusation against Sir Charles might not be true, but it was one of the 'offences morally worse than murder, and including in their complicated criminality almost every conceivable degree of moral baseness and unnatural vice'.[35]

As so often when prominent Victorians were accused but not found guilty, the suspicion of a cover-up was not far away. According to the *Pall Mall Gazette*, 'the belief that the whole thing was 'a put up job' is almost universal', and "They were squared, of course they were', is the remark which is heard everywhere.'[36] Yet another reason for Dilke to clear his name.

The political ramifications of the case were given an extra twist by an anonymous letter to the *Pall Mall Gazette*, which spoke up for Dilke, while agreeing with the gravity of the charges against him – 'He is either worse than a brute in bestiality and worse than a fiend in hypocrisy, or he is one of the most unlucky and most injured of men.' According to the letter-writer, Dilke had intended to go into the witness-box but had been dissuaded at the last minute by none other than his friend Joseph

Chamberlain, who was soon to resign from Gladstone's government over Home Rule, and was as controversial a politician as Gladstone himself. Stead tried to persuade Chamberlain to answer the accusation but, although the acrimonious correspondence between the two men was published in the *Pall Mall Gazette*, he failed to do so. He also tried to get Gladstone to intervene, because the judge's decision seemed to indicate that to obtain a divorce a husband had only to appear in court and say that his wife had committed adultery.[37]

There was a way for Dilke to give evidence. Under the Divorce Act, six months separated the jury's pronouncement of a decree nisi and the date when the divorce became effective with a decree absolute. During that period an official called the Queen's Proctor could intervene if he thought that evidence had emerged to prevent the divorce. Dilke used this means to reopen the case. He proved a very bad witness, under cross-examination by the same Henry Matthews who had not committed adultery with Mrs Chetwynd. Mrs Crawford was a good witness – and frank:

'He asked me to meet him at another house. I refused for a long time. I did not know what he meant but at last I promised to go . . .'

'Did he tell you how to go there?'

"I was to go in a hansom, and change into another one on the way. Then I was to get out at the corner of Warren-street, and walk up to the house; and when I had arrived at it a woman would let me in. I was to go upstairs into a back room on the first floor, and was not to speak to anybody, and he would be there waiting for me.'

'Did you go there on the day?'. . .

'I did . . . A woman opened the door, but I did not look at her or speak to her, but went straight upstairs into a back bedroom on the first floor. There was a large bed standing against the wall.'

'. . . I am obliged to put the question to you, Mrs Crawford, and mind how you answer it. Did Sir Charles Dilke commit adultery with you on that occasion?'

'Yes, he did.' (Sensation).

But even that was not Mrs Crawford's most sensational evidence:

'Did he say anything about yourself in connection with your mother?'

'He said I was very like my mother, and that was why he took a fancy to me.'

'During the year 1883 did Sir Charles Dilke ever mention a person named Fanny to you?'

'Yes . . . He said that she was a girl who used to sleep with him, and spend the night at his house.'

'Yes, what else?'

'He told me that she was very nice, and that she was my age; and he asked me if I would like to see her at his house. I said I would not like to see her at all.'

. . . 'Tell us the circumstances under which you first saw her?'

. . . 'He had asked me to see her several times. He said he wanted to see us together, and one day when I was at Sir Charles Dilke's house speaking to him in the blue-room, he said she was in the house then, and he asked me if I would see her. I said I did not want to. Then we went upstairs, and after we had been upstairs in his bedroom, he brought Fanny into the next room.'

'Was she dressed or undressed?'

'I do not think it necessary that I should go through all this.'

'Very well, I will not ask you. What happened when he brought her into the room?'

'He wanted me to talk to her, and I would not, and he sent her away. He told me that I would never see her again if I did not want to.'. . .

'When did you see her again?'

'I saw her again in the spring of 1884, when we came back to London. He spoke to me about her a good many times, at least several times, and asked me to see her again, and I did not want to at all. He called me into the room when I was there, and she remained there for a minute or two, and I asked him to send her away.'

'Did you ever see her again?'

'I saw her about a week or two after that at his house in the same way. He told me I was very silly not to like her. She stayed in the room ten minutes or so, and she helped me to dress.'

'Were you all three in bed together?'

'Yes.'[38]

To prevent the divorce the Queen's Proctor had to prove that Dilke had not committed adultery with Mrs Crawford, even though she said he had. He failed, and Dilke's fall was complete. The music-halls had a field day:

> Master Dilke upset the milk
> When taking it home to Chelsea
> The papers say that Charlie's gay –
> Rather a wilful wag!
> This noble representative
> Of everything good in Chelsea
> Has let the cat – the naughty cat
> Slip out of the Gladstone bag.[39]

By no means all Victorians were as censorious as Stead. Although Dilke had lost his seat in the general election between the first and second trials, the swing against him had been smaller than that against the Liberals nationally. Perhaps his constituents in Chelsea – which incidentally a hundred years later returned Alan Clark as its MP – were particularly relaxed about sexual scandal. On the other hand, although Dilke never became a minister again, six years later he was returned to Parliament by another constituency – in the face of virulent opposition from Stead, and *The Times'* refusal to report his speeches.

Dilke was not the first or the highest-ranking Victorian politician to be cited in a divorce case. Lord Palmerston was prime minister and was within ten days of his 79th birthday when an Irish radical journalist called Kane claimed that he had committed adultery with Mrs Kane. Kane lost his case, but there was a great deal of hilarity in view of Palmerston's age. The most popular joke was 'She was Kane, but was he Able?'[40] But that had been in 1863 when the electorate was smaller and party-political feeling was not running as high as it was in 1886. And Dilke, a politician on the way up, was more vulnerable than Palmerston, who was regarded as a national institution and a law unto himself.

In November and December 1886, *Reynolds's Newspaper* ran and reran the headline 'Lord Colin Campbell's Divorce Suit – Revolting Revelations'. The Campbell v. Campbell case opened four months after the second Crawford trial. A *Pall Mall Gazette* cartoon showed two news-vendors representing the *Evening News* and the *Standard*, two of Stead's fiercest critics over 'The Maiden Tribute of Modern Babylon'. One says,

'This 'ere Colin Campbell licks Charles Dilke into smash, don't 'e?' The other replies, "E do just.'[41] The music-halls also linked the two cases:

> Some young men do not care to stick to one sweet bit of silk,
> That was the case with Colin Campbell and with Charlie Dilke.[42]

The *Pall Mall Gazette* was sparing in its coverage of the Campbell trial, which Stead used to revenge himself on the rivals who had persecuted him the year before: 'The deliberately detailed reports of the case which are published every morning and evening by nearly every paper in the country must have surprised those who did not at the time see through the hypocrisy of these same papers when they condemned the mere mention of certain topics as prejudicial to public morals.' As well as the *Standard*, which had 'easily outdistanced every competitor' in its detailed stories of 'the filthiest case every reported', he singled out the *Observer*, which had been surpassed by few in its denunciations of 'The Maiden Tribute' and now shortened its usually long list of church services to make way for 'the details of the filthiest divorce case on record'.[43]

Lord Colin Campbell was the fifth son of the Duke of Argyll, a former cabinet minister. His older brother, the Marquess of Lorne, was the husband of Princess Louise. Lord Colin's wife, formerly Miss Gertrude Blood, accused him of adultery and cruelty, alleging that he had passed on to her the venereal disease which he knew he had contracted before their marriage. He accused her of adultery with a duke, a doctor, a general and the chief of the London Fire Brigade.[44]

The only amusing exchange in the doctor's evidence came when he was reproached for having been in his patient's, Lady Colin's, bed-room for an awfully long time, and replied that he had gone to sleep. The general - General Butler - never turned up in court and was widely reviled for failing to defend the honour of a lady. A music hall song was to compare Butler unfavourably with Colonel Baker:

> How is it General Butler has been made a KCB?
> That's what the country wants to know.
> Why has he been forgiven by Her Gracious Majesty?
> That's what the country wants to know.
> Once at the Campbell trial he refused to show his face,
> The 'Butler' is forgiven, while the 'Baker''s in disgrace,

The 'revolting revelations' of the Campbell divorce case even eclipsed the Crawford trial. One cartoon showed two newsvendors in dialogue: "'This 'ere Colin Campbell licks Charles Dilke into smash, don't 'e?" "'E do just"'.

When shall we call brave Baker Pasha back to fill his place?
That's what the country wants to know.[45]

Captain Shaw, the chief of the London Fire Brigade, is remembered
today because, in Gilbert and Sullivan's *Iolanthe*, the fairy queen wants his
help in extinguishing her passion for a mere mortal:

> On fire that glows
> With heat intense
> I turn the hose
> Of common sense,
> And out it goes
> At small expense! . . .

> Oh, Captain Shaw!
> Type of true love kept under!
> Could thy Brigade
> With cold cascade
> Quench my great love, I wonder!

Insiders knew of Captain Shaw's reputation as a ladies' man, so the idea
of his putting out the fires of passion was a good joke. At the opening
night of *Iolanthe*, he sat next to Lady Colin Campbell.

However, the most notorious co-respondent was the Marquess of
Blandford, as he was when the events discussed in court had happened,
and the 8th Duke of Marlborough, as he had become by the time of the
trial. He had been divorced by his wife, who had accused him of hitting
her while she was pregnant. His divorce followed his appearance as co-
respondent in the sensational Aylesford v. Aylesford divorce case of 1878.
Both Blandford and Aylesford, like Colonel Baker, were friends of the
Prince of Wales. Unlike Baker, who was in disgrace, Aylesford had accompanied the Prince to India. While he was away Blandford and Lady
Aylesford, the sister of General Owen Williams who was to hit the headlines at Tranby Croft, had an affair and ran off to Paris together. The
divorce proceedings showed up the rackety lifestyle of all three protagonists, as *Reynolds's Newspaper* gleefully pointed out:

The revelations in the Aylesford divorce suit are of a most hideous and revolting kind. Lord Aylesford appears therein as a sot, a spendthrift, an adulterer and pretty well all that is foul and filthy . . . As for the Marquis of Blandford, who took advantage of his friend's absence in India to seduce his wife, and elope with her, he also is a married man and a father of a family, and a precious specimen of our 'old nobility'. Lady Aylesford was known, before the scandal which ruined her reputation was made public, as one of the many fast ladies of high life who drove four-in-hands, frequented race-courses, hunt meetings and such like places of resort for the loungers and butterflies of society . . . According to the evidence of servants, waiters, brothel-keepers and others, Lord Aylesford's life was one of the lowest sort of dissipation. His favoured resorts were those frequented by harlots and debauchees of his own stamp. When such places closed, he drove off to the Marlborough Club, an 'institution' as the Prince of Wales would style it, considered the most 'select' of its kind in London, as having the heir to the throne, ex-Colonel Valentine Baker of unsavoury notoriety, and other 'gentlemen' of rank and fashion as its members.[46]

The evidence of servants was vital in such cases, but it was vulnerable to attack. They might have a grudge, they might have been bribed by either side, or they might be frightened to speak the truth. One of the Campbells' servants, James O'Neill, told the court, 'I knew that a lot of wrong had been done, but it was not my business to say anything . . . If I made any trouble, I thought I might not get another situation in this city.'

In O'Neill's most sensational piece of evidence, he described what he had seen through a key-hole.

'Now with regard to your keyhole performances. Was this the first time you had ever gone through a performance of that nature?'

'Yes, sir.'

'This is Captain Shaw. You know him very well?'

'Oh, yes.'

'You are sure you are not drawing on some recollections of an American brothel?'

'No, sir.'. . .

'Would you mind going through that story again, for I should just like to hear it?'

'Well, Captain Shaw rang the bell, the area bell, and asked for her ladyship. I said she was out, but his lordship was in. He said he would call again. But as he was going, Lady Colin Campbell drove up in a cab . . . I told her ladyship that his lordship was in the drawing-room. She pushed Captain Shaw into the dining-room. I shut the door, and was proceeding to go downstairs, and when I got to the top of the staircase, her ladyship opened the dining room door, and either called or beckoned me. I went to her, and she told me to tell his lordship that she was either out or going out. I then went downstairs . . . Almost as soon as I entered the kitchen, my attention was drawn by the cook to the noise overhead.'

'Upon hearing this, your suspicions were aroused, and you came upstairs?'

'Yes.'

'How long did you remain at the keyhole?'

'A few moments.'[47]

O'Neill went on to describe the exact positions in which he had seen Lady Colin and Captain Shaw on the carpet, but not even *Reynolds's Newspaper* reported this. Sir Charles Russell, who led for Lady Colin, later seemed to have proved that it was not possible to see through the keyhole in question, but after the jury had trooped off to the house to examine it they decided that it was.

Neither of the Campbells was granted a divorce and it was his death a few years later that brought the wretched marriage to an end. She failed to prove adultery against him – her only witness was her mother – so her other accusations became irrelevant. Perhaps more surprisingly, Lady Colin was also cleared of adultery. She was described in the press as 'a sex goddess', possessing 'the unbridled lust of a Messalina and the indelicate readiness of a common harlot' and of having a life story 'of immorality and obscenity without parallel'.[48] The all-male jury might have believed her evidence, been charmed by her, or motivated by chivalry or compassion. Had she been branded an adulteress, the shame would have been overwhelming. As it was, she lost her position in society. Happily she had talent as well as beauty – unlike her husband. She took up journalism, one of the few professions open to women – especially women with a louche reputation.

Four years later the O'Shea divorce case destroyed Charles Stuart Parnell. His political fall was even more dramatic and significant than

Dilke's. When Captain O'Shea's case came to court in 1890, Parnell still enjoyed the sympathy he had earned from the exposure of Pigott's forgeries, and seemed to have a reasonable chance of delivering Home Rule. He made it hard for himself by refusing to take part in the trial, and Mrs O'Shea would not call witnesses or have her husband's cross-examined. She seemed to be saying that there had been no adultery, but that her husband had connived in it. Her confusion was understandable: the lovers needed the divorce so that they could marry, but Parnell's innocence had to be established for political reasons. In the event Parnell, a bachelor, was disgraced for his affair with a married woman, and the Home Rule Party split between those who still wanted him as leader and those who wanted him out.

The case made Parnell a laughing stock. Caroline Pethers, the O'Sheas' cook, was asked what had happened when Parnell was in the drawing room with Mrs O'Shea, and her husband suddenly arrived home:

'I went up to light the gas. The door was locked. I heard persons in the room, but I could not get in. Mrs O'Shea said it did not matter about the gas. Captain O'Shea rang the front door bell. My husband answered it. Captain O'Shea went into the dining room, and then went upstairs, and ten minutes after that Mr Parnell rang the front door bell and asked to see Captain O'Shea.'

(Laughter).

'Could he have gone down by the stairs?'

'No, there was a balcony outside the drawing room. There were two rope fire-escapes from the window. This happened three or four times. On these occasions Mr Parnell was in the sitting-room, and he did not come down the staircase.'[49]

It was thought hilarious that the 'uncrowned king of Ireland', known for his cold, haughty demeanour, had had to dash down the fire escape to ring the front-door bell as if he had just arrived.

Can you wonder that the foes of Erin jeer and jape?
Hasn't her 'uncrowned king' turned out a jackanape?
Fancy Robert Emmet sliding down that fire escape!
Oh! What will become of poor old Ireland?

Charlie Parlie! Charlie Parlie! Naughty, naughty boy!
Who would think he would upset another fellow's joy?
Won't the lawyers giggle and grin when they take up his pelf;
He wants Home Rule for Ireland but he can't Home Rule
   himself.[50]

Of course, many newspapers took a high moral line, none more so than *The Times*, which took its revenge for its humiliation over the Pigott letters:

Domestic treachery, systematic and long-continued deception, the whole squalid apparatus of letters written in the intention of misleading, houses taken under false names, disguises and aliases, secret visits and sudden flights make up a story of dull and ignoble infidelity, untouched so far as could be seen by a single ray of sentiment or a single flash of passion, comparable only to the dreary monotony of French middle-class vice, over which M. Zola's scalpel so lovingly lingers.[51]

Nothing could be more damning in matters of sexual morality than a comparison with the French, especially when Zola, widely regarded as a pornographer, was brought into it. However, Parnell was passionate about Mrs O'Shea, and as soon as he met her realised she was the only woman for him. Nor was *The Times* correct when it added that O'Shea's character had been vindicated. It seems clear now that he connived in the relationship.

The Times's reaction was predictable. It was the attacks by the Liberal papers which damaged Parnell, because only the Liberal Party was prepared to grant Home Rule to Ireland. The *Pall Mall Gazette* asked if any sane man believed that the Home Rule cause would benefit if 'the hero of many aliases' was retained, or that the fire escape would be the bridge to return waverers to the Liberal Party. An eminent Baptist wrote in the *Star* that the conscience of the nation had been aroused. 'Men legally convicted of immorality will not be permitted to lead in the legislation of the kingdom'.[52] Parnell had fallen foul of Irish Catholics *and* English Nonconformists, who were overwhelmingly Liberal. Gladstone dared not remain his ally, and Irish Home Rule ceased to dominate English politicsas it had during the 1880s.

In 1883, the discovery of a homosexual ring at Dublin Castle, the seat of the British government in Ireland, in fact failed to do serious damage. Two Irish Nationalist MPs brought some aspects of the affair to light in the Home Rule paper *United Ireland*. One was the paper's editor, William O'Brien, whose imprisonment in 1887 led to the events of 'Bloody Sunday' in Trafalgar Square. The writer of the unsigned article which started the row was Tim Healy, Parnell's most implacable opponent after the O'Shea divorce.

The head of the CID in Ireland, James Ellis French was sexually involved with young police officers and initiated the first in a series of libel actions. That he was later described as 'chief spy and agent provocateur to the English government in Ireland'[53] shows how politically sensitive the case was, but he delayed his action for so long that O'Brien was able to have it dismissed. French's superior, George Bolton, and the secretary of the General Post Office were among other high officials involved. Some were ruined, but the damage to the British government in Ireland was contained. No substantial body of British opinion wanted to inflate a scandal at Dublin Castle, and Irish Catholics did not welcome lurid revelations on such a subject. The pressures against disclosure in the press emerged when the foreman of the jury in one case asked the judge to ban publication of the evidence. His Honour preferred to appeal to 'the discretion and Christian forbearance' of the press. The British and Irish papers heeded his appeal, and did not publish the evidence in later cases either.[54]

Although the Dublin Castle scandal was controlled, the authorities were less successful in hushing up the Cleveland Street Affair, named after the London street between Oxford Street and Marylebone Road, which harboured a male brothel. In September 1889, the *North London Press* ran the following headline: 'The Earl of Galloway Examined Before the Sheriff. Noblemen Concerned in an Unspeakably Gross Case in the West End Are Allowed To Escape While Their Panders Are Mildly Punished.' The paper had a circulation of only a few thousand, but the article was reprinted the next day in *Reynolds's Newspaper*. It brought together two separate stories. The one about the Earl of Galloway made less impact in the long run, but it was pretty sensational at the time. A man in Dumfries told of what he had seen in the street there:

> I saw about fifty yards in front of me a man dressed in a black-coloured coat and white trousers, wearing a soft felt hat. I distinctly saw the man commit indecencies upon a little girl upon the wall. The spot is close to

the town-clerk's residence. I saw the man for about four minutes . . .
There were two or three little children about the place who called to the
girl to come down off the wall, but she answered that she could not as
the man was holding her. Several persons came up and joined in the
altercation. The man then walked off, and I followed him as I was
going in the same direction. I lost sight of him in English Street. While
on the road I saw a railway servant touch his hat to the man. The official was asked who the man was, and he replied, 'Lord Galloway.'[55]

The Earl of Galloway was a former MP and Lord High Commissioner
of the General Assembly of the Church of Scotland. He had married the
half-sister of the Prime Minister, Lord Salisbury. He was eventually put
on trial but acquitted, much to the indignation of the *North London Press*,
which argued that the prosecuting counsel had been so half-hearted
that it might as well have been acting for the defence. They suspected a
cover-up, and another in the second case mentioned in the headline:

The other case to which we direct attention is a scandal of so horrible
and repulsive a character that it would be better unmentioned if it were
not necessary to expose the shameless audacity with which officials
have contrived to shield the principal criminals. At the Old Bailey last
week George Daniel Veck, aged forty, described as a minister, and
Henry Horace Newlove, aged eighteen, clerk, were sentenced by the
Recorder to four months and nine months respectively for attempting
to conceal abominable crimes. Their 'trial' practically took place in
secret. At the close of the day they were hastily placed in the dock, their
plea of guilty taken, and sentence pronounced all in a few minutes.[56]

The Cleveland Street Affair came to light during a robbery inquiry
when a telegraph boy at the main Post Office was found to have more
money than he could have acquired honestly. To show that he was not a
thief, he revealed that he had been paid to take part in certain activities at
a Cleveland Street house. The establishment was presided over by a man
called Hammond, who fled to the Continent in July, and three months
later, in a curious echo of an earlier sensation, sailed for New York under
the name of Boulton.[57] The *North London Press* wondered how he had
scented danger, but was more interested in Newlove:

When taken, Newlove made a keen breast of the whole horrible business. He gave the names of men highly placed in the nobility who patronised the house, whose money passed through the hands of Newlove, and was used to corrupt the boys. Amongst these were the heir of a duke, the younger son of a duke, and an officer holding command in the Southern district, who, we may at once say, is not General Maitland. The names of these men are in our possession, and we are prepared to produce them if necessary. Week after week the wretched youth Newlove and the more infamous Veck were remanded by the Marlborough-street magistrate, ostensibly to allow the ramifications of this unspeakable iniquity to be traced out, but really to give the rich and influential patrons of Hammond's hell time to secure their immunity by flight or otherwise. Then, when the time was ripe came the committal to the Old Bailey, a few moments in the dock in an empty court, and the farcical sentence of nine and four months imprisonment. To properly appreciate the scandalous character of the Recorder's decision, one has only to recall the fact that the Hackney minister who some twelve months ago was convicted of an isolated offence of this kind . . . was given a life sentence from which hope of release was expressly eliminated.[58]

The 'heir of a duke' was the Earl of Euston, son of the Duke of Grafton. He sued the editor of the *North London Press*, Ernest Parke. When Parke was sentenced to a year in prison, his paper folded. Euston admitted that he had gone to Cleveland Street, but only once. A card had been handed to him in the street, advertising displays of nude female beauty at that address. When he had realised his mistake he had left. *Reynolds's Newspaper* was not inclined to believe him:

Judge Hawkins seems to us to have committed a grave error when he evidently intended the jury to believe that Lord Euston's statement, although utterly and entirely unsubstantiated, was a plain, unvarnished truthful statement . . . However, as judge and jury have exculpated and whitewashed the future Duke, it is to be hoped his ardour for witnessing exhibitions of nude females will be somewhat cooled by recent circumstances.[59]

The following week the paper launched another attack on the judge:

In his virulent address to the jury, and when passing what we can but consider a most vindictive sentence on the accused, Judge Hawkins emphatically declared that the libel was one of the grossest ever published without a single extenuating circumstance. Now we contend that the circumstance of a person knocking at the door, or ringing the bell of any particular house, being instantly admitted, remaining there, never mind how short a time, and then coming out and walking away, might naturally, and, indeed would obviously lead to the conclusion in the mind of anybody who witnessed all this, that he was a frequenter of the place into which he had so readily gained admission. But Hawkins refused to recognise any extenuating circumstance in the case, and Mr Parke's was made an example to others who dare tamper with the name of our virtuous and noble aristocracy.[60]

On the facts as stated in court, Parke had to be guilty. He had weakened his case by saying that the Earl had fled to Peru, which was untrue. For some reason Newlove was never called, leaving as Parke's main witness a homosexual prostitute who had offered to give evidence at the Dublin Castle trials.

The 'younger son of a duke' was Lord Arthur Somerset, the third son of the Duke of Beaufort, and a member of the Prince of Wales's household. He had been seen frequenting Cleveland Street, and was given time to escape to France. When his mother died, he returned for the funeral, but was allowed to leave for the Continent a second time. He never returned.

Most newspapers were afraid of the case. An exception was *Truth*, owned and edited by the maverick radical MP Henry Labouchere, at whose house Pigott had called a year earlier to confess to his forgery of the Parnell letters. It had been Labouchere who inserted the clause in the Criminal Law Amendment Act that made all homosexual acts illegal.

On 28 February 1891 he raised the Cleveland Street affair in the House of Commons and showed that he was very well informed: he described how Hammond had been watched in Belgium by English police, who could not move because the government would not apply for extradition, just as the police had had to stand by helplessly, without an arrest warrant, when Lord Arthur Somerset attended his mother's funeral. By the time a warrant was issued, it was too late. Labouchere's most sensational accusation concerned the Prime Minister, Lord Salisbury, who, he said, had obstructed the investigation all along. When he had met Sir Dighton Probyn, a senior aide to the Prince of Wales, on King's Cross station, he had allegedly tipped him off that a warrant was about to be issued for Somerset's arrest, which had enabled him to take flight. 'What was this case but a criminal conspiracy, by the very guardians of public morality and law, with the Prime Minister at their head, to defeat the ends of justice?'[61]

The Parnell Commission's judgements on the Irish Members of Parliament had just been published, and this gave the debate an intriguing Irish dimension. In trying to explain to the House why it had taken the government so long to move, the Attorney-General said charges should not be brought hastily because once they were made, 'however much a man might clear himself, there were people foolish and wicked enough still to believe in them'.

There were ironic cheers from the Irish Nationalists. Labouchere pointed out that Parnell had been accused of giving money to a man to help him escape justice. Giving information for the same purpose was no different. If an inquiry into Salisbury's conduct was refused, it would show that one code of ethics governed treatment of the Irish leader and another the Conservative leader! Labouchere was suspended from the House when he said, 'I assert, if I am obliged to do it, that I do not believe Lord Salisbury.'[62] Sitting in the Lords, Salisbury could not be questioned by Labouchere. Later he made a statement brushing aside the accusation against him.

It has not been proved, and probably cannot be. However, as his latest biographer, Andrew Roberts, points out, Salisbury had once written that it might be acceptable to tell white lies to help 'a fugitive who is in danger or a friend who is in trouble'; Lord Arthur Somerset's father was an important Tory supporter, and Salisbury was acutely aware of how much the power of the upper classes rested on their social prestige.[63]

Lord Arthur Somerset might not have been the biggest fish whom the Prime Minister was protecting. Rumours were flying around London that another visitor to Cleveland Street had been the Prince of Wales's eldest son, Albert Victor, known as Prince Eddy. Certainly Somerset wrote to his friends that he had fled to protect a more important person than himself. When the *North London Press* named names, it added: 'These men have been allowed to leave the country, and thus defeat the ends of justice, because their prosecution would disclose the fact that a far more distinguished and more highly placed personage than themselves was inculpated in these disgusting crimes.'[64]

That was as far as any British paper could go. However, the American press was more open. A correspondent to the *New York Herald* wrote, 'I have heard, though I have not actually seen the paper, that a New York journal recently published an article on certain abominable scandals, with a portrait of Prince Albert Victor in the middle of it.' The *New York Times* described Prince Eddy as combining the 'worst attributes of those sons of Georges, at whose mention history still holds her nose. It is not too early to predict that such a fellow will never be allowed to ascend the British throne.'[65] In fact, he died a few years later.

There are reasonable grounds for supposing that Prince Eddy was homosexual.[66] The Boulton and Parke affair would have been even more sensational than it was if the Duke of Newcastle's son had lived to be charged. Similarly, in the Cleveland Street affair, had another duke's son faced trial, the scandal would have been even worse, and Prince Eddy's name might have been mentioned. Labouchere stressed his belief that, unlike Lord Salisbury, the Prince of Wales had been anxious to get at the truth. Not all writers about the case have agreed with him,[67] and the Prince had good reason to protect his son.

A year later, Oscar Wilde published *The Picture of Dorian Gray*. One reviewer wrote that 'if he can write for none but outlawed noblemen and telegraph boys', the sooner he took to a decent trade the better.[68] Public awareness of the Cleveland Street Affair affected perceptions of Wilde, whose disgrace was often described as another 'society scandal'.

Wilde's fall was precipitated by the Marquess of Queensberry, the father of Oscar Wilde's lover, Lord Alfred Douglas. He left a card at Wilde's club, accusing him of posing as a sodomite (Queensberry's spelling and handwriting were so bad that the exact wording is disputed.) Wilde sued him for libel, but Queensberry pleaded justification and supplied the court with so much evidence that Wilde's chief counsel, Sir Edward Clarke, who had not been afraid of the Prince of Wales in the Tranby Croft affair, was reduced to arguing that his client was not a sodomite, although he might seem to have posed as one. There were cheers in court when Queensbury was acquitted and Wilde was arrested. He was charged, along with an Alfred Taylor, of indecency and sodomy. The first jury failed to agree, and it was only at the end of his second trial that Wilde received the maximum sentence, two years' hard labour. All three trials were quickly held in April and May 1895. Wilde's *An Ideal Husband* had opened on 3 January, and *The Importance of Being Earnest* on 14 February. He was a sensation throughout the first five months of 1895.[69] His nearest rival was W G Grace, who, aged 46, became the first batsman to score 1,000 runs in May, the month when he also became the first to make his hundredth first-class century.

Oscar Wilde was the most prominent Victorian to be convicted of homosexual offences. His peculiar reputation at the time of his fall made the sensation unique. By 1895, he had been newsworthy for at least fifteen years. As an aesthete in the early 1880s, he had been the butt of George du Maurier's cartoons in *Punch* and W S Gilbert's satire in *Patience*. Until 1890 his literary reputation rested on his poetry, which is little read today and even then was read by few. His fame, however, rested on his witticisms, the way he dressed and his genius for self-advertisement – he anticipated the celebrities of our own age who are famous for being famous. He was almost the only public figure immediately recognisable by his Christian name, witness the frequent press references to 'Oscar'.

However, in the five years leading to 1895, Oscar Wilde had also achieved stature as a writer, and almost everything that makes up his literary reputation today dates from this period, notably *The Picture of Dorian Gray* and his four sparkling comedies, which are still staged, unlike the vast majority of nineteenth-century plays. At the time of his case against Queensberry, he was described as 'the man who had materially assisted to make the dramatic history of the nineteenth century, and who practically was better known for his "peculiar" literary ability than any man of the present day'.[70]

The crash of his fall was all the louder because so many disliked Wilde – which was inevitable because he advertised himself so relentlessly, and was so much cleverer than most of his adversaries. Also, he insisted, scandalously, that aesthetic values mattered more than moral ones. The Victorians set high store by morality, and Wilde actually claimed in court that there was no such thing as a moral or immoral book, that books were either well or badly written. After he was sentenced, the *Daily Telegraph* published a leader that opened with an attack on art for art's sake, and, doubtless to the bemusement of many readers, invoked the names of Kant, Lessing, Schiller and Hegel.

The same article rehearsed the unpopular elements of Oscar Wilde's public persona – 'his foolish ostentation, his empty paradoxes, his insufferable posturing, his incurable vanity' – and suggested that those who had been unduly influenced by him were 'Young men at universities, clever sixth form boys at public schools, silly women, who lend an ear to any chatter that is petulant and vivacious, novelists who have sought to imitate the style of paradox and unreality'.[71] There was another reference to public school boys in one of the few attempts to make a point or two in Oscar Wilde's favour. It came from W T Stead, of all people, now founder-editor of the *Review of the Reviews*: 'If all persons guilty of Oscar Wilde's offences were to be clapped into gaol,' Stead wrote, 'there would be a very surprising exodus from Eton and Harrow, Rugby and Winchester, to Pentonville and Holloway.'[72] (Holloway was not yet a women's prison.)

When Wilde was first arrested with Taylor and brought before a magistrate at Bow Street, he was refused bail. Sir John Bridge, the magistrate said, in justification, 'I think there is no worse crime than that with which the prisoners are charged'.[73] Although this remark has been seen, with some justice, as the epitome of Victorian homophobia, Stead's *Pall Mall Gazette* had described the seduction of a young bride, as alleged against Sir Charles Dilke, as 'morally worse than murder'.

Oscar Wilde paraded his partners in public, and was openly camp in his behaviour. He did not go as far as Boulton and Park, who had worn makeup and women's clothes in the street, but they were small fry and he was a celebrity. Yet he was no campaigner for homosexual rights: when Sir Edward Clarke asked, before he agreed to take the brief, if there was any foundation for the charges, Wilde said there was not.[74] He was acting by society's values rather than his own. He showed a great deal of bravery during the course of his downfall, but he denied his homosexuality. Given the prevailing views of the period, it would be unreasonable to expect him to have done otherwise.

In the libel case against Queensberry, even Clarke referred repeatedly to 'the greatest of all offences'.[75] When Oscar Wilde was in the dock, Clarke said the jury should remember that 'he was a man of high intellectual gifts – a person whom people would suppose to be incapable of such acts as were alleged'. When reporting this, *The Times* added that, leaving aside Oscar Wilde's abilities, 'he belonged to a class of people' whom it would be difficult to imagine committing such offences. The paper still held, as it had during the Boulton and Park case a quarter of a century earlier, that homosexuality was a working-class vice.

Reynolds's Newspaper *fed what it itself deplored as 'morbid' public interest in the Wilde trial: far from drawing a veil over the case, it sold a full and graphic account of proceedings for a penny.*

As with the Boulton and Park affair, the newspapers varied in how much of the unsavoury evidence they were prepared to report. The *St James's Gazette* refused to print any at all. *The Times'* coverage was remarkable for its brevity as well as its discretion. Even Oscar Wilde's now much admired peroration on 'the love that dare not speak its name' was not reported, except for a reference in the judge's summing-up.

At the other extreme, *Reynolds's Newspaper* was once again remarkable for its frankness; far from wanting to draw a veil over the case, it sold a separate account of the Bow Street proceedings for a penny. Its founder, G W M Reynolds, was long dead, but the paper was still exploiting the class angle and flaying the aristocracy – Queensberry had 'considerable natural gifts when compared with the majority of the hereditary automatons who happen to be of his own rank'. It added, 'The morbid interest which the persons in the street have taken in the case throughout suggests certainly that there is a lack of moral stiffening – a decadence in the community.' In deploring this 'morbid interest' while at the same time feeding it, the paper was worthy of today's popular press.

Unlike its rivals, *Reynolds's Newspaper* reported this exchange: "He asked me into his bedroom, which opened off the sitting-room. We went there." "Did you undress?" "Yes." "Both of you?" "Yes." "Did you take them all off?" (Bluntly) "Yes." "Both went naked into bed?" "Yes." "I don't propose to take this further." There was a reference to the state of the sheets in Oscar Wilde's bed at the Savoy Hotel: when the housekeeper was asked, 'What did you see on the sheets?' she replied, 'I refused to look at them.' It also recorded that of the eight pairs of trousers found in Taylor's room, 'seven had the sewing of the pocket cut on one side, so that anyone could pass their hands straight through. (Sensation.)' However, there were limits: readers were told that although in court details of 'acts of indecency' were insisted upon, 'the evidence, [was], of course, unreportable'.[76]

Perhaps the most interesting coverage came in the *Illustrated Police Budget*, which specialised in reports of sensational crime, copiously illustrated with line drawings. It did not print the salacious evidence, which, it suggested, should have been heard *in camera*, but reported Oscar Wilde's every move in a special supplement, which was published after Queensberry won the libel case. The editor had instructed his journalist to 'Pick Oscar Wilde up tomorrow morning and never leave him until he either goes abroad or is arrested.' The journalist followed his prey across London, including the journey from the Cadogan Hotel to Bow Street.[77]

COMMITTED.

SIR JOHN BRIDGE: "HAVE YOU ANYTHING TO SAY, WILDE?"
OSCAR: "NOTHING AT PRESENT, YOUR WORSHIP."

The Illustrated Police Budget *specialised in copiously illustrated reports of sensational crime. It obsessively reported Wilde's every move in a special supplement, published after Queensberry won the libel case.*

In his article he made much of Wilde's background in the lap of luxury then described the 'ill-lit, ill-furnished and uncomfortable cell' in which he now found himself. 'The quilt is not pretty, and must considerably upset the artistic being of a man like Wilde.'[78] The following week there was a blow-by-blow illustrated account of how 'one of the most sensational prisoners of the nineteenth century' had to take his compulsory morning and afternoon exercise, with the other remand prisoners, in the yard at Holloway.[79]

If Wilde anticipated modern trends in consciously manufacturing celebrity status for himself, he became a celebrity scandal victim against his will. Exile was inevitable after his release from prison, not only because Victorian society abhorred homosexuality but because, in questions of morality, it drew no distinction between the personal and public spheres.

The heterosexual Colonel Baker also served time in prison, then went into exile. Unlike Wilde though, he inspired a campaign to forgive him and bring him home. Even so, despite powerful friends, it failed: there was no way back from a Victorian disgrace. It paid, however, to have powerful protectors who might prevent a scandal in the first place. It is remarkable how many cover-ups were linked to the Prince of Wales. Although, under Queen Victoria, newspapers advanced a long way towards the commanding position they now enjoy, the socially privileged were more or less safe from press intrusion. Class loyalty and social cohesion made leaks from their circle unthinkable. The Divorce Court was a magnificent innovation for sensation-seekers because it was the only place where the rich and famous had to reveal their disreputable secrets. Public prurience was fed there as nowhere else. No less than their descendants, Queen Victoria's subjects were avid not just for sensation, but for sensation involving sex.

CHAPTER 5:

Murder

'There's nothing beats a stunning good murder, after all.' *Broadside seller to Henry Mayhew*[1]

On the morning of 6 May 1840 Lord William Russell was found in bed in his Mayfair home, his throat cut, a towel clotted with blood over his face, and a bloodstained pillow behind his head. However, brutal as the crime was, there were too many murders for it to have created the sensation it did without other factors being involved. One of these was the high social standing of the victim. Lord William, 73, belonged to one of the oldest and most prestigious families in the land. He was the brother of two dukes of Bedford and uncle to a third. Lord John Russell, a future prime minister, was his nephew.[2]

Lord William lived alone, apart from his servants, and his murder was an inside job. The chief suspect from the start was the Swiss butler and valet, François Courvoisier. The upper classes were suddenly terrified of their servants killing them while they slept. As the *Sunday Times* put it, 'The excitement produced in high life by the dreadful event is almost unprecedented, and the feeling of apprehension for personal safety increases every hour, particularly among those of the nobility and gentry who live in comparative seclusion.' One manifestation of this excitement, as was so often the case, was the impulse to visit the scene of the crime. 'During the whole of Thursday, a great number of the nobility and gentry, in carriages, on horseback and on foot, passed through Norfolk-street for the purpose of taking a passing view of the house in which the appalling deed was committed.'[3] Ordinary members of the public followed, anxious to get a glimpse of their betters, and crowds arrived in Norfolk Street until attention switched to the Old Bailey. When Courvoisier was hanged, it was noted that 'The number of man-servants present was remarkable as evincing the fearful interest taken in the culprit's fate by the class to which he had belonged.'[4]

A murder sensation always grew if the accused had an interesting personality, and Courvoisier did. He spoke good English, and was most agreeable, even charming. His previous employers testified at the trial to his good character. He dealt coolly with the police, even when rings, cufflinks, a fob watch and silver spoons were found to be missing, and later discovered in the butler's pantry. The night before the murder he had fetched beer for two female servants, which they drank, and afterwards slept more heavily than usual. After the arrest, the police found among his possessions suspicious objects that they had previously missed. Courvoisier's defence lawyer claimed that they had been planted – suspicion over police methods has a long history.

Interest in the Russell murder did not flag even after Oxford's attempt on the Queen's life on 10 June. Benjamin Disraeli wrote to his sister, 'All the world is talking of Courvoisier, and very little of the quasi regicide.'[5]

In an ideal murder drama at this period there were three acts: the crime, the trial and the hanging. The trial was the most important because every detail relating to the crime was rehearsed, and it had to end satisfactorily to make the hanging possible. In addition, the lucky few could not only read about the trial but attend it. With comparatively few ways to amuse themselves, the Victorians prized even minor trials at local assizes because they provided a free spectacle. Of course, murder trials were the most popular. According to Charles Dickens, portraits of murderers were 'rife in the print shops', their autographs 'stuck up in shop windows'; 'high prices were offered for their clothes at Newgate', and turnpike trusts grew rich from the tolls paid by sightseers travelling to look at murderers' houses or the scene of the crime. Dickens's reference to murderers under sentence of death 'followed into their cells and tracked down from day to day, and night to night' foreshadows press coverage of Oscar Wilde in prison and suggests that Wilde was treated like a murderer.[6]

The day the Courvoisier case opened, crowds tried desperately to get into the Old Bailey, even though all the tickets had been taken. The privileged few packing the courtroom included a duke, three earls and the Archbishop of Canterbury's private secretary. 'The presiding judge was so

AN ELIGIBLE INVESTMENT.

*Punch's satirical cartoon was based on fact. An estimated 40,000 spectators
gathered to watch Courvoisier's execution: positions at the windows of
neighbouring houses were let out for large sums, and roofs were crowded.*

hemmed in by the extensive draperies of the surrounding ladies that he
had scarcely any room to move, and looked disgusted at the indecency of
the spectacle.'[7]

All the evidence against the accused was circumstantial, and he handled himself so well that an acquittal seemed likely. However, on the last
day there was a sensation in court: silver spoons, engraved with the Russell
crest, were still missing, but a woman who kept a hotel off Leicester
Square had read about the case and realised that Courvoisier had left
them with her just after the murder. At the last minute she came forward,
and sealed his fate, despite defence attempts to discredit her as the keeper
of a house of ill-repute.

Another valued ingredient of the murder sensation was the murderer's
confession, preferably on the scaffold. It was so popular that, if necessary,

writers of broadsheets invented them. While he was still in prison, Courvoisier obliged with no fewer than three different confessions. At one point he said he had got the idea of cutting his employer's throat from reading *Jack Sheppard*, Harrison Ainsworth's novel of criminal life. This was the literary sensation of the day, with 3,000 copies sold in the first week of publication alone, but the book's many critics believed it encouraged crime and that the Courvoisier case proved their point.[8] It certainly highlighted the vast market for murder in fiction as well as fact.

According to some estimates, 40,000 spectators gathered to watch Courvoisier's execution. Positions at the windows of neighbouring houses were sold for large sums, and roofs were crowded. Six hundred 'persons of distinction' were said to be there, including several Members of Parliament but, more importantly, William Makepeace Thackeray and Charles Dickens, whose accounts of the occasion have ensured that it is still remembered.

Thackeray was up at three thirty in the morning to be in position early. He described the crowd as consisting of 'all ranks and degrees – mechanics, gentlemen, pickpockets, members of both houses of parliament, street-walkers, newspaper-writers'. The experience turned him against the death penalty:

> I came away from Snow Hill that morning with a disgust for murder, but it was for *the murder I saw done*. This is the twentieth of June, and I may be permitted for my part to declare that, for the last fourteen days, so salutary has the impression of the butchery been upon me that I can see Mr Ketch at this moment, with an easy air, taking the rope from his pocket; that I feel myself shamed and degraded at the brutal curiosity which took me to that brutal sight, and I pray to Almighty God to cause this disgraceful sin to pass from among us, and to cleanse our land of blood.'[9]

Dickens did not publish his description of the Courvoisier hanging until five and a half years later, when he was campaigning against the death penalty. It appeared in the *Daily News*, of which he had been the first editor. At one point his tone was similar to Thackeray's: 'It was so loathsome, pitiful and vile a sight, that the law appeared to be as bad as he, or worse; being much the stronger, and shedding around it a far more dismal contagion.'

However, the two accounts are different. Thackeray's targets are the authorities for carrying out what he sees as judicial murder and himself for witnessing it. The crowd in his description is decent enough: 'There is great heaving and pushing, and swaying to and fro; but round the women the men have formed a circle, and keep them as much as possible out of the rush and trample.' Dickens launches a ferocious attack on the crowd: from the moment of his arrival at midnight, he says, he did not see one emotion suitable to the occasion. 'Nothing but ribaldry, debauchery, levity, drunkenness and flaunting vice in fifty other shapes. I should have deemed it impossible that I could have ever felt any large assemblage of my fellow-creatures to be so odious.'[10]

Three years after the Russell murder, in March 1843, another killing struck at the heart of the governing class. Edward Drummond, the private secretary to the Prime Minister, Sir Robert Peel, was shot dead by a man who mistook him for Peel. Within a few days another man had been charged with threatening to shoot both the Prime Minister and the Queen, and yet another with threatening the Chancellor of the Exchequer. In the days when it was still possible not to know what the Prime Minister looked like, few could have recognised the Chancellor.

An attempt on the Prime Minister, in which a man was killed, was all the more sensational because the only assassination of a British prime minister, Spencer Perceval, had taken place within living memory, in 1812. The *Observer* claimed that the excitement over the trial of Daniel MacNaghten for Drummond's murder 'has not been surpassed by any of the extraordinary events of a similar character which have taken place during the last quarter of a century'.[11] However, by far the most important feature of the trial was the verdict: in a new legal development, MacNaghten was acquitted on grounds of insanity, and so gave his name to the 'MacNaghten rules', which were used for more than a hundred years to define who was and who was not insane. The innovation was highly unpopular. 'Who after this is safe?' people asked. The guilty man's escape from the gallows was supposedly 'filling the heart of the country with horror and alarm',[12] but the public was indignant at being deprived, unfairly as it thought, of act three of the drama. 'Mad or not, the prisoner ought to have been hanged. Such was no uncommon expression, and a general denunciation of mad doctors, and some not very complimentary remarks upon lawyers, might not unfrequently be heard.'[13]

Just as the Russell murder held its own against Oxford's sensational

USEFUL SUNDAY LITERATURE FOR THE MASSES;

OR, MURDER MADE FAMILIAR.

Father of a Family (reads). "The wretched Murderer is supposed to have cut the throats of his three eldest Children, and then to have killed the Baby by beating it repeatedly with a Poker. * * * * * In person he is of a rather bloated appearance, with a bull neck, small eyes, broad large nose, and coarse vulgar mouth. His dress was a light blue coat, with brass buttons, elegant yellow summer vest, and pepper-and-salt trowsers. When at the Station House he expressed himself as being rather 'peckish,' and said he should like a Black Pudding, which, with a Cup of Coffee, was immediately procured for him."

The market for reports of murder cases was vast. A highly valued ingredient of the sensation was the murderer's confession, preferably on the scaffold. Such confessions were so popular that, if necessary, broadside writers would invent them.

attack on the Queen, the case against the Mannings was no less riveting because cholera was rife in the land. During the preliminary hearings in Southwark there was a day of 'humiliation and prayer' when the shops were closed and the streets deserted, but the crowds continued to mass outside the court. One witness died of the disease. Cholera comes in waves and its victims die quickly, and the epidemic of 1848–9 was the worst to hit Britain in the nineteenth century, with more than fifty-three thousand deaths in England and Wales. This was a sensational epidemic, but nothing could blunt the impact of the Mannings' case.[14]

On 17 August 1849, two policemen discovered a body under the flag-stones in the kitchen of Mr and Mrs Manning's house in Bermondsey. The skull was fractured in two places, and a bullet protruded under the skin over the right eye. The deceased was a Customs House employee and part-time usurer, Patrick O'Connor, who had been a frequent visitor to the house. There followed an exciting hunt for the Mannings with many false trails. A ship that had left London for New York was stopped and boarded, only for the police to find a different Manning among the passengers. Eventually Mrs Manning was arrested in Edinburgh, where she was trying to sell railway shares stolen from the murdered man, and her husband was found in Jersey.

It was her personality that caught the public imagination – in comparison, her husband was a nonentity. After the murder, Maria Manning had twice been bold enough to visit O'Connor's lodgings from which she had removed the railway shares and other valuables. Even her defence counsel wrote later that he suspected her to be 'the power that really originated the deed of blood'.[15] *The Times* was not alone in referring to her as 'Lady Macbeth', but it added 'Jezebel, the daring foreigner, the profane unbeliever . . . the ready arguer, the greedy aggrandizer, the forger, the intriguer, the resolute, the painted and attired even unto death'.[16]

Like Courvoisier, Maria Manning was Swiss, and, also like him, she had been a servant in high society. There was even an untrue rumour that they were related. She had married a railway worker from Taunton, where they lived until they moved to London early in 1849. Mrs Manning had had an affair with O'Connor – after which husband *and* wife did away with the lover, a variation on the standard theme.

Did the couple really act together or was one guilty? As soon as he was arrested, Manning laid the blame on his wife. She refused to talk until the trial, but she said then, 'The villain, it was him that did it, not me.'

Manning claimed, improbably, that after his wife had committed the murder, he had fainted and did not know that the body had been buried in the kitchen. He eventually confessed to having finished off O'Connor: Maria had shot him and he had battered his head with a crow-bar. 'I never liked him very much,' he said.

If they had stuck to their original stories, in which they blamed each other they might have got off. Only six months later, a couple were acquitted of murdering their 14-year-old servant because the jury could not decide which of them had killed her.[17] However, this strategy ensured that each spouse had to face two sets of prosecuting counsel: one employed by the Crown and the other by their spouse's defence team. It also emphasised the contrast between Maria's proud demeanour, and the unimpressive Manning, who was widely despised for trying to hide behind his wife. As they were handcuffed after the death sentence had been pronounced, he was abject, while she reportedly uttered the splendidly melodramatic line, 'Damnation seize ye all!'[18]

It was the same on the day of the public hanging at Horsemonger Lane gaol. 'She walked to her doom with a firm, unfaltering step' while his step was so 'feeble and tottering' he had to be supported by two turnkeys.[19] His counsel had told the jury to disregard the idea that the male is always stronger than the female. 'History teaches us,' he said, 'that the female is capable of reaching higher in point of virtue than the male, but that when once she gives way to vice, she sinks far lower than our sex.' The Victorian obsession with wicked women often surfaced in fiction and on the stage. As Judith Knelman points out in her study of Victorian murderesses, murder by a woman did not fit the patriarchal ideology of Victorian England: it had to be explained away as 'the action of a whore, witch, monster or mad woman'[20] – as in the case of Maria Manning.

Many people commented on Maria's attractive figure, not least at her execution. According to the *Morning Chronicle*, 'Even the distortion consequent upon the mode of death she suffered could not destroy the remarkably fine contour of her figure as it swayed to and fro by the action of the wind.'[21] Judith Knelman, who emphasises the sexual attraction of the Victorian murderess both in the dock and on the scaffold, quotes this description along with Thomas Hardy's of another murderess whom he saw swing: 'What a fine figure she showed against the sky as she hung in the misty rain, and how the tight black silk gown set off her shape as she wheeled half-round and back.'[22] Mrs Manning's gown was of black satin, and it was widely believed for years afterwards that because of this black satin became unfashionable immediately after her execution.[23] In another case from 1849, a pretty 18-year-old servant called Sarah Thomas was hanged for the murder of her mistress; her age and appearance, and her struggles on the scaffold, made her death seem particularly abhorrent.[24]

Charles Dickens saw the Mannings hang, and interrupted his work on *David Copperfield* to write to *The Times* calling for an end to public executions: 'When the day dawned, thieves, low prostitutes, ruffians and vagabonds of every kind, flocked on to the ground, with every variety of foul and offensive behaviour. Fightings, faintings, whistlings, imitations of Punch, brutal jokes, tumultuous demonstrations of indecent delight when swooning women were dragged out of the crowd by the police with their dresses disordered, gave a new zest to the general entertainment.' He wrote of the 'upturned faces, so inexpressibly odious in their brutal mirth or callousness, that a man had cause to feel ashamed of the shape he wore. When the two miserable creatures who attracted this ghastly sight about them were turned quivering into the air, there was no more emotion . . . no more restraint in any of the previous obscenities, than if the name of Christ had never been heard in this world.' *The Times'* report was less emotional. It recorded that more than 30,000 people were kept in order by 500 police, and 'They did not behave worse than other mobs under similar circumstances have done.'[25] That was Dickens's point: he was campaigning against public executions. On the death penalty, he thought that opinion was too entrenched to be moved.

Dickens could not get the Mannings out of his mind. He mentioned them repeatedly in his magazine *Household Words*.[26] Three years after the case, he described himself lying awake at night, thinking of the hanging, 'those two forms dangling on the top of the entrance gateway – the man's a limp loose suit of clothes, as if the man had gone out of them; the woman's a fine shape, so elaborately corseted and artfully dressed, that it was quite unchanged in its trim appearance as it swung slowly from side to side'.[27] His imagination was fired by Maria Manning, on whom he based the murderous foreign maidservant Hortense in *Bleak House*. References to the Mannings appear in two great sensation novels of the period, *The Woman in White* by Wilkie Collins and *Lady Audley's Secret* by Mary Braddon.[28]

Even before the trial, fictional accounts of Maria's memoirs appeared.

In a particularly imaginative version, she is about to enter a nunnery when she runs off with a bandit chief.[29] The murderous couple were also a favourite subject for broadsides although, as so often, the accuracy of the woodcuts could not be trusted – as Henry Mayhew pointed out, a supposed portrait of O'Connor was a reused cut of King William IV.[30] Some broadsides, of course, were in verse:

> At length they planned their friend to murder,
> And for his company did crave,
> The dreadful weapons they prepared,
> And in the kitchen dug his grave.
> And, as they fondly did caress him,
> They slew him – what a dreadful sight,
> First they mangled, after robbed him,
> Frederick Manning and his wife . . .
>
> Old and young, pray take a warning,
> Females, lead a virtuous life
> Think upon that fateful morning,
> Frederick Manning and his wife.[31]

The Mannings were popular subjects for the waxwork shows that were then found all over Britain. The most important, because of its size and its site in central London, was Madame Tussaud's, which bought up and displayed anything that could be linked to a famous murderer. (In 1849 the aged Madame Tussaud still had another year to live.) Around this time *Punch* commented, 'In these days no one can be considered positively popular unless he is admitted into the company of Madame Tussaud's celebrities in Baker Street.'[32] It went on to fulminate, 'Talk of cholera, Sir, and miasma, is there not a worse moral poison and does it not reek from the Chamber of Horrors, contaminating not only Baker Street, but all London?'[33] The effigies of the Mannings provoked the greatest scorn: 'There she stands in silk attire, a beauteous thing to be daily rained upon by a shower of sixpences. George Manning is greatly improved in his appearance in the hands of Madame Tussaud. He has a look of a very clean undertaker . . . Fortunately the low brutes who behaved so ill at Horsemonger Lane will not be able to disgust a thinking public by their licence in Baker street. They can't afford it.'[34]

The Mannings were often coupled with James Blomfield Rush. The Rush and Manning trials were the most sensational of four that received specially extended coverage in *The Annual Register for 1849* on the grounds that they involved 'crimes so enormous in their inception, so ruthless and so reckless in their execution, and [were] attended with circumstances so enthralling in their detection and punishment'. The reader might well ask himself, 'Can these things be, and yet our boasted progress be more actual than a dream?'[35] Horrific crime posed a threat even to the self-confidence and optimism of the Victorians, suggesting that its impact among thoughtful people might have been occasioned by more than a taste for sensation.

Rush was the tenant of three farms in Norfolk, but was convinced that he was their true owner. When his landlord, Isaac Jermy, a prominent local figure, threatened him with eviction, Rush shot him, his son and his daughter-in-law. The daughter-in-law survived, but lost an arm. The sex angle in the case was provided by a young woman who lived with Rush, his accomplice in forgery. Rush's personality also contributed to the excitement: his unusual decision to conduct his own defence allowed him to emerge as a disturbing and saturnine figure – defendants were excluded from the witness box. He was also thought to be a dangerous political radical. There seems to be no evidence for this, but much that was written about him was fiction.[36] Dickens, incidentally, did not see him hanged but visited the scene of the crime.[37]

Punch, whose attacks on Madame Tussaud were relentless, declared that she 'displays the names of the MANNINGS and RUSH as the manager of a theatre would parade the combination of two or three "stars" on the same evening'. In the theatre the depiction of living people was banned, and the censor had stepped in to prevent Rush being portrayed on stage. *Punch* also attacked the *Observer*, which had denounced a publisher for trying to persuade Rush to write his life-story by offering £500 to each of his children. Allegedly, the *Observer* had also exploited the Rush children by publishing an untrue report that the eldest daughter was dying from shock.[38] An amusing satire showed the proprietors of the *Sunday Drop*, the *Scaffold Weekly News* and other imaginary sensationalist sheets petitioning Parliament for executions to be switched to Saturdays from Mondays and Tuesdays.[39] Another of *Punch*'s targets was the Eastern Counties Railway Company, which had laid on special trains to Norwich for the hanging.

Punch was not alone in recognising the role of Madame Tussaud in contributing to the Rush sensation. A street patterer interviewed by Henry Mayhew thought of asking her to treat him to something with which to drink to 'the immortal memory of Mr Rush, my friend and hers'.[40] Mayhew explains that patterers were men who made as much noise as possible on the streets to sell their broadsides. Only a few words needed to be audible – when the subject was murder, they might shout 'murder', 'horrible', 'barbarous', 'love', and mysterious'. 'If, however, the "paper" relate to any well-known criminal such as Rush, the name is given distinctly enough.'[41] Naturally Rush aroused special interest in Norfolk, and one of Mayhew's informants described how 'he saw, one evening after dark, through the uncurtained cottage window, eleven persons, young and old, gathered round a scanty fire'. An old man was reading to the others, by the firelight, a broadside on Rush's execution – perhaps even the one that Mayhew was told achieved the highest sale of all. He described it as the best he had seen, but criticised the sympathy shown to the murderer. According to custom, the murderer was supposed to have composed it in his cell.

> If Jermy had but kindness shown,
> And not have trod misfortune down,
> I ne'er had fired the fatal ball
> That caus'd his son and him to fall.
>
> My cause I did defend alone,
> For learned counsel I had none;
> I pleaded hard and questions gave,
> In hopes my wretched life to save.[42]

The patterers also did well from the sale of Rush's supposed confession to the prison chaplain, which claimed that he had murdered his mother and his wife. The sales figures Mayhew gives should be treated with caution but they establish a popularity league table: at a time when no newspaper had a circulation of 100,000, Rush and the Mannings each sold 2.5 million copies of various broadsides. Courvoisier is next at nearly 1.6 million.[43]

The 1850s saw the poisoner's rise to prominence. Those who weren't worried about being stabbed or shot were afraid of being poisoned. An article in *Household Words* said that between 1839 and 1849, there had been 249 deaths by poison but only 85 convictions. In other words, two-thirds of the poisoners had escaped justice. It also pointed out that while shop-keepers needed a licence to sell tea, coffee, tobacco and snuff, they could sell arsenic freely.[44] A later article claimed that sellers of poisons often did not keep a record of the names and addresses of all purchasers, despite the provisions of the 1851 Sale of Arsenic Act. The great danger of poisoning was that it 'admits more readily of a fiendish sophistication in the mind of the perpetrator than any other form by which murder is committed. No violence is used; the destroyer can stop short of the final dose . . . and if the victim dies some time later, it is pretended that it is a broken constitution that has given way.'[45] As late as 1886, the Elephant and Castle Theatre, advertising one of its melodramas, claimed that the number of deaths by poisoning had risen alarmingly, 'the unsuspecting one receiving his death draught from the hands of those whom he believes to be his best and dearest friends'.[46] Three years later, *The Times* said that poisonings made strangely attractive cases because they implied domestic treason. It also mentioned that some doctors missed the part played by poison in some deaths.[47]

The most famous of all Victorian poisoning cases starred William Palmer of Rugeley, Staffordshire. Lord Chief Justice Campbell entered in his diary that Palmer's trial was the most memorable of the past 50 years, 'engaging the attention of not only this country but of all Europe'.[48] Palmer's biographer of 1925, George Fletcher, remembered how when he was a boy 'My father sent me to buy any daily paper at Birmingham New Street Station during the trial, for which I had to pay fabulous prices, especially the last four days of the fortnight's trial in London – often three or four shillings a copy for *The Times*.'[49] Four shillings was 12 times the cover price, and the circulation of *The Times*, which was up to 60,000 at this period, could be almost doubled by a sensational trial like Palmer's. A shilling account, which was hastily published as soon as Palmer had been executed, said that his name 'has hung incessantly on the lips of people of all classes and conditions, for weeks – nay, for months past'.[50] Local prejudice against him was so great that Parliament hastily passed a law which enabled the trial to be moved to the Old Bailey. It lasted two weeks, and the day of national rejoicing to celebrate the end of the Crimean War, with its illuminations, firework displays and free theatre performances, was the only event that briefly distracted public attention.[51]

Although Palmer was described as a doctor, he had given up medicine two or three years earlier to devote himself to horse-racing. However, the high social standing of the medical profession made his fall a salutary moral lesson. *The Times* referred to his descent 'from gambling to insolvency, from insolvency to forgery, from forgery to murder of the foulest kind'.[52] The case certainly opened a window on to the louche world of the turf. Palmer owned a valuable stud, and when it was eventually sold, Prince Albert bought one of his brood mares. The murder for which Palmer was convicted was of a young racing associate, John Parsons Cook. Had he escaped the gallows on that count, he would have been charged with the murders of his wife and brother, whose bodies were exhumed after an inquest jury decided that he had murdered Cook. Two more coroner's juries entered verdicts of murder against him, although in the case of the brother a grand jury decided later that the cause of death could not be satisfactorily ascertained. This was largely because of the state of the body: when the coffin was opened, the stench was so dreadful that 15 people were taken ill with vomiting.

It seems very likely that among other possible victims, who included several legitimate and illegitimate children, Palmer also killed his mother-in-law. She died within two weeks of going to live with him, and he inherited property on her death. Palmer was certainly a serial killer, even if he was not guilty of all 16 murders that some versions of his story attribute to him. As with many racing men, his problem was debt, and he was constantly in the clutch of money-lenders. His main strategy in the losing struggle to keep solvent was to insure the life of someone he could poison. He insured his wife for £13,000. As she was only 27, the first year's premium was £760, more than six per cent, but only one premium was ever paid because she died a few months later. Although Palmer appeared overcome with grief at her funeral, it was well known that he had neglected her for the turf and loose women. His mistress, who became pregnant by him, was a servant living in the house. The insurance company had its suspicions but paid up reluctantly. Palmer still could not satisfy the money-lenders, and tried to insure his brother for more than £80,000, but the insurance company would only agree to a much smaller sum. When he tried to insure the life of an under-groom, George Bates, he told the company that Bates was financially secure and of high social standing. They sent a police inspector to investigate and he found Bates manuring a field; he advised them not to pay out on the brother, or to accept Bates for insurance. Then Palmer turned to Cook.

The crisis came at Shrewsbury races, where Palmer lost a lot more money, but Cook cleaned up on a winning horse, which he owned. The money-lenders were pressing Palmer hard and, having already forged his mother's name to try to keep up with the payments, he committed more forgery to get hold of Cook's money. If Palmer did not act soon, his mother would be sued, and he persuaded the Rugeley postmaster to intercept letters addressed to her to prevent her knowing what was going on. He took Cook with him to Rugeley and put him up at the Talbot Inn, opposite his own house. There Cook was taken ill, and died six days later, during which time Palmer administered food and medicines. Palmer quickly ordered a coffin without consulting the deceased's stepfather, who became suspicious when he discovered that Cook's betting book and other papers were missing. The doctor who attended Cook was over eighty, and had been persuaded to certify that the man's death had been due to apoplexy. However, Palmer was known to have bought strychnine and was suspected of having substituted it for the pills the doctor had prescribed. The post-mortem demanded by Cook's stepfather was a disgrace. Palmer was allowed to attend, and caused the contents of the dead man's stomach to be spilled. Then he tried to bribe a cab-driver to overturn his cab so that the jar containing the material being sent for analysis would smash. When a London expert wrote to a Rugeley solicitor with the results, Palmer tried to bribe the postmaster to intercept the letter.

It was clear that Palmer was a murderer, but the evidence was circumstantial. The problem for the prosecution was one of conflicting medical evidence. Even before the trial began, the *Illustrated London News* was warning its readers that the defence would want to confuse the jury into thinking that 'there is no such thing as absolute truth in science',[53] and the leading counsel for the prosecution lost no time in giving the same warning. The jury had every right to be confused: forensic medicine was in its infancy, and the medical witnesses were grappling with the first case of alleged strychnine poisoning – most poisoners used arsenic. All sorts of possible causes of death were put forward because no strychnine was found in the body – perhaps because of the way the stomach had been treated at the post-mortem. On the gallows Palmer said that he was innocent of poisoning Cook by strychnine, which left open the possibility that he had used some other substance.

The case highlighted the defects in the insurance industry, as well as in the medical profession, and led to the passing of a law to prevent someone insuring another's life for more than the insured party was worth. Also, the inhabitants of Rugeley seem to have been exceptionally tolerant, or perhaps too willing to look the other way, given the long list of Palmer's likely victims. They were taken in by a superficially charming man, who was popular in the area especially with the horse-racing fraternity. But the *Illustrated London News* declared that Palmer seemed without a redeeming quality: 'That he was a favourite with grooms, chambermaids, and servants generally, with whom he liked to joke, and to whom he gave a good deal of money, may be set at its value, and in most persons' minds will scarcely go to the favourable side of the account.'[54]

Many members of both Houses of Parliament were at the trial, including Gladstone. He recorded in his diary that 'I liked ill both the looks and the demeanour of the prisoner.'[55] Dickens was also unimpressed by Palmer's self-assurance: in a *Household Words* article entitled 'The Demeanour of Murderers', he described him as 'the greatest villain that ever stood in the Old Bailey Dock'. He continued 'The public has read from day to day of the murderer's complete self-possession, of his constant coolness, of his perfect equanimity,' but argued that a murderer like Palmer had no sensibility or sentiment left, and that the blacker his guilt, the more likely that he could appear self-assured.[56]

Although the press was universally hostile to Palmer, street ballads showed him the sympathy they had offered Rush.

> In Rugeley I was once respected.
> A gentleman, lived at my ease,
> With noblemen I was once connected,
> And sporting men of all degrees.
> Although a Doctor, no one knew me
> To do anything amiss,
> Now each one strives to undo me,
> I never thought I'd come to this.[57]

The Lord Chief Justice, the senior of the three judges at the trial, ordered that Palmer should be sent back to Stafford for his public hanging. *The Times* reported, 'The express train and others from London on Friday night brought a great number of well-dressed persons; but these

Ever yours

Wm Palmer

THE ONLY AUTHENTIC LIKENESS OF WILLIAM PALMER.

Demand for news of the Palmer trial was immense: The Times *sold for 1200% above its cover price and its circulation, around 60,000 at this period, could be almost doubled by a sensational trial like Palmer's.*

bore no comparison in point of force with the crowds who kept constantly arriving during the night by railway and other means of conveyance from the adjoining towns for fifty miles round, including the Pottery districts, Birmingham, Wolverhampton, Walsall, Tipton and the rest of what is called "the black country".' Despite the rain almost every vantage point was occupied by four o'clock in the morning. The crowd was mainly made up of 'young men and lads, labourers, artisans, but also the better class', and 'free from the savage brutality which is said to characterize a mob assembled on similar occasions in front of the Old Bailey.'[58]

The sensation of the following year, 1857, involved a woman charged with murder by poisoning, who escaped the gallows through a Scottish verdict of 'not proven', even though she was widely held to be guilty.[59] It was one of a number of examples in which the combination of murder and feminine sex appeal proved irresistible.

Madeleine Smith was a lively young woman of 21 from a prosperous middle-class family in Glasgow. She took as her lover a Jersey man, Pierre Émile L'Angelier, nine years her senior, who was earning ten shillings a week as a warehouse clerk. Her parents disapproved of him so the relationship was kept secret. Eventually a suitable husband turned up, whom Madeleine agreed to marry. She was happy to ditch L'Angelier but he still had her passionate love letters, which made clear that she had lost her virginity to him, and he threatened to send them to her father. In Scottish law, evidence of intercourse constituted a legal marriage.

Madeleine bought several amounts of arsenic from local chemists. Arguably she was indebted to John Stuart Mill for the ability to do so: a draft version of the Sale of Arsenic Act would have allowed only men to buy it but pressure from Mill forced a change. However, the shop-keeper had kept an account of all purchases, as the law now demanded. Madeleine claimed that she diluted the arsenic with water and used it as a cosmetic on her face and arms. Nevertheless, Émile was ill with stomach complaints on three occasions. On the first, Madeleine had just been to the opera, ironically *Lucrezia Borgia*, about the most famous female poisoner in history. On the last occasion Émile died. A post-mortem showed that he had more than eighty-two grains of arsenic inside him, the remains of what one expert estimated had been half an ounce, a huge dose. However, while the prosecution could prove that Madeleine had bought arsenic, they could not prove that she had been with Émile, and vice versa. His memorandum book, which surfaced after the trial, recorded several more occasions when they had been together. The book was the source of many rumours: according to the *Glasgow Herald*, it was supposed to damage the reputation 'of at least one highly respected lady connected with our own city', but her husband had been assured officially that neither his wife's name nor his own was in it.[60]

The case created such a furore that the trial was moved to Edinburgh, under the recently-passed Palmer Act. A letter to the *North British Mail* described the crowd trying to get into the court: 'Cries of murder, screams and groans, with people sinking on the pavement, only expand the energies of the strong, and the people are carried in, rolled in, tumbled in, they know not how.' And according to the *Ayrshire Express*, 'In the evening thousands gather in the streets to see the cab in which she is borne back from the court-room to the prison.'[61] Not even the first reports of the Indian mutiny could deflect public interest.

It was widely believed that Madeleine Smith escaped the gallows because she was a beautiful young woman. However, contemporary pictures of her do not prove this. Maria Manning had been seen as a fascinating creature, but neither is there evidence in her case of remarkable good looks. The fascination came from her bold demeanour and the wishful thinking of millions of men who had no photographs to guide them. Belief in Madeleine Smith's beauty seems to stemmed from the same sources. *Reynolds's Newspaper* gave a favourable but not conclusive description: 'The personal appearance of Miss Smith is more than ordinarily prepossessing. Her features express great intelligence and energy of character . . . Her profile is striking, the upper part of her face exhibiting considerable prominence, while the lower part is cast in a more delicate mould, and her complexion is soft and fair. Her eyes are large and dark, and full of sensibility . . . Her figure seemed to be less than middle-sized, and girlish and slight.'[62] On the other hand, *The Times* reported, 'Her eyes are deep-set, large and some think beautiful, but they certainly do not look prepossessing . . . Her nose is prominent but is too large to be taken as a type for the Roman, and too irregular to remind one of Greece.'[63]

What is not in doubt is her extraordinary self-assurance and coolness in the dock. If these qualities were remarkable in Palmer, a man in his thirties, they were far more so in a single woman of 21, charged with murdering her lover, in an age when young women were expected to be chaste and look demure. 'Miss Smith never ceases surveying all that goes on around her, watching every witness, returning every stare with compound interest, glancing every second minute at the down-turned eyes of the side-galleries, and even turning right round on the reporters immediately behind her to see how they got along with the note-taking which is carrying her name and deeds into every British home.'[64] She weakened and put her hands to her face only when the most intimate of her letters were read out. Her self-possession was described as either 'a proud consciousness of innocence' or as a sign of 'almost unparalleled self-control'.[65]

The letters were the sensation's special ingredient.[66] Like Mrs Chetwynd's diary, they provided the newspapers with a unique record of a woman's sexual feelings. They were read out in dry, emotionless tones by an elderly court official, but it was extraordinary to hear such intimate details of a relationship between an unmarried couple. Although his letters were unavailable, Émile and Madeleine seemed to be speaking in court through hers. Neither the dead man nor the accused woman could have done so in any other way. When a representative sample is placed in chronological order, a dramatic story emerges.

3 September 1855: You know not how I love you, Emile. I live for you alone; I adore you. I never could love another as I do you. Oh dearest Emile, would I might clasp you now to my heart.

27 June 1856: I am now a wife, a wife in every sense of the word... Oh how I love that name of Mimi. You shall always call me by that name, and, dearest Emile, if ever we should have a daughter, I should like you to allow me to call her Minnie for her father's sake. As you ask me, I shall burn your last letter. I must go to bed, as I feel cold, so good night. Would to God it were to be by your side . . . I am thine for ever, thy wife, thy devoted, thy own true Mimi L'Angelier.

15 July 1856: Our intimacy has not been criminal, as I am your wife before God, so it has been no sin our loving each other. No darling, fond Emile, I am your wife.

11 August 1856: Would you leave me to end my days in misery? For I can never be the wife of another after our intimacy.

1857: Oh, sweet darling, my heart and soul burns with love for you, my husband. What would I not give at this moment to be your fond wife . . . I weep to think of our fate. If we could only be married, all would be well; but alas, I see no chance of happiness for me.

1857: You may be astonished at this sudden change of heart, but for some time back you must have noticed a coolness in my notes. My love for you has ceased, and that is why I was cool. I did once love you truly and fondly . . . I know you will never injure the character of one you so fondly loved. No, Emile, I know you have honour, and are a gentleman. What has passed you will not mention. I know when I ask you that you will comply . . . For God's sake do not bring your once-loved Mimi to open shame. Emile, I have deceived you. I have deceived my mother . . . I deceived you by telling you she knew of our engagement. She did not . . . Oh Emile, do not be harsh to me. I am the most guilty miserable wretch on the face of the earth. Emile, do not drive me to death. When I ceased to love you, believe me it was not to love another. I am free from all engagement at present. Emile, for God's sake, do not send my letters to papa . . . I am mad, I am ill. Emile, my father's wrath would kill me. You little know his temper . . . I put on paper what I should not . . . On my bended knee I write to you, and ask you as you hope for mercy at the judgment day, do not inform on me – do not make me a public shame . . . I have destroyed the best of men. You may forgive me, but God never will. For God's love, forgive me and betray me not . . . Oh! You will not for Christ's sake denounce me. I shall be undone. I shall be ruined. Who would trust me? Shame will be my lot. Despise me, hate me, but make me not the public scandal.

21 March 1857 (last letter): Why, my beloved, did you not come to me? Oh, my beloved are you ill? Come to me. Sweet one, I waited and waited for you, but you came not. I shall wait again tomorrow night – same hour and arrangement. Oh, come sweet love, my own dear love of a sweetheart. Come, beloved and clasp me to you heart.

The stirring nature of the letters offered a remarkable contrast with the cool young woman in the dock. They also showed her to be a persistent liar. A draft had been discovered of one of Émile's letters to her from the latter part of the correspondence. It said, 'Your cold, indifferent and reserved notes without a particle of love in them . . . and the manner you evaded answering the questions I put to you in my last, with the reports I hear, fully convince me, Mimi, that there is foundation in your marriage with another. Besides, the way you put off our union till September without a just reason is very suspicious.'

More than sixty of Madeleine's letters were read out, but they were just a selection. 'Only those effusions were read in full which were absolutely necessary to the case, of numbers only a few sentences were read, and all objectionable expressions, all gross and indelicate allusions were carefully and studiously omitted. In some instances, we understand, particular words were altered in the reading in order that the feelings of the prisoner might not be overwhelmed by such a terrible publicity.'[67] This, of course, allowed the imagination full rein.

The prosecuting counsel spoke of 'the almost incredible evidence that discovers a scene of degradation' and 'those feelings of commiseration and horror which the age, the sex and the condition of the prisoner must produce in every mind', but he thought it quite right that the letters should have been made known to Madeleine's father. 'There is much that is dishonourable in this case but not that. It would not have been honourable to allow the prisoner at the bar to become the wife of any honest man.'

The verdict was greeted with jubilation: this time the public was not furious to be deprived of a hanging. The cheers from the crowded court were loud and long, and were returned from the square outside. The judge scowled and the court officials shouted for silence, but order was not restored until a man was arrested. According to one account, Madeleine 'has become quite a heroine with the great majority of the opposite sex, who view her as a thoughtless but most interesting and warm-hearted young woman – one who in the simplicity of her heart, in her first love affair, abandoned herself to the man of her choice, with an amount of confiding love and outspoken artlessness of purpose, which, censure or regret as they may, they cannot regard without sympathy and admiration.'[68] Some Glasgow tradesmen raised a subscription 'to testify their sympathy' for her. This, for a young single woman who had lost her virginity, was surely an act of rebellion against the prevailing moral code.

It was a help to Madeleine that the man in an illicit relationship was assumed to have been the seducer, and that Émile, who was poorer than she, was seen as a fortune hunter. He had also boasted about his alleged attractiveness to women, and about the drugs he had taken – large quantities of poppy seeds on one occasion, and arsenic. A witness had found him vomiting some years earlier – 'Cholera had lately been in the town, and we got very much frightened.'

Reactions to the verdict were largely emotional. Some people thought that Émile had got his just deserts, and, although they believed Madeleine guilty, they rejoiced in her escape from hanging. Jane Carlyle revealed contrasting prejudices: she wrote to her husband Thomas that she did not believe 'the girl' guilty of poisoning, 'but she is such a little incarnate devil that the murder don't go for much in my opinion of her'.[69]

People never forgot Madeleine Smith. Nearly sixty years later, Henry James remembered how, when he was a boy of 14, the daily reports of the trial in *The Times* reached his parents in Boulogne, 'and how they followed it and discussed it in suspense and how I can still see the queer look of the "not proven" seen for the first time, on the printed page of the newspaper'. James expressed his surprise at the verdict, but added 'she was truly a portentous young person... And what a pity she was almost of the pre-photographic age – I would give so much for a veracious portrait of her *then* face.'[70]

Nearly twenty years later, there was another sensation in which an attractive woman who had taken part in an illicit sexual relationship was thought to have used poison to kill a man who might have been after her fortune. She was not convicted either. According to the *Illustrated London News*, 'It is scarcely an exaggeration to say that the attention of the nation has been monopolised for the past two or three weeks by the inquiry which has been reopened to elucidate what is commonly called the "Balham Mystery."'[71]

Before describing the death of Charles Bravo, it is necessary to outline the background of his wife Florence,[72] whose family lived in some style. In 1864, when she was 19, she married a Guards officer called Ricardo, whose great-uncle was the famous economist, whose uncle was the 5th Earl of Fife and whose father was a member of parliament. Ricardo was also a violent alcoholic. After seven years of marriage his third attack of delirium tremens proved fatal; by then he was living with another woman in Cologne.

The crisis in her marriage had led to Florence becoming the patient of Dr James Gully, a pioneer of homeopathic medicine. His celebrity patients at Great Malvern ranged from Tennyson to Darwin, from

Disraeli to Florence Nightingale. He was nearly forty years older than Florence Ricardo but much younger than his own wife. Separated from him for thirty years, she was in her eighties but still in good health. Gully developed a friendship with Florence, whom he comforted in her distress, and they became lovers. It seems clear that they would have married, had Gully been free. The relationship estranged Florence from her parents, but they were reconciled when she dumped Gully to marry a young lawyer, Charles Bravo.

Four months into the marriage, on 18 April 1876, Bravo returned home, pale and in pain after his horse had run away with him. He seemed better at dinner time, but by midnight he had emerged from his bedroom calling urgently for hot water to make himself sick. An emetic was prepared, Bravo took it, went back to his room and threw up out of the window. Over the next two and a half days six doctors were called, but on 21 April he died.

The inquest was held at the Bravos' home in Balham. No accurate account of the proceedings was kept, and the press was not informed. Mrs Cox, Florence's friend, companion and housekeeper, emerged as a key witness. She testified that the dying man had told her when she was alone with him in his bedroom, 'I have taken poison; don't tell Florence.' However, a friend of Charles insisted that he was not the kind of man to commit suicide. The post-mortem concluded that he had died from the poisonous effects of antimony, but the evidence did not show how it had got into his body.

There had been tension and rows in the marriage; on occasion Charles had hit his wife and stormed out of the house. She resented his attempts to make her curb her spending, as all their money had come from her and she lived within her income. One of the economies he wanted was to get rid of Mrs Cox – who was therefore seen, like Florence, as a prime suspect. Dr Gully also fell under suspicion, as did a groom Charles had sacked, who had been heard to say that his former master would be dead within a few months. During his illness, Charles insisted to the doctors that he had applied laudanum to his gums but had taken no other poisonous substance. However, antimony was used in the stables to worm the horses: could the wine that only Charles had drunk at dinner have been poisoned? Or the water in his bedroom? Antimony is tasteless in water.

As suspicion grew, it was recalled that Mrs Cox had recently been seen with Dr Gully, who still lived nearby, although she said they had met by chance. He had prescribed medicine for Florence, which the chemist had labelled 'poison'. It emerged that Charles, whom Florence had told about the pre-marital relationship, had often thrown the doctor's name at her, even though he had promised not mention it if she did not bring up his own pre-marital affair and his illegitimate child. He been enraged by an anonymous letter that had accused him of marrying Gully's mistress for money. It was certainly the conventional view that only a fortune-hunter would knowingly marry a woman with a 'past'.

A clamour began largely fanned by the *Daily Telegraph*: the Home Secretary was questioned in the House. A second inquest was held over 23 days in July and August 1876 and an obscure death became a sensation. The same incompetent coroner presided. In effect Florence Bravo and Mrs Cox were being tried for murder but they could be cross-examined in a coroner's court, which would not have been possible in a criminal trial. The protagonists were represented by counsel, and the Attorney-General acted for the Crown. Mrs Cox now said that Charles had told her that he had taken poison 'for Dr Gully'. She had previously omitted the last three words to protect Florence. In answer to the Attorney-General she admitted that Dr Gully had been Florence's lover, but refused to define the word. In those days the meaning was less clearly sexual than it is now. However, the Bravo family's solicitor would not let her off easily:

'What was it she told you?'
'Of her intimacy with Dr Gully.'
'What do you mean by intimacy?'
'You may draw your own conclusions.'
'No, I decline to do that – tell me, Madam, was it a *criminal* intimacy with Dr Gully that she told you of? Answer my question, Madam.'
'Yes, a criminal intimacy.' (Sensation.)[73]

Florence had lied when she had sworn that the relationship had not been sexual. It had taken place between her marriages, and Dr Gully had comforted her in her distress. There was no evidence that she wanted to go back to him. However, a 30-year-old widow, a sexually experienced woman, was treated more harshly than the younger, less experienced Madeleine Smith: to the prurient, her affair seemed to make Florence a more likely murderess. Charles Bravo's was not mentioned.

Yet the ferocity with which George Lewis questioned Florence, for the Bravo family, created a backlash. According to *The Times*, 'That a cross-examination, even in a Coroner's Court, of a crushed and humiliated woman should have been pushed to the lengths it was at Balham, was a disgrace to the Court which allowed it, and to the manliness of everyone who was in the least degree responsible for it.' Florence also invoked manliness on the one occasion when she rounded on her tormentor: 'I have been subjected to sufficient pain and humiliation already, and I appeal to the Coroner and the jury, as men and Britons to protect me.' The Bravo case launched George Lewis on a dazzling career as the solic-itor of the rich and famous. His clients included the Irish leaders at the Parnell Commission. *The Dictionary of National Biography* records that he also had a 'practical monopoly of those cases where the seamy side of soci-ety is unveiled, and where the sins and follies of the wealthy classes threaten exposure and disaster'. Those cases included the Tranby Croft affair, where he acted for the defendants.

After Florence's dramatic ordeal, the appearance of the famous Dr Gully in the witness box was only a minor sensation, although his repu-tation, too, was destroyed. As the *Illustrated London News* put it, 'Public interest in the Bravo case may be said to have increased with the cross-examination of Mrs Cox, and to have culminated in the appearance of Mrs Charles Bravo in court.'[74] It was, of course, a bonus that the woman being harried about her fornication could be described as 'a handsome lady of about thirty years of age, with large expressive blue eyes, chestnut hair tinged with gold, and having a graceful figure'.[75] Her hair was not naturally chestnut. The *Medical Times and Gazette* said 'her detractors proved that she dyed her hair, but they did not prove that she poisoned her husband.'[76]

On the other hand, her name was not cleared: the jury found that Charles had been poisoned but 'there is not sufficient evidence to fix the guilt upon any person or persons'. It was tantamount to a 'not proven' ver-dict on Florence and Mrs Cox.

One of the strangest aspects of the mystery is that Charles Bravo was perfectly calm during the two and a half days he survived and accused nobody. Yet if he had wanted to commit suicide, he would surely not have chosen to use antimony, whose effects are so painful. According to one suggestion, he tried to kill Florence for her money and took the poison by mistake.[77] The latest book on the case, which includes some new evidence, claims Florence as the murderer, with Mrs Cox as her accomplice.[78] According to another theory Florence, who had suffered two miscarriages, had intended to give Charles just enough poison to prevent him having sex with her but, having drunk two bottles of sherry that evening with Mrs Cox, she had overdone the dose.[79] She had admitted to her lawyer, 'When we were first married, he thought I took too much sherry, and I gave it up to please him.' Two years later she died of drink, still in her early thirties.

In 1889, Florence Maybrick was accused of poisoning her husband. She, too, was a prosperous and good-looking young woman, who suffered from the hostility of her husband's family and the public exposure of her sex life. There were admiring references to her hair and eyes, and to her 'rounded figure, well-developed bust and hips, slender waist'.[80] She created a furore, which was prolonged by anger at what *Reynolds's Newspaper* called the 'sensational and unexpected' guilty verdict. The same journal described the case as 'full of unsavoury details' and, unfairly, as containing 'almost every element of low intrigue and sordid crime'.[81]

James and Florence Maybrick had married in 1881. They lived in Liverpool where James was a member of the Cotton Exchange. They had two children, and Florence, an American of good family, was 24 years younger than her husband. Like Émile l'Angelier, James used drugs, but he was a hypochondriac who took anything, however dangerous, including arsenic, strychnine, morphia and dilute prussic acid.

When Maybrick was taken ill in late April 1889, with vomiting and diarrhoea, nothing seemed to do him any good. Short periods of recovery alternated with periods of pain, and he died on 11 May. Some of his family, friends and servants had always disliked Florence, and now they suspected her of murder. During his last few days she was banned from his bedroom.[82]

There had been quarrels between husband and wife. He had given her a black eye, and had changed his will leaving her only enough to keep her respectable. Worst of all, a young servant had opened a letter from Florence to her 'paramour'. Poisons were found in the house, although no attempt had been made to hide them. They included a bottle labelled 'arsenic' and another of meat juice that contained arsenic. Florence later claimed that her husband had begged her to empty a paper from his pocket into the meat juice, but she had not known what the contents were. In any case he had fallen asleep and never taken it. It was also established that Florence had bought fly-papers containing arsenic. She said that she soaked out the arsenic to use it as a cosmetic, and it was remembered that Madeleine Smith had offered the same excuse. Florence was arrested as she lay ill in bed.

It did not help her that her main support was her mother, whose third marriage had already failed, and who was reported to have had lovers since. Like mother, like daughter, some thought - the greatest sensation of all was the adultery. The *Liverpool Echo* reported that when a waiter at a London hotel began to give evidence about the nights Florence and her lover spent together, 'There was a manifest commotion and excitement, especially on the part of the female auditors who leaned forward and craned their necks to catch every word of the details . . . This event was brief, but to the court it seemed to be the tit-bit of the trial, and the "lady" listeners made no attempt to conceal the evident interest and relish they took in the miserable story.'[83]

As in the Palmer trial, the medical experts contradicted each other. Some said Maybrick had died from arsenic poisoning, others that it was gastroenteritis, cause unknown. But if arsenic had killed her husband, did Florence administer it? It is widely believed that the judge's summing-up turned the jury against her. Stressing the adultery, he said that she had good reason to be free of her husband so that she could live with the man 'for whom she had made the greatest sacrifice that a woman could make'.[84] The court was not told that the deceased had fathered three illegitimate children before his marriage and two after it.

The judge was James Fitzjames Stephen, a highly respected lawyer and man of letters who had written for the *Cornhill* magazine under Thackeray's editorship. Unfortunately he had suffered a stroke four years before the trial, and seems never to have completely recovered. His wish to be fair was unquestionable. He even took the almost unprecedented step of allowing Florence to make a brief statement from the dock, leading to the headline 'MRS MAYBRICK SPEAKS. EXTRAORDINARY SENSATION IN COURT'.[85] He also condemned the law that kept her out of the witness box. However, he repeatedly muddled dates and, astonishingly for a judge sitting in Liverpool, seemed not to know what the Grand National was. Two years later he was admitted to an asylum for the insane.

When Florence Maybrick was sentenced to hang, there was a huge outcry – in the United States as well as Britain because she had been an American citizen. As *The Times* put it, 'The public are not thoroughly convinced of the prisoner's guilt.'[86] According to the London correspondent of the *New York Times*, 'There is candidly more acute excitement throughout the kingdom over the fact that Mrs Maybrick is under sentence of death than any other event has produced over the past ten years'.[87] Immediately the verdict was known, an impromptu mass meeting to demand that it be reversed took place on the steps of St George's Hall, Liverpool, where the trial had been held. There were 17,000 names on one of the many petitions for clemency sent to the Home Secretary, Henry Matthews, who received separate petitions from lawyers, and from doctors offended by the judge's joke that a physician spends his time putting drugs of which he knows little into a body of which he knows less.

Not everyone supported Florence. Because of the conflict of medical evidence, the *Lancet* reviewed the case in detail and thought that the verdict was fair. Labouchere, who as proprietor and editor of *Truth* had built a journalistic career on sensation, said that he had expected Florence to be acquitted but, having studied the evidence, had decided that the writers to the papers on her behalf had less reasoning faculty than a costermonger's jackass.[88] Broadsides, which were otherwise in almost terminal decline, were sold and sung on the streets again, both for and against Florence, in order to satisfy all tastes.[89]

The advocacy of Sir Charles Russell, representing Florence, was widely admired. She had been hissed at and spat on when she was first driven to court, but within a couple of days public opinion turned in her favour, and she never lost it. Neither did the Home Secretary's decision to commute the death sentence to life imprisonment end the furore: he found that she had tried to murder her husband but that there was reasonable doubt as to whether she had succeeded. It was pointed out that she had never been charged with attempted murder.

Repeated attempts to have Florence released kept her name before the public. One petition was signed by the members of the American cabinet, the speaker of the House of Representatives and the Vice President of the United States. Nevertheless, she served 15 years and was released in January 1904.

Although the crimes of professional criminals were usually too routine to cause much excitement, the case of Charley Peace was an exception. In February 1879 two sensations transfixed the country: news of the British defeat in Zululand, the biggest ever at the hands of a non-European army; and Peace's trial for a murder that had taken place in Sheffield over two years earlier. The murder in itself was scarcely sensational. Peace, a professional burglar, had pestered his neighbours Mr and Mrs Dyson with his persistent visits, until in July 1876 he had pushed a revolver into Mrs Dyson's face, and threatened to blow her husband's brains out. They moved house to avoid him, but one night in November when Mrs Dyson went out into her yard, Peace was there, threatening her again with a revolver. Her husband heard her screams and followed Peace into the road. Two shots rang out and the second killed Dyson with a bullet in the left temple. Peace climbed a wall at the end of the road, and disappeared.

His ability to elude the police for nearly two years established him as a master criminal. At last in October 1878 a constable arrested a burglar in Blackheath, despite having been shot in the arm. To their surprise and delight, the police had Charley Peace in custody. Now his extraordinary way of life was revealed. By day he had lived as a respectable citizen, popular with the neighbours for his regular churchgoing and his early nights, but by night he was transformed into an active cat burglar. He lived this dual existence, under various guises, in one area of London after another; when arrested, he was a 'Mr Thompson' of Peckham. Violins were among his favourite swag, and he sometimes played to the neighbours. The contrast between the daring criminal of the night and the respectable, artistically inclined citizen of the day gripped the public imagination as the murder of Dyson alone could never have done. [90]

Peace was sentenced to life imprisonment for shooting the constable, then sent to Leeds to be tried for the murder. On the way, he threw himself out of a train travelling at 45 miles an hour but was recaptured without serious injury. The trial brought out his reputation as a lady-killer, and there were suggestions of impropriety with Mrs Dyson, who claimed to have repulsed his advances. After only 12 minutes the jury found him guilty. Before he was hanged, Peace confessed to an earlier murder of a policeman for which another man had been convicted but fortunately not executed. This enhanced his reputation for worsting the police, even though he had served several gaol sentences. Moralists argued that, despite his prosperity, he looked old and frail during his final court appearance, but it was pointed out that this might have been due to his fall from the train.

The publicity given to a dangerous burglar led to increased fear among the public of armed robbery, especially where Peace had been active. 'Respectable householders are now buying revolvers. Burglary is in the ascendancy. The south of London is scarcely safe.'[91] As Peace's criminal activities had been brought to an end, this was hardly rational.

However, the public's fascination with him was widespread. A catalogue for an Edinburgh waxwork display attributed it to 'his unusual courage, and the notion that he was a kind of criminal gladiator, always staking himself against society'. It also commented on the rare contrast between his artistic side and his criminal callousness.[92] Peace's musical instruments sold for high prices: the 'morbid and unhealthy taste' for a murderer's relics was compared with the fascination that had attached to the black satin gown in which Mrs Manning had been hanged, and Palmer's snuff-box and betting book.[93] People who had been burgled began to boast of it, having convinced themselves that they had been among Peace's victims.

The newspapers played up Peace's versatility, from his strength and agility as a cat burglar, despite a maimed hand, to the violin-playing and his skill in carving picture frames. They ascribed every unsolved murder of the previous dozen years to him, and could not print his supposed confessions fast enough. All sorts of stories were reported and believed, including his boast that he had visited Scotland Yard to look at his 'wanted' poster. There is no doubt that the press inflated the sensation for its own benefit.

The same applies to the greatest murder sensation of the Victorian era, although admittedly it was a big enough story in its own right. Although violent crime was routine, this case involved exceptional brutality. However, many other factors were involved, notably the number of linked crimes and the failure of the police to solve them, which made the personality of the murderer a particularly potent factor. As he was never caught, there was no limit to the possibilities, and the public imagination ran riot.

It is still disputed how many murders were due to 'Jack the Ripper', possibly there were five, although several more were ascribed to him at the time.[94] These horrific killings occurred over about fifteen months from April 1888. They were all committed in Whitechapel, in the East End of London, except one that took place a short distance away in the City. The location helped to make the story sensational. Respectable people feared to tread the ill-lit lanes and alleys of one of the capital's poorest areas. All of the victims had been prostitutes, which did not prevent respectable ladies fearing for their lives. Where the series of female poisoning cases revealed the passions seething behind middle-class respectability, the Ripper story was one of desperate women, often abandoned by their partners for their heavy drinking, trying to earn money for the next meal or the next night's room in some sordid, vice-ridden lodging-house. Ironically, it was the nature of their trade that they accompanied men to where they would not be disturbed.

A murder was attributed to the Ripper when the body had been disembowelled or was in the process of being so when the murderer was disturbed. It is not necessary to catalogue here the revolting state of the bodies – even the papers, although full of graphic detail, played down the Ripper's fascination with the female sex organs.

'Jack the Ripper' was the pen name of the author of letters and a postcard to the Central News Agency. Whether or not they were authentic, they were accepted as such at the time. Later suggestions that they were concocted by a journalist adds a new dimension to the press's exploitation of the sensational. In one letter, the writer says, 'I am down on whores and I shant quit ripping them till I do get buckled [arrested].' In another, 'If she was a whore, God will bless the hand that slew her . . . I never harm any others or the Divine power that protects and helps me in my grand work would quit for ever.'[95] Ironically, some of the thousands of prostitutes on the London streets, the only women at risk, were the least scared. A police inspector reported, 'For the sake of fourpence to get drunk on, they will go in any man's company, and run the risk that it is not him. I tell many of them to go home, but they say they have no home, and when I try to frighten them and speak of the danger they run they'll laugh and say, "Oh, I know what you mean. I ain't afraid of him. It's the Ripper or the bridge with me."'[96]

On Sunday 9 September 1888 *Reynolds's Newspaper* revealed the atmosphere engendered by the killings. A week earlier, on 31 August, the body of Mary Ann Nichols had been found. Her windpipe had been severed, and a bruise on her face seemed to show that the murderer had clamped his hand over it before cutting her throat from ear to ear. She had been disembowelled. Now the paper offered the headline 'ANOTHER FIENDISH MURDER IN WHITECHAPEL/HORRIBLE DISCOVERY YESTERDAY/EXCITEMENT IN THE EAST END'. Annie Chapman's head had been nearly severed and various organs had been removed from her body. In addition to this report, there is an account of a later incident at Spitalfields market, in which a man knocked a woman down, kicked her and pulled out a knife. Some other women who were on the way to join the enormous crowd at Hanbury Street, where Annie Chapman had met her end, shrieked, 'Murder.' Their screams reached Hanbury Street, and some of the crowd pulled back to see what was happening. The man with the knife fell on his victim and stabbed her several times before he was pulled off. He turned out to be a blind lace-seller, and the woman had been leading him around. Her wounds were not serious. It is not clear whether her removal to hospital gave rise to a rumour, reported in the same edition of the paper, that a young woman had been found in a square at the back of the building with her throat cut and 'ripped'. There was a rush to the hospital, where the rumour was found to be untrue. There could scarcely have been a better picture of the fear and excitement endemic in the East End.

Equally characteristic were groups of men and boys yelling anti-Jewish slogans. 'At about ten o'clock a gang of vagabonds marched down Hanbury-street, shouting "Down with the Jews!" "It was a Jew who did it." "No Englishman did it."'. There were several fights, but the police, who were out in force, managed to cope.

Whitechapel was full of recent Jewish immigrants from Poland and Russia and their story crosses with that of Jack the Ripper at several points. After the discovery of the body of Catherine Eddowes in Mitre Square, Aldgate, just outside the bounds of Whitechapel, her blood-stained apron was found and on the wall above it, 'The Jewes are the men that will not be blamed for nothing.' Sir Charles Warren, the police commissioner, wrote that if the police had not wiped out the words, 'there would have been an onslaught upon the Jews, property would have been wrecked, and lives probably would have been lost'.[97] The MP for Whitechapel, Samuel Montague, was a prominent Jew who offered a reward to show the world, in Warren's view, that the Jews wanted the Chapman murder cleared up to divert the strong feeling that was growing up against them.

A Polish Jew called Pizer, a shoemaker known locally as 'Leather Apron' was suspected of the Chapman murder until the police cleared him. When Elizabeth Stride, an immigrant from Sweden, was found dead three weeks after Annie Chapman, it was in the backyard of a socialist working men's club where a discussion had been taking place between ninety to a hundred people who seem to have been mostly Jewish. Warren thought that a secret society might have been responsible but not a socialist one: an attempt was being made, he thought, to discredit 'the Jews and Socialists or Jewish Socialists'.

According to Robert Anderson, who became head of the CID during the Ripper murders, 'The conclusion we came to was that he [the Ripper] and his people were low-class Jews, for it is a remarkable fact that people of that class in the East End will not give up one of their number to Gentile justice.' He added that a madman in an asylum was identified by a Jewish witness until he discovered that the suspect was Jewish and refused to swear.[98] The idea that Jews would protect the murderer infuriated the *Jewish Chronicle*, which commented, 'Here was a whole neighbourhood, largely composed of Jews, in constant terror lest their womenfolk, whom Jewish men hold in particular regard – even "low-class Jews" do that – should be slain by some murderer who was stalking the district undiscovered.' It was not surprising that the witness hesitated before denouncing a Jew, as the 'callous brutality' of the crimes was quite foreign to Jewish nature. After Anderson had written to the paper expressing 'sincere distress' that he should be thought to have cast aspersion on Jews, the paper repeated that it did not object to Anderson saying the murderer was a Jew, although he would have been well advised to keep quiet, 'knowing the peculiar condition in which we are situated, and the prejudice that is constantly simmering against us'.[99]

'Leather Apron' might have won substantial libel damages from the newly founded newspaper the *Star*, which had printed reports such as 'LEATHER APRON THE ONLY NAME LINKED WITH THE WHITECHAPEL MURDER. A Noiseless Midnight Terror. The Strange Character who Prowls About Whitechapel After Midnight. Universal Fear Among the Women. Slippered Feet and A Sharp Leather-Knife'.[100] However, a young journalist fobbed him off with fifty pounds and the assurance that another paper, which had been equally libellous, would give him the same. This bright young man was none other than Ernest Parke, who, in his spare time from the *Star*, edited the *North London Press*, where he exposed the Cleveland Street Affair the following year. He earned high marks from his editor for his Ripper coverage.[101]

There were plenty of other suspects. The police considered themselves hampered by sensational journalism and hoaxers, but their greatest problem was that the public was *too* co-operative. They spent endless time following up leads and suggestions that came to nothing. Butchers and abattoir workers were deemed highly suspicious. An early suspect was

Joseph Isenschmid, a Swiss butcher, who had become depressed after his business failed, and spent ten weeks in the asylum at Colney Hatch. After his release he carried his large butcher's knives around with him. In fact, the bodies had been expertly dissected rather than butchered, and many thought that the Ripper must have had a surgeon's training. Another theory made him a seaman who sailed in and out of the Port of London regularly because the murders took place only at certain times of the month. Visitors flocked to the East End. The *New York World* reported that 'slumming' in Whitechapel was fashionable again, and that every night scores of young men who had never been there before 'prowl around the neighbourhood where the murders were committed'. The police did not interfere as long as two men kept together without becoming a nuisance, but 'if a man goes alone and tries to lure a woman of the street into a secluded corner to talk with her he is pretty sure to get into trouble'.[102]

The government was deeply worried. When Mary Kelly, perhaps the last of the Ripper victims, was murdered in a rented room rather than in the street, the cabinet offered a pardon to anyone except the murderer who could contribute to an arrest. Nevertheless, police reluctance to offer a reward led to the belief that they knew who the Ripper was but did not want to catch him. One journalist saw fit to deny that Lord Salisbury had concealed Jack the Ripper at his home, and that the Home Secretary had instructed the police to discontinue inquiries because Jack was a member of the House of Lords.[103] The inspiration for this might have been Labouchere's accusation against Salisbury, a week earlier, of a cover-up in the Cleveland Street Affair. Such rumours were current for a long time, especially in the East End. It is still suggested that the Ripper was a famous man or of noble birth, and Prince Eddy has been mentioned in the long list of unlikely suspects. Rumour, speculation and uncertainty, fanned by the popular press, are essential ingredients in the Ripper story, and help to explain why, for both his contemporaries and ours, it was perhaps the greatest Victorian sensation of all.

CHAPTER 6:

The 'Sensation Novel'

If a scandal of more than usual piquancy occurs in high life, or a crime of extraordinary horror figures among our causes célèbres, the sensationist is immediately at hand to weave the incident into a thrilling tale.[1]

Shootings, poisonings, adultery and bigamy all sold newspapers, so it is hardly surprising that novels too should exploit the same themes. The 'sensation' novelists even drew on specific crimes for their material, and sometimes tackled issues of public concern. Charles Reade said he found his plots in the pages of *The Times*, and Wilkie Collins, like his friend Charles Dickens, was fascinated by real-life murder cases. The heroine in his *No Name* reads a newspaper account of a brutal murder, in which the murderer's confession takes 'a fearful hold on her mind'.[1]

Dickens's *Oliver Twist*, which was being serialised when Victoria came to the throne, would have been called a 'sensation novel', had the term existed then. The same applies to its successor in *Bentley's Miscellany*, Harrison Ainsworth's even more popular *Jack Sheppard*, which, as we have seen, was believed to have inspired Courvoisier's crime. Both of the latter stories featured a criminal milieu and brutal murder. Dickens's ability to clothe sensational incidents in artistic respectability made him the key literary influence on the sensation novel, and particularly after *Bleak House*, with its combination of murder, mystery and a densely plotted narrative, was published.

The term 'sensation novel' was applied to certain works of the 1860s when the concept of 'sensation' was all the rage. In fact, modernity was one of its essential characteristics. As a critic of the time put it, 'A writer who takes boldly in hand the common mechanism of life, and by means of persons, who might all be living in society for anything we can tell to the contrary, thrills us into wonder, terror and breathless interest, . . . has accomplished a far greater success than he who effects the same result through supernatural agencies . . . or violent horrors of crime.'[2] This defines the achievement of the 'sensation' novelists. They inspired 'wonder and terror' by 'bigamy, adultery, illegitimacy, disguise, changed names, railway accidents, poison, fire, murder, concealed identity, false reports of death, and the doubling of characters or incidents'.[3] Madness, and wicked women − not only criminals, but those seen as unduly assertive or using their sexuality to gain their ends − were also popular subjects.

According to one overheated critic, the influence of such novels was 'on the whole, so infamous, the principles contained in many of them so utterly demoralising; the conversations retailed so revolting for their looseness, wickedness and blasphemy; the scene represented so licentious or so horrible, that it becomes the duty of each one who can find his way into print to protest against them'.[4] This wild diatribe reflects how powerfully 'sensation novels' affected their readers, but grotesquely misrepresents their moral orientation. Even when, as often happened, they challenged conventional morality, good invariably won out in the end. The texture of the novels cannot be communicated by merely listing the sensational elements, which were subservient to the aim of instilling in the reader the 'sensations' of excitement, surprise, fear, dismay and so on. The authors understood that the best way to achieve this was not to pile up external 'sensations' but to use them selectively within an everyday setting that the reader would recognise and identify with. Sensation novelists represented what one contemporary called 'the aristocratic branch of sensation literature' as opposed to 'the cheap publications which supply sensation for the million in penny and halfpenny numbers'.[5] These consisted of eight pages, with a dramatic woodcut on the front. Each was packed with incident, usually culminating in a cliffhanger ending.

Mary Braddon was one of the most important sensation novelists, and her first stories were published in penny numbers, but she understood the difference between that kind of fiction and 'the aristocratic branch' to which she graduated. In *The Doctor's Wife* she satirizes a penny novelist who has never achieved the dignity of a bound volume. The illustration for his next instalment shows 'a man with his knee upon the chest of another man, and a knife in his hand', while the flavour of his masterpiece emerges when he is asked if it contains a suicide. 'Why, it teems with suicides.

There's the Duke of Port St Martin's, who walls himself up alive in his own cellar; and there's Leonie de Pasdebasque, the ballet-dancer, who throws herself out of Count Caesar Maraschetti's private balloon; and there's Lilia, the dumb girl – the penny public like dumb girls – who sets fire to herself from the – in fact, there's lots of them.'[6]

If Mr G. W. Reynolds be the Mr Reynolds who is the Author of the Mysteries of London . . . I hold his to be a name with which no lady's, and no gentleman's, should be associated. *Charles Dickens*[7]

G W M Reynolds was the most interesting and able of the authors of the fiction Mary Braddon satirized. She confessed that at the start of her career she had aimed to combine 'as far as my powers allowed, the human interest and genial humour of Dickens with the plot-weaving of G W M Reynolds'.[8] Reynolds's stories were immensely popular among working-class readers and his sales figures dwarfed even Dickens'. He used many of the ingredients that reappeared in the sensation novel, but added a lavish helping of sex and violence, which mainstream authors were not permitted.

Reynolds is an important figure in the story of Victorian sensation for both his journalism and his fiction, which were written in the same spirit. He was the founder editor of *Reynolds's Newspaper*, which features so often in these pages because of its readiness to print material and language too sensational for other papers. It reflected Reynolds's own views as a left-wing republican, and attacked the abuses he targeted in his novels. For example, *Reynolds's Newspaper* campaigned for years against flogging in the army, which was the theme of one of Reynolds's best known stories, *The Soldier's Wife*.

One theme recurs again and again: the evils of the aristocracy.

Show us a class of persons, on the face of God almighty's earth, more thoroughly heartless than the English aristocracy. No – you cannot! . . . Talk of the donations which they make to charitable institutions – it is a despicable farce . . . And even if they were really charitable and truly bounteous – even if they gave largely to the deserving poor, and dispensed gold by handfuls in secret benevolence – they would only be rendering back to the people a portion of that inordinate wealth which they derive from the thews, sinews, fibres, vitals and heart's blood of the toiling – wretched – starving millions!'[9]

An extract from a Reynolds novel, this could easily have appeared in his newspaper. And wherever it appeared, it would have been unacceptable to conventionally minded readers.

From the late 1830s until the end of the 1850s, Reynolds's output of fiction seemed inexhaustible. Some of his stories are in the Gothic horror tradition, some historical, some about contemporary life. Sex and violence feature most strongly in *The Mysteries of London*, and in *The Mysteries of the Court of London*, which first appeared in weekly penny numbers from 1844 to 1856. They were published in hard covers in four and eight volumes respectively; each volume contained 400 pages of small print in double columns. Reynolds accurately described the two series, which he kept going over 624 weeks, as 'an encyclopaedia of tales'.[10] The exact number of his other novels is disputed, but must be over thirty.

The violence in them was often gruesome: an old man kicked almost to death then finished off with a ferocious stamp on his mouth; a fight between two thugs in which one's eye is gouged out and the other's nose bitten off before the bloodsoaked but exultant victor deals the final blow with a knife.[11] A streak of sadism in Reynolds undoubtedly led to gratuitous violence.

On the other hand, sex, although often intended only to titillate, sometimes illustrates important themes that more respectable authors would not touch. There is an obvious parallel here with the almost uniquely uninhibited reporting of *Reynolds' Newspaper*. In one episode, a man and his wife are living in one room with their grown-up sons and daughters in a London slum:

> Shame and decency exist not amongst them – because they could never have known either. They have all been accustomed from their infancy to each other's nakedness, and, as their feelings are brutalised by such a mode of existence, they suffer no scruples to oppose that fearful inter-course which their sensuality suggests. Thus – for we *must* speak plainly, as we speak *the truth* – the very wretchedness of the poor, which com-pels this family commingling in one room and as it were in one bed, leads to incest – horrible revolting incest![12]

In the same story, in similar surroundings, a woman takes in young children:

> It was a regular pig-stye, in which we wallowed like swine: and like that

of brutes also was the conduct of the eldest boys and girls. If the other rooms of the house were used as a brothel by grown-up persons, no stew could be more atrocious than our garret. The girls were more precocious than the boys, and the latter were corrupted by the former. Mere children of nine and ten practised the vices of their elders. But, my God! Let me draw a veil over this dreadful scene.[13]

These were serious issues, but too sensational for a middle class readership. The same applies to the candour with which some of Reynolds's female characters refer to their sexual feelings. They are often unashamed of them, and not always wicked. *Rosa Lambert* is the story, told in the first person, of a clergyman's daughter who yields her virtue to save her brother from being exposed as a criminal. She then becomes a high class courtesan and although, in the end, she sinks into prostitution and dies, she is mostly treated sympathetically as she passes from one lover to another.

> His eyes were looking down fondly into mine: he drew nearer, and he became bolder: his arm encircled my waist – my head sank upon his shoulder – he joined his lips to mine. To be brief, I forgot all my obligations to Lord Alfreton; and Claudius Sydenham quitted not the house until after breakfast on the following morning . . . There was no particle of *sentiment* in the mood wherein I had surrendered myself up to him: my weakness arose entirely from the *sense*: it was sheer wantonness.[14]

In a hypocritical advertisement for the book Reynolds claimed that it 'will contain nothing to shock even the most sensitive delicacy',[15] but a bookshop kept by his publisher sold his work alongside even more explicit material.[16]

Reynolds's young women are invariably well endowed, and their bosoms heave, palpitate and throb whenever their passions are engaged. 'Again did the enraptured Harley imprint a thousand kisses upon her flushed and glowing countenance: again and again did he clasp her to his breast – and he could feel her bosom throbbing against his chest like the undulations of a mighty tide ebbing to and fro. Octavia was lost as it were in a new world of ineffable bliss.'[17] Reynolds's readers seem to have enjoyed both his revolutionary diatribes and the sex and violence; it is not clear which his detractors found more deplorable.

The Mysteries of the Court is set in the Regency period. The early chapters are probably the most titillating in all Reynolds's fiction. In one scene a young nobleman dresses and makes himself up as a woman to insinuate himself into the bedroom of the object of his desire.[18] In another, a crowd of low criminals are having an orgy in which 'two or three of the younger women present stripped themselves stark naked and danced madly under the influence of brandy. Their lascivious movements, disgusting attitudes, and abominable freaks raised the delight of the spectators to a positive delirium.' It is typical of Reynolds's blend of salaciousness and moralizing that in the preceding paragraph he attacks the English hypocrites who oppose slavery in America. 'Slavery is a black spot upon their civilisation, it is true, but that spot is absolutely white when compared with the stain of hellish dye which the miseries of our own poor stamp upon the name of England!'[19]

Sex and politics come together in the *Mysteries of the Court*. The arch lecher of the series is the Prince of Wales, later George IV. The Prince, making ruthless use of his wealth and power, entices several young women into his bed, but Reynolds allows others either to reject him or to use desperate means to escape. There is also a working-class anti-hero, a criminal thug called 'the Magsman', whose wife has left him and risen in society as the keeper of a high-class brothel, frequented by the Prince. When the two men meet, the thug treats the prince as an equal: 'You are the Prince of all the rakes and demireps at the West End – and I'm the Prince of all the buzgloaks, prigs, cracksmen, and flash coves elsewhere.' (Mary Braddon attacked George IV too, in *Aurora Floyd*.[20])

The link between penny fiction and sensation novels was both acknowledged and deplored. A critic who described the latter as 'one of the abominations of the age', proclaimed that Mary Braddon 'may boast, without fear of contradiction, of having temporarily succeeded in making the literature of the Kitchen the favourite reading of the Drawing room'. Another writer claimed that sensation novels had passed 'from the parlour to the kitchen'.[21]

Reynolds's outpouring of fiction dried up as the sensation novelists came into vogue. In this coming together of above- and below-stairs taste perhaps they picked up his readership.

Take of foolscap half-a-ream,
Take, oh take, a convict's dream,
Lynch pin, fallen from a carriage,

Forged certificate of marriage,
Money wrongly won at whist,
Finger of a bigamist,
Cobweb from mysterious vaults,
Arsenic sold as Epsom salts,
Pocket-knife with blood-stained blade,
Telegram, some weeks delayed . . . *W S Gilbert*[22]

Wilkie Collins' *The Woman in White* was the first sensation novel, and did much to define the genre. It was published in three volumes in 1860 after being serialized by Dickens in *All The Year Round*. It sold out on publication day and six more impressions followed within six months. The publisher George Smith, of Smith Elder, was told by a lady sitting next to him at dinner, 'Everyone is raving about it. We talk *Woman in White* from morning to night.' Smith had offered Collins a mere £500 to publish it and admitted in his memoirs that he could have offered ten times as much, and still made a handsome profit.[23]

Gladstone recorded in his diary, 'I did not get to the play last night from finding *The Woman in White* so very interesting.'[24] The delight of the public was not always reflected in the reviews, but the novelist Mrs Oliphant, in an article that mounted a vigorous attack on sensation fiction, praised Collins as a writer who 'by means of persons who might all be living in society for anything we can tell to the contrary, thrills us into wonder, terror, and breathless interest, with positive personal shocks of surprise and excitement'.[25] As Henry James put it, Collins introduced into fiction 'those most mysterious of mysteries, the mysteries which are at our own doors'.[26]

When the story begins, the eponymous woman appears suddenly on a moonlit night to Walter Hartright, an artist, who is walking to London from Hampstead. In gothic fiction she would have been a ghost, but this woman is made of flesh and blood. She is called Anne Catherick, and the central mystery of the story revolves around her true identity, and why she obtrudes into the life of Walter's beloved Laura Fairlie.

Walter first meets Laura when he is employed as drawing master, then the male equivalent of the governess, to her and her half-sister, Marian Halcombe. He is brought close to Laura, but his inferior status makes touching her even more than usually taboo. Collins describes sensuality with a delicacy which has no place in the explicit scenes penned by

Wilkie Collins' The Woman in White *was the first 'sensation novel', and was also a sensational bestseller. The first impression sold out on publication day, and six more followed in the next six months.*

Reynolds: 'It was part of my service, to live in the very light of her eyes – at one time to be bending over her, so close to her bosom as to tremble at the thought of touching it.'

Marian is largely responsible for solving the mystery, and is the first of a line of strong women in sensational fiction. The villain, an enormously fat but intelligent Italian, Count Fosco, is attracted to her for her strength of character and intellect, rather than her figure. For many contemporary readers the cynical, ruthless Fosco was the mesmerising force of the novel, and his duel with Marian overshadowed the genteel relationship between the insipid Walter and Laura.

In *The Woman in White* Collins tells the story through a sequence of narrators. While watching a criminal trial in 1856, he had been struck by the way in which each witness made a contribution to the chain of evidence, and resolved to use the same process in fiction. As he put it in the first chapter, 'The story here presented will be told by more than one pen, as the story of an offence against the laws is told in Court by more than one witness.' In *The Moonstone*, where he uses the same technique, the reader is compared with 'a Judge on the bench'.[27]

The technique is not always successful: many of the narratives are in the form of letters and diary entries, and in a bid to make them dovetail with each other Collins was led to make some improbably long. The most sensational trial of 1856 was William Palmer's, and it is likely that Collins attended it.[28] As it happens, *The Times'* review of *The Woman in White* linked the novel with Palmer: Collins need not have warned reviewers so fiercely against divulging the plot, it said, because 'the great pleasure which the public take in such a trial as that of Palmer's is not in the expectation of new facts, but in the purely intellectual study of the evidence already known, worked up as it is by logical minds into a demonstration'.[29] In Mary Braddon's *Aurora Floyd* Palmer is mentioned three times.[30]

Posterity has preferred *The Woman in White* to Braddon's *Lady Audley's Secret*, but the latter was more popular in its day: in 1862 eight editions were published in three months. Miss Braddon freely acknowledged her debt to *The Woman in White*, but Lady Audley is her own creation: 'The innocence and candour of an infant beamed in Lady Audley's fair face, and shone out of her large and liquid blue eyes. The rosy lips, the delicate nose, the profusion of fair ringlets, all gave to her beauty the character of extreme youth and freshness.'[31] In fact she is a villainess in disguise, a new type of female protagonist, notably satirized by W S Gilbert as 'the beautiful fiend with yellow hair and the panther-like movement.'[32] Helen Tallboys, the future Lady Audley, is left behind when her husband, George, sails to Australia to make his fortune. She leaves their son with her father, puts an announcement of her death in the paper and, under a false name, becomes a governess in the family of the elderly Sir Michael Audley, whom she marries bigamously for his money. When George returns unexpectedly, Lady Audley pushes him down a well and leaves him for dead. Later, she kills a minor character, while trying to murder the man who is on her trail. He is George's friend, Sir Michael's nephew, Robert Audley, and is determined to solve the mystery of George's disappearance after his return to England.

Braddon perhaps discovered from Collins' work that she could create enormous tension in her story by throwing together the villain and his or her antagonist in apparently normal domestic circumstances. In *The Woman in White*, Marian lives under the same roof as Count Fosco, at one point, and cannot make a move without being terrified that he will spot it. Similarly Robert, who suspects that Lady Audley had something to do with the disappearance of his friend, wages a battle of wits with her when he is a guest at Audley Court. The tension is all the greater here because he is aware that if he succeeds in proving her guilt he may destroy his beloved uncle, who dotes on her.

Like Lady Audley, the eponymous heroine of Miss Braddon's *Aurora Floyd* is a bigamist. The two novels appeared at the same time both as magazine serials and in book form. *Aurora Floyd* was almost as popular as *Lady Audley's Secret*, and the 27-year-old Mary Braddon was a double sensation in 1862. It is due to her that sensation novels became associated with bigamy. Readers who were disturbed by this would have been even more alarmed to know that the author was living with a man whose wife was in an Irish madhouse, and that Braddon bore him several children before his wife's death enabled them to marry. She was not alone in living a life that diverged from the Victorian ideal: Wilkie Collins commuted between mistresses in two different households; Charles Reade was a bachelor without being celibate; Bulwer Lytton consigned his wife to an asylum for a while; and Charles Dickens threatened to do the same when his marriage broke up.[33]

Aurora Floyd disobeys her father to run off with a handsome groom, and marries him in secret. The groom is unfaithful and treats her cruelly, and she knows she could divorce him, but does not 'for my father's sake'.

SPECIAL NOTICE.

More than Fourteen Years have passed since the Drama, in Two
Acts, founded on Miss Braddon's popular Novel,

LADY AUDLEY'S SECRET

Was produced at the St. James's Theatre, when, thanks to the zeal
and energy of all concerned in the representation, a gratifying and
unqualified success was assured.

Having regard to the intensity of interest developed in the Story,
and bearing in mind the advanced constructional exigencies of the
day, the adapter has remodelled, and in a measure re-written the
Play, which is this Evening submitted to the Public, in Four Acts,
with New Scenery, Costumes, &c.

After LADY AUDLEY'S SECRET, will be produced (First
Time), a Petit Drama, in One Act, freely adapted and arranged
from FRANÇOIS COPPÉE'S "Le Luthier de Crémone," entitled THE

VIOLIN-MAKER OF CREMONA

By HENRY NEVILLE.

Box Office open daily from Eleven till Five.
NO BOOKING FEES.
PRICES OF ADMISSION.

Private Boxes, One to Three Guineas. Stalls, 7s. 6d. Dress Circle, 5s.
Boxes (Bonnets), 4s. Pit, 2s. Amphitheatre, 1s. 6d. Gallery, 1s.

Doors open at 7.   Commence at 7.30.

Refreshment Department under the Management of
Mr H. HARVEY.

Lady Audley's Secret, *by Mary Braddon, was possibly even more popular
with the Victorians than* The Woman in White. *It went through eight
editions in three months during 1862, and stage adaptions attracted
enthusiastic audiences for the rest of the Victorian era.*

Instead she returns to live with her father. Nobody knows about her marriage and she receives two proposals, which she turns down. When she reads in the paper a (mistaken) report that her dastardly husband is dead, she becomes engaged to the aristocratic Talbot Bulstrode. However, although he is unaware of her previous marriage, he discovers that a year is missing from her life, which she cannot explain, and backs out. 'God forgive you, Aurora Floyd; by your own confession you are no fit wife for an honourable man. I shut my mind against all foul suspicions; but the past life of my wife must be a white unblemished page, which all the world may be free to read.'[34]

Later Aurora marries a trusting Yorkshire squire, who needs no explanation of the missing year. Then her first husband turns up, blackmails her and is shot dead. Aurora's bloodstained marriage certificate is found sewn into his clothing and her husband suspects her of the murder. The identity of the murderer is never really in doubt, but the evidence is only found after a detective has been engaged to investigate the crime.

It is clear from the story that Aurora is a moral woman who has a bad time of it. She is maltreated by her first husband, blackmailed, and wrongly accused of murder. Yet the self-appointed upholders of Victorian morality did not think that she had been punished enough. Aurora's sexuality counted against her. Bulstrode compares her to Cleopatra, Nell Gwyn, Lola Montes and Charlotte Corday. He thinks that 'she is like everything that is beautiful and strange, and wicked and unwomanly, and bewitching'.[36] In other words, she is trouble, a danger to the good order of Victorian society, but likely, of course, to attract large numbers of readers.

Female sinners painted in attractive colours were especially alarming, and their female creators were held to be leading other women astray. 'Shame to women so to write,' Mrs Oliphant declared, 'shame to women who read and accept it as a true representation of themselves.' She was equally dismissive of the infant women's rights movement: 'We have most of us made merry over Mr [John Stuart] Mill's crotchet on the subject.' She defended the Victorian double standard, whereby 'the wickedness of man is less ruinous, less disastrous to the world in general, than the wickedness of woman'. Mrs Oliphant regretted that 'Mr Trollope's charming girls do not, now that we know them so well, call forth half so much notice from the press as do the Aurora Floyds of contemporary fiction,' and in particular that *The Times* had given these books 'the crowning glory of its approval'.[36]

SIXTH EDITION

Dedicated To

MISS E. BRADDON.

Aurora Floyd

GALOP

BY

Gerald de Boutville

Ent. Stat. Hall.

By the same Composer
"THE BRIDAL BELLS" MAZURKA, (4TH EDITION) 3/

Price 3/0

LONDON.

JOHN BLOCKLEY, 3, ARGYLL STREET. REGENT STREET, W.

Madness and bigamy, central features of Braddon's 1862 Aurora Floyd, *were rooted in the author's own experience. Unknown to her readers she had several children with a man whose wife was in an Irish madhouse, before the wife's death enabled them to marry.*

The Times was as little given to stirring up revolution in literature as it was in any other sphere, but it showed a more sympathetic understanding of the sensation novel than Mrs Oliphant. Its review of *Lady Audley's Secret* accepted that 'this is the age of lady novelists, and lady novelists naturally give first place to the heroine', and it would not do to depict them as passive and insipid. They had to be 'high-strung women full of passion, purpose and movement – very liable to error'. As the most interesting side of a woman's character is in relation to the opposite sex, there were now 'descriptions of the most hidden feelings of the fair sex which would have made our fathers and grandfathers stare'.[37] The writer was correct in stressing the role of 'lady novelists' in this development, but Wilkie Collins also played a part.

The most famous example of adultery in a sensation novel is that of Lady Isabel Vane in Mrs Henry Wood's *East Lynne*, who leaves her virtuous husband, Archibald Carlyle, to run off with a bounder. The story was serialised over 20 months from January 1860, and published as a book in the summer of 1861. Nearly forty years later it was described as 'still one of the most popular novels on the shelves of every circulating library'.[38] Much of its initial success has been credited to a review in *The Times*, which did not appear until January 1862, after which, according to the author's son, 'the libraries were besieged, and Messrs. Spottiswoode, the Queen's Printers, had to work night and day upon new editions'. *The Times* did not review novels regularly, and a favourable notice 'directed the whole English-speaking world to the work'.[39]

Lady Isabel mistakenly believes that her husband is betraying her with a family friend, Barbara Hare. Barbara is indeed in love with him, but her frequent meetings with Archibald are to discuss the plight of her brother Richard, who has run away from home after being unjustly accused of murder.

Lady Isabel runs off with Captain Levison, and it is clear that she finds him far more attractive than her husband. 'She was aware that a sensation all too warm, a feeling of attraction towards Francis Levison was working within her; not a voluntary one; she could no more repress it than she could repress her own sense of being.'[40] Yet Mrs Wood emphasises Lady Isabel's jealousy and plays down her sexual motive for absconding. She also passes up the opportunity to introduce bigamy: Archibald remarries after hearing that Lady Isabel has been killed in a railway accident, but Mrs Wood has already made sure that he is safely divorced. He is the only character in a well-known sensation novel to take advantage of the new Divorce Act – divorce took place in the open while bigamy was shrouded in secrecy, and thus lent itself naturally to a gripping plot.

Mrs Wood makes Lady Isabel pay dearly for her sins. Disfigured in the train crash, she returns in disguise to the Carlyle home as governess to her own children, whom she is desperate to see. This leads to the most appalling mental suffering. The greatest selling point of the novel was not the murder, the adultery or the train crash, but the painful experiences which the reader, especially the woman reader, shares with the heroine. She witnesses Archibald's love for Barbara Hare, his second wife, and the death of her son to whom she cannot reveal her true identity.

> Oh reader, believe me! Lady – wife – mother! should you ever be tempted to abandon your home, so will you awake! Whatever trials may be the lot of your married life, though they may magnify themselves to your crushed spirit as beyond the endurance of woman to bear, *resolve* to bear them; fall down upon your knees and pray to be enabled to bear them.. bear unto death, rather than forfeit your fair name and your good conscience; for be assured that the alternative, if you rush on to it, will be found far worse than death.[41]

It seems hard to criticise *East Lynne* from the standpoint of conventional Victorian morality, but Mrs Oliphant objected that Lady Isabel only becomes interesting after she has sinned, and that this is 'dangerous and foolish work'. 'Nothing can be more wrong and fatal,' she protested, 'than to represent the flames of vice as a purifying fiery ordeal, through which the penitent is to come elevated and sublime.' She disapproved of wicked or morally flawed characters being depicted sympathetically. While praising the vivid portrayal of Fosco in *The Woman in White*, she objected to the way in which 'he seizes on our sympathies more warmly than any other character in the book'.[42]

Lady Isabel's culpability is undeniable: she deserts a loving husband for a villain. However, there are extenuating circumstances: she married a man for whom she felt affection rather than love to escape abject poverty. Many Victorian women did this, but few would have experienced the disaster from which Lady Isabel's marriage saves her: she falls from luxury to destitution because of the profligate ways of her father, an earl, whose huge debts are revealed only by his death. Poverty also brought about

Lady Audley's bigamous marriage to Sir Michael. Her husband, George Tallboys, had left her penniless when he disappeared to Australia and, like Lady Isabel, she made it clear to her rich suitor that she respected but did not love him.

Both Mrs Wood and Miss Braddon seem to have felt that they were on dangerous ground and tried to backtrack. While the former piles up Lady Isabel's suffering, the latter tries a different approach: when Robert survives Lady Audley's attempt to burn him to death, which shows her that the game is up, Lady Audley tells him, in one of the most sensational moments of the novel, 'You have conquered – a MADWOMAN!'.[43]

But a woman whose crimes emanate from rational, if immoral, decisions is not mad, and Lady Audley's supposed madness unconvincing. As the American critic, Elaine Showalter, has written, 'Lady Audley's unfeminine assertiveness, so different from the plastic passivity of a Laura Fairlie, must ultimately be described as madness, not only to spare Braddon the unpleasant necessity of having to execute an attractive heroine, with whom she in many ways identifies, but also to spare the woman reader the guilt of identifying with a cold-blooded killer.'[44] In an 1877 stage production of *Lady Audley's Secret*, the villainess's cry of triumph after pushing George Tallboys down the well 'Free, free once more!' elicited a tremendous cheer from the audience. The critics declared that it was prompted by the brilliant acting, but it is more likely that the audience was expressing its sympathy with the character.[45] In making Lady Audley mad, Braddon was trying to temper this response.

In his second sensation novel, *No Name*, Wilkie Collins presents another attractive young woman who acts immorally for understandable reasons. However, she commits no crime; good and bad are more finely balanced in Magdalen Vanstone than they are in Lady Audley.

Magdalen and her sister, Norah, have been reduced from gracious living to destitution by the death of their father. In their case it is because, as a young man, he was lured into marriage by a wicked adventuress. Although he left her, she would not divorce him, so he had not married their mother. When news comes that his wicked wife has died, Magdalen and Norah's parents marry, but their father's will was made when his daughters were illegitimate and the bequest of his fortune to them is invalid. He dies before he can make a new one and the money goes to his effete nephew, Noël Vanstone.

The main strand of the story deals with Magdalen's vengeful attempt to recover the money by luring Noël into marrying her. She enlists the help of an eccentric rogue called Captain Wragge but is opposed by Mrs Lecount, Noël's housekeeper, the dominating force in his life. The two sides fight an exciting duel of plot and counter-plot.

The novel's special flavour comes from the fact that readers, gripped by the twists and turns of the story, sympathises with Magdalen, despite the fact that her actions are immoral. The reader knows that the beautiful, brave and talented woman is fighting dirty, against an ill-looking, mean-spirited untalented man. And, in any case, Magdalen is deeply divided. 'If I can marry him – the journey to the church, if the profanation of myself is more than I can bear – the journey to the grave.'[46]

The novel also took an inflammatory stand in the sympathy shown for the rights of children born out of wedlock. The family lawyer says that a law that bars two sisters from their inheritance is a disgrace to the nation – even their parents' eventual marriage made no difference to their plight. At least one critic argued that, in championing the children, Collins was defending the illicit relationship to which they owed their existence. He accused Collins of rigging the evidence by presenting a vicious wife and a virtuous 'concubine' – the mother of Magdalen and Norah. 'A different set of circumstances would have told as heavily against Wilkie Collins's argument as those in the story do in favour.'[47]

After Magdalen has married Noël, he is persuaded to cut her out of his will just before he dies. However, her sister and the next heir fall in love and marry. Thus the morally impeccable sister, who has adopted the conventional means of staving off poverty by becoming a governess, gains the fortune that has eluded the more enterprising but morally dubious Magdalen. According to the family lawyer, Magdalen is 'one of the most reckless, desperate and perverted women living',[48] and Collins knew that it would have been unacceptable to his readership to allow such a woman to win.

The female protagonist of Collins's next work, *Armadale*, makes Magdalen Vanstone look like a saint. Her name is Lydia Gwilt, and she too marries for money, using her sexuality as a snare. Allan Armadale is a rich young squire whose fortune Miss Gwilt covets, but although she bewitches him, his ardour cools. Undeterred she succeeds in marrying his best friend, Ozias Midwinter. She knows that Midwinter's real name is also Allan Armadale, although the squire does not. By marrying Midwinter under this name, she obtains a marriage certificate showing that she has married Allan Armadale. The couple go to live in Italy, with the squire, and all Lydia has to do is to arrange for the latter to be murdered, leave her husband, whom she believes will remain abroad, and return to England to claim the squire's fortune as his widow.

However, Armadale and Midwinter, as they had better be called for clarity's sake, are linked by a bond that only the latter knows about: Midwinter's father murdered the squire's and he feels a brotherly affection for the young man, which becomes mutual. Midwinter has worked hard to protect his friend from the experienced 35-year-old Miss Gwilt, but this does not prevent him falling in love with her himself. The murder plot fails, and *both* men return to England where Lydia lures them into a sanatorium for the mentally deranged. There she tries to murder Armadale but almost kills Midwinter by mistake. Believing that she has done so, she commits suicide in despair, because she has found that she reciprocates his love. At one stage, she is on the point of warning him: 'I am a fiend in human shape.'[49]

Lydia Gwilt is abetted in her ensnarement of men by a sinister old woman called Mrs Oldershaw, who, it is hinted, is involved in all sorts of shady practices, including abortion. Her most public occupation is as the proprietress of a 'Ladies' Toilette Repository', where 'I have had twenty years' experience among our charming sex in making up battered old faces and worn-out old figures to look like new.'[50] The character is based on the notorious Madame Rachel, who kept a shop in Bond Street and claimed to restore youth and beauty to those who had lost them. She was eventually sentenced to five years' penal servitude for fraud and false pretences.

Before the novel begins, Lydia Gwilt lived a life of crime. She committed forgery at the age of 12, when it was said of her that 'no creature more innately deceitful and more innately pitiless ever walked this earth' – a strong statement to make of a 12-year-old so perhaps John Sutherland's suggestion that she could have had a sexual relationship with the man who instigated the crime is correct.[51] As a young woman in Brussels, her sexual allure brought her into a criminal milieu. She enticed a rich young man into marriage, and poisoned him, after taking a Cuban seafarer as her lover. The death sentence passed on her was not carried out: after a campaign on her behalf, influenced by her beauty rather than the facts of the case, she was pardoned, and imprisoned for two years' for robbery – reminiscent of the charming Madeleine Smith's escape from the gallows.

Wilkie Collins earned more from Armadale than any other novel. This time George Smith, impressed by the success of *The Woman in White*, offered Collins the huge sum of £5000 for the copyright and serialization rights in *Armadale*. It would appear in the *Cornhill*, an upmarket magazine, which also published Thackeray and Trollope. However, over the course of serialization, the *Cornhill* lost about three thousand readers, unable to stomach the evil Miss Gwilt. They were well represented among the critics: the *Athenaeum* described her as 'one of the most hardened female villains whose devices and desires have ever blackened fiction – a forger, a convicted adulteress, murderess and thief';[52] For the *Spectator*, she was 'a woman fouler than the refuse of the streets', and even though she dies a typical villain's death, it was said that Collins had 'overstepped the limits of decency, and revolted every human sentiment'.[53] However, perhaps Miss Gwilt was a symptom of a greater problem of excess: in the eyes of contemporaries, not only was she too wicked but the novel contained too many sensational incidents, one piled on top of another, almost *à la* Reynolds. Collins was trying too hard to write the most sensational sensation novel of them all. But *Armadale* is still a terrific read.

Charles Reade's *Hard Cash* also contained sensational material that hampered its sales. It was published as *Very Hard Cash* in 1863 in *All the Year Round* and lost the magazine around the same number of readers as the *Cornhill* lost with *Armadale*. They disliked the descriptions of the treatment meted out to inmates of private lunatic asylums.

The fear of madness and incarceration is ever-present in sensation novels. Mary Braddon writes in *Lady Audley's Secret*:

> Madhouses are large and only too numerous; yet surely it is strange they are not larger, when we think of how many helpless wretches must beat their brains against this hopeless persistency of the orderly outward world, as compared with the storm and tempest, the riot and confusion within; when we remember how many minds must tremble upon the narrow boundary between reason and unreason, mad to-day and sane tomorrow, mad yesterday and sane to-day.[54]

When Robert Audley puts Lady Audley into a madhouse, he does to her what she has tried to do to him. She warns him that 'such fancies', as she describes his accusations, 'have sometimes conducted people, as apparently sane as yourself, to the lifelong imprisonment of a private lunatic asylum'.

He takes her threat seriously. 'Robert Audley was no coward, and yet a shiver of horror, something akin to fear, chilled him to the heart.'[55]

In *No Name*, Captain Wragge tries to convince Noël Vanstone that his housekeeper, Mrs Lecount, is mad. *Armadale* features the sinister 'sanatorium' for the deranged in which Lydia Gwilt tries to murder the rich squire, while earlier in the story Armadale and Midwinter see a shrieking madman captured by his keeper as he leaps over rocks on the coast of the Isle of Man. In *Aurora Floyd*, the jealous women who resent the marriage of Aurora's father to a wife socially his inferior ask why his relations did not 'show a little spirit – institute a commission of lunacy, and shut their crazy relative in a madhouse? He deserved it.'[56] The bride, who has not realised that her husband is an enormously rich man, 'remonstrated with her new master, fearing that his love had driven him mad, and that this alarming extravagance was the first outburst of insanity'. Moreover, after his wife's death, the widower's love for his daughter Aurora 'was a weakness, almost verging upon a madness. Had his nephews been very designing men, they might perhaps have entertained some vague ideas of that commission of lunacy for which the outraged neighbours were so anxious.'[57] The nephews stand to lose financially from the unexpected marriage of their 47-year-old uncle, and it was not unusual for relatives to lock a man or woman in an asylum for their own financial gain.

In *East Lynne*, Archibald Carlyle's marriage to Lady Isabel Vane provokes the wrath of his sister Cordelia, who lashes out: 'He must have been stark staring mad to go and do it; and had I gathered an inkling of the project I would have taken out a commission of lunacy against him.' A little later she expands on the theme: 'Better have confined him as a harmless lunatic for a couple of years, than suffer him to go free and obtain his fling in this mad manner.'[58] These remarks are not made entirely seriously, but they express a precise threat. 'You are mad' could not be said as lightly in those days as it can now. Famously, *The Woman in White*, which set so many trends for sensation novelists, begins with the startling appearance of a woman who has escaped from a madhouse. Later, when Lady Glyde, formerly Laura Fairlie, is also unjustly incarcerated in the same institution, Collins writes, 'Faculties less delicately balanced, constitutions less tenderly organized, must have suffered under such an ordeal as this. No man could have gone through it, and come out of it unchanged.'[59]

In *Hard Cash*, however, the hero undergoes a similar ordeal, and *does* come out unchanged. That is why he is a hero. Reade demurred at being described as a 'sensational novelist', arguing in the preface to the first edition of *Hard Cash* that 'this slang term is not quite accurate as applied to me'. He claimed to 'mix a little character, and a little philosophy, with the sensational element'. This is a bit pompous: presumably all sensation novelists would have claimed 'a little character' for their work, and for Reade's 'philosophy' read 'propaganda'. *Hard Cash* is a work of propaganda against the laws relating to insanity and the system by which the insane and supposedly insane were dealt with.

Alfred Hardie, the hero, has discovered that his banker father is a swindler. To silence him, the father has him lured to a house where he is shut up, and told that he has been put in an asylum to cure him of his 'delusion': 'At this fatal word 'asylum', Alfred uttered a cry of horror and despair, and his eyes roved wildly round the room in search of escape.' There is no escape and, despite his desperate struggles, there begins a terrible experience, which, Reade insists, might happen to anyone: 'Pray think of it for yourselves, men and women, if you have not *sworn* never to think over a novel. Think of it for your own sakes; Alfred's turn today, it may be yours to-morrow.'[60]

Alfred and the other inmates of the asylum are subject to brutal violence:

> Every art has its secrets: the attendants in such madhouses as this have been possessed of one they are too modest to reveal to justices, commissioners, or the public: the art of breaking a man's ribs, or breast-bone, or both, without bruising him externally . . . They subdue the patient by walking up and down him on their knees . . . Thus died Mr Sizer in 1854, and two others quite recently. And how many more God only knows; we can't count the stones at the bottom of a well.[61]

When Alfred is locked up, he is about to marry Julia, the daughter of the sea captain whom Alfred's father has swindled out of his money. The first night of his incarceration is all the worse because it was to have been his wedding night: instead of sharing a bed with his beloved, he lies helpless in handcuffs and leg irons, unable to ward off the insects that attack him. 'In conjunction with the opiates, the confinement and the gloom . . . they had driven many a feeble mind across the line that divides the weak and nervous from the unsound.'[62]

The erotic theme is developed in the character of the lovely Mrs Archbold, a woman of 30 who is one of the keepers at the asylum and lusts after Alfred. Imagine what Reynolds might have done with this situation! But, although he is young, strong, fit, and cut off from his bride, Alfred resists her blandishments. One night Mrs Archbold goes to his cell and kisses him as he lies asleep: 'She had sucked fresh poison from those honest lips, and filled her veins with molten fire. She tossed and turned the livelong night in a high fever of passion.'[63]

Shortly afterwards Alfred is transferred to another asylum, which allows Reade to broaden his exposé of the system. Asylum keepers did not want to lose income by releasing their patients, and doctors benefited financially from consigning cases to them. Thus corrupt doctors were easily induced to sign certificates authorising a victim to be shut up. Alfred travels between asylums by train and appeals to fellow passengers for help, but they shy away when his keepers produce the certificates. In the second asylum Reade targets more malpractices. Morphia is administered to the inmates: 'the accursed drug with which these dark men in these dark places coax the reason away out of the head by degrees, or with a potent dose stupefy the victim'. Women patients are 'tanked': 'For the least offence, out of mere wantonness, they would drag a patient stark naked across the yard, and thrust her bodily under water again and again, keeping her down until almost gone with suffocation, and dismissing her more dead than alive with obscene and insulting comments ringing in her ears.'[64]

Mrs Archbold reappears, as passionate as ever. '"You couldn't love me like a man; you shall love me like a dog." "How will you manage that, pray?" he inquired with a sneer. "I'll drive you mad." She hissed this fiendish threat out between her white teeth.'[65] For the sane person, the danger of being driven mad in the asylum overshadowed all its other torments.

Julia's father, the sea captain, who has been driven into insanity by being swindled out of his life savings, is confined in the same asylum as Alfred. When the building is set on fire they escape together. However, Alfred has another disaster to face: his sister has been killed by a maniac, too poor to get into a private asylum and ineligible for a public one as he has not hitherto physically harmed anyone. As Reade puts it, 'If a poor man is as mad as a March hare, his friends cannot by force of law and without favour get him into a public asylum, unless he has earned that privilege by killing or maiming a fellow-citizen.'[66] In the end Alfred's wicked father loses his reason and ends up in a madhouse, a fitting punishment for his crimes.

The asylum scenes make up only about a fifth of the story, but this element created uproar because it was an issue that many did not want to confront. In an earlier work, *It Is Never Too Late To Mend*, Reade had exposed the horrors of the prison system to similar devastating effect. He was a propagandist to an extent that makes Wilkie Collins's attack on the laws of inheritance in *No Name* seem mild: even in Collins's later work the propaganda, which has been widely blamed for the drop in literary quality, is not as obvious as it is in Reade's.

Charles Reade bombarded the newspapers with his views on public issues. He had attacked every abuse fictionalised in *Hard Cash* in letters to the press, even recounting his own experience in befriending a young man who had escaped from an asylum. But an uninhibited propagandist was a problem for an editor. Dickens had published three of Wilkie Collins's best known sensation novels in *All the Year Round*, but he was mortified by *Hard Cash* and not only because of the fall it caused in his magazine's circulation: one of the corrupt asylum keepers is based on John Conolly, whom Dickens had praised in public as 'a distinguished gentleman who was not more remarkable for his talent than he was for possessing the kindest and tenderest heart'.[67] Admittedly, that had been six and a half years earlier, but Dickens's close friend John Forster was a lunacy commissioner, responsible for inspecting and licensing asylums. In Reade's story, the men carrying out these tasks are shown to be easily fooled by the asylum keepers into overlooking cruelty and dishonesty. It is no wonder that Dickens published a disclaimer, with the last episode of *Hard Cash*, emphasising that Reade's views were not necessarily his.[68]

In 1868 Reade wrote *Foul Play* jointly with Dion Boucicault, whose sensation dramas were a feature of the decade. The collaboration neatly encapsulates the link between the sensation novel and the sensation play. Here, the authors campaigned against shipowners who arranged for their vessels to sink so that they could claim insurance on the cargo. Arthur Wardlaw, the shipowner of *Foul Play*, does not know that his own fiancée, Helen, is on board the scuttled ship. When it sinks, she manages to reach a desert island, where she finds herself alone with Robert Penfold, a young man who is deeply in love with her. Eventually a rescue ship arrives with her father on board. When he learns about her young companion, he immediately thinks that the relationship might have developed in a way that, in fact, has not occurred to Helen. How often it has occurred to Robert, who happens to be a clergyman, is up to conjecture. To Helen's complaint that the young man has concealed his identity, her father replies, 'You are a little fool, and, in your ignorance and innocence, have no idea how well this young fellow has behaved on the whole.'[69]

It is a nice touch on Reade's part that Wardlaw, for all his villainy, is sincerely in love with Helen. When he loses her to Penfold, and his misdeeds are exposed, he goes mad, like the villain in *Hard Cash*, although in this case the madhouse is seen as an alternative to prison.

Foul Play deals with several contemporary issues apart from ship-scuttling. Early in the story, Robert Penfold has been imprisoned for a crime he did not commit, and he first catches sight of Helen when he has been released on a 'ticket of leave', which gave a convict a conditional discharge before his sentence had expired. The new leniency towards convicted criminals provoked controversy in the 1860s, and one of the most popular plays of the decade, *The Ticket-of-Leave Man* by Tom Taylor, featured another convict unjustly imprisoned and discharged early. Needless to say, in *Foul Play* as in Taylor's drama, the hero's innocence is eventually established. Another contemporary element lies in Wardlaw's fears for the future of his bank in 'the panic of '66' when 'Overend and Gurney broke'. Overend and Gurney's was the most sensational banking failure of the period, comparable with the more recent collapse of Baring's, but at this period Baring's was riding high, and when Robert eventually comes into a fortune, the money is paid to him 'in drafts on Baring'.

While *Foul Play* was being published, *The Moonstone*, Wilkie Collins' last sensation novel of the 1860s, was appearing in *All The Year Round*. It was another huge success. According to William Tinsley, who published the story in three volumes, no other novel, not even *Great Expectations*, gained Dickens' magazine more readers. On the days when the final instalments were published, crowds of readers gathered outside the magazine's office just off the Strand. 'I know of several bets that were made as to where the moonstone would be found at last. Even the porters and the boys were interested in the story, and read the new numbers in sly corners, and often with their packs on their back.'[70]

The story begins with a short prologue in which a disreputable member of the Verinder family loots the Moonstone, a fabulous diamond, from an Indian temple. Thereafter the reader is repeatedly reminded of the stone's origins by the presence of three Indians near the family home. They are obviously determined to get it back, and they are suspected of robbery when it is stolen from the room of Rachel Verinder, who has inherited it.

Collins' The Moonstone and Charles Reade's Foul Play (dramatized as The Scuttled Ship) were among a number of sensational novels whose stage adaptations became huge and long-running successes.

In fact, the Indians have not taken the Moonstone, but they get it in the end by murdering the villain of the piece. Readers last see the jewel back where it belongs, mounted in the statue of a Hindu god. Although the three Indians are murderers, their crime is mitigated because it is a response to an insult to their faith, and because their victim is the villain. *The Moonstone* was published in 1868, little more than ten years after the Indian Mutiny, and its tenderness towards Hindu susceptibilities was conspicuously lacking in other writers, notably Dickens.

Collins was what we should now call 'liberal' in matters of colour and creed. In *Armadale*, the mother of the swarthy Ozias Midwinter (alias Allan Armadale) is a Creole. He is a sympathetic character, and far more intelligent than the other Allan Armadale, who is Anglo-Saxon in appearance: Midwinter has repeatedly to rescue the Anglo-Saxon from his foolishness. John Sutherland has pointed out that this seems to have been a deliberate riposte to Thackeray's *Philip* in which the hero is fair-haired and blue-eyed, and the villain, of the very deepest dye, a mulatto. *Philip* had been serialised in the *Cornhill* two or three years before *Armadale*.[71]

The looting of the Moonstone brings a curse on the Verinder family. No sooner has Rachel's beloved, Franklin Blake, brought it from the lawyer's to the family home than it goes missing. This, of course, is one of the story's sensations, although the disaster is not so much the loss of the jewel as the devastating impact on relationships within the family circle. Another sensation is the suicide of a housemaid, Rosanna Spearman, desperately in love with Franklin, who allows herself to be sucked into quicksand. As she has a prison record, she is a prime suspect for the theft. Then there is the discovery of a night shirt with a tell-tale paint stain which is supposed to prove that the wearer committed the robbery. Franklin narrates this part of the story and brings this instalment to a sensational conclusion: "'If time, pains and money can do it, I will lay my hand on the thief who took the Moonstone' – I had left London with those words on my lips. I had penetrated the secret which the quicksand had kept from every other living creature. And, on the unanswerable evidence of the paint-stain, I had discovered Myself as the Thief.'"[72]

The Moonstone is widely considered to have been the first detective story – the detective in *Aurora Floyd* is a minor character. Sergeant Cuff, who is hired from Scotland Yard by Rachel's mother, was preceded by

Inspector Bucket in *Bleak House*, but the plot of Dickens' novel is so wide-ranging and complex that it transcends the detective genre.

Several elements of *The Moonstone* derive from a real-life crime of 1860. The horrific murder of a little boy called Francis Kent was not replicated in the novel, but Sergeant Cuff is based on the inspector who investigated the case in which a missing nightdress loomed large. The hostility of the Kent family to the police is also reflected in the novel: the old retainer, Betteredge, despite his repeated attacks of what he calls 'the detective fever', protests that 'to be held up before my mistress, in my old age, as a sort of deputy-policeman, was, once again, more than my Christianity was strong enough to bear'.[73] In the Kent case, the detective suspected Constance, an older sister of Francis, but nothing was proved against her until she confessed to the crime five years later. Many people did not believe her confession, and some inclined to Dickens' theory that she was covering up for her father, whose love-making with the nursemaid had been disturbed by the little boy.[74] There is a secret passion in the Verinder household too: it is because of Rachel's undeclared love for Blake that she suffers so much after seeing him take the jewel, which explains her mysterious resentment of the attempts to get at the truth.[75]

The murder in the book draws on another real-life killing of a few years earlier. In July 1861, a man covered with blood was seen at the window of a house in Northumberland Street, near the Strand in London. He had battered to death a money-lender who, he claimed, had lured him to the house, then shot and wounded him. The Northumberland Street Affair became famous because the fight was so violent, desperate and bloody. Thackeray wrote about it in his *Roundabout Papers*, it inspired a play as late as 1882, and then a celebrated music-hall sketch. Collins places the house to which the murder victim is lured, and where he is murdered by the Indians, in Northumberland Street. Contemporary readers would not have missed the reference.

After the 1860s, middle-class readers turned away from sensation novels, partly because the best ones had already been written. Miss Braddon and Mrs Henry Wood continued to be prolific writers of fiction, but explored other avenues. Wilkie Collins' powers declined, although his later works are not without merit. In *The Law and the Lady* of 1875, he created the first woman detective – an amateur, of course. Valeria Woodville is a worthy addition to Collins' succession of strong women – Marian

Halcombe, Magdalen Vanstone, Lydia Gwilt – and, to some extent, Rachel Verinder. Valeria is 'a far better man' than her feeble husband, Eustace. That she is so deeply in love with him is the least credible aspect of the novel.

The first mystery of the story is why Eustace married her under a false name. Valeria discovers that he has been married before, and was the accused in a sensational murder trial – she did not know about it because conveniently she was living abroad. In an echo of the Madeleine Smith case, Eustace was accused in Scotland of poisoning his wife, but the verdict was 'not proven'. He is so ashamed of not being cleared that he runs away from Valeria as soon as she finds out. She is convinced that he is innocent and sets out to prove it.

The Law and the Lady is a sensation novel in the old Collins mode and has several thematic links with earlier works. Madness reappears as a theme, Collins attacks the law, as he did in *No Name*, and arsenic poisoning again plays its part.

Sensation novels were criticised on their first appearance for concentrating too much on plot and not enough on character. Literary critics of later generations have endorsed this enthusiastically, disregarding the art of telling a good story. In fact, the best of these books are compelling page-turners – although they share one significant defect in their reliance on coincidence and improbability, which the Victorians swallowed more easily than we do.

For example, Mrs Henry Wood hit on a brilliant situation when she made Lady Isabel Vane governess to her own children, the unrecognised witness to the death of her little boy and to her wronged husband's love for his second wife. However, to get to that point her beauty had to be ruined by a railway accident and she had to meet someone who could arrange for her to fill that particular job vacancy. It doesn't do to question her decision to return to her old home or her ex-husband's failure to penetrate her disguise. Other improbabilities include a man standing for Parliament in the very constituency where he has committed a murder.

Similarly, in *Armadale*, we have to accept that two men meet by chance, the father of one having murdered the father of the other. Aurora Floyd risks daily contact with her first husband, whom she believed dead: we are expected to believe that of all potential grooms available her husband has hired this man and that Aurora, although warned of it, does not protest. And, although the characters in sensation novels do not spend much time reading newspapers, they always pick one up just when it contains information they need to know. In *Lady Audley's Secret*, George Tallboys happens to see the very edition of *The Times* which contains the announcement of his wife's supposed death.

Despite their limitations, though, the finest sensation novels were runaway bestsellers, and are still immensely readable today. If they have one quality that strikes a particularly modern note it is in the depiction of women. When, like the protagonists of *Lady Audley's Secret*, *East Lynne*, *No Name* and *Armadale*, a minor female character in *The Law and the Lady* marries a man she does not love, the heroine responds 'When a woman sells herself to a man, that vile bargain is none the less infamous (to my mind) because it happens to be made under the sanction of the Church and the Law.'[76] Elsewhere such marriages are not condoned, but it is acknowledged that they were often the only way out of poverty for some women. The circumstances leading up to them imply a criticism of society, which Mary Braddon makes explicit in *The Doctor's Wife*: 'A bright young creature, with the soul of a Pitt, sits at home and works sham roses in Berlin wool; while her booby brother is thrust out into the world to fight the mighty battle.'[77]

The 1860s were, after all, the decade of the first women's suffrage committee and of John Stuart Mill's *On the Subjection of Women*. The female characters who foreshadowed the future most strongly were not the villains, Lady Audley or Miss Gwilt, but the strong, resourceful women who took upon themselves more responsibility than their men ever expected of them, like Marian Halcombe, Valeria Woodville, and even Magdalen Vanstone. They were the precursors of the 'New Woman' of the 1890s, when the limitations on women's role in society and in marriage became the major themes of women novelists. In the 1860s, these themes were beginning to surface, and nowhere more strongly than in the sensation novel.

CHAPTER 7:

The 'Sensation Drama'

One result of the enormous popularity of the *Colleen Bawn* at the Adelph has been the introduction of a new word into the theatrical vocabulary. A manager who brings out a piece in which the interest of the audience is visibly concentrated on one particular scene, which thus stands in strong relief to the rest of the action, boasts that he has produced a 'sensation drama', and the scene which justifies the use of this term is called a 'sensation scene'.[1]

Like the sensation novel, the sensation drama was a phenomenon of the 1860s. Melodrama was the dominant dramatic form of the Victorian age, and the sensation drama was a branch of it. *The Colleen Bawn* was to the sensation drama what *The Woman in White* was to the sensation novel. Each of these pioneering works largely defined its genre, and they were both born at the same historical moment. *The Colleen Bawn* received its London première at the Adelphi Theatre on 10 September 1860, less than three weeks after serialization of *The Woman in White* had been completed in *All The Year Round*.

To qualify as a sensation drama, a play had to contain one or more 'sensation scenes' showing some overwhelming experience, often a disaster – a fire, an earthquake, an avalanche, a shipwreck, a train crash. (Murder had always featured in melodrama of all kinds.) As the real-life versions of these phenomena were copiously reported in the press, it is clear that theatres, booksellers and cheap newspapers were catering for similar tastes. Sensation scenes were exciting in themselves, but the audience also marvelled at the technical feat involved in replicating aspects of life that seemed beyond the resources of the stage. Eventually the term 'sensation scene' referred to any lavishly mounted sequence in a melodrama which took the audience's breath away, or any scene of intense emotional upheaval.

There had always been a theatre of spectacle, but by the 1860s sophisticated new stage mechanics and elaborate three-dimensional scenery, manipulated by an army of stage hands who were readily and cheaply available, were achieving stunning effects. For years, the scene painter had been so important that in many theatres he was more likely than the dramatist to see his name on the bill, and if his efforts received enough applause, he was called to the footlights to take a bow. Now he maintained his position, despite the increased use of solid scenery rather than painted backcloths alone.

However, to make its greatest impact a sensation scene needed careful preparation. As *The Times* put it, it is 'not so easily contrived as might commonly be supposed. Not only should the scene-painter do his best, but the dramatist should so contrive his leading incident that it requires the pictorial illustration to give it completeness.'[2]

———

'The new drama of 'Uncle Tom's Cabin', being received on each representation with the acclamation and tears of crowded Audiences, will be Repeated Every Evening'. *From a playbill*[3]

As an American import, set in America, *Uncle Tom's Cabin* would not have been described as a sensation novel, even if the term had been in use a decade earlier, but the best stage adaptations might have been termed sensation dramas. They certainly contained a sensation scene, and Mrs Stowe's story made such an overwhelming impact on both page and stage that it cannot be left out of an account of Victorian sensation.

According to Charles Reade, not to read the novel was tantamount to ignoring *The Times* for a week.[4] As there was no copyright agreement with the United States, more than twenty different editions came out within a year of publication in America, at least ten in October 1852 alone; a million and a half copies were sold within 12 months in Britain and the colonies.[5] Stage productions sprang up all over the country: the theatre managers, like the publishers, did not pay Mrs Stowe a penny. Such was the hurry to get the story on to the stage that a repertory company might give the job of adapting it to one of its own members who had little or no playwriting experience: the different versions varied greatly in

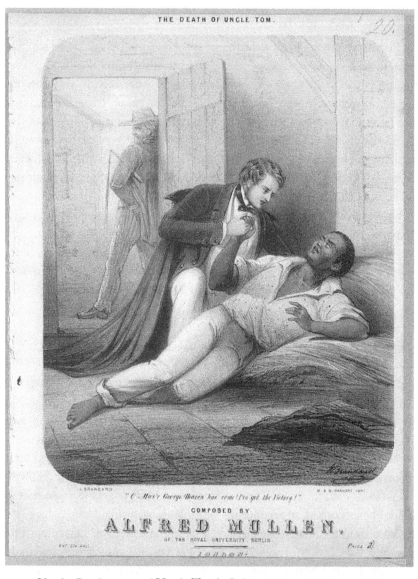

"O - Mas'r George! Heaven has come! I've got the Victory!"

COMPOSED BY

ALFRED MULLEN,

OF THE ROYAL UNIVERSITY, BERLIN.

Price 2/.

Charles Reade wrote of Uncle Tom's Cabin *that not having read the novel was like not having read* The Times *for a week. 1,500,000 copies were sold within 12 months in Britain and the colonies.*

quality. *Uncle Tom's Cabin* remained popular in the stage repertoire for the next 30 years.

Of the play's many attractions, the two greatest were the chance to see Mrs Stowe's characters in action, moving and talking, and what, ten years later, would be dubbed the sensation scene, in which the fugitive slave, Eliza, escapes with her baby over the frozen Ohio river to freedom. She is pursued by the henchmen of the wicked slave owner, and often real dogs were used in the hunt, although it was sometimes difficult to get them to show any ferocity. Audiences gasped at the might of the 'frozen river', and thrilled to the human drama of the escape, cheering Eliza when she reached safety. The slave-auction scene, in which the villain bids triumphantly for Uncle Tom, Eliza and her child, elicited howls of rage and booing while the death of Uncle Tom reduced many to tears.

In those days theatre bills were long and varied. At Christmas 1852 *Uncle Tom's Cabin* was often performed before the pantomime. Indeed, this happened at Drury Lane: the theatre usually put on Shakespeare and other classics, but it had been going through a bad patch so the management fell back on the title most likely to bring in an audience. The production was one of the many to be written and staged in haste and the author, Edward Fitzball, provided two other theatres with different versions. At the Pavilion in London's East End, *Uncle Tom's Cabin* was the pantomime, a reminder that although most adaptations were serious and theatre-goers were indignant at the treatment of American slaves, blacks were associated with broad farce, partly because of the growing popularity of the (blacked-up) minstrel show. One critic complained that at Drury Lane Uncle Tom delivered a boring sermon, which 'might have been supplemented to advantage by the bones and the banjo'.[6]

The name of Mrs Stowe's hero was used as an attraction in productions that had nothing to do with the book. Although *Uncle Tom's Crib*, a farce at the Strand Theatre, was supposedly 'suggested by the popular novel, the reading of which is now a mania among the Million',[7] Uncle Tom was the landlord of a public house at which the other black characters met. In another farce, *Those Dear Blacks*, in which an American black comes to England to find a white servant, the author pokes fun at the craze for *Uncle Tom's Cabin* in his portrayal of a crowd taking the air on a seaside pier while they were all absorbed in the book.[8]

At Astley's, the home of equestrian drama, the audience paid *Uncle Tom's Cabin* the compliment of not showing the least impatience to get on

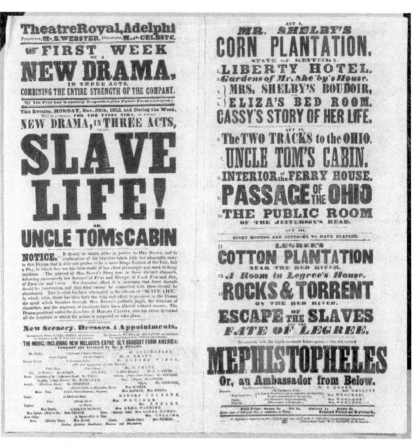

Uncle Tom's Cabin *was a popular part of the stage repertoire for 30 years, but the period of greatest excitement followed the book's publication: in London alone, there were 11 productions by the turn of 1853.*

to the pantomime. In the best traditions of the house, horses were used in the pursuit of the escaped slaves, and a runaway horse was introduced on the pretext that he, too, loved freedom. Horses appeared in other productions of the play, notably at the Royal Pavilion Circus in Brighton.[9]

In the popular production at London's Adelphi theatre, Topsy, played by an actress who 'moved spectators to unlimited admiration', was more prominent than usual, and Uncle Tom was killed with a Bowie knife. As early as December 1852 a reviewer asked 'What reader of light literature is not acquainted with the book? and what inveterate playgoer has not seen it dramatised?'[10] The best of the early London versions, however, was at the Surrey, where Uncle Tom was less prominent than George Harris and Eliza, who were the hero and heroine. Adapters changed the story as they thought fit, and at the Surrey Eliza escaped only to be returned to slavery on Simon Legree's plantation. There the wicked slave owner made an unsuccessful assault on her honour, and was about to set his dogs on her little boy when George came to the rescue. George's anti-slavery speeches 'were received with bursts of applause that proved how thoroughly an English audience are imbibed with the spirit of freedom'.[11] The political aspect was a factor in the success of both the play and the novel: the public combined a genuine sympathy for the abolitionist cause, with nationalistic pride that Britain had already outlawed slavery. Meetings calling for abolition were numerous at this time, with women especially prominent in calling on their American sisters to convert their menfolk to the cause. In 1853, Mrs Stowe visited Britain, and was given a heroine's welcome.

In some provincial cities, too, there were rival versions at different theatres. In Leeds, business was no better than tolerable at the Theatre Royal, apparently because the adaptation was weak, but two months later the production at the Princess's 'caused an unprecedented furore', and the theatre was crowded every night. In Manchester, the production at the Theatre Royal eventually did well, even though several postponements allowed the Queen's Theatre to get in first with a run of 60 nights, excellent for that time.[12]

Uncle Tom's Cabin was played late into the century, both in London and the provinces, and a number of American touring companies crossed the Atlantic with it; some included black performers. It has been calculated that as many as forty-nine troupes were travelling in America and putting on the play as late as 1879, and that the first year without a full tour there was 1930.[13]

———

Miss Braddon is fast acquiring amid the play-going public the amount of celebrity enjoyed by Mrs Beecher Stowe in the days when a theatre seemed to be scantily furnished unless it was provided with a version of *Uncle Tom*.[14]

The sensation drama and stage adaptations of sensation novels were different. Most of the latter were intended to satisfy the public's delight in seeing the characters of a popular novel on stage. Most were unsuccessful or achieved only fleeting success. The problem was that novelists had to stretch out their story to fill three printed volumes, and serialisation induced them to pile on the complications. Dramatists had to condense their story into a couple of hours.

Adaptations meant that the less exciting episodes had to be skipped. This was only a minor problem when the story of the novel was still fresh in the minds of the audience, who could fill in the gaps, but an insurmountable one later. The most successful adaptation of *Bleak House* restricted it to one strand of the plot and left out several major characters.[15] A dramatic version of *The Woman in White*, produced in the wake of the novel's publication, was almost unintelligible to those who had not read the book.[16]

However, in 1863 *Lady Audley's Secret* transferred from page to stage as successfully as *Uncle Tom's Cabin* and as the century wore on, it continued to hold audiences of the less sophisticated public spellbound. In the early days its appeal had been general: one of the first productions had run at the St James's Theatre, one of the most fashionable in London, to packed houses. All around the theatre ladies were seen explaining aspects of the plot to their menfolk, proof, if it were needed, that women were greater novel-readers than men.[17]

The two main assets of *Lady Audley's Secret* from the dramatist's point of view were a marvellous part for a leading actress and a comparatively simple plot. Only *East Lynne* matched its double achievement of creating a theatrical sensation hot on the heels of the literary one and becoming a long-term fixture in the stage repertory. *East Lynne*, too, provided the female lead with plenty of opportunity, and most adapters simplified the plot by having Lady Isabel already married when the curtain rises. It focused attention on her elopement, and the tear-jerking scenes after her return as a governess to the Carlyle home. It is one of the dramatisations, and not the novel, which contains the famous line, 'Dead, dead, and never called me Mother!'

The dramatist with a keen perception of the theatrical wants of his age, and the immense mechanical advantages which the modern theatre affords, seized boldly upon the materials afforded by contemporary life, and transplanted boldly to the stage realistic pictures of that life as it appears to our own eyes.[18]

Dion Boucicault's *The Colleen Bawn*, the first sensation drama or play, was also based on *The Collegians* by the Irish novelist, Gerald Griffin. The 'colleen bawn', or 'fair girl', of the title is Eily O'Connor, a simple Irish peasant married to a gentleman, Hardress Cregan, who has kept the marriage secret because, although he loves her, he is ashamed of her simple ways and unsophisticated language. He keeps her isolated in a remote hut, and is tempted to contract a bigamous marriage with his rich cousin, Anne Chute, to save his mother from eviction and ruin at the hands of the villain, who has a mortgage on her property.[19]

While the sensation novel was set against a familiar British background, one of the charms of *The Colleen Bawn* was the representation of beautiful Irish scenery, romantic and unfamiliar to an English audience. A far greater attraction, though, was the character Myles na-Coppaleen (Myles of the Ponies), played in the first London production, and repeatedly thereafter, by Boucicault himself. The Irish 'broth of a boy' was a stock character, but by general agreement no other example was invested with such wit and humour, such colour and warmth as it was by Boucicault, who himself was Irish, born in Dublin.

The great sensation scene, the highlight of the play, is set on a moonlit lake in Killarney. Eily appears in a rowing boat, with Danny Mann, a hunchback who is fanatically devoted to Hardress. When she refuses to give up her marriage certificate, Danny pushes her from a rock into the water, but Myles appears, shoots Danny, dives into the lake and saves Eily from drowning. While stressing that the play was too good to depend for its success on this scene alone, one playgoer mentioned the 'incidents of plunging, swimming, drowning and fishing up, of which the illusion provokes rounds of applause'.[20]

In its review of the first night, *The Times* oddly referred to the attempted drowning of Eily as 'perhaps too really horrible',[21] but later acknowledged repeatedly the thrilling impact of 'the famous header'. The scene was endlessly reproduced on playbills, and on the covers of the sheet music for *The Colleen Bawn* waltz, quadrille, galop, and other musical novelties written to cash in on the play's success. The effect was achieved not with real water, but with gauze, and a trap-door through which Eily sank before resurfacing.

The Colleen Bawn was the first play to achieve a long run of modern proportions, even though the winter of 1860–1 was severe enough to harm business at nearly all of the other London theatres. The number of consecutive performances would have been greater had Boucicault and his wife, who played Eily, not left the Adelphi from time to time for Ireland or the provinces. However, when the play reopened almost exactly a year after the first night, it was the 232nd Adelphi performance. This was all the more extraordinary because, without the advantages of modern transport, even theatres in central London had a small catchment area compared with now. A packed house honoured 'the famous header' 'with all the appearance of admiring wonder', and was as anxious about Eily as if they had not already known that she would be saved. 'Have you seen *The Colleen Bawn*? became 'one of those questions which everyone asked and which nobody cared to answer in the negative'.[22]

The play was still going strong in November 1861, when another Irish sensation drama, clearly inspired by it, took London by storm. The author, Edmund Falconer, had played Danny Mann to Boucicault's Myles. As *The Times* reported, on the first night the Lyceum Theatre 'exhibited all the signs of a decided 'sensation'. Not only were the audience more numerous than usual, but the buzz of expectation went about, which infallibly shows that something extraordinary is anticipated.'

The sensation scene did not disappoint. As with *The Colleen Bawn*, it showed the spectacular rescue of a young woman from the clutches of a would-be murderer. The scene was of a quarry only accessible via a bridge. The hero's sister has been lured down to the quarry floor by a thug engaged by the villain to end her life. While she hides from him among the rocks, he wrecks the bridge so that the floor of the quarry is cut off. He is about to club her to death when the hero appears above. How can he get down to affect a rescue? 'The precipice at his feet affords no pathway even for a skilful climber, but, maddened by excitement, he seizes the summit of a tree which has its roots at the bottom of the chasm.' He swings down into the quarry on the tree, and rescues his sister by killing her assailant, while his faithful sidekick Barney roars triumphantly from above. 'All this is admirably done, and on Saturday raised a shout of admiration that shook the theatre to its base. Such a thrilling incident, and such a specimen of scene painting are not often to be witnessed.'[23] *Peep o' Day* ran for 346 nights at the Lyceum before transferring to Drury Lane. When it was revived at the Adelphi, in 1877, the audience followed every scene with the keenest interest and 'the remarkable sensation effects were applauded vehemently'.[24]

Queen Victoria never saw *Peep o' Day*. Prince Albert's death, in December 1861, had brought her playgoing to an end. However, she had seen *The Colleen Bawn* on three occasions, the third time being her last ever visit to the theatre.[25] In the summer of 1862 Boucicault moved his production from the Adelphi to the huge stage of Drury Lane. The great exhibition of that year, the first since the one in the Crystal Palace 11 years earlier, filled London with visitors, and 'though the piece has been played in every city, folks fresh from the provinces will be curious to see how it looks in a big London house, where the gentleman who has written it subjects himself to the "header" which has contributed not a little to his fame'.[26] When Boucicault did not tour the play himself, he authorized other companies to do so, and even allowed it to be staged at Astley's – without horses. Naturally there were many parodies, like *The Colleen Drawn from a Novel Source* with Heartless Och Cregan, Miles Smugglegin and a great 'whiskey and water scene'. Even this travesty was apparently more recognisably related to the original than the straight production staged in Paris. Boucicault was unhappy with Julius Benedict's operatic version, *The Lily of Killarney*, which was first performed at Covent Garden in February 1862. Nevertheless, both opera and play were successes simultaneously.

Boucicault was a master craftsman, and he knew it. He wrote to *The Times* 'to repudiate the cant word "sensation" attributed to me' by the paper, 'and which, in truth, I was the means of bringing into use. It is a bad word, and I beg pardon for it.' This denial is about as convincing as Charles Reade's denial that he was a sensation novelist. However, the letter argues more plausibly that the success of *The Colleen Bawn* did not depend on its most famous scene, which had been introduced only after the play had already become popular in America.[27] Without it, though, *The Colleen Bawn* would not have been a Victorian sensation. As the characters are so well drawn, and the play is so well constructed, it is still possible to enjoy modern productions of the play that cannot afford spectacular Victorian stage effects.

The same could not be said for the vast majority of sensation dramas. Only a handful by Boucicault can hold the stage today. On the other hand, his dominance of the Victorian stage was brought about by quantity as well as quality. When he returned to London in 1860, after a seven-year absence, he brought with him not only *The Colleen Bawn*, but other plays unseen by British audiences which had been staged to great acclaim in New York. With the addition of new works, he had enough material to fill one or sometimes several London theatres for the next decade. Usually he had written a meaty part for himself.

Boucicault's earlier melodramatic successes, which dated from before he went to America, were still being played all over the country. His version of Alexandre Dumas' *The Corsican Brothers* had caused almost as much theatrical excitement in early 1852 as *Uncle Tom's Cabin* did later in the year. Queen Victoria saw it five times, and sometimes managers wanting to offer a special treat staged both plays in the same evening. *The Corsican Brothers* tells the story of identical twins, who are played by one actor. The twin living in Corsica has a vision of the other being killed in a duel outside Paris, then wreaks his revenge on his brother's killer. The remarkable scene of the vision was not a sensation scene before its time, because the supernatural element was the product of an earlier tradition, but it showed Boucicault's mastery of stage mechanics. Another of his early adaptations of French melodrama, *Louis XI*, about a fifteenth-century king of France, was also a public favourite.

It is only possible to refer to some of the sensation dramas which after 1860 poured forth from Boucicault's pen. In November 1861 *The Octoroon* followed *The Colleen Bawn* at the Adelphi. In its theme of American slavery, and particularly the slave-auction scene, it showed the influence of *Uncle Tom's Cabin*. But the big sensation scene, in a night of sensations, was the destruction of a steamboat by fire on the Mississippi. However, although the play made a spectacular impact, it suffered from following *The Colleen Bawn*, the hit of a lifetime, and from the different susceptibilities of British and American audiences. Zoë, the heroine, is an 'octoroon', and therefore only one-eighth black; but in the American South before the Civil War, this was enough to prevent her marrying the white man she loved, and she commits suicide at the end of the play. 'Of the blood that feeds my heart, one drop in eight is black – bright red as the rest may be, that one drop poisons all the flood; those seven bright drops give me love like yours – hope like yours . . . but the one black drop gives me despair.' However, a British audience saw no need for despair: why could not Zoë leave the Deep South and marry her lover, especially as she was played by the attractive and popular Mrs Boucicault? The enthusiastic first-night applause which greeted the curtain after each of the first four acts was not matched after the last.

A Victorian play with an unhappy ending was at a severe disadvantage, and Zoë's life was soon spared. Boucicault announced on the playbill that the new last act had been 'composed by the Public, and edited by the Author'.[28] The change underlined the fact that the motive force of sensation drama was not art but profit. It also showed that not every American sensation crossed the Atlantic successfully. When the play was revived in 1868, more changes were made, and Boucicault reverted to the part he had played in America. Instead of Salem Scudder, a gentlemanly Southerner, he became once again the Comanche Indian who conceives a terrible hatred for the villain, hunts him down through a Louisiana swamp, and kills him after a tremendous fight. His only dialogue consisted of a few ejaculations, allegedly in one of the Indian languages, 'but Mr Boucicault has shown a singular feeling for the picturesque, and all the bodily movements supposed to be characteristic of the red man are executed with the nicest accuracy'.[29]

The sensation scenes of *The Trial of Effie Deans*, based on Sir Walter Scott's *Heart of Midlothian*, included a mob breaking open a prison, and an incident that does not feature in the novel, in which Meg Murdockson kills her own daughter, the insane Madge Wildfire, because Madge has swapped cloaks with Jeannie Deans, the intended victim. The play was staged in January 1863, at the same time as the first productions of *Lady Audley's Secret* and *Aurora Floyd*. Boucicault not only directed and acted in his own work but produced it at Astley's, which he had taken over and converted into a conventional theatre. He was praised for his skill in making intelligible the story of a 55-year-old novel whose plot ordinary playgoers could no longer be expected to remember. He did this by not following the original too closely, unlike the rival adapter of Scott's work at the Surrey. In the Surrey's great sensation scene, Jeannie escaped from Meg over a huge cataract of real water. However, the Surrey could not match Boucicault's trial scene: he had built up the role of the defence lawyer as a star part for himself. He was the supreme theatre craftsman, who always won in a direct comparison.

In the following year came *The Streets of London*, which had begun life in America as *The Streets of New York*, and was first produced in England as *The Streets of Liverpool*. It was an ingenious idea to change the title and the sets of the play in line with the city in which it was being performed: audiences liked elaborate stage sets that represented places they knew well, and those who gathered at the Princess's Theatre in Oxford Street for *The Streets of London* were treated to a section of Charing Cross and Trafalgar Square, complete with street singers, and sellers of baked-potatoes, playbills and matches. One of the play's many revivals was staged in 1877 at the Adelphi, not a hundred yards from where this scene was set.

Packed houses greeted it rapturously, and it was described as 'one of the most effective set scenes ever witnessed, even on the Adelphi stage. The illuminated windows of the distant houses, the passage of vehicles from street to street, and the variety of characters crossing and recrossing made altogether one of the most realistic pictures imaginable.'[30] (In New York the equivalent scene had shown Union Square.) The great sensation scene was of a house on fire across the whole width of the stage, with firemen scaling ladders and a real fire engine. *The Times* referred to 'the best burnt house ever destroyed on stage'.[31]

Arrah-na-Pogue (Arrah of the Kiss), first produced in London in 1865, shared with *The Colleen Bawn* some beautiful Irish scenery and a lovable Irish scallywag played by Boucicault. Later generations of Irishmen, not least Bernard Shaw who admired his work, accused him of offering the English an Irish stereotype which confirmed their prejudices. However, at the play's first night in Dublin when 'he came lumbering on in the heavy-caped coat of the Irish carman with his whip hung over his shoulder, he was received with peal after peal of applause, which it seemed would never end'.[32] The play was rewritten for London, the first city to witness the scene in which Shaun the Post (Boucicault's character) escaped from prison by getting out of a window and climbing up the ivy-covered tower by the sea in which he was confined. Special stage machinery brought about a change from the inside to the outside of the prison, and lowered the tower as the actor climbed, so that it looked as if he was ascending an immense height.[33] A controversial aspect of the play was the song 'The Wearing of the Green', an old Dublin street ballad with new words reflecting Irish resentment of British rule: 'Then since the colour we must wear is England's cruel red,/ Sure Ireland's sons will ne'er forget the blood that they have shed.' A revival in 1867, starring the Boucicaults, coincided with the Fenian bomb explosion at Clerkenwell prison, and the song was banned throughout the British Empire.[34]

The Long Strike of 1866 was produced by Boucicault under the management of Charles Fechter, another dominant figure in the London theatre. Fechter, who began his acting career in France, had caused a sensation when he crossed the Channel in 1860 to act in English for the first time. He had starred in the original French production of *The Corsican Brothers*, which he later played in English, and had been the first French Armand Duval in *The Lady with the Camellias*. He was considered a thrilling actor, and English audiences did not object to his accent, even when he played Hamlet. His management of the Lyceum Theatre attracted enormous interest, and he paid the Boucicaults a compliment in giving over his stage to them for a production in which he did not appear.

Charles Dickens, a friend of Fechter, was a great admirer of *The Long Strike*, and even involved himself in the production. The play is set in Lancashire, and its heroine is Jane, a working class girl, who loves a young man from the same background as herself, but is chased by a capitalist. She faces an agonising situation when her sweetheart is accused of the capitalist's murder, which, she knows, has been committed by her father. This was clearly inspired by Mrs Gaskell's novel of northern industrial life *Mary Barton*, but Mrs Gaskell could not have conceived of the small but highly effective part written by Boucicault for himself – that of the hero's friend, an Irish sailor. Moreover, the great sensation scene was entirely up to date.

To establish the hero's alibi, it is essential to contact the sailor, but he has gone to Liverpool and his ship is about to sail. A friendly lawyer takes Jane to a telegraph office, 'an instance of the great effect which a bit of closely copied reality has upon a modern audience. The stage becomes for the nonce an actual telegraph office, with its clerks employed like real clerks, and its dials working with the correct click.' The audience watch spellbound, only to learn that there is no reply from Liverpool because the telegraph operator has gone home. Eventually, however, a click is heard; unexpectedly the man has returned. But the message is that the Irish sailor's ship has sailed. Despair again. No! The lawyer pays for a pilot-boat to overtake her, and all is well. 'The rise and fall of these difficulties, accompanied by the minutiae of telegraphic correspondence, raises the audience to a high pitch of excitement, and there is no doubt that this scene will be considered the great attraction of the piece.'[35] It was, and it stayed in the memory, although *The Long Strike* did not have the run pre- dicted for it: after a month the mercurial Boucicault and his wife, who played Jane, left the cast.

Presumably he was busy with his next play, which opened the Holborn Theatre the following month, although he did not act in it. The epony- mous hero of *Flying Scud* is a racehorse who must win the Derby if villainy is to be confounded and virtue to triumph. As the race is about to start, Flying Scud's jockey falls off because the villains have given him drugged brandy. However, in the best showbusiness traditions, the hero- ine's grandfather, a veteran jockey is at hand to grab the jockey's colours, mount the horse and start the race, which takes place at the back of the stage with cardboard horses. Naturally, Flying Scud is the winner, and the old jockey leads on a real horse to accept the cheers of the audience. On the first night, 'They watched the progress of the mimic race with an anxiety that could scarcely have been surpassed if every one of them had actually put his money on Flying Scud. The shout from pit, boxes and gallery that greeted the old jockey when he came forward as the victor expressed not only violent approbation but a strong sense of relief.' At least one critic thought the sensation scene of *Flying Scud* less successful than those in *The Streets of London* and *The Long Strike*: the painted figures at the back of the crowd – a common dodge in Victorian crowd scenes – did not harmonise with the performers in the foreground.[36]

On the other hand, the spectacle of the Derby aroused an enthusiasm among Victorians which is scarcely imaginable now: until 1892 Parliament adjourned for the day so that Members could watch the race. *Derby Day*, 'Mr Frith's celebrated picture' on which much of the staging was based, had been an artistic sensation when first shown only eight years earlier. The play's run of more than two hundred performances demonstrated once again Boucicault's extraordinary ability to give the public what it wanted. It also inaugurated a new genre, the racing melodrama, which was popular into the twentieth century.

Two years later in *After Dark*, Boucicault staged the most famous of all sensation scenes, in which a character lies helpless on a railway line at the mercy of an oncoming train. 'The whistle of the locomotive is heard, and the destruction of the prostrate man seems inevitable; but he is perceived and snatched up at the right moment . . . and then the train sweeps across the stage, raising the audience to a perfect fervour of excitement.'[37] It did not matter that it was not Boucicault's idea, and had been done before: it was new to the West End of London, it had never been done as well, and Boucicault, up-to-date as ever, added another twist by making the railway on which the dramatic scene is enacted the Metropolitan line of the Underground, the first in the world and opened only five years earlier.[38]

After Dark ran from August 1868 to May 1869, with no break for a Christmas pantomime – a sign of exceptional popularity. The great sensation scene alone would probably have been enough to bring this about, especially as railways were very much in the news. A week after the play opened, the Chester–Holyhead express hit two wagons containing

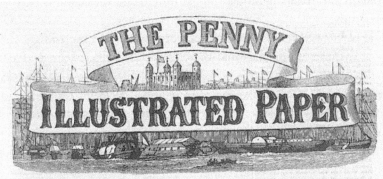

REGISTERED AT THE GENERAL POST OFFICE FOR TRANSMISSION ABROAD.

No. 360.   LONDON, SATURDAY, AUGUST 22, 1868.   Vol. XV.

SCENE FROM MR. BOUCICAULT'S NEW DRAMA OF LONDON LIFE, "AFTER DARK," AT THE PRINCESS'S THEATRE:
THE RESCUE ON THE UNDERGROUND RAILWAY.—SEE PAGE 118.

In the most famous of all sensation scenes, Boucicault's After Dark
*involved the rescue of a character from an oncoming train. In a
contemporary touch Boucicault set the scene on the newly-opened
Metropolitan line of the London Underground.*

petroleum and reducing 33 passengers were reduced to cinders within a few seconds.

The play contained other backdrops of London life, including a close copy of Victoria station and what Boucicault called 'Blackfriars Bridge on crutches' – the bridge was being rebuilt at the time. *After Dark* and *The Streets of London* are the two plays in which Boucicault explored most extensively one of the great themes of Victorian melodrama: London as the most sinful as well as the greatest city in the world.

Such was the fascination with London that such scenes could also be used in the provinces, despite the nationwide taste for familiar locales. A *Times* critic claimed that scenery was also shipped off to Paris and New York, 'the pre-eminence of the English in the art of stage decoration being admitted all over the civilized world'. The remark was made within a few weeks of *After Dark* opening, in a review of *Land Rats and Water Rats* at the Surrey Theatre. The title refers to two types of London criminal operating on the streets and on the river. Here Hetty, a Covent Garden flower girl, was stretched across a railway line in front of an oncoming train. It was thought that to have a woman rather than a man in this situation provided an extra frisson, and that the show had an advantage over *After Dark* in that the scene was kept until the end of the play. In fact when the curtain fell the audience did not know quite what had happened to Hetty. However, in obedience to a tumultuous clamour it rose again to show her in the arms of her doting husband with her father, who had disapproved of the match, looking on benignly. *The Times* critic asked whether the story would have been left incomplete if the audience had not reacted with such enthusiasm, then answered his own question: that a lesser response to such an exciting scene would have been impossible.[39]

In 1869, Boucicault's *Formosa, or the Road to Ruin* created a sensation, even if, by the strictest definition, it was a lavishly staged melodrama rather than a sensation play. Formosa is the *nom de guerre* of a high-class tart, or, as *The Times* put it, 'one of those meteoric beauties, who frequently change their name, inhabit superb villas and whose public scene of action is Rotten Row' where they picked up their rich and fashionable clients. She had the hero in her toils, and the outcry was not only against the character but against her appearance at Drury Lane, for so long the shrine of English drama. The moralists should not have worried: just as she is indulging in a wicked triumph over her rival, her parents appear and 'she is stricken to the earth with shame and contrition'. Boucicault welcomed the controversy, of course, and allegedly stirred up and extended it by writing anonymous letters attacking himself whenever interest flagged. He shared £12,000 with the theatre manager from the run of 117 nights.[40]

Love of scandal was one obvious reason for the play's success, but the stage resources of Drury Lane also played a part. Formosa's villa on the Thames at Fulham was awesomely lovely, and its luxury needled the puritans. Also, Boucicault presented another great spectacle of Victorian sport: the university boat race. This was sure to bring in the crowds, even though, like the Derby Day scene in *Flying Scud*, the beautiful view of the Thames from the foot of Barnes bridge left room for improvement on the first night: the weaknesses were in the painted crowd and 'the profile boats by which the race is performed'.

After 1870, Boucicault came up with just one more new sensation, *The Shaughraun*. It was the third in his trilogy of Irish dramas. Some consider it his best, but the main sensation scene, although spectacularly staged, was only a clever variation of the escape from prison offered in *Arrah-na-Pogue*. There is also a boisterous Irish wake in which the corpse, a lovable Irish rogue played, of course, by Boucicault, suddenly springs to life. One of the most interesting features of the play was that the pro-Fenian characters were presented sympathetically but in such a way that English audiences were not antagonized. The villains are Irish spies and sycophants, living off the British government in Ireland.

Many thought that Boucicault went too far in the new year of 1876 in writing an open letter to the Prime Minister, Disraeli, demanding the release of Irish political prisoners. His assumption that enthusiasm for *The Shaughraun* reflected support for Irish nationalism was not widely shared, and certainly not by Disraeli, who ignored the letter. Also, he was unwise to boast that the Prince and Princess of Wales had been to see the play: they were hardly likely to support the release of Irish rebels. A writer to the *Era* sneered, '*The Shaughraun* could not be launched in England without an outburst of Irish enthusiasm, and so came about that marvellous letter to Lord Beaconsfield [as Disraeli had become] demanding the release of the political prisoners which served to advertise the new drama, and was promptly put behind the fire by the Prime Minister.'[41] The letter was published during a row Boucicault had provoked: he had contributed an article to an American magazine on the decline of the drama, for which he partly blamed the press. Many held Boucicault responsible, however, and attacked the lack of literary ambition in his plays. According to another of the *Era*'s correspondents,

> Mr Boucicault, the high priest of sensationalism, has contributed more to the Decline of the Drama than all the critics and newspapers in the world. His runaway engines, steamboats, revolving towers, horse and boat races, &c have much to answer for. In the imitation of him others have dragged into their plays diving bells, balloons, circular saws, steam forge hammers, pile drivers, windmills and heavens knows what besides.'[42]

So, 'sensational' could be applied to plays – novels and newspaper stories too – in a derogatory sense. However, earlier that year a theatre critic had attacked the use of the word to damn the artistic quality of Boucicault's works, arguing that their exploitation of modern stage machinery did not make them inferior, and that in every art a minority sneered at popular taste.[43]

Other sensation dramatists owed much to Boucicault, but Charles Reade owed less than most, despite the collaboration over *Foul Play*. Reade's *It's Never Too Late To Mend*, which opened at the Princess's Theatre in October 1865, was derived from his own bestselling novel of the same title, which had been published in the previous decade. Unlike Boucicault, Reade was a social reformer: *It's Never Too Late To Mend*, *Hard Cash* and *Foul Play* were driven by the same reforming zeal. Reade's creative method, which involved accumulating a great mass of documentary evidence on which to base his novels and plays, owed nothing to Boucicault, but was avowedly influenced by Mrs Stowe and *Uncle Tom's Cabin*.[44]

Reade was determined to expose the cruelty of prison life. The second act of *It's Never Too Late To Mend* shows, with brutal realism, the physical maltreatment of a young boy by sadistic prison staff, and his death when he is on the point of hanging himself. The scene has been compared with the sequences in *Uncle Tom's Cabin* involving the brutal slave owner, Simon Legree.[45] On the first night the actress in the part of the boy was said to have fainted because the prison warders were over-vigorous. Certainly, her shrieks were so heartrending and natural that a thrill of horror went round the house. However, the first night became notorious because the venerable drama critic of the *Morning Advertiser* rose from his seat in the stalls to voice his disgust. Sensation! The actor-manager, who was playing the hero, made matters worse. He advanced to the footlights and, in the course of an excited defence of the play, told the critics that they should behave more circumspectly because they were guests of the theatre who had not paid for their tickets. Journalists never like to be reminded of such things and, after furious shouts of 'Apologise!' he did just that.[46]

The *Times* critic expressed his distaste in both the brevity of his review and its content. The act showing the interior of the prison, complete with treadmill, was 'exceedingly revolting to the more refined part of the audience'. The play was magnificently staged, but 'it would be folly to commend a piece, the second act of which is almost as repulsive as an accurate representation of the tortures of the Spanish Inquisition'. Even if what was shown was true, he argued, it was not a good enough reason for showing it.[47] This was the kind of squeamishness displayed twenty years later by those readers of the *Pall Mall Gazette* who had not liked Stead's exposure of child prostitution. Henry Morley, in his *Journal of a London Playgoer* observed that the manager had 'spent his chief energies in the way of scenic effect' on this scene, 'a perspective of radiating prison corridors seen from the centre of a model prison, with practicable tiers of galleries, and iron staircases, and cells, and gas-lights'; however, the scene was a 'repulsive excrescence, which does not advance the story by a syllable'.[48] As well as the torture and death of the boy, who had been imprisoned for committing a minor theft when he was near starvation, it also contained a tremendous fight between the hero and the brutal warders. Needless to say, this all ensured that the play was immensely popular.

Reade's collaboration with Boucicault over *Foul Play* inevitably involved a drama as well as a novel. It was, according to *The Times*, a 'decided and deserved success'.[48] The most sensational scene involved the mate of the scuttled ship, Wylie, after his return to England. At the wicked shipowner Wardlaw's behest he has carried out the scuttling, but he gives up his villainy for love of his sweetheart Nancy. However, he has hidden the gold, which is supposed to have been lost at sea, in a house next door to Nancy's, and he announces his return melodramatically by stretching his hand down the chimney of the room in which she is sitting. This is a bad move as the detective in pursuit of Wylie handcuffs the two lovers together. They make a sensational escape by bringing down a large part of the room in a shower of lath and plaster. In another dramatic scene Wylie is locked up in a cellar by the dastardly Wardlaw and left to die of starvation, until the detective rescues him.

Nine years later, Reade rewrote the play, and called it *The Scuttled Ship*. The programme proclaimed that the original novel 'presents many thrilling incidents of Love, Adventure, Crime and Retribution. It also deals with those abuses of Maritime Insurance, which have since been so fully exposed by the patriotic efforts of MR SAMUEL PLIMSOLL M. P.'. The reviews are mainly interesting for their revelation of how a young man and woman of the period would be dressed – or undressed – when marooned on a desert island. According to one account, the heroine disported herself 'in costumes gorgeous enough for Scarborough, and silk stockings of lovely hues which might be the envy of Ryde Pier'.[50]

The production of *The Scuttled Ship* in May 1877 began a remarkable season of sensation at London's Olympic theatre – and as *The Shaughraun*, *East Lynne*, *After Dark*, *The Streets of London*, *The Colleen Bawn* and *Aurora Floyd* were all playing in London at the same time, it is clear that sensation was still very much alive. *The Scuttled Ship* was followed by *Lady Audley's Secret*, then Wilkie Collins' own dramatization of *The Moonstone*, and a revival of a stage version of Miss Braddon's *Henry Dunbar*.

The production of *The Moonstone* demonstrated again the difficulty in adapting sensation novels for the stage. In the very first act, Rachel Verinder sees Franklin Blake, walking in his sleep, go to the cabinet in her room, and take the jewel. Her cry of 'My God, a thief' is an effective curtain line, but there is no longer a mystery. There is also an effective ending to the second act when Rachel has found Franklin's dressing gown and is about to remove the tell-tale stain. Sergeant Cuff comes in, with Franklin, and asks, 'Whose dressing gown is that?' 'Mine,' cries Franklin, and the curtain falls. Another gripping scene comes in Act Three, when Franklin confronts Rachel and demands that she explain why she has treated him so coldly. When she exclaims, 'You villain! I saw *you* steal the Moonstone,' he falls senseless to the ground. However, an inept piece of writing broke the tension by making Rachel take up a tract, left behind by the tedious Miss Clack, and read out the title: 'Soft Soap by a Converted Laundress'.[51] The play ran for only 54 nights, no more than respectable at this period.

Henry Dunbar worked better, although it was no *Lady Audley's Secret.* The heroine, Margaret, began life as another of the sensation novel's strong women. On stage too, she relentlessly pursues the man whom she believes to have murdered her father, but when she comes face to face with him, it is her father she sees: he is the murderer and has been posing as his victim. She changes sides and works to shield her father from the law. The sensational moment of recognition, as played in the original production of 1865, was marred by too much dialogue. As *The Times* reviewer pointed out, a shriek and a few words before the curtain fell would have been enough. Unfortunately, Margaret was allowed to recover from her shock and deliver a long speech on the difference between repentance and remorse.[52] This does not seem to have drawn comment at the Olympic production, so perhaps the text had been pared down. Henry Neville, usually a romantic hero, received special praise for his playing of the murderer. He was especially commended for the scenes where 'tremblingly he acknowledges that his victim seems ever with him, staring at him with glaring eyes, and where, his daughter having effected her purpose, he stands cowering and conscience-stricken before her; and finally for the terrible realism of the death scene'.[53] In the novel the character does not die, but this change was almost forced on the adapter: on the Victorian stage a murderer could not be allowed to live, however sympathetic his daughter.

Two years later Charles Reade recorded his greatest triumph in the theatre with *Drink,* based on Émile Zola's *L'Assommoir.* It opened on 2 June 1879, and was not even overshadowed by Sarah Bernhardt's sensational London début the same night. The sophisticated few knew that the novel had created a furore in France with its brutally realistic depiction of Parisian working-class life, and that the dramatization had been playing to crowded houses in Paris for the past six months. However, the vast majority knew nothing of this, and certainly had not read the novel. The attraction lay in three sensational scenes.

The first was a fight in a public wash-house between the heroine, Gervaise, and her arch-enemy, Virginie. A fight between two women was a daring innovation, and soon copied by other dramatists. Several women were shown with their arms plunged into washtubs, apparently scrubbing real linen with real soap. The combatants hurled pails of real water at each other, and the audience roared with delight when the wicked Virginie was drenched. On the first night they called for the actresses at the end of the scene – as still happens in opera today – but it was explained that they had been told to hurry back to their dressing rooms to get dry.

The turning point of the play comes in what could be called the sensation scene proper, when Gervaise's husband, Coupeau, who is repairing a roof, falls dramatically from the scaffolding on which he is perched, 'putting into the shade some of the "sensations" of other days'. It was so tremendous that even spectators who knew how dummies were used in the theatre believed that they had seen the actor crash to the ground. In fact, a dummy had been placed out of sight: the actor screamed, disappeared behind a chimney and the dummy hurtled down. Then the curtain descended for a few seconds, during which the actor slid down a ladder and took his place on the ground while the dummy was removed. It had been made to the actor's measurements, wore exact replicas of his wig and costume, and a mask created from a plaster cast of his face by the famous wig-maker, Willie Clarkson.

In the third great sensation scene, Coupeau died in a fit of delirium tremens. Horrific scenes of drunkenness were nothing new on the Victorian stage, but this one 'made men and women gasp and want to get away,' and it made a star of the actor, Charles Warner, who had recently been playing the hero in *It's Never Too Late To Mend*. For a few years, Reade's drama and *Drink* were the only two productions, apart from pantomimes, that could fill every seat of the vast Standard Theatre in Shoreditch.[54]

Drink did not offer Zola 'neat': that would not have been to the taste of the public and, in any case, the censor would have stepped in. Adapting from the French went hand in hand with bowdlerization. In Reade's play, Gervaise had a husband before she married Coupeau, not a lover as in the original. Moreover, far from descending into drink herself, she takes brandy only once. Nor does she die of despair: she is given hope by the love of the temperance campaigner, Goujet. Some found his speeches tedious, but their anti-alcohol message drew people to the theatre who would otherwise have stayed away. However, it did not escape notice that, whenever the play was staged, the theatre bars did especially good business, and the manager of the first production was criticized for allowing beer to be drunk in the gallery. There was a song, which went:

> You've read of a piece by Charles Reade that's called *Drink*,
> You can go nap on that.

It teaches us all from the liquor to shrink
> You can go nap on that.
And yet on the night when I'd seen *L'Assommoir*,
I sought the saloon that's above the first floor,
And never have seen it so crowded before,
> And you can go nap on that.[55]

The number of parodies and music hall impersonations of Warner were further tributes to the play's popularity, which was helped by heavy poster advertising. *The Saturday Review* singled out *Drink* in an article on 'The Horrors of Street Advertisements': 'On every empty wall the drunken plumber, or whatever he was, is falling headlong from the housetop, and the washerwomen are tossing Mr Reade's second-hand soapsuds in each other's faces.' The writer deplored the omnipresence of the street poster, and complained 'No one can avoid it; it cries as loud as bad colour, bad drawing and bad taste can cry.'[56] It was no use complaining: by the late 1870s, the street poster was a permanent fixture in the modern world.

Drink, like *It's Never Too Late To Mend*, was first produced at the Princess's Theatre in Oxford Street, where many of Boucicault's plays were revived. While provincial theatres wanted any kind of London hit, London houses specialized: many theatres would not touch sensation drama, but the Adelphi, the Lyceum and the Olympic relied on it for long periods. South of the river, the main centres of sensation were the Surrey and – until the high-minded Emma Cons took over – the Victoria; in the East End, it was the Standard and the Pavilion.

Most plays staged at these theatres were ephemeral, but some contained scenes that were long remembered. At the Surrey, in *Ashore and Afloat*, the villain left the heroine stranded down a mine. Excitement reached fever pitch when the hero came down in the basket that the villain had raised to the surface, took in the swooning girl, and was bringing her up to safety – when a falling beam brought them to a halt. At the same time the mine was filling with water. The resourceful hero cut a cord, let the basket fall, climbed up the rope with the girl in his arms, and was reaching the surface when the curtain fell. *The Times* predicted correctly that people would talk about this scene 'when the intricacies of the plot have faded from the memory'.[57]

The great sensation scene in *The Orange Girl*, at the same theatre, showed a frozen tarn, skirted by craggy rocks. The heroine had agreed to meet one of the villains there, but, 'oppressed by care and terror' as she crossed the ice, disappeared through a hole he had dug and then covered up. Almost immediately her aunt, looking for her, was seen on the crags above. She dashed down and also disappeared through the ice, with a tremendous crash, but swam to the spot where her niece had vanished and rescued her. The villain produced a gun and was about to shoot them, when the arrival of some travellers saved the day. *The Times* commented that 'As a means of producing a "sensation", the scene of the frozen tarn has perhaps never been excelled,' and commended another scene in which the villain and the hero were handcuffed together as prisoners in the Portland convict settlement. The hero dragged his rival up a mass of rock and was about to jump into the sea with him, when the police intervened. This, *The Times* said, produced a new sensation in an audience that had already been kept 'in a state of strong emotion'.[58]

This last scene was taken a step further 13 years later at the Victoria, a neighbour and rival of the Surrey. *In The Wearing of the Green, or The Lover's Leap* – title and subject reflect Boucicault's influence – Talbot O'Moore was a captain both in the British army and, apparently, of the Irish Whiteboy rebels. The man who informed against him lured the heroine to the 'lover's leap'. O'Moore 'seizes him by the collar, drags him step by step to the top of a rock, and the excitement of the spectators reaches a climax when he hurls the miserable little wretch into the foaming waters below'.[59]

At the Standard, the otherwise forgettable *Humanity, or A Passage in the Life of Grace Darling* contained a fight in which every available object was used as a weapon, a staircase collapsed and both combatants were killed. 'It seems almost too real for the stage, and we venture to say that nothing more exciting has been witnessed behind the footlights in the history of terrific stage struggles ... When that staircase falls with a crash and leaves the villains struggling upon the floor, each seeking the life of the other, the effect is nothing short of thrilling.' In fact, the staircase was really being lowered from the side of the stage with invisible wires. The author admitted freely that the scene had been inspired by the Northumberland Street Affair.[60] It was so popular that it eventually acquired a life of its own as a music-hall sketch.

In *The Ruling Passion*, also first staged at the Standard, the sensation scene involved a balloon ascent from the Crystal Palace. After its guy-lines were cut, the huge balloon was seen floating through the air with a female lunatic on board. She had bitten the fingers of the balloonist who had been hanging on to the basket to stop it taking off. Eventually the balloon seemed to be falling into the sea, but as it crumpled and the basket seemed to be sinking, a lifeboat manned by eight men came dashing across the water just in time to effect a rescue.[61]

Woman and Wine, first produced at the Pavilion, featured a sensational stage fight between two women, much more brutal than the one in *Drink* nearly twenty years earlier. The reviewer of the *Era* asked his readers what they thought of the spectacle of 'a couple of demi-mondaines, who, with tiger-like audacity, stripping off their dresses, fight a duel with butcher's knives'. Whatever his readers thought, audiences in the working-class districts of London and in the provinces loved it. The *Era* referred to the play's 'Zola-like realism', and concluded reluctantly that it would be popular with the masses. The fight, at dawn in the Paris flower market, was between two rivals in love, and ended with the loser stabbed to death. It was made even more dramatic, and more distasteful, by a ghoulish man looking on, who took obvious delight in the violence, and even sharpened the knives for the women.[62]

To the more fastidious here was an example of nineties' decadence – such a play was never offered to West End audiences. However, if they did not like sadism, they enjoyed sensation. During the last 20 years of the Victorian era, the middle classes flocked to Drury Lane, where they were offered melodrama as sensational as *Women and Wine*, but without the coarseness.

The man responsible was Augustus Harris, who took over Drury Lane in 1879, the year of the triumphant first production of *Drink*. Acutely aware that Shakespeare and intellectual drama lost money, he spent huge sums on spectacle, for both the annual melodrama and the Christmas pantomime, which between them held the stage for most of the year. Every scene in a Harris production was lavishly mounted, except those played in front of a backdrop whose main purpose was to distract the audience's attention while the scene shifters were busy. Hordes of extras filled battle scenes, race meetings and society balls. The characters lived in mansions, palaces and other luxurious surroundings. Critics often described this scenic splendour as 'sensationalism', but in the 1860s sense this could only be applied to certain scenes, which were admittedly plentiful in Harris melodramas.

For example, *Pluck* of 1882, which was billed as 'a new sensational and domestic drama', featured a double railway accident. An accomplice of the villain damages the line and knocks out Jack, the hero, as he tries to repair it. The train crashes, with the villain and the detective who has him under arrest on board; the villain escapes; Jack comes to, and rescues Ellen, one of the heroines, from the wreck. Then:

> *Ellen*: My child, my child is in the carriage.
> *Guard*: Here's the down train coming, and it must smash into us. Stand aside, everyone, for your lives!
> *Ellen* (screams): My child – my child! For God's sake, save my child!
> (*During all this, people are being carried out of carriages.*)
> *Guard*: Too late, it is certain death!
> (*Business. Increasing noise of train approaching and blowing whistle. The train enters and dashes into the other one as Jack rushes from the carriage, and throws the child into Ellen's arms.*)
> (Second crash) Grand Tableau![63]

In fact, the property trains were not impressive enough to make the scene as dramatic as it is written, and one critic claimed that *Pluck* was 'one of the worst plays of its kind which has ever been placed on the stage of a West-End London theatre'.[64] This does not seem to have worried Harris, who was its part-author and himself played Jack. He had given himself some spirited lines for the scene in which a mob bays for the blood of a Jewish banker whose bank has failed. In reply to cries of 'Down with the Jew!' Harris, who was Jewish, shouted in the role of Jack, 'And what if he be a Jew? He's a man as well! Whose names are foremost in every good and noble cause? The Jews – the Jews who handed down to you the grand sacred book you put into your children's hands to guide their hearts and minds to truth and right.'[65]

Harris soon gave up acting, but continued with co-authorship, and the following year he helped concoct *A Sailor and His Lass*, in which a London street is blown up and a ship scuttled. G A Sala clearly had him in mind when he wrote that same year that 'these 'sensational and domestic dramas' of London life' were becoming played out. He claimed that the public were growing tired of 'stage houses on fire, explosions, railway disasters, shipwrecks, lodging-house cellars, steamboat collisions, and struggles between assassins and their victims'.[66] The record of Drury Lane over the next 30 years proved him wrong.

In 1886, Harris staged his first racing drama, in which Goodwood was lovingly created on stage, and eventually plays featuring the Derby and the Grand National. They were all 'out of' Boucicault's *Flying Scud*. *The Derby Winner* of 1894 even repeated Boucicault's idea of the drugged jockey who has to be replaced at the last moment. Unfortunately, on the first night the stage machinery did not work properly, and Harris had to appear before the curtain to assure the audience, on his honour, that the right horse had won.[67]

Reviewing *The White Heather* of 1897, *The Times* commented that there were 'four or five scenes which may each be called a triumph of sensationalism', among which it mentioned the interior of the Stock Exchange, where a member falls dead from the shock of being 'hammered', Battersea Park at the height of the bicycle craze, and a fancy-dress ball. However, in Boucicault's sense there was one great sensation scene: a fight to the death between two deep-sea divers at the bottom of the sea, armed with knives. 'In all our experience of the sensationalism of Drury Lane and the Adelphi we do not recall a more effective scene than this.'[68] The illusion of being under water was perfect, down to the fish and the absolute silence in which the fight was carried on. Eventually the villain was killed when his antagonist cut his air-tube, and he was asphyxiated.

Harris died in 1897, but his successor, Arthur Collins, kept to the same policy, as the autumn drama of 1898 showed. This was *The Great Ruby*, in which the big sensation scene featured a fight in the sky. Thieves steal the ruby, but a sleep-walker removes it from its place of safety, in a scene surely inspired by *The Moonstone*. Later, an amateur balloonist makes off with the stone by mistake. His balloon is stationed on Hampstead Heath where the gang arrive, along with a young Indian prince who is in love with a woman in league with them. The prince reaches the balloon, gets into the basket, touches a lever and ascends into the air. One of the thieves is clinging to the basket, and the two men fight as, by means of a moving backcloth of clouds, the balloon is shown sailing further and further up into the heavens. The prince beats the thief off from the balloon, hurling him to his death.

The balloon scene provided a special talking point. The British public in 1898 knew of only one Indian prince: Kumar Shri Ranjitsinhji was the most famous Indian of his day and the first non-European international sports star. Few who watched him bat for Sussex and England had ever seen another Indian. 'Ranji' had secured a place in history two years earlier with 62 and 154 not out against the Australians in his first test. He had just toured Australia with the England team. And the Indian prince in *The Great Ruby* was portrayed as a brilliant cricketer.

The problem was that he was also portrayed as a killer. The journalists dared not mention Ranji for fear of being accused of libel. According to one paper, 'The authors could have had no idea of the suggestion they were conveying to ninety-nine people in every hundred in making the Indian prince a popular cricketer, or they would surely have omitted cricket from the accomplishments of the native Indian Prince, educated at an English university [as Ranji had been], who becomes a thief and a murderer.'[69]

In fact, the prince was quite a sympathetic character, and was given one of the few interesting speeches ever uttered in late-Victorian Drury Lane melodrama in which dialogue was notoriously subordinate to scenery, costumes and stage effects. He moans that the India Office has advised him to go home, and explains,

> Now it has thoroughly unfitted me to go there – now it has taught me that all men of my blood are a subject race, that their gods are idols, that their country is a hell, while my heaven is Piccadilly - now that I am as much an alien there as here. Conquer us as you have – rule us as you will, but let it be like men, don't make us a mockery of ourselves, don't make more what you've made me – neither good white, nor bad black, a monument of Piebald Patriotism and Educated Native.'[70]

The great sensation scene of 1899 in *Hearts Are Trumps* was an avalanche, which killed the villain but fortunately not the heroine. Boucicault had included an avalanche in *Pauvrette* more than thirty years earlier. In 1900, the last year of Victoria's reign, the Drury Lane melodrama was *The Price of Peace*. Its plot was not only improbable but so brazenly so that it constituted a sensation in itself. According to one paper, the audacity with which it challenged conventional morality was worthy of Balzac. However, Balzac would not have had a British prime minister, in the presence of two other cabinet ministers, shoot dead a Russian spy because his knowledge of vital state secrets threatened the lives of 5,000 British soldiers.[71] Nor, presumably, would Balzac have had the prime minister drop dead of a heart attack in the House of Commons after making a speech defending what he had done. There were more conventional sensation scenes, too, including one in which a yacht was struck by a steamer and sunk, and the villain was drowned after a terrific fight with a revengeful Chinaman. Like its predecessors, *The Prince of Peace* was panned by the critics, but brought in the crowds, not only at Drury Lane but also on tour.

At the very end of the Victorian era, the British public had lost none of its taste for sensation in the theatre, and found it in plentiful supply. After all, it made a lot of money. Drury Lane melodrama continued until the First World War, and even briefly after it, but by that time no sensation scene could compete with the cinema in achieving spectacular effects.

CHAPTER 8:

Stars of Entertainment

I freely confess that what success I have had in my life may fairly be attributed more to the public press than to nearly all other causes combined. There *may* possibly be occupations that do not require advertising, but I cannot well conceive what they are. *P T Barnum*[1]

Of course, there was a simpler way to cause a sensation in the entertainment world than by staging an avalanche, an underwater fight between divers or a race meeting: find a big star. One of the definitions of a 'sensation', after all, is 'an event or person which creates' one. In all branches of entertainment, including literature but above all in the performing arts, great efforts were made, as they are now, to *create* sensations – especially where individual stars were concerned: success or failure of the enterprise depended on them. Promoting stars was easier for the Victorians than for their predecessors because of the unprecedented circulation of newspapers. Developments in transport were crucial too in creating international stars for the first time. However, showmanship was essential, and early in Victoria's reign, even before the great expansion of the press, the greatest showman and sensationmonger of the nineteenth century visited Britain.

On 3 February 1844 an incongruous pair arrived in Liverpool aboard the packet *Yorkshire*, which had sailed from New York 18 days earlier. The showman was more than six feet tall; the star in the making not much over two and weighed little more than a stone. The American impresario Phineas T Barnum was accompanied by Charles H Stratton, better known by the name Barnum had given him: 'General Tom Thumb'. Together, they taught the British public a unique lesson in how to create a sensation.[2]

Tom Thumb was six years old, although Barnum gave him out to be 12. He was one of those Victorian 'infant phenomena', performing children, whose most famous fictional example appears in Dickens's *Nicholas Nickleby*, published only five years before. Of the many in real life, none was such a star as Tom Thumb, or remained so big a draw after reaching adulthood.

'Dwarfs' and 'midgets', to use the now discredited but then usual terms, were common in Victorian entertainment but were usually misshapen and had little talent as performers. Tom Thumb's small but perfect form, engaging personality and real, if perhaps limited, performing abilities had attracted big audiences in the United States, and these assets were to provide the substance of his success in Britain. However, it would not have been possible without the hype provided by Barnum, then aged 33. It was Barnum who first established the reputation of American showbusiness entrepreneurs as masters of publicity.

He lost no time in offering Tom Thumb to the public in Liverpool, and then at the Princess's Theatre in London, billing him with typical panache as 'the hero of Lilliput, the Pride of Kentucky, the Monarch of Dwarfs'.[3] The audience was clearly amazed to see such a little fellow appear on stage, where he was announced by Barnum in person. His first London appearance was described as that of 'an infant that has by some magic process jumped out of its cradle and has adjured pap for popularity'. His tiny physique was much admired, although some considered his head a little large for his body. He received generous applause and good reviews, although at least one critic preferred him dancing the hornpipe and singing 'Yankee Doodle Dandy' to posing in imitation of famous classical statues.[4] He made enough of a stir to become the subject of all sorts of jokes and rhymes:

> He's five and twenty inches high,
> One inch too tall, for who'll deny
> That almost everyone we meet
> Will run about upon two feet?[5]

Even bad jokes are good publicity. At the Princess's, Tom Thumb was only one item on a mixed bill, and Barnum quickly transferred him to the Egyptian Hall in Piccadilly, where he could star in his own right. He did good business, without being a sensation, but Barnum's plan to make him one was well under way.

The first stage was to attract the cream of society, which would impress and attract a mass public. Barnum rented a house in a fashionable part of town, and invited influential people to visit Tom Thumb: he announced in the papers that, the General 'is now holding a series of levees at his residence in Grafton Street'.[6] These invitations, which were enthusiastically taken up, cleared the way for Tom Thumb to be admitted to high society. The press was always kept informed, and it was reported that when he visited the mansion of Baroness Rothschild 'he excited the greatest admiration and wonder', and that on his departure 'The Baroness presented him with a splendid purse *thickly lined with gold*.'[7] But Barnum was aiming higher than a Baroness. One day a notice appeared on the door of the Egyptian Hall: 'Closed this evening, Tom Thumb being at Buckingham Palace by command of Her Majesty'. The second stage of the operation had begun.

Acceptance by the Queen had been central to Barnum's strategy all along and, considering how doubtful it was of success, it was brave as well as brazen of him to proclaim it openly from the beginning. He had announced Tom Thumb's departure from New York as 'for the purpose of visiting Her Majesty Queen Victoria and the nobility of England'.[8] As soon as he arrived in London, the public was told that Tom would be exhibited to Her Majesty on her arrival in town, but if that proved impossible, he would proceed to Paris. This implied that without royal patronage Barnum could not create the sensation he was aiming for, and would have to move on.

When the *Yorkshire* had docked at Liverpool the court had been in mourning for the death of Prince Albert's father and could not be approached. This was a reminder to Barnum that he was taking a huge risk: he had no contacts in royal circles. However, he had an introduction to the American minister at the Court of St James, through whom he made the breakthrough. It was a difficult job but he succeeded. Queen Victoria was charmed by Tom Thumb. The main source of information for what went on between the pair is Barnum's memoirs, but he was a self-proclaimed liar and, to use his word, 'humbug'. However, in this matter he has never been contradicted, and his account is backed up by what is known of Tom Thumb's personality, the presents the Queen gave him, and the fact that in 1844 he was invited to Buckingham Palace three times.

Barnum's memoirs had yet to be written, but he achieved a tremendous coup on the first visit to the Palace by persuading the official responsible for the *Court Journal* to include a piece on Tom Thumb in the next edition, in more or less Barnum's own words. No publication could have been more authoritative.

Where the Queen led, her subjects followed, and they flocked to the Egyptian Hall. To cater for the bigger audiences, Tom Thumb took over a larger hall from George Catlin and his portraits of American Indians. The portraits stayed behind as one of the supporting attractions to the General, who repeated his Princess's Theatre repertoire. His imitations of classical statuary included one of Cupid which was particularly popular as he shot tiny arrows at the ladies who made up a large part of his audience. In mid-April it was reported that 'the public curiosity to behold this human wonder has now become a furore, and the Egyptian Hall is daily thronged with the aristocracy of the metropolis, the man of science and the sightseeker [sic].'[9] The aristocracy included the aged Duke of Wellington, considered the greatest living Englishman. He was particularly taken with Tom Thumb's appearance in costume as a diminutive Napoleon, marching up and down the platform, apparently deep in thought. When the Duke asked what was on his mind, the General gave an answer that was widely repeated as evidence of his wit. 'I was thinking of the loss of the battle of Waterloo.' At least, that is the version given in Barnum's memoirs, but at the time *Bell's Life in London* attributed the remark to Barnum,[10] who was certainly capable of attributing it to Tom Thumb for publicity purposes. More good publicity was gained from the presents on display, given by Queen Adelaide, William IV's widow, and the Queen of the Belgians, as well as by Victoria, and from Barnum's repeated announcements that the show was about to close – then that it stayed open by popular demand.

An effigy of Tom Thumb was on display at Madame Tussaud's, but everyone who could was prepared to pay the high entrance price to see the real thing – one shilling with no reductions for children, although Barnum had been told in Liverpool that the British public would not pay more than a penny or twopence to see a dwarf. When the show finally closed in July, takings had averaged £500 a day against expenses of £50. The grandiloquent announcement that 'The General continues to wait on the Nobility and Gentry, at their residences, on due notice' meant that he was available to appear at private parties at eight to ten guineas a time.

At the end of his run, Tom Thumb abandoned the Egyptian Hall in the evening, but only to appear at the Adelaide Gallery, dancing the polka with a suitably tiny partner. Barnum did not miss a trick: 1844 was the year of polka mania. Only the new dance rivalled Tom Thumb as a sensation, and the combination of the two must have seemed irresistible.

There followed a long tour of Europe, where Tom Thumb was as popular with continental monarchs as he had been with Queen Victoria. When he reappeared at the Egyptian Hall at Christmas 1845, their gifts, too, were on show. Then the provinces paid homage, before he returned to London in March 1846. He followed his daytime appearances at the Egyptian Hall with evening performances at the Lyceum Theatre in the title role of *Hop o' My Thumb*, a play written especially for him. It was a burlesque, which enabled its star to show a gift for comedy that won him repeated curtain calls. Today to burden a child with such a heavy schedule would be regarded as exploitation, and one journalist commented at the time, 'How the poor little devil goes through it after morning "levees" and what not we are at a loss to understand; but that he sustains his little bustling part unflaggingly to the close, and then comes forward game as a pebble, to ask the people to visit him again, is the literal and stupendous fact.'[12]

During Tom Thumb's final series of appearances at the Egyptian Hall, the painter Benjamin Robert Haydon was exhibiting his work in another part of the building. His room remained empty while Tom Thumb's overflowed. The humiliation contributed to Haydon's suicide on 22 June 1846. When Barnum's memoirs were eventually published, revealing the promotional tricks he had used, outraged readers remembered guiltily how they had neglected Haydon. However, posterity has confirmed their judgement of his paintings.

Tom Thumb and Barnum finally left for the United States on 4 February 1847. They missed the arrival of the Swedish soprano, Jenny Lind, by two and a half months. This demure, devoutly religious exponent of high art made such a sensation in Britain that afterwards Barnum engaged her to tour America under his management.

Jenny Lind's Continental triumphs, especially in Germany, meant that British opera lovers were desperate to see her. While Barnum had had to break down barriers on behalf of the General, the only problem with Jenny Lind was her reluctance to come. Strenuous efforts had been made previously to bring her to Britain and had failed – she had once committed herself to Drury Lane but then backed off. At last she was lured by Her Majesty's Opera House in the Haymarket: its finances were so fragile that only Jenny Lind, it seemed, could keep it open.[13]

Hence the air of expectancy at the beginning of May 1847. As the *Era* put it, 'All has been expectation and anticipation without the walls of the theatre, and within all was business and bustle . . . We shall be much disappointed if Jenny Lind does not produce even a greater enthusiasm in England than she has in Germany.'[14] She did, as the huge prices paid for tickets demonstrated: five pounds for reserved seats in the stalls, and twenty guineas for boxes.

On 4 May 1847, there was chaos in front of the theatre. Inside the house was full to overflowing, and the star received an ovation before she had sung a note. 'The whole scene seemed more like a nation's rejoicing for a great victory than that of congregating to witness the first appearance of a young girl from foreign parts.'[15] The highest hopes were not disappointed by Lind's performance as Alice in Meyerbeer's *Robert the Devil*. It was punctuated by long bursts of applause and, at the end, the audience rose to its feet, cheering, clapping and waving hats and handkerchiefs. To meet the censor's religious scruples, the nuns required by the plot and the tombstones by the stage directions were nowhere to be seen. Nobody cared: what mattered was the quality of the diva's voice, her superb acting and stage presence. The reviewers were as ecstatic as the audience. According to *The Times*, 'that wondrous thing, a new sensation was actually created',[16] and the *Era* reported that, 'the Queen in her palace, the lady in her boudoir, the men at the clubs, the merchant on Change, the clerk in his office, and indeed all sorts of people from the most exalted to the lowest members of society spoke of Jenny Lind'.[17]

If it were possible, she was an even greater hit the following week in *La Somnambula*. The first sleepwalking scene inspired the comment, 'On no former occasion has such a scene been beheld within the walls of a theatre.' Excitement was high outside those walls, too. 'Every morning the stage door is regularly besieged by hundreds, anxious to get a sight of the lion of the day . . . The Lind fever has not abated.'[18] She appeared next in the title role of *Norma* and in the first London production of *The Daughter of the Regiment*. She also starred in the world premiere of *I Masnadieri*, with Verdi, the composer, conducting two performances. and ended her season as Susannah in *The Marriage of Figaro*.

It is hard to imagine two more different entertainers than Tom Thumb and Jenny Lind, but their triumph had one factor in common: the Queen. She had already heard the Swedish Nightingale several times in Germany, and Lind seems to have been her favourite performer of all. On that dramatic London opening night, Victoria threw her a bouquet from the royal box, an unprecedented gesture.

May 24 was the Queen's birthday:

> At night the west-end of town was a blaze of lights. Besides the profuse illuminations displayed at the government offices and other public buildings, the clubhouses, theatres, exhibitions and gardens were lighted up with variegated lamps and gas. Her Majesty's tradesmen and several others who had no claim to the honour of serving the Queen testified their loyalty by illuminating their houses. Several beautiful devices were exhibited in the Strand, Fleet-street, Ludgate-hill and other parts of the city. Crowds of admirers of illuminations paraded every part of London till a late hour.[19]

And where was the Queen during all this? In the opera house applauding Jenny Lind in *The Daughter of the Regiment*. In June Her Majesty arrived at a gala performance of *Norma* in a procession of nine state carriages, with an escort of Life Guards. She also honoured the star by inviting her to sing privately for her.

The Queen, as well as the singer, benefited enormously from the relationship. When Jenny Lind opened her second London season with *La Sonnambula*, 'there were two first appearances, that of Victoria, Queen of England, and Jenny Lind, Queen of the Lyric Art'.[20] It was the Queen's first public appearance since her latest confinement. Chopin, who was there, was impressed by both women, and even more so by the Duke of Wellington, 'sitting beneath the royal box, like an old monarchical watchdog in his kennel beneath his royal mistress'.[21] When the Queen arrived after the first act, attention moved away from the stage and the National Anthem was played. 'The late seditious demonstrations gave a special character to the scene – each line was seized with avidity, and responded to with cheers. What a lesson to the continent of Europe of the blessings of a well-balanced constitutional monarchy.'[22]

The King of the French had lost his throne that year, and the Queen had not been seen since the Chartists had been faced down less than a month earlier. 'Thank God,' she had written.[23] In contrast, monarchy as well as music was being celebrated inside the appropriately named Her Majesty's. Not only did the royal patronage add to Jenny Lind's glory, but the Queen, accompanied by Prince Albert, was associating herself with a unique standard of excellence. The vast opera house was filled with the court and the aristocracy, and an audience who were equally anxious to see the Queen and to hear Jenny Lind. Each woman was basking in the approval of her own admirers, and in the adulation accorded to the other.

It is more surprising, perhaps, that an opera singer should be a sensation with *all* classes. Sheet music was sold, not only of arias in her repertoire, but also of Jenny Lind waltzes, quadrilles, polkas, and dances of every description. One of the many songs and street ballads reflecting her fame included these verses:

> Oh is there not a pretty fuss,
> In London all around,
> About the Swedish nightingale
> The talk of all the town . . .
>
> As to a liquor shop you go
> To drink your wine or gin,
> The landlord begs that you will taste
> His famous Jenny Lind . . .
>
> Now everything is Jenny Lind
> That comes out new each day
> There's Jenny Lind shawls and bonnets too,
> For those who cash can pay . . .
>
> If to a butcher's shop you go
> To buy a joint of meat,
> It's buy, oh buy, my Jenny Lind
> She's tender and she's sweet.[24]

Her name and her picture were used – no payment to her – to promote every commercial article under the sun. A particularly cheeky advertisement, for Moses and Son, tailors, put these words into her mouth at the start of her second London season:

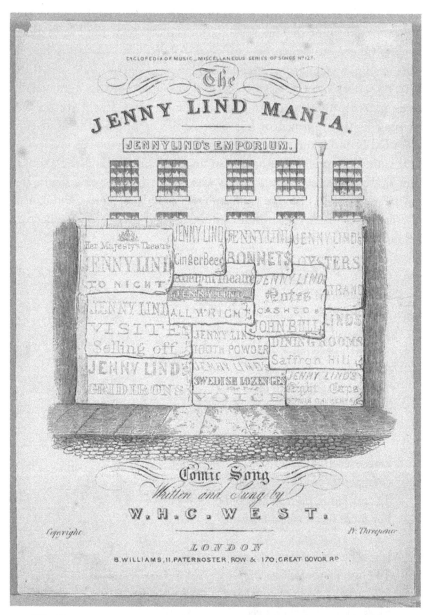

The Times *wrote of Jenny Lind, 'that wondrous thing, a new sensation was actually created'. Lind's name and picture were used, with no profit to her, to promote every conceivable commercial article.*

How oft have I gazed from the brightly lit stage
On the elegant dresses around,
Who furnished attractions that well might engage,
And proved Messrs Moses had honoured the age,
And deserve to be widely renowned.

I return to the city where Moses and Son
Their elegant fashion display,
Which fashions the highest approval have won,
As beautiful articles equall'd by none –
The style and the pride of the day.[25]

No other performer was so exploited commercially, or so admired. Pauline Viardot who was appearing at Covent Garden was a comparative failure. Hector Berlioz conducted a concert of his music, but he was not a sensation. The public was used to the great ballet star Taglioni. Only once were comparisons made that were not entirely in Jenny Lind's favour: some thought that she was less well cast as Norma than the Italian diva Giulia Grisi, who was singing the part at Covent Garden. Others admired the two singers equally: 'Jenny Lind is the betrayed and heart-crushed woman; Grisi the jealous mistress panting for vengeance for her wrongs. We are awe-stricken and oppressed by Grisi; softened into womanish tears by Lind.'[26]

Jenny Lind was a deeply religious woman, and as time went on she became increasingly convinced that acting out the grand passions on stage was incompatible with her beliefs, a view shared by many Victorians. When she came to London in 1849, she tried to meet her obligations by giving six performances without acting or staging. The first attempt, with *The Magic Flute*, resulted in her only failure, so she reluctantly gave six full performances, which were her last. From then on she was heard only in concerts and oratorios. However, the British public continued to love her, the more so as she made her home in England from 1858 until her death in Malvern in 1887. No one forgot 1847 and 1848, the years of Lind mania, when opera-goers were overwhelmed by her genius, and other people to whom opera meant nothing, by her reputation as a sweet, good woman, the admired of the Queen, and by the commercial exploitation of her name.

Most of the sensational performers of the period were imported. Some, like Jenny Lind, had built up a reputation abroad which made their very arrival intensely exciting. International stars also had the advantage of being able to leave before the public appetite was sated. But two Englishmen, Charles Dickens and Henry Irving, held the public in thrall for many years. No great writer has been more popular in his lifetime than Dickens. To catch sight of him was exciting; to see him perform even more so; and to see and hear him perform *his own works* was sensational.

Dickens was an enthusiastic amateur actor in public performances, which he staged for charity with many of his celebrity friends. It was generally agreed that he was good as an amateur but many thought he ranked with the professionals. However, they might have been swayed by their admiration for his novels, their delight at seeing him on stage, or indulgence towards an actor performing for good causes. The classical actor W C Macready expressed in his diary the other point of view. He was commenting on Dickens' production of Ben Jonson's *Every Man in His Humour*, in which the great novelist played Bobadil. On 15 November 1845 Macready wrote, 'As an amateur production it is exceedingly good, but the commendation is held of no account with the actors, and they desire to be judged on positive grounds . . . The performance would not be endured from ordinary, or rather regular actors by a paying audience. They seem to me under a perfect delusion as to their degrees of skill and power in this art, of which they do not know what may be called the very rudiments.'[27] Macready might have had the professional actor's disdain for amateurs, but he was one of Dickens' closest friends.

Even as a reader Dickens was a part-timer, albeit a superb one. There were often long intervals between his reading tours, which gave him the same advantage as a foreign star whose public never had time to grow disenchanted with him. On the other hand, the five hundred or so readings he gave were never near to satisfying public demand. Charles Kent, who was in the audience many times, says in his book *Dickens as a Reader*:

Attracting to themselves [his readings] at the outset, by the mere glamour of his name, enormous audiences, they not only maintained their original *prestige* during a long series of years – during an interval of fifteen years altogether – but the audiences brought together by them, instead of showing any signs of diminution, very appreciably, on the contrary, increased and multiplied. Crowds were turned away from the doors, who were unable to obtain admittance . . . Densely packed from floor to ceiling, these audiences were habitually wont to hang in breath-less expectation upon every inflection of the author-reader's voice, upon every glance of his eye, – the words he was about to speak being so thoroughly well remembered by the majority before their utterance that, often, the rippling of a smile over a thousand faces simultaneously anticipated the laughter which an instant afterwards greeted the words themselves when they were articulated.[28]

This was no exaggeration. Dickens read in public for the first time on 27 December 1853 at the town hall, Birmingham, when he gave a reading for charity of *A Christmas Carol*. He read *The Cricket on the Hearth* on the twenty-ninth, and repeated the *Carol* the following day. Despite the bad weather the hall was packed, but on the last occasion prices were reduced because Dickens wanted an audience of mainly working people. The readings were vastly popular with all classes and the Birmingham audiences were not daunted by their lasting three hours; even so, Dickens learned quickly to condense and adapt his chosen passages.

Those first Birmingham readings led to a flow of requests for him to read elsewhere, far more than he could possibly meet, and he travelled all over the country. The first London reading was on 30 June 1857. Again, it was *A Christmas Carol*, now down to two and a half hours, at St Martin's Hall in Long Acre, and was to raise money for the widow of Dickens' friend, the author Douglas Jerrold. Writing more than fourteen years later, Charles Kent remembered, 'as though it were but an incident of yesterday, the enthusiasm of the reception then accorded to the great novelist by an audience composed for the most part of representative Londoners. The applause with which he was greeted, immediately upon his entrance, was so earnestly prolonged and sustained, that it threatened to postpone the Reading indefinitely.'[29]

Dickens read again at St Martin's Hall to earn money for himself. On 29 April 1858, he began a series of 16 readings, which was followed by a tour of the provinces; audiences often numbered up to two thousand people. The question of whether a serious novelist debased himself and his profession by becoming a professional reader was much debated among Dickens' friends, and led him to defend his position on that first occasion – but the public does not seem to have considered it an issue. There were 87 readings in this first series, over about three and a half months.

The triumphant reading tours continued until within a few months of Dickens' death. His letters are full of not very modest references to the public's acclaim:

> Last Thursday I began reading again in London – a condensation of Copperfield; and Mr Bob Sawyer's Party from 'Pickwick' to finish merrily. The success of Copperfield is astounding. There were eighteen hundred people in the place, and numbers were turned away. It made an impression that *I* must not describe – I may only remark that I was half dead when I had done, and that although I had looked forward, all through the summer when I was carefully getting it up, to its being a London sensation, and that although Macready hearing it at Cheltenham told me to be prepared for a great effect, it even went beyond my wildest hopes. I read again next Thursday, and the rush for places is quite furious.[30]

Macready's approval is significant, considering his opinion of Dickens as an actor and that Dickens acted out the parts of the various characters. According to Dickens, Macready's reaction to the *Copperfield* reading was:

> No – er – Dickens! I swear to Heaven that as a piece of passion and playfulness – re – indescribably mixed up together, it does – er – No, er, really Dickens! amaze me as profoundly as it moves me. But as a piece of art – and you know – er that I – No Dickens! By God! – have seen the best Art in a great time – it is incomprehensible to me. How it is got at – er – how it is done – er – how one man can – well! It lays me on my – er – back, and it is of no use talking about it.[31]

The following year, an eye-witness recorded the effect of *The Trial from Pickwick* on Thomas Carlyle. This must have been one of the few occasions when the grim Scottish sage was seen convulsed with merriment: 'Carlyle sat on the front bench and he haw-hawed right over and over till he fairly exhausted himself. Dickens would read and then he would stop in order to give Carlyle a chance to stop . . . I laughed till my jaws ached, and I caught myself involuntarily stamping.'[32]

Those familiar with Dickens' life story will know how much the readings meant to him – how much he needed the adoration of his audiences, and how the exertion, especially acting out the murder of Nancy in *Oliver Twist*, along with the wear and tear of travel, helped to wreck his health. Eventually, on doctor's orders, he had to give up. The final reading on 15 March 1870, at St James's Hall in Piccadilly, was one of the most sensational episodes in the history of professional performance in Britain.

Everyone knew that they would never hear Dickens read again; nearly everyone could be sure that they would never see him again. The knowledgeable few would have understood how ill he was. The readings were *A Christmas Carol* and *The Trial from Pickwick*, probably the most popular of all. When Dickens appeared on the platform, the audience of 2,000 rose to their feet and cheered him for several minutes. In the words of the *Penny Illustrated Paper*, 'The hearty applause subsiding, the eyes of all were centred on that one spare figure, faultlessly attired in evening dress, the gas-light streaming down upon him illuminating every feature of his familiar flushed face, lined with literary hard work, the eloquent blue eyes particularly seeming to indicate much recent study.'[33]

After the reading was over and 'the resounding applause' had died away, 'there was a breathless hush as Charles Dickens, who had for once lingered there upon the platform, addressed to his hearers, with exquisitely clear articulation, but with unmistakably profound emotion', a few simple words of farewell.[34] And he had broken his wise rule not to give readings while he was writing a novel. He spoke of how delighted and encouraged he had been by the public's response to his readings over many years:

Nevertheless, I have thought it well, at the full flood-tide of your favour, to retire upon those older associations between us, which date from much further back than these, and henceforth to devote myself exclusively to that art which first brought us together. (*Applause*). Ladies and gentlemen, in but two short weeks from this time I hope that you may enter, in your own homes, on a new series of readings [*The Mystery of Edwin Drood*], at which my assistance will be indispensable; but from these garish lights I vanish now for evermore, with a heartfelt, grateful, respectful and affectionate farewell.[35]

The choice of words reveals the ham actor in Dickens, but it was magnificent ham, and intensely moving. Then,

Leaving the platform amid acclamations of the most tumultuous kind, he proceeded to his retiring-room with quite a mournful gait, and tears rolling down his cheeks. But he had to go forward once again, to be stunned by a more surprising outburst than before, and dazzled by the waving of handkerchiefs. Respectfully kissing his hand, Mr Dickens retired for the last time.[36]

Those present remembered the occasion for the rest of their lives. Dickens died less than three months later.

The 1860s were the heyday of Dickens as a reader – but also of a trapeze artist and a tightrope walker. In the summer of 1861, when Dickens was planning a new reading tour for the autumn, two Frenchmen provided their own sensations.

François Gravelet, known as Blondin, had become 'the hero of Niagara' two years earlier, by performing amazing stunts on an 1,100-foot rope stretched across the Falls. Jules Leotard's reputation had been made on the continent with his new invention, the flying trapeze. Both benefited from clever press publicity. Shortly before Leotard arrived in England, an article appeared in the *Era*, purporting to give a brief history of man's attempts to fly, and continuing:

> What will be thought when we say that there exists at the present day a man whose marvellous feats seem to have almost realised the inconceivable prodigy of vanquishing the laws of eccentric and concentric forces, who defies the laws of gravity, who hovers in the air like a bird, and supplies his want of wings by his elasticity of muscle . . . The feats of Leotard must be seen to be believed. The enthusiasm Leotard has called forth in Paris, Vienna, St Petersburg and Berlin is unprecedented; everyone is unanimous in styling him the *flying man*. Whether there is any exaggeration in these reports we are not in a position to decide, but fortunately we shall shortly be able to judge for ourselves, as daily advertisements in the morning papers and numerous posters all over London inform us that Leotard will (by consent of Mr T. B. Simpson) appear on Whit Monday at the Alhambra and shortly afterwards at Cremorne.[37]

The posters and publicity worked. When Whit Monday arrived, the Alhambra music-hall was full to overflowing to see Leotard perform from eleven thirty in the evening until midnight.

No mere description can convey an idea of what he does during that intensely exciting half-hour. Literally throwing himself through the air at an immense altitude, he gyrates as he goes, clings for a second to one of the intervening bars, and then projects himself twenty feet forward to the next bar, where he hangs by his feet and then turns backward somersaults through the air back to his original starting point, with no greater impetus than what is acquired from the oscillation of the ropes with which he swings himself onwards in his aerial progress. Nothing like it has ever been seen in England before . . . All who want a new sensation will be sure to number themselves among the Alhambra audience during his engagement, and whatever they may have previously seen in the way of proofs of physical courage and alacrity, they must be sure here of seeing greatly surpassed. It is emphatically one of those performances that once witnessed are never afterwards to be forgotten.[38]

Leotard's fine body looked good in 'the simplest style of athletic costume' which now bears his name, but it was even more clearly displayed when clad only in a loincloth in a 'cabinet-sized' photograph; they were widely available in the mid-Victorian period. His appeal to women inspired one of the most popular music-hall songs of the 1860s:

> He smiled from the bar on the people below
> And one night he smiled on my love.
> She winked back at him and she shouted 'Bravo!'
> As he hung by his nose up above!
>
> He'd fly through the air with the greatest of ease,
> A daring young man on the flying trapeze,
> His movements were graceful; all girls he could please;
> And my love he purloined away.[39]

Two weeks after Leotard's first London performance, Blondin made his début, on 1 June 1861. Understandably the two artists were linked in the public mind: 'Great excitement has of late come thick and fast upon us, and the interest caused by one outstanding performance has scarcely had time to lose any of its keenness before another "excitement" has taken hold of the minds of the amusement-seeking portions of the people.'[40] On the other hand, although Blondin was French, he was also associated with the United States, the land where 'sensation' had allegedly originated. Even before his arrival in Britain, *All The Year Round* had coupled his name with that of the Prince of Wales, in an article on 'American Sensations'.[41] As the first heir to the throne to visit America, the Prince had inevitably made a sensational impact, and he had contributed to the Blondin sensation by being present at his feats over Niagara Falls.

Blondin performed in the costume of an Indian chief – emphasising the American connection – 170 feet above the central transept of the Crystal Palace, and, on some later occasions, outside on the terrace where the rope was suspended high over the fountains between three enormous masts. There were gasps of excitement when he walked across it blind-folded, in a sack which left only his legs free. In his most spectacular feat, he carried a cooking stove strapped to his shoulders. It weighed 50 pounds, and cooking dishes, a tray and a broom were attached to it. Still on the rope, he proceeded to cook an omelette while the band played 'Home, Sweet Home'.

Danger, of course, was essential to the kind of sensation which Blondin and Leotard offered. Neither used a safety-net. However, Leotard never stressed the danger or sought to terrify his audiences. The ease and grace of his performance made for wonder rather than fear. Blondin, on the other hand, played up the danger, and exploited the possibility that he might trip by pretending to do so. This provided *too much* excitement for some, and there were demands that these false steps should be discontin-ued, 'as with spectators of any sensibility at all, the sensation produced is sickening'.[42] In deference to this criticism, Blondin performed at the Crystal Palace, on at least one occasion, only a few feet from the ground, but fear was part of the sensation which the audience came to enjoy.

Blondin was to settle in London, and make it the centre of his inter-national career, but Leotard was to return only once before his early death in 1870. Blondin also stayed longer than Leotard during that first sensa-tional season of 1861, but the latter had an easier time of it. Controversy arose as to whether Blondin's feats had been performed in Britain before. A number of the tight-rope walking fraternity maintained that they had, and that the only novel aspect of his performance was the extraordinary height at which they were carried out.

Before his arrival, Blondin had published warnings in the press against unworthy imitators, probably as an advertising ploy. However, unlike Leotard, he had to face imitators and rivals, including a Mr D'Alberte, whose selling point, despite his name, was that he was British, and more than one female Blondins, whose selling point was that they were female. One fell to her death. Mr D'Alberte issued an aggressive advertisement claiming that the Frenchman 'could scarcely put one foot before the other on the rope but it is reported in *The Times* and other papers and called WONDERFUL PERFORMANCES'. He added that he would do anything that Blondin could do – 'except cooking omelettes, but he, Mr D'Alberte, is quite ready to cook good old-fashioned English pancakes'.[43]

Blondin had other problems that summer. At Margate he insisted that the rope had been placed too low, and had it raised to 80 feet. The result was that hundreds of spectators outside the grounds, which were much smaller than those of the Crystal Palace, could see almost as well as those who had paid their shillings, and a great deal of revenue was lost.[44] Elsewhere, however, Blondin's 1861 provincial appearances were as successful as those in London. The venues were carefully chosen to allow special excursion trains to arrive from all directions. In Sheffield, for example, it was claimed that he attracted a crowd of 90,000. Blondin's photograph was on display everywhere, and even Blondin handkerchiefs were on sale. He was so famous that a farce *Blondin* and a dramatic sketch *Caught in a Line, or The Unrivalled Blondin* were performed at London theatres.

Even the criticism was good publicity. Those who found the performances *too* sensational suggested, wrongly, that there might be less appetite for them in Britain than in the United States, 'the land where everything of an abnormal character appears to obtain'.[45] Such hostility to America may have been influenced by the fact that civil war had started, although sour grapes were a factor, as in the case of the rival who claimed to have equalled Blondin's feats 'notwithstanding the absence of Yankee puffing'.[46]

1861 was a vintage year for sensation in the world of entertainment. Leotard and Blondin were appearing, *The Colleen Bawn* and then *The Octoroon* were on at the Adelphi, and *Peep o' Day* at the Lyceum. What was more, before the year was out, the long and sensational career of another American import, or rather re-import, had begun.

The actor Edward Askew Sothern was an Englishman who had gone to the United States, and fetched up in New York, playing a small and boring part in *Our American Cousin*, by the English dramatist and future editor of *Punch*, Tom Taylor. In despair of making anything of the role of

Lord Dundreary, he began to introduce extravagant business, skipping about the stage, stammering and sneezing, using every possible trick to gain the audience's attention. He was so disillusioned that he did not care what damage he did to the play – but audiences loved him. The part grew and grew, as Sothern added new business and new lines, so that his contribution overshadowed Tom Taylor's. Lord Dundreary became a hit in his own right as a grotesque parody of the effete and stupid English nobleman. It is not surprising that he was so popular in mid-century America, where there was a strong current of Anglophobia, but the British public loved him just as much.

Although he had played Dundreary more than eight hundred times in the United States, Sothern had never acted in London before when he opened at the Haymarket theatre on 11 November 1861. The house was far from full, but it was soon convulsed with laughter. The then amazing run of nearly five hundred nights was probably due more to word-of-mouth recommendations than to the reviews: 'Accepting it as a hasty work manufactured to suit the American market, it will have its recommendation as a sort of dramatic curiosity.'[47] There had been no substantial advance publicity, but the theatre quickly announced in the newspapers that Sothern was being 'encored nightly'.

Soon his appearance was immediately recognisable everywhere – his long frock coat, his monocle, and the long side whiskers, which became known as 'Dundrearies'. According to his biographer, Sothern's dressing room at the Haymarket

> ... was crowded with parcels sent by energetic haberdashers, who knew that if, by wearing it on the stage, he would set the fashion for a certain make of necktie or a particular pattern of shirt-cuff, or collar, their fortunes would be half made; and hatters and bootmakers followed in the haberdashers' wake ... Concerning *Dundreary* quite three parts of England went more than half mad, and not to know all about him ... was to argue yourself unknown.[48]

Dundreary adorned the covers of at least sixteen pieces of sheet music. Silly jokes became known as 'Dundrearyisms', and, showing that Dundreary existed for his audiences as vividly as a character in a modern soap opera, little books were sold in thousands at street corners about his imaginary doings and those of his relatives.

THEATRE ROYAL, HAYMARKET.

LICENSED BY THE LORD CHAMBERLAIN,

To Mr. JOHN BALDWIN BUCKSTONE, Actual and only Responsible Lessee and Manager, 18, Suffolk Street.

MR. SOTHERN

Second Week since his return from Paris, in his famous character of

LORD DUNDREARY!

Nightly received with

Shouts of Laughter and Applause,

And the accustomed Encore to the Reading of

BROTHER SAM'S LETTER.

MISS ROBERTSON,
AND
MR. J. T. RAYMOND,

ALSO EVERY EVENING.

THE WINNING CARD!
EVERY EVENING.

This Evening, MONDAY, November 4th, 1867, and during the Week,

To commence at SEVEN with the New successful Comedietta, entitled

THE WINNING CARD

Baron de Rocombole - (Governor of the Citadel)	-	Mr. ROGERS
M. Mendheim - (Burgomaster)	-	Mr. P. WHITE
Florian (Aide-de-Camp of the King)		Mr. WALTER GORDON
Pepin - (a Gardener	-	Mr. COMPTON
Cecile - (Daughter of the Burgomaster)	-	Miss DALTON
Madlle Euphemia de Rocombole (the Baron's Sister)		Mrs. LAWS
Jacqueline (Ceciles' Maid)	Mrs. E FITZWILLIAM	

SCENE

A SMALL TOWN ON THE PRUSSIAN FRONTIER.

Period - The Reign of Frederick the Great.

Sothern opened at the Haymarket theatre on 11 November 1861. His Lord Dundreary was soon 'encored nightly', enjoying a – then extraordinary – run of nearly 500 nights.

The most important relative was his brother Sam; in the most famous scene Dundreary reads aloud a letter from him which says he has discovered his old nurse is his mother. Dundreary tries, without success, to work out who his own mother can be. In another passage, Sam has expressed concern that his last letter might not have arrived, as he forgot to put a name and address on the envelope. 'Then I suppose that's the reason I never got it,' Dundreary says, ' but who could have got it? The only fella that could have got that letter is some fella without a name. And how on earth could he get it? The postman couldn't go about asking every fella he met if he'd got no name.'[49] An actor who could make lines like those hilarious must have been brilliant. Six years after he first opened there, the Haymarket was still boasting 'Lord Dundreary nightly received with shouts of Laughter and Applause and the accustomed encore to the reading of Brother Sam's letter'.[50] No other major English actor attempted the part, except Sothern's son, who could not match his father.

Adah Isaacs Menken was establishing her sensational reputation in New York in June 1861, when Blondin and Leotard were thrilling Londoners. The role, the only one for which she was famous, was that of the eponymous hero in *Mazeppa*, a play based on a poem by Byron. In 1864 she brought it to London. Menken, who had failed as a serious actress, and had served at one time as Blondin's assistant, had the physical attributes to provide what passed in the 1860s as a sex and nudity scandal. Of course she did not appear naked, although the woodcut illustration on the playbill made it look as though she did, and the pink 'fleshings' covered by only a brief white vest and trunks, gave that impression.

Mazeppa is about a hero who turns out to be the King of Tartary, and suffers grievously at the hands of his Polish enemies. However, the plot was subordinate to the scenes on horseback, when Mazeppa was strapped, helpless, to 'the fiery untamed steed of Tartary', which then galloped off in 'its wild career'. Menken's figure and her bravery in this scene made her a sensation. The venue for her triumph was Astley's. When Boucicault had taken it over, he had got rid of the circus ring and made it into a conventional theatre, but he had been bankrupted by his enormous outlay on rebuilding. Neither *The Colleen Bawn*, *The Trial of Effie Deans* nor even the pantomime which he had written around the character of Lord Dundreary could save the day, so the circus ring was back. Mazeppa had always been played in the past by men, none of whom had been brave enough to do his own stunt, let alone appear apparently naked. Braver and better-looking, Menken played the scene herself rather than make way for a dummy. There were other more conventional scenes on horseback, and she received splendid reviews – as action woman rather than actress.

Her reputation as a dangerous woman in her private life provided good publicity. Most of the rumours about her were untrue, but one of her husbands had been the handsome Irish American John C Heenan who, four years earlier, had fought the famous bare-knuckle fight against the English champion, Tom Sayers. The beautiful Menken was a gift to journalists. She had great charm and a number of leading literary figures, including Dickens, took an interest in her. During the two months leading up to opening night on 3 October 1864, she had made herself as conspicuous as possible and, helped by the manager of Astley's, fed journalists with plenty of copy:

Miss Adah Isaacs Menken, the popular young American actress, is now in London. Every fine afternoon she appears among the aristocracy in Hyde Park, either mounted on her famous black mare and escorted by a groom in full livery, or else airing herself in an open carriage with a liveried coachman and footman complete. Her equipage is much admired by the fashionable.

The public watch Ada Menken, day after day, driving up the Mall with her team of ponies. Duchesses, even if they are young and beautiful, pass unnoticed when La Belle Menken is in sight.[51]

Foreshadowing the demands of subsequent American stars visiting Britain, Menken insisted on an unprecedented financial deal, and a more luxuriously equipped dressing room than had previously been available. All this helped the publicity machine, which excelled itself in advertising the forthcoming spectacle. And a sure way to create a showbusiness sensation has always been to start an argument about sex, about what is permissible and what is not. In the Menken case, an article in the *Orchestra* raised the temperature nicely:

There have been imported many corruptions from America already, corruptions in language, in religion – or, at least, that superstition which does duty for it – in art. It would be the more painful, therefore, to have

to point out to a London manager that the public morals are not yet so
sunk as to tolerate a performance which would be hooted everywhere,
save in a Yankee audience, or among their kindred spirits in a Sepoy
community.[52]

In her indignant reply, which of course fuelled the controversy, Menken
referred to her interest in classical sculpture, and compared her costume
favourably with the scanty attire of the ladies of the ballet and of burlesque. When the show opened, she had the satisfaction of finding not
only overflowing houses but that most of the critics agreed with her.

There were many predictable jokes about getting to the 'bare facts'
and the 'naked truth', and songs and rhymes abounded:

> Here you are! Here you are!
> Morning papers, just come out –
> Great sensation! Conflagration!
> Latest death through crinoline!
> Adah Menken in *Mazeppa*
> Sweetest woman ever seen![53]

The crinoline, then at the height of its vogue, was dangerous. A woman
could easily bring its outer extremities close to an open flame without
realising it, and find herself ablaze on all sides in a moment. As it
extended a long way in all directions, it also kept men at more than arm's
length. Menken wore the crinoline when in society, and the contrast with
her stage costume seemed particularly amusing. In the flurry of bad jokes,
Punch was not to be left out:

> Here's half the town – if bills be true –
> To Astley's nightly thronging,
> To see the Menken throw aside
> All to her sex belonging,
> Stripping off woman's modesty,
> With woman's outward trappings –
> A bare-backed jade on bare-backed steed,
> In Cartlich's old strappings![54]

Cartlich had played Mazeppa 30 years earlier. When Menken gave way to the annual Astley's pantomime, she toured the provinces, where the arguments raged as fiercely as they had in London. In 1864–5 Menken was the most talked about woman in England. Then she began to lose her appeal, and within four years of her London opening night she was dead.

If the stars of the 1860s were, above all, circus performers like Leotard, Blondin and Menken, the 1870s belonged to a classical actor, Henry Irving. However, he shot to fame in what was claimed as a tragedy but was surely a melodrama. On 25 November 1871, the opening night of *The Bells*, Irving was 33. He had been in the cast when Sothern had taken Lord Dundreary to Paris, and had played the villain in *Formosa*, but although he had been a professional actor for 15 years, nothing he had done had prepared the theatre world for what he was to do now. The *Observer* commented that 'there are possibly very few who were aware that this actor possessed so much undeveloped power'.[55] *The Times* went further: 'As a valuable actor, especially of bad men in good society, Mr Irving has for some years been recognised by the London public . . . But when he appears as a tragic artist, with the duty of sustaining a serious drama single-handed, he may almost be said to be making a début.'[56]

The Bells was an adaptation of a French play about Mathias, an innkeeper who has become the wealthy burgomaster of a small Alsatian town, as a result of having robbed and murdered a rich Polish Jew 15 years earlier. The drama centres on the contrast between Mathias's outward respectability and his guilt. He is haunted by the memory of the winter night when the Jew arrived at his inn in the sledge whose bells give the play its title. In the great scene of the play, he enacts a terrible nightmare in which he relives and is put on trial for his crime. As his family knock on the bedroom door to wake him for his daughter's wedding day, Mathias, who believes that the hangman's noose is around his neck, dies of guilt and terror.

Stage machinery played no part in this great scene. It depended entirely on Irving's acting. He made the part of Mathias his own and it remained in his repertoire for the rest of his life, an unforgettable performance. Edward Gordon Craig, who acted with him, remembered how, as the villagers reminisce about the Polish Jew, Irving 'glides up to a standing position; never has anyone seen another rising figure which slid slowly up like that. With one arm slightly raised, with sensitive hand speaking of far-off apprehended sounds, he asks, in the voice of some woman who is frightened, yet does not wish to frighten those with her. "Don't you . . . don't you hear the sound of sledge-bells on the road?"[57]

By contrast, in the dream scene, pretence was at an end. The *Times* critic wrote after the first night:

> The struggles of the miserable culprit, convinced that all is lost, but desperately fighting against hope, rebelling against the judges, protesting against the clairvoyant, who wrings his secret from him, are depicted by Mr Irving with a degree of energy that, fully realizing the horror of the situation, seems to hold the audience in suspense. On Saturday it was not until the curtain fell, and they summoned the actor before it with a storm of acclamation, that they seemed to recover their self-possession. Nevertheless, so painful is the interest of the scene that, notwithstanding the excellent manner in which it is played, we would suggest its reduction to a smaller compass.[58]

The *Era* took a similar line, suggesting that during the trial scene Irving's acting inflicted pain on the audience for too long. He was particularly powerful in the re-enactment of the murder:

> We see him strike the blow, clutch the treasure which was the fateful temptation to the deed, and finally stagger under the weight of his victim to the lime kiln where the body was consumed, thus defeating all chances of discovery. Mr Irving's acting in this scene was positively appalling. It was terrible realism of a kind such as we have rarely witnessed, and for its awful truth was therefore painful. It was a scene which one watches and listens to with breathless horror, and a few among the audience were disposed to express some disapprobation. Speedily, however, these signs gave way to loud and continuous applause.[59]

Irving's performance was essentially melodramatic – 'the best actor we have of crime, remorse, villainy, ambition, sin'.[60] He continued to star in *Louis XI* and *The Corsican Brothers* during the 1890s, when intellectual critics thought them irredeemably old-fashioned. That he failed as Romeo but excelled as Mephistopheles and Richard III gives a fair indication of his gifts. Melodrama was so central to Victorian theatre that, without this melodramatic flair, Irving could not have appealed to all classes of audience, become a truly national figure, and kept public interest in him at a high pitch over 30 years. However, his conquest of fashionable play-goers would scarcely have been possible had he not thrilled them in Shakespeare.

There was intense excitement when, on 31 October 1874, he opened as Hamlet. Everyone knew that, in electing to play the most famous part in world drama, Irving was making a bid for the leadership of his profession. On the opening night of *The Bells* the audience, according to his most authoritative biographer, 'had been neither numerous nor distinguished'.[61] Now it was both. Hours before the curtain was due to rise, the pit and gallery entrances of the theatre were thronged with people and 'When the doors finally opened, the flower of artistic and literary society were seen in the stalls and boxes. The less fashionable parts of the house were full of what one reporter called the good old backbone of intelligence, which alas! has for some time not been constantly found at our theatres.'[62]

Irving was determined to offer a sensational interpretation of Hamlet which would fly in the face of all tradition. He succeeded. The critics agreed that it was different from all the readings of the part they had seen. Irving did not merely speak the words; he appeared to think them, and to show a mind at work. This was in itself a casting aside of tradition. At that time, there were generally accepted interpretations of particular speeches; particular intonations and emphases associated with particular lines. In our day, when novelty and innovation are the norm, it is hard to imagine what a sensation Irving's approach caused. In *Hamlet*, as in *The Bells*, the first night audience was taken aback and needed time to adjust. The *Era* said that 'at first the performance was far too subtle'. However, what he was doing gradually became clear and, by general consent, the turning point came in the third act. According to Clement Scott, the *Daily Telegraph* critic, 'the scene with Ophelia turns the scale, and the success is from this instant complete'. He described how it was done:

According to Henry Irving, the very sight of Ophelia is the keynote of the outburst of his moral disturbance. He loves this woman . . . and he seems mentally to suggest what might have happened if he had been allowed to love her, if his ambition had been realised. The more he looks at Ophelia, the more he curses the irony of fate. He is surrounded, overwhelmed, and crushed by trouble, annoyance and spies. They are watching him behind the arras. Ophelia is sent on to assist their plot.

They are driving him mad, though he is only feigning madness . . . The
distraction of the unhinged mind, swinging and banging about like a
door; the infinite love and tenderness of the man who longs to be soft
and gentle to the woman he adores; the horror and hatred of being
trapped, and watched, and spied upon, were all expressed with con-
summate art.[63]

This scene provoked a spontaneous burst of applause throughout the
house, and from then on 'Mr Irving had conquered'. The play lasted until
after midnight, but the cheers and repeated curtain calls at the end confirmed his triumph. The first night of *Hamlet*, following the sensation of
The Bells, led to a brilliant career and Irving became the first actor knight.

No British actress of the period made the same impact. The most popular was Ellen Terry, whose strongest asset was charm, and whom Irving
overshadowed because, during her long service under his management,
the plays were chosen to suit him and not her. It is an extraordinary fact
that the two most sensational actresses on the English stage during the
Victorian period performed only in French. Sarah Bernhardt was Irving's
contemporary, and the sensation she made reminded older playgoers of
Rachel who, in 1841 at the age of 20, had taken London by storm.

On 10 May of that year, Elisa Rachel Felix, who used only her middle
name professionally, opened at Her Majesty's Theatre. She played
Hermione in Racine's *Andromaque*; the character does not appear in the
first act, which was therefore considered a terrible bore. It was with the
scene in which Hermione is determined to bring about the death of the
man she loves that the ferocity of Rachel's acting made her as great a sensation in London as in Paris.

From then on, for eight summer seasons up to 1855, Rachel thrilled
British audiences in French seventeenth-century tragedy. Charlotte
Brontë saw her twice in 1851, and wrote in a letter:

Rachel's acting transfixed me with wonder, enchained me with interest
and thrilled me with horror. The tremendous power with which she
expresses the very worst passions in their strongest essence forms an
exhibition as exciting as the bull-fights of Spain and the gladiatorial
combats of old Rome, and (it seemed to me) not one whit more moral
than these poisoned stimulants to popular ferocity. It is scarcely human
nature that she shows you; it is something wilder and worse, the feelings

and fury of a fiend. The great gift of genius she undoubtedly has; but, I fear, she rather abuses it than turns it to good account.[64]

Brontë adapted some of this passage for her novel *Villette*, in which the actress Vashti is modelled on Rachel.

Here again is the Victorian dislike of the uncomfortable. The element of danger in acting repelled as well as attracted, just as Blondin's exploitation of *physical* danger did. Queen Victoria shared in this equivocal reaction: her admiration contributed to Rachel's success, but she preferred the gentler stage personality of Jenny Lind. After seeing Rachel as Racine's Phèdre, the Queen wrote in her diary that her acting 'was very fine . . . but French Tragedy is not pleasing and extremely unnatural'. As Hermione, Rachel had acted beautifully, but the character was 'abominable'.[65]

The fierce intensity of Rachel's performances foreshadowed those of Bernhardt. Contemporary descriptions of the two actresses make this clear. As Roxane in Racine's *Bajazet*, Rachel

> stalked silently upon the stage, approached the front, and remained gazing at the audience. A hush came over them; women involuntarily turned away from that glance, men breathed more heavily, and wished that she would break that painful silence. Subdued by the power of that fierce look, the awful reality of vengeful power which it expressed, they shivered and grew uncomfortable. Then when the silence seemed wholly intolerable, the pent-up rage, the anger of the wronged woman, burst forth with the irresistible force of a torrent. The tall figure, drawn to its utmost height, the heaving breast, the swaying arms, the pale face, the firmly compressed mouth, were so intensely fierce, that the actress and her artificial surroundings were forgotten, and the audience deemed it true.[66]

Compare that with Clement Scott's description of Bernhardt in a part written for her, although now known only through Puccini's operatic version of the play:

> The cries of the despairing Tosca, as her lover is being tortured, literally sent a shudder of horror around the house. She made the audience feel the double pain – his physical agony, her mental suffering even more

acute . . . [And when she murders Scarpia] She looked superb, pale as death, with distended eye and the fierce glare of a Judith. The grandeur of her tragic acting is awakened by such a scene as this, that through-out caused a silence in the house which could almost be felt in its intensity . . . The woman was transformed into a beast of prey, and seemed possessed with strength superhuman.'[67]

In 1879, when Bernhardt, as a member of the Comédie Française, landed for the first time at Folkestone, a band of admirers was there to welcome her. They had already cheered her in Paris. Oscar Wilde threw an armful of lilies at her feet. Like Rachel, she first conquered London in Racine. On 2 June she played the second act of *Phèdre* at the Gaiety Theatre, which set London alight. Her success over the season persuaded her to leave the company and strike out on her own.

The differences between Rachel and Bernhardt are as instructive as the similarities. In 1841, Rachel, the daughter of a Jewish pedlar, was such a sensation with her fashionable audiences that she was invited to the best drawing rooms, including the one at Windsor Castle. In later years, how-ever, when news of her lovers and illegitimate children leaked out (she never married), the invitations dried up. Bernhardt, too, had many love affairs, but they helped to make her name familiar, as Rachel's never was, to millions who would never have gone near a play in French. Both women openly displayed their sexuality on stage, something rarely allowed their English contemporaries, and in Bernhardt's case this chimed with her lifestyle: it was widely known that she slept in a coffin, and kept a cheetah as a pet.

She was also in tune with the times in her choice of plays. Rachel mostly failed in the few new plays she attempted. The classics counted for less in Bernhardt's career, although Phèdre long remained one of her best parts. In 1881 *Vanity Fair* denied that Bernhardt was a great actress, and even claimed that her Phèdre was flat, but

> give her a modern play, and a strong passionate motive for that play, and Sarah Bernhardt flings her whole nature into the scene with startling effect . . . As a woman she is fascinating; as an artist she has learned how, night after night, to reproduce that fascination. It is this produc-tion of her own individuality, this power of self-projection into the characters she portrays, that I fancy constitute her secret . . . With the

personal life of an artist of any sort of course one has nothing to do; but there are sometimes tones, expressions and movements given to us on the stage that strike home with this thought – 'You who portray this for us *must* have felt this passion, and passed through this, in some similar moments yourself'; and these moments are very rare, very touching and of extraordinary value.[68]

Her personal life *was* relevant. Its melodrama added interest to the melodrama on stage. Bernhardt's leading man was often her latest real-life lover or even her husband, employed despite his lack of talent. Bernhardt's relationship with her public was like that of a pop or film star today, very different from that of her contemporaries. Like Irving's, Bernhardt's acting suited the melodramatic nineteenth century. One of her great hits was *The Lady of the Camellias*, which, like *Tosca*, became an an opera, *La Traviata*. Bernhardt's operatic style helped her overcome the language barrier.

It was a style little suited to the portrayal of 'ordinary people', and Bernhardt played queens and princesses, high-life adventuresses and courtesans. Her death scenes were particularly moving, and she was often called upon to murder an enemy or a lover. Bernard Shaw, who never fell under her spell, wrote that she would come every season with a new play 'in which she killed someone with any weapon from a hairpin to a hatchet'.[69]

In 1893, the Italian Eleanora Duse played the Lady of the Camellias in London for the first time, in a restrained, naturalistic style, which was the opposite of Bernhardt's. From then on the loyalty of theatre-goers was split between the two actresses. For Oscar Wilde, Duse was 'a fascinating artist though nothing to Sarah'.[70] Bernard Shaw disagreed, but even the Duse camp knew that any actress aspiring to fame would be measured against Bernhardt.

During that first visit to London by the Comédie Française in 1879, Irving played host to the company. He had become the ambassador of the acting profession in England to visiting celebrities, and gave a supper party in their honour when they visited the Lyceum. In 1886, Franz Liszt received the treatment after seeing Irving play Mephistopheles in *Faust*. The theatre orchestra played one of his compositions, a Hungarian march, in his honour, and Liszt acknowledged the applause from his box, which had been nailed shut to protect him from well-wishers. He had to leave through the royal box next door.

Liszt had arrived in London for two weeks on 3 April 1886. He had been in England several times as a boy prodigy of the piano, and his last visit had been 45 years earlier. It was not a success, partly because of his relationship with a married woman. Another pianist-composer of genius, Frédéric Chopin, who had also played to English and Scottish audiences in the 1840s, had fared scarcely better. In 1848 (when he met Jenny Lind in London), Chopin had written of his British experience, 'To please the middle class you need something sensational, some technical display, which is out of my sphere.'[71]

As a pianist Liszt excelled in technical display, but the sensation he created in London during April 1886 did not depend on it. He never promised to play: each time he walked up to the piano, it was intended as a spontaneous gesture of appreciation to his hosts. His public hoped desperately to hear him, but they knew that his days as a touring virtuoso were long past, and were content merely to see the genius whose reputation as a wild romantic had given way to that of a 74-year-old *abbé*. After Liszt had played to her at Windsor Castle, the Queen, one of the few who remembered him from 1841, wrote that whereas all those years ago he had seemed 'a wild fantastic looking man', he now looked 'a quiet benevolent old priest, with long white hair and scarcely any teeth'.[72]

Liszt attended a ceremony at the Royal Academy of Music to inaugurate the Liszt scholarships for young British composers and pianists. There was a concert; and, when it was over, he consented to play. In later life a student said, 'No piano has ever sounded the same to me before or since.'[73] The centrepiece of the visit was the first complete performance in Britain of Liszt's oratorio *St Elizabeth*. It took place at the St James's Hall, where Dickens had given his last reading. The audience burst into applause when Liszt entered, and afterwards the Prince of Wales went to his box to congratulate him, and invited him to Marlborough House. At the end of the performance, he received one of the greatest ovations of his career. Standing in the middle of the orchestra, he was showered with applause by the singers and players as well as the audience. The performance was so successful that another was hurriedly arranged for the Crystal Palace where a group of cab drivers, who knew about celebrities even if they did not know about music, raised their hats to 'Habby Liszt', as they called him.

At a concert at the Grosvenor Gallery, Liszt played a piece by Schubert and a Hungarian rhapsody of his own. Sir George Grove, who was there, recorded, 'Directly he sat down, he dismissed that very artificial smile which he always wears, and his face assumed the most beautiful serene look with enormous power and repose in it.'[74]

Top international musicians were drawn to London in the 1880s by the money to be earned. However, to have *Liszt* in town was of a different order. It was claimed that during his 17-day visit he was 'fêted as no artist has ever been in this country'.[75] He had not aroused such enthusiasm since the days of continental 'Lisztomania' 40 years earlier, and the feeling that the British public's response had been inadequate then may have made it more tumultuous now. As he left, Liszt said that he hoped to return, but little more than three months later he was dead.

The following year, 1887, saw the Queen's Golden Jubilee. The procession through the streets of London and the great ceremony in Westminster Abbey were at the centre of the festivities. However, there was one spectacle worthy to be compared even with this sumptuous pageantry. It was previewed in print by Henry Irving, who had seen it in America:

> I saw an entertainment in New York which impressed me immensely. It is coming to London. It is an entertainment in which the whole of the most interesting episodes of life on the extreme frontier of civilization in America are represented with the most graphic vividness and scrupulous detail. You have real cowboys with bucking horses, real buffaloes and great hordes of steer which are lassoed and stampeded in the most realistic fashion imaginable. Then there are real Indians who execute attacks upon coaches driven at full speed. No one can exaggerate the extreme excitement and 'go' of the whole performance. It is simply immense, and I venture to predict that when it comes to London it will take the town by storm.[76]

He was right. It was a masterstroke to bring over Buffalo Bill's Wild West Show for the first time when London was packed for the Jubilee. It was the most popular part of an American exhibition at Earl's Court, and it was well ensconced by the time the main jubilee celebrations started in June. To whet the public appetite important people were invited to previews, including Gladstone, whose conversation through an interpreter with Red Shirt, the American Indian, was widely reported. The show opened on 5 May. When 'the entire company rode out on the arena from an ambuscade of rocks, the American Indians in full war paint, the sensation they produced was instantaneous and electric'. The Prince of Wales was there, and Queen Victoria attended a private performance. That was a great coup: the Queen never went to the theatre now, and the theatrical profession was jealous of Buffalo Bill. The *Era* protested: 'It is still fresh in the minds of the public and the profession that Her Majesty conferred a similar honour on the entertainment supplied by the Paris Hippodrome Company at Olympia. Now that the French and American shows have been patronised by the Queen, we may hope that Her Majesty will consider the propriety of encouraging native enterprise.'[77]

Victoria was so delighted with the show that she commanded a performance at Windsor Castle on the morning of 20 June, the day before the great jubilee celebrations. On the day itself, Buffalo Bill and his troupe rode through the streets of central London to the delight of the crowds waiting for the Queen.[78]

Never had England seen so many American Indians or so many exotic North American animals as they saw at Earl's Court. Who had seen *one* bison (or 'buffalo') before? The famous Deadwood stage coach had been brought over especially for the Indians to attack, and they also attacked an immigrant wagon train and a settler's hut, with lots of gunpowder and war-whooping, before Buffalo Bill and his scouts rode to the rescue.

If the spectacle of the Wild West was a great attraction, Buffalo Bill, or William Cody, was the star at the centre of it all. He was a legendary figure who had lived the frontier life on display at Earl's Court. At 41, he had kept his fine figure, and his riding, shooting and lassoing skills thrilled his London audiences (as did the marksmanship of the 20-year-old Annie Oakley, now best remembered from the musical *Annie Get Your Gun*.) Like other visiting stars before him, Cody gained useful publicity by mixing in high society. He was made an honorary member of various London clubs, where he met public figures, including Irving, an early visitor to the show. Irving invited the American Indians to see *Faust*, but they did not seem to enjoy it.

It was all so new to London – a remote and romantic way of life from across the ocean. Bronco riding was another novelty, and visitors enjoyed being allowed to roam around the Indian encampment where the Indians watched them impassively.

A welcoming article in the *Illustrated London News* hints at why the Wild West show caught the mood of the times:

It would be unnatural to deny ourselves the indulgence of a just grati-
fication in seeing what men of our own blood, men of our own mind
and disposition in all essential respects, though tempered and sharpened
by more stimulating conditions, with some wider opportunities for
exertion, have achieved in raising a wonderful fabric of modern civilization and bring it to the highest prosperity across the whole breadth
of the Western continent . . . and we take it kindly of the great kindred
people of the United States that they now send such a magnificent representation to the motherland, determined to take some part in
celebrating the jubilee of Her Majesty the Queen.[79]

There are some interesting misapprehensions there: if the Wild West
wanted to celebrate the jubilee, it was as a way of making money. The pro-
portion of Americans for whom Britain was the motherland was getting
smaller each day. The splendour of the jubilee concealed an uneasy feeling that Britain's power might be in decline. Many people wanted to
believe that, through ties of blood, the United States would inevitably be
an ally in any important struggle, and this seemed to be confirmed by the
huge exhibition in London of American strength and vitality. In 1887, the
British wanted to love America and, even more, to be loved by her.

Four years earlier, however, American showmen, and one in particular,
had been out of favour. More than 40 years after he had brought Tom
Thumb to Europe, Phineas T Barnum was still looking for sensations to
import into America. He had once failed to buy Shakespeare's birthplace,
which he wanted to ship in sections to New York, but in 1882 he succeeded in carrying off a beloved national treasure in the face of a
tremendous outcry: Jumbo had been London Zoo's first African elephant. He had been quite small when he arrived in 1865, and, it was
thought, about four years old. However, by 1882, he had grown to about
twelve feet high, and was one of the most popular sights in London. A
generation had grown up with fond memories of feeding Jumbo and
riding on his back.[80]

The trouble was that by about 1880 Jumbo had begun to misbehave,
smashing up his house, and inflicting some nasty injuries on himself in the
process. Even worse, he was a potential danger to others; it was thought
prudent to buy an elephant gun, and, when he was in a bad mood, to suspend the children's rides. The Zoo was delighted to sell Jumbo to
Barnum.

Strangely, there was no great public reaction when *The Times* first published the story in January 1882. The turning point came on 17 February when Barnum's men arrived with a crate to take Jumbo to London docks. The horror of the situation now dawned on Jumbo's fans and, it seemed, on Jumbo himself. He lay down and refused to budge. Crowds gathered, and were greatly moved by the sight of Jumbo in chains. A national sensation resulted when the press took up the subject as a patriotic issue. Jumbo was depicted as a hero, bravely resisting the Yankee aggressor. The Zoo authorities were reviled for betraying an old and dear friend. Their opponents dwelt on the distress to children, and a relationship was assumed between Jumbo and a female African elephant called Alice, who had been at the Zoo nearly as long as he had. As a music hall song put it:

Who doesn't remember when 'doing' the Zoo,
The gambols they've had on the green,
Little children all scrambling on Jumbo's broad back,
The pleasantest sight to be seen;
The young ones unselfishly going him halves
With their buns and their oranges too.
Whoever once thought in those moments of joy
He'd be taken away from the Zoo? . . .

Now if *you* were an elephant, Jumbo by name,
And Alice the name of your wife,
Would *you* from your spouse like to be torn away,
And mis'rable be made for life?[81]

The furore made Jumbo the most famous elephant in history, and gave his name to the English language. While he was still refusing to get into his crate, questions were asked in the House, *Vanity Fair* started up a Jumbo Defence Fund, John Ruskin pitched in on Jumbo's side, and the numbers visiting the Zoo, to catch a last sight of him, rose to 60,000 a week. Barnum was delighted at the publicity – he was already Jumbo's legal owner, and knew that the outcry had come too late. The story goes that when his agent cabled New York to ask what should be done about Jumbo's intransigence, Barnum replied, 'Let him lie there a week, if he wants to. It's the best advertisement in the world.'

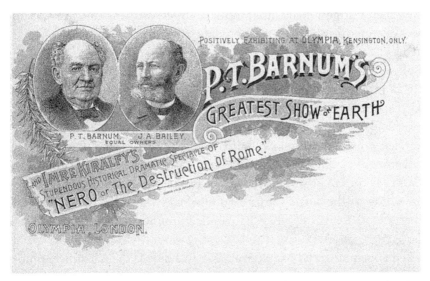

*Barnum and Bailey's 1889 'Nero or The Destruction of Rome', was billed
as 'the Most Stupendous and Regal Historical Production of any Era',
a claim backed up by – among other features – the involvement of
a thousand performers.*

Dissident fellows of the Zoological Society challenged the legality of
the sale. They lost, but by that time Jumbo had missed two transatlantic
liners. His picture was everywhere, on songs and sheet music, and advertisements of every kind; the newspapers and magazines were full of Jumbo
cartoons; everybody was making Jumbo jokes, a common theme being
that Jumbo should be kept at home, and Gladstone, Bradlaugh, or some
other hate figure sent to America instead. All this time presents for Jumbo
poured in – fruit, buns, sweets and cakes – but also oysters, wines, spirits
and beer, although these last were said to have been put 'where they
would do most good'. On 20 March 1882, 18,500 visitors to the Zoo were
the last to see Jumbo in London. The next day he was finally lured into his
crate, but it took nearly three hours to chain him inside by all four legs,
and many more to make the crate safe from his rage, and get it outside the
Zoo grounds. The Jumbo sensation had reached its peak, and now, per-
force, died down.

For the next three years Jumbo toured America with Barnum and
Bailey's Circus. In September 1885 he was killed in a railway accident but

even then Barnum made him profitable by showing his stuffed skin and his skeleton. In 1889, they were brought to England when the circus visited Olympia.

This was Barnum's last sensation on British soil. At 79, he made as big an impact on a huge scale as he had in miniature with Tom Thumb 45 years earlier. The three-ring circus is supposed to have been invented by the British showman, Lord George Sanger, but, if so, nobody noticed when *Barnum and Bailey* opened on 11 November 1889 at Olympia. Nor did any one care about Bailey. 'The Greatest Show on Earth', as the circus was billed and on all sides acknowledged to be, had to be due to the world's greatest showman, who received the loudest cheers of the evening when he paraded around the arena in an open carriage.[82]

The opening grand parade – or, as it was billed, 'the magnificent hippodramatic, wild beast and equestrian procession and pageant' – was worth the entrance money in itself. It included 'the golden chariot revelries of Mother Goose' and 'the pageant tales of dazzling fairy land', not to mention zebras, camels, 13 elephants and other animals. The only criticism of the show was that there was so much going on at once in the three rings that it was impossible to take it all in, but this brought spectators back to see what they had missed. The three rings were dispensed with during the last hour of the performance, which consisted of a spectacle called 'Nero or The Destruction of Rome', billed as 'the Most Stupendous and Regal Historical Production of any Era'.[83] This claim was backed up by the appearance of 1,000 performers and a large number of the animals. The scenes included chariot races, races for elephants and camels, gladiatorial combats, and a riot of Roman citizens. Nero committed suicide against a background of burning Rome and a final 'glorious apotheosis' and 'celestial vision' of the dawn of Christianity. The action was mimed, and accompanied by an orchestra and a great choir singing hymns and Christian odes.

In addition, spectators could visit many side shows outside the arena for no extra charge. If the two manifestations of dear old Jumbo were the most poignant, there were also the mermaid, the thin man, the fat woman and Barnum's usual collection of freaks. The lowest price for it all was only a shilling, the same as Barnum had charged to see Tom Thumb all those years ago. In its emphasis on size and value for money, 'the Greatest Show on Earth' was a truly American entertainment. Barnum, an impresario not a performer, had become a star in his own right, and given a lesson in how to create sensations through size, planning, advertising and razzmatazz. Those who had sneered in the 1860s, and who had associated sensation with America, had been more prophetic than they knew. In 1889, as with Tom Thumb in 1844, Barnum led the way into the twentieth century.

Afterword

Much has been written of how remote the Victorians are from us. Their inflexible thinking on social issues, the severity of their moral code, the hypocrisy with which they broke it have been much derided. They have been seen as monsters of repression and restraint. This book, however, has attempted to redress the balance, to show how like us they were in their love of sensation, scandal, melodrama and excess.

In referring to 'the Victorians' most people mean 'middle-class Victorians'. There is no doubt that the much larger numbers of the less educated social strata loved sensation in all its forms, and melodrama was the most popular form of entertainment. However, if the sensation play was mainly performed to working-class audiences, the middle classes were avid readers of the sensation novel.

The impact of the sensation novel is the easiest Victorian sensation to recapture today, and that of the sensation play the most difficult. With the exception of Boucicault's best works, it is impossible to stage such pieces now: their intrinsic worth is too slight to justify the enormous expenditure of money and manpower. On the other hand, it is possible to relive the Victorian novel-reading experience by turning to the works of Wilkie Collins or Mary Braddon. Admittedly, a few references have become obscure and their literary innovations, re-used by countless imitators, are now familiar, but even titles long out of print are back in the bookshops, largely because the best of these tales are as exciting as they ever were.

The vast majority of sensations emerged from real life. In some cases, the excitement they produced was negative in tone – for instance, when it was associated with subjects such as birth control, or child prostitution. It was not only the middle classes who shied away from discussing them openly but these issues could no longer be avoided in an age when press reporting was gathering momentum. The strength of resistance to public acting of a taboo subject made the sensation all the greater when it failed.

Most types of sensation gave immense pleasure to the public, especially the unsavoury revelations of murder trials, and the lurid tales of adultery, domestic cruelty and violence that emerged from the Divorce Court. Like many of us, the Victorians often relished the discomfiture of others, particularly if they were rich, famous, powerful, or any combination of the three. Many Victorian newspapers were not so different from their modern-day equivalents in zestfully reporting what they claimed to deplore.

The two Victorian sensations best known to the twenty-first century were enjoyed by millions of people who might not have admitted to their enjoyment. One was the fall of Oscar Wilde. The revelations in court inspired revulsion, but also delight that Wilde received what was believed to be his just deserts. A jury's decision was as exciting then as today we might find the result of a football match – and provoked the same sort of partisan reaction. The second was Jack the Ripper, who inspired disgust and horror – but horror stories and films show that fear can be accompanied by pleasure: this case provided a real-life horror story combined with a murder mystery. The real and the imaginary were juxtaposed in an extraordinary way during the late summer of 1888 when the Ripper was most active. The American actor Richard Mansfield was appearing in London in *Dr Jekyll and Mr Hyde*, the first dramatisation of R L Stevenson's novel. One playgoer remembered Hyde's first entry: 'The ill-shaped monster appeared in the moonlight behind a french window, with his hands up to his head, and making a horrible hissing intake of the breath. Never did I see an audience so frightened ... On the Saturday afternoon I went to see the play for the second time, and, on emerging into the Strand, after the performance, the first thing that met my eyes was the poster of the *Globe* newspaper announcing that two more murders had been discovered that day.'[1]

The Oscar Wilde and Jack the Ripper sensations are exceptional for their longevity: few sensations last, unless their interest is mainly political. Tom Thumb's first visit to Britain, the nun who sued her Mother Superior for libel, the ecstatic reception given to Blondin and Leotard, even the great Tichborne case are virtually forgotten. Sometimes their most lasting impact was on the English language; but even that has tended to fade. Many people will be aware that the leotard was named after a trapeze artist, but fewer, perhaps, that 'tich' means a small person because a famous music-hall star called himself 'Little Tich' in a joking reference to the corpulent Tichborne Claimant.

The ephemeral nature of most sensations is of particular interest to a historian. If the Victorians share with us a taste for sensation in general, their sensations were necessarily of their own time. Events which engage millions of people at a particular point in history characterize it all the more strongly. That Lord Dundreary and the Tichborne Claimant kept the public interested for years was their most extraordinary achievement: they give a fascinating insight into what millions of Victorians were prepared to swallow in the 1860s and 1870s. By contrast, Garibaldi's sensational visit was confined to a single month, and showed much about the Victorians of April 1864: their behaviour in crowds, their concept of a hero, and the Government's fear of popular sentiment. Similarly, *The Maiden Tribute of Modern Babylon* reveals a great deal about Victorian society in the summer of 1885: its attitudes to sex, its idea of respectability, the power of the press. Whatever the time-scale, the evidence can be used, of course, to contribute towards a picture of the Victorian age as a whole.

Although these sensations were ephemeral, in that their time was soon past, they had an afterlife beyond the weeks, months, or even years during which they held the public in thrall. They lingered in the minds of everyone who lived through them. They provided a common experience and then a common memory for whole generations, something to talk about at the time and something to refer back to. Sensations offer no greater pleasure than this. We have the advantage over the Victorians in that, as their descendants, we can not only enjoy our own sensations in this way but also relive to some extent the events that so moved them. Of course, the whole experience cannot be recaptured, but we can console ourselves for what is lost with the knowledge that we have come a little nearer to Queen Victoria's subjects. As it is to be hoped this book has shown, they were not only our ancestors but our brothers and sisters under the skin.

CHRONOLOGY OF THE
MAIN EVENTS MENTIONED

1837

20 June   Victoria becomes Queen.

1838

9 November   Publication of *Oliver Twist* in book form

1839

January–   First instalment of *Jack Sheppard* in *Bentley's Miscellany*
February 1840
4 November   Newport rising of Chartists

1840

13 January   Chartist leaders of Newport rising sentenced to death
26 January   Abortive Chartist rising in Bradford
1 February   Death sentence on Chartist leaders commuted to deportation
10 February   Victoria marries Albert
6 May   Lord William Russell found dead in bed with his throat cut
10 June   Edward Oxford tries to kill the Queen
20 June   Courvoisier sentenced to death for murdering Lord William
                     Russell
6 July   Courvoisier hanged
22 November   Princess Victoria born
3 December   'The boy' Jones found in Buckingham Palace

1841

10 May   Rachel's first London appearance
9 November   Prince of Wales born

1842

30 May	John Francis tries to shoot the Queen
3 July	John William Bean tries to shoot the Queen

1843

20 January	Daniel MacNaghten shoots Edward Drummond, mistaking him for Prime Minister, Sir Robert Peel
25 January	Drummond dies
4 March	MacNaghten escapes death penalty on grounds of insanity

1844

3 February	Barnum and Tom Thumb arrive in England
20th March–20 July	Tom Thumb's first season starts at Egyptian Hall, London
22 June	Benjamin Robert Haydon kills himself

1847

4 February	Tom Thumb returns to USA
4 May	Jenny Lind's first appearance in London
27 May	Jenny Lind, in *The Daughter of the Regiment*

1848

10 April	Mass meeting of Chartists – later aborted – on Kennington Common
4 May	Jenny Lind opens second London season in *La Sonnambula*
25 May	Jenny Lind in *Lucia di Lammermoor*
28 November	James Blomfield Rush murders Isaac Jermy

1849

29 March	Rush trial opens
21 April	Rush hanged
10 May	Jenny Lind appears in opera for the last time
19 May	William Hamilton fires at the Queen
17 August	The body of Patrick O'Connor found under the floorboards of the Mannings' kitchen in Bermondsey
25–6 October	Trial of the Mannings opens
13 November	Mannings hanged

1850

27 June	Robert Pate strikes the Queen
4 September	General Haynau attacked by Barclay & Perkins brewery workers

29 September	Nicholas Wiseman created Archbishop of Westminster
5 November	Effigies of the Pope and Wiseman burned
7 November	Publication of letter from Prime Minister, Lord John Russell, to Bishop of Durham, denouncing 'Papal Aggression'
11 November	Wiseman reaches England from Rome

1851

| 23 October | Lajos Kossuth begins triumphant visit to Britain |
| 19 November | Kossuth leaves for USA |

1852

| 24 February | *The Corsican Brothers* opens |
| September | Publication of *Uncle Tom's Cabin* |

1853

| 27 December | Charles Dickens' first public reading, at the town hall, Birmingham |

1856

27th May	William Palmer sentenced to death
14th June	Palmer hanged
19 October	Stampede at Surrey music-hall, during Charles Spurgeon's first service there, killed seven

1857

30 June	Madeleine Smith trial opens
9 July	Madeleine Smith verdict: 'not proven'
30 June	Charles Dickens' first London reading

1858

| 1 January | Divorce Court opens |
| 29 April | Charles Dickens' first reading for his own profit |

1859

| 26 November– 25 August 1860 | *The Woman in White* serialized in *All The Year Round* |

1860

| January– August 1861 | *East Lynne* serialized in *The New Monthly Magazine* |
| 10 September | British premiere of Boucicault's *The Colleen Bawn* |

1861

25 March	Opening of Spurgeon's Metropolitan Tabernacle
20 May	Leotard's first London appearance
1 June	Blondin's first London appearance
9 November	Opening of Edmund Falconer's *Peep o' Day*
11 November	Edward Sothern appears in London as Lord Dundreary
18 November	Opening of Boucicault's *The Octoroon*
14 December	Prince Albert dies

1862

1 October	*Lady Audley's Secret* published in book form

1863

10 March	Prince of Wales marries Princess Alexandra

1864

3 April	Giuseppe Garibaldi arrives in Britain
11 April	Garibaldi arrives in London
28 April	Garibaldi leaves Britain
29 July	First Contagious Diseases Act passed
1 August	Opening of Boucicault's *The Streets of London*
3 October	Adah Isaacs Menken makes first London appearance as Mazeppa.
November–June 1866	*Armadale* serialized in *The Cornhill Magazine*.
16 December	The Chetwynd divorce case opens

1865

20 January	Chetwynd divorce case ends; jury finds for Mrs Chetwynd
22 March	London opening of Boucicault's *Arrah-na-Pogue*
4 October	London opening of Charles Reade's *It's Never Too Late To Mend*

1866

23 July	Great Reform League demonstration in Hyde Park
11 June	Second Contagious Diseases Act passed
15 September	Boucicault's *The Long Strike* opens
6 October	Boucicault's *The Flying Scud* opens

1867

12 July	Sultan of Turkey begins his visit to Britain
18 September	Fenian prisoners rescued from police van in Manchester; policeman killed
24 November	Three Fenians hanged in Manchester
12 December	Fenian bomb at Clerkenwell prison

1868

4 January– 8 August	*The Moonstone* serialized in *All The Year Round*
26 May	Michael Barrett the last man to be publicly hanged in Britain
28 May	Reade and Boucicault's *Foul Play* opens
12 August	Boucicault's *After Dark* opens

1869

3 February	Saurin v. Starr trial opens
5 August	Boucicault's *Formosa* opens
11 August	Third Contagious Diseases Act passed

1870

16 February	Insanity trial of Lady Mordaunt (Mordaunt divorce case) opens
21 February	Prince of Wales in witness box
15 March	Charles Dickens' last public reading
28 April	Arrest of Boulton and Park
29 April	Boulton and Park charged at Bow Street police court
30 May	Boulton and Park committed for trial

1871

21 March	Marriage of Princess Louise with Marquess of Lorne
9th May	Trial of Boulton and Park opens
10th May	First Tichborne trial opens
15 May	Boulton and Park acquitted
25 November	Henry Irving opens in *The Bells*

1872

27 February	National day of Thanksgiving for recovery of Prince of Wales from typhoid
29 February	Arthur O'Connor accosts Queen with loaded pistol
6 March	End of first Tichborne trial and arrest of the Claimant
16 August	Voting in Colchester by-election

1873

23 April	Second Tichborne trial opens
17 June	Moody and Sankey arrive in Britain
18 June	Shah of Persia begins visit to Britain

1874

28 April	The Claimant sentenced to 14 years' penal servitude
31 October	Henry Irving opens in *Hamlet*

1875

16 February	Dr Edward Vaughan Kenealy elected MP for Stoke-on-Trent
9 March	Moody and Sankey hold first revival meeting
22 June	Moody and Sankey service attended by Eton boys after protests in Parliament
22 July	Samuel Plimsoll, MP creates dramatic scene in Commons over 'coffin ships'
2 August	Colonel Valentine Baker appears at Croydon Assizes, convicted of indecent assault
4 August	Moody and Sankey return to the USA
19 August	Royal yacht, with Queen on board, causes three deaths
4 September	Opening of Boucicault's *The Shaughraun*

1876

10tJune	First of a series of reports in *Daily News* of Turkish massacres of Bulgarians
11 July	Second inquest on Charles Bravo opens
6 September	Gladstone publishes *Bulgarian Horrors and the Question of the East*
9 September	Gladstone speaks on Bulgaria at Blackheath
29 November	Charley Peace murders Arthur Dyson

1877

18 June	The Queen v. Charles Bradlaugh and Annie Besant trial opens
25 June	Bradlaugh and Besant sentenced

1878

24 February	Pro-government and pro-Russian demonstrations in Hyde Park
16 July	Beaconsfield (Disraeli) returns from Congress of Berlin proclaiming 'Peace with Honour'

1879

4 February	Charley Peace sentenced to death for murder of Arthur Dyson
25 February	Charley Peace hanged
2 June	Sarah Bernhardt's first appearance in London
2 June	Opening of Charles Reade's *Drink*
13 June	Sarah Bernhard opens in *Phèdre*
24 November	Gladstone's first Midlothian campaign begins
8 December	Midlothian campaign ends

1880

2 April	General election: Liberals win large majority. Kenealy loses his seat at Stoke. Bradlaugh elected for Northampton
25 May	Sarah Bernhardt opens second London season
23 June	Bradlaugh taken into custody for refusing to leave the House.

1881

9 April	Bradlaugh elected for Northampton for second time
11 June	Sarah Bernhardt opens in *La Dame aux Camellias*
3 August	Bradlaugh forcibly ejected from House of Commons

1882

10 February	Bradlaugh administers the oath to himself
17 February	Barnum's men arrive at London Zoo to remove Jumbo.
2 March	Roderick Maclean fires on Queen; Bradlaugh elected for Northampton for third time
21 March	Jumbo removed from London Zoo to be shipped to America
5 August	*Pluck* opens at Drury Lane Theatre.

1883

21 April	House of Commons repeals Contagious Diseases Acts
3 May	House of Commons rejects a Bill to allow Bradlaugh to affirm
15 October	*A Sailor and His Lass* opens at Drury Lane Theatre

1884

| 11 October | The Claimant released on ticket-of-leave |

1885

| 6–10 July | Stead publishes *The Maiden Tribute of Modern Babylon* on child prostitution in the *Pall Mall Gazette* |
| 10 August | The Criminal Law Amendment Bill becomes law, raising the age of consent, and making all homosexual acts illegal |

| 10 November | Stead sentenced to three months in prison for 'abducting' Eliza Armstrong |
| 23 November | General election: Bradlaugh elected for Northampton for fourth time |

1886

13 January	Speaker Peel allows Bradlaugh to take the oath
8 February	Social Democratic Federation rally in Trafalgar Square, riots in the West End
12 February	Crawford v. Crawford divorce case, Sir Charles Dilke is cited as co-respondent
3 April	Liszt arrives in Britain
16 July	Dilke reopens the Crawford case
26 November	Campbell divorce case opens
20 December	Campbell divorce case ends: neither party granted a divorce

1887

18 April	*The Times* publishes facsimile of a forged letter in Parnell's handwriting condoning the Phoenix Park murders
5 May	Buffalo Bill's Wild West Show opens at Olympia
21 June	Golden Jubilee processions
13 November	Bloody Sunday in Trafalgar Square

1888

3 April	Murder of Emma Smith, sometimes included among victims of Jack the Ripper
7 August	Murder of Martha Tabram, Ripper victim
31 August	Murder of Mary Ann Nichols Ripper victim
8 September	Murder of Annie Chapman, Ripper victim
30 September	Murder of Elisabeth Stride and Catherine Eddowes, Ripper victims
17 September	Parnell Commission begins work

1889

20–21 February	Sir Charles Russell cross-examines Pigott before the Parnell Commission
26 February	Pigott fails to appear
1 March	Pigott commits suicide in Madrid
17 July	Murder of Alice McKenzie, sometimes included among Ripper victims
31 July	Trial of Florence Maybrick opens

22 August	Florence Maybrick's death sentence commuted to life imprisonment
28 September	*North London Gazette* breaks the story of the Cleveland Street Affair
11 November	Barnum & Bailey's Circus opens at Olympia
22 November	Last day of Parnell Commission hearings

1890

15 January	Editor of *North London Gazette* sentenced to a year in prison for libelling Lord Euston
13 February	Parnell Commission issues its report
15 February	Last night of Barnum & Bailey's circus
28 February	Henry Labouchere accuses Lord Salisbury of a cover-up in the Cleveland Street Affair, and is suspended from the House of Commons

1891

13 February	Murder of Frances Coles, sometimes included among Ripper victims
1 June	Opening of Sir William Gordon Cumming's libel case, the Tranby Croft Affair
2 June	Prince of Wales gives evidence about playing baccarat

1894

| 15 September | Opening of *The Derby Winner* at Drury Lane Theatre |

1895

3 April	Oscar Wilde sues Lord Queensberry for libel
26 April	Trial of Oscar Wilde for committing 'indecent acts'; the jury cannot reach a verdict
22 May	Wilde's second trial opens; he is sentenced to two years' hard labour

1897

| 21 June | Diamond Jubilee procession |
| 16 September | *The White Heather* opens at Drury Lane Theatre |

1898

| 1 April | The Claimant dies |
| 15 September | *The Great Ruby* opens at Drury Lane Theatre |

1899

16 September   *Hearts Are Trumps* opens at Drury Lane Theatre

1900

17 May   Rumours reach London of the Relief of Mafeking
18 May   Rumours confirmed
20 September   *The Price of Peace* opens at Drury Lane Theatre

NOTES

INTRODUCTION

1. 'The Great Sensation Song', Frank Hall and Frederic Archer, London, 1861.
2. *The Shorter Oxford English Dictionary*, 1947.
3. *Manchester Guardian*, 10 November 1841.
4. *The Annual Register for 1849*, Appendix to Chronicle, p. 429.
5. *Household Narrative of Current Events*, 29 October to 28 November 1850, p. 247.
6. *Punch*, vol. 41, p. 31.
7. *All The Year Round*, vol. IX, no. 222, 25 July 1863, p. 517.
8. Collins, *No Name*, Sc. 4, Chapter 13.
9. *The Times*, 31 May 1895.
10. Charles Edwardes, 'The New Football Mania' in *Nineteenth Century*, October 1892.
11. Henry Mayhew, *London Labour and the London Poor*, London, 1864, vol. 1, p. 236.
12. Serjeant Ballantine, *Some Experiences of a Barrister's Life*, 1882, p. 72.
13. *The Times*, 29 October 1849.
14. *Pall Mall Gazette*, 4 December 1890.
15. *Tomahawk*, 5 March 1870.
16. *Punch*, vol. 17, no. 434, p. 181.
17. *The Times*, 2 July 1857.
18. *Reynolds's Newspaper*, 5 July 1857.

1: ROYALTY

1. Quoted in Cecil Woodham-Smith, *Queen Victoria: Her Life and Times 1819–61*, London, 1975, p. 264.
2. 'The Four Georges. II: George the Second', in *Cornhill*, August 1860, p. 189.

3. Quoted in Cecil Woodham-Smith, *Queen Victoria*, p. 204.

4. *Lloyd's Newspaper*, 29 June 1838.

5. The same account of the fair appeared in a number of London papers, e.g. *Bell's Life in London*, 1 July 1838. See also Thomas Frost, *The Old Showmen and the Old London Fairs*, London, 1874.

6. Woodham-Smith, *Queen Victoria*, p. 205.

7. Ibid., p. 208.

8. Adherents of Chartism, the UK parliamentary reform movement of 1837–48. It took its name from *The People's Charter*, in which its principles were set out.

9. *Sunday Times*, 9 February 1840.

10. *The Pilgrim Edition of the Letters of Charles Dickens*, vol. 2, ed. Madeleine House and Graham Storey, 1969, p. 23.

11. John Ashton, *Modern Street Ballads*, London, 1968, p. 277.

12. *Sunday Times*, 9 February 1840.

13. *Letters of Charles Dickens*, vol. 2, p. 16.

14. *Observer*, 16 Feburary 1840.

15. *The Times*, 11 June 1840.

16. *Sunday Times*, 14 June 1840.

17. John Guille Millais, *The Life and Letters of Sir John Everett Millais*, London, 1899, pp. 20–1.

18. *The Times*, 13 June 1840.

19. *Sunday Times*, 14 June 1840.

20. Ibid.

21. *Observer*, 14 June 1840.

22. *The Times*, 12 June 1840.

23. *Sunday Times*, 14 June 1840.

24. *The Times*, 4 December 1840.

25. *The Times*, 5 December 1840.

26. Ibid., 4 December 1840.

27. 'The Boy Wot Visits the Palace', James Bruton, arranged by Henry Giffin; author's collection.

28. G W M Reynolds, *The Mysteries of London*, vol. 1, chapters LVIII and LIX.

29. *The Times*, 11 November 1841.

30. Ibid., 10 November 1841.

31. Ibid., 12 November 1841.

32. Ashton, *Modern Street Ballads*, pp 279–80.

33. Dorothy Thompson, *The Chartists*, London, 1984, p. 300.

34. *The Times*, 16 November 1841.

35. *The Times*, 31 May and 1 June 1842.

36. Ibid., 24 July 1866.
37. *The Times*, 28 June 1850.
38. *The Times*, 1 March and 12 April 1872.
39. *The Times*, 3 March 1882.
40. Dana Bentley Cranch, *Edward VII – Image of an Era*, London, 1992, p. 46.
41. *Letters of Charles Dickens*, vol. 10, ed. Graham Storey, 1998, p. 221.
42. Mary Elizabeth Braddon, *John Marchmont's Legacy*, chapter XXXV.
43. Sir Sidney Lee, *Edward VII: A Biography*, 1925, pp. 160–1.
44. For the Mordaunt case I have relied heavily on Elizabeth Hamilton, *The Warwickshire Scandal*, 1999.
45. This is the compressed account from *The Times*, 17 February 1870, in which the questions are omitted. The exchange is quoted in full in Hamilton, *Warwickshire Scandals*, p. 331.
46. Ibid., pp. 350–1.
47. *The Times*, 24 February 1870.
48. Dudley W R Bahlman (ed.), *The Diary of Sir Edward Walter Hamilton*, London, 1972, p. xv.
49. *Punch*, vol. 59, p. 181.
50. Quoted in *The Entr'acte*, 17 June 1871.
51. Anon., 'The Wedding of Louise and Johnny of Lorne', printed by Disley, High Street, St Giles.
52. *The Entr'acte*, 24 December 1870, did not rate it highly.
53. *Illustrated London News*, 1 April 1871.
54. *Daily Telegraph*, 21 March 1871.
55. Quoted in Roy Jenkins, *Dilke: A Victorian Tragedy*, London, 1996, pp. 69–70.
56. *The Times*, 24 November 1871.
57. Ibid., 13 December 1871.
58. Ibid., 28 February 1872
59. *Illustrated London News*, 2 March 1872.
60. *Manchester Guardian*, 28 February 1872.
61. Ibid.
62. 'England Greets Thee Prince of Wales', Frank Green and Henry Parker.
63. *Manchester Guardian*, 28 February 1872.
64. *The Times*, 13 July 1867.
65. Ibid.
66. *The Times*, 23 July 1867
67. *The Times*, 13 July 1867.
68. *The Times*, 16 July 1867.
69. *The Times*, 20 July 1867.

70. *Foreign & Commonwealth Office*, published for the Foreign & Commonwealth Office, 3rd edition, 1996.
71. *The Times*, 22 July 1867.
72. *The Times*, 19 June 1873
73. Sir Henry Ponsonby, *Sidelights on Queen Victoria*, London, 1930, p. 118.
74. 'Have You Seen the Shah?', Bracey Vane.
75. *Entr'acte*, 5 July 1873, review of London Pavilion music-hall.
76. *Era*, 21 September 1873, review of Forester's music-hall.
77. *Era*, 6 July 1873.
78. *The Times*, 21 June 1873.
79. *The Times*, 24 June 1873.
80. *The Times*, 26 June 1873.
81. See note 55.
82. I have relied on Michael Havers, Edward Grayson and Peter Shankland, *The Royal Baccarat Scandal*, London, 1988.
83. *The Royal Baccarat Scandal*, pp. 197–8.
84. Quoted in *Reynolds's Newspaper*, 7 June 1891.
85. 'Oh Billy Cumming, Can It Really Be the Truth?' J P Harrington and Orlando Powell.
86. 'The Scandals are 'Cumming', a Baccarat Song', Charles D Hickman, arranged by Warwick Williams,.
87. *Era*, 13 June 1891, reviews of the Forester's and the Washington music-halls.
88. *Reynolds's Newspaper*, 7 June 1891.
89. Ibid.
90. *Baccarat*, Havers et al, p. 117.
91. *Reynolds's Newspaper*, 7 and 14 June 1891.
92. Reprinted in the *Pall Mall Gazette*, 9 February 1886.
93. *The Times*, 20 and 21 August 1875.
94. Ibid., 28 August; and Stanley Weintraub, *Victoria*, 1987, p. 415.
95. *The Times*, 11 April 1876.
96. *The Times*, 22 June 1887.
97. Ibid.
98. William Baker and William M Clarke (eds.), *The Letters of Wilkie Collins*, vol. 2, London, 1999, p. 541.
99. 'Oh! The Jubilee', James Tighe.
100. *The Times*, 23 June 1887.
101. *The Times*, 22 June 1887.
102. Details of the Diamond Jubilee: *Manchester Guardian* 22 June 1897.
103. *Manchester Guardian*, 23 June 1897.

2: POLITICAL MOVEMENTS

1. 'Model England' Harry Dacre and Edgar Ward.
2. John Ashton, *Modern Street Ballads*, 1968, p. 335.
3. Asa Briggs, *Chartism*, 1998, p. 1.
4. Dorothy Thompson, *The Chartists*, 1984, preface.
5. *Monmouthshire Beacon*, 9 November 1839; and Dorothy Thompson, *The Chartists*, pp. 79–86.
6. *Northern Star*, 9 November 1839.
7. Ibid., 16 November 1839.
8. Anon., 'Chartism' in *Fraser's*, May 1848, XXXVII, 579 ff.
9. *Monmouthshire Beacon*, 9 November 1839.
10. *Northern Star*, 4 January 1840.
11. Ibid., 9 November 1839.
12. Ibid., 4 January 1839.
13. Thompson, *Chartism*, pp. 321–2.
14. Quoted in T Charles-Edwards and B Richardson, *They Saw It Happen. An Anthology of Eyewitness's Accounts of Events in British History 1689–1897*, Oxford, 1958.
15. *Fraser's*, see note 5.
16. *Reynolds's Newspaper*, 8 June 1851.
17. *The Pilgrim Edition of the Letters of Charles Dickens*, vol. 5, ed. Graham Storey and K J Fielding, p. 274.
18. *The Times*, 11 April 1848.
19. From Thomas Frost, 'Forty Years Recollections' in Charles-Edwards and Richardson, *They Saw It Happen*.
20. *The Times*, 11 April 1848.
21. 'General Haynau & The Draymen', Thomas Ramsay, 1850.
22. Henry Mayhew, *London Labour and the London Poor*, vol. 2, London, 1864, p. 15.
23. See note 20.
24. M G Wiebe, J B Conacher, John Matthews and Mary S Millar, *Benjamin Disraeli Letters*, vol. 5 (eds), Toronto, London, 1993, p. 486.
25. *Reynolds's Newspaper*, 2 November 1851.
26. Reynolds's Newspaper, 26 October 1851.
27. *Reynolds's Newspaper*, 10 April 1864.
28. This and the following account is taken from *The Times*, 4 April 1864 onwards.
29. John Morley, *The Life of William Ewart Gladstone*, London, 1908, vol. 1, p. 555.
30. Quoted in Derek Beales, *Gladstone and Garibaldi*, Peter J Jagger (ed.),

Gladstone, London, 1998, pp. 140–1.

31. *Reynolds's Newspaper*, 17 April 1864.
32. Quoted in Jagger, *Gladstone*, pp. 138–9.
33. *Gladstone Diaries*, vol. VI, ed. H C G Matthew, p. 269.
34. *Daily Telegraph*, 24 July 1866.
35. Llewellyn Woodward, *The Age of Reform*, 1962, p. 184.
36. *The Times*, 14 December 1867.
37. *The Times*, 19 September 1867.
38. *The Times*, 24 September 1867.
39. *The Times*, 25 September 1867.
40. *The Times*, 25 November 1867.
41. Robert Kee, *The Bold Fenian Men*, London, 1976, p. 51.
42. 'The Tichborne Romance' by A Barrister At Large (A Steinmedz) , 1872, p. 3. The press quotes are on pp. 219.
43. My main source is Douglas Woodruff, *The Tichborne Claimant, A Victorian Mystery*, London, 1957.
44. *Vanity Fair*, 12 February 1876.
45. *Disraeli's Letters to Lady Bradford and Lady Chesterfield*, vol. 1, 1929, p. 133; for the 'infamous impostor' see Woodruff, Tichborne Claimant, p. 386.
46. Woodruff, *Tichborne Claimant*, p. 284.
47. Ibid., p. 297.
48. The Earl of Oxford and Asquith, *Memories and Reflections*, London, 1928, p. 63.
49. Arabella Kenealy, *Memoirs of Edward Vaughan Kenealy*, London, 1908, p. 287; and *Englishman*, 23 May 1874.
50. See, for example, *Entr'acte*, 31 August 1872.
51. 'The Tichborne Trial and What Became of It', Frank Green and Alfred Lee, 1872.
52. *Era*, 22 June 1873.
53. Ibid., 21 March 1875.
54. *Entr'acte*, 24 April 1875.
55. Ibid., 29 May 1875.
56. 'I'm The Fellow That Tells The Truth', Fred Gilbert, 1884.
57. Bradford A Booth and Ernest Mehew (eds), *The Letters of Robert Louis Stevenson*, vol. 7, London, 1995, p. 254.
58. 'There's a Cry from the East', Frank Halland M Hobson, printed in the programme for the Oxford Music Hall, 20 October 1877.
59. The two reports were published 23 June and 8 July 1876.
60. Robert Blake, *Disraeli*, 1969, p. 600.
61. *Daily News*, 23 June 1876.

62. R T Shannon, *Gladstone and the Bulgarian Agitation*, 1963, p. 110.
63. H C G Matthew, *Gladstone 1875–1898*, 1995, pp. 31–2.
64. Benjamin Disraeli, *Letters to Lady Bradford and Lady Chesterfield*, ed. Marquis of Zetland, 1929, p. 73.
65. *The Times*, 11 September 1876.
66. Roy Jenkins, *Gladstone*, London, 1996, p. 407.
67. Hugh Cunningham, 'Jingoism', in *Victorian Studies*, vol. XIV, no. 1, September 1990, p. 432.
68. *The Times*, 25 February 1878.
69. Hugh Cunningham, 'Jingoism', in *Victorian Studies*, June 1971, p. 449.
70. 'Macdermott's War Song', G W Hunt, 1877.
71. *Entr'acte*, 5 May 1877.
72. J A Hobson, *The Psychology of Jingoism*, 1901.
73. *Era*, 23 September 1893.
74. 'The Lion and the Bear', 'the most popular song of the day', W Johnson, 1878.
75. *Punch*, vol. 74, p. 196.
76. *Referee*, 19 May 1878.
77. *Era*, 8 December 1878.
78. 'I Don't Want to Fight', Henry Pettit and Vincent Davies.
79. Morley, Gladstone, vol. 2, pp. 146–7.
80. *The Times*, 28 November 1879.
81. Ibid., 26 November 1879.
82. Ibid., 28 November 1879.
83. Morley, *Gladstone*, vol. 2, p. 151.
84. Quoted in Eberhard Voigt, *Die Music Hall Songs und das Öffentliche Leben Englands*, Greifswald, 1929, p. 160.
85. *Saturday Review*, 29 November 1879.
86. *The Times*, 29 November 1879.
87. 'There Never Were Such Times', written by John S Baker.
88. *Pall Mall Gazette*, 9 February 1886.
89. The account, including the quotations from other papers, is taken from the *Pall Mall Gazette*, 9 and 10 February 1886.
90. Details are taken from 'Remember Trafalgar Square, Tory Terrorism in 1887', *Pall Mall Gazette* 'Extra' No. 37, and from *The Times*, 14 November 1887.
91. *Reynolds's Newspaper*, 13 and 20 November 1887.
92. 'I Can Tell It By Your Bumps', J P Harrington and George Le Brunn, 1889.
93. R Barry O'Brien, *The Life of Lord Russell of Killowen*, 1902, p. 231.
94. Quoted in O'Brien, *Russell*, p. 241.

95. The account of the Commission is based on F S Lyons, *Charles Stewart Parnell*, chapter 13. The quotation expressing pity for Pigott is on p. 420.

96. Song by F V St Clair, in *Era*, 26 May 1900.

97. *The Times*, 18 May 1900.

98. This and what follows from *The Times*, 19 May 1900.

99. This and what follows from *The Times*, 21 May 1900.

100. Thomas Pinney (ed.), *The Letters of Rudyard Kipling*, vol. 3, Basingstoke and London, 1996, p. 18.

101. *The Times*, 21 May 1900.

102. Thomas Pakenham, *The Boer War*, 1971, p. 417.

3: RELIGION AND MORALITY

1. *The Times*, 21 October 1856.

2. Ibid., 5 July 1848.

3. William Ward, *The Life and Times of Cardinal Wiseman*, London, 1897, vol. 1, p. 543.

4. *The Times*, 14 October 1850.

5. Ibid., 19 October 1850.

6. Ibid., 25 November 1850.

7. Ward, *Wiseman*, pp. 550–1.

8. *Household Narrative*, 29 October to 28 November 1850, p. 248.

9. Ward, *Wiseman*, pp 551–2.

10. *Household Narrative*, 29 October to 28 November 1850, p. 249.

11. Henry Mayhew, *London Labour and the London Poor*, London, 1860, vol. 3, pp. 72–3.

12. Ibid., Henry Mayhew, *London Labour and the London Poor*, London, 1860, vol. 3, pp. 72–3.

13. Ward, *Wiseman*, p 547.

14. Mayhew, *London Labour*, vol. 1, p. 243.

15. *The Times*, 19 June 1884.

16. Quoted in Ernest W Bacon, *Spurgeon, Heir of the Puritans*, 1957, p. 42, and pp. 50–1, where the Sheffield paper is not identified.

17. *Pall Mall Gazette*, 13 July and 28 September 1885.

18. *Morning Advertiser*, in Bacon, Spurgeon, p. 52.

19. *Punch*, vol. xl, p. 146.

20. *The Times*, 20 October 1856.

21. *Reynolds's Newspaper* 26 October 1856.

22. *Charles Spurgeon, The Early Years*, London, 1962, (a revised edition of his autobiography), pp. 432–4.

23. *Reynolds's Newspaper*, 3 January 1858.

24. 'The Great Sensation Song', Frank Hall and Frederic Archer.

25. *The Times*, 19 June 1884.

26. Morley, *Life of Gladstone*, vol. II, p. 104.

27. Bacon, *Spurgeon*, 1967, pp. 76–7.

28. See Walter L Arnstein 'The Murphy Riots: A Victorian Dilemma' in *Victorian Studies*, XIX, September 1975.

29. Except where otherwise stated, the source is *The Times*, which covered the case 4–26 February 1869, with a leader 27 February.

30. *Reynolds's Newspaper*, 7 March 1869.

31. *Daily Telegraph*, 27 February 1869.

32. *The Times*, 27 February 1869.

33. *Tablet*, 6 March 1869.

34. *The Times*, 10 March 1875, quoted in J C Pollock, *Moody without Sankey*, 1963, p. 137.

35. Pollock, *Moody*, p. 138.

36. *Daily News*, 10 March 1875.

37. James Findlay Jr, *Dwight L. Moody, American Evangelist*, 1969, p. 155.

38. Ibid., p. 157.

39. Pollock, *Moody*, 1963, p. 130. Also Michael Holroyd, *Bernard Shaw*, vol. 1, 1990, p. 39.

40. Pollock, *Moody*, p. 138.

41. W R Moody, *The Life of Dwight L Moody*, 1900, p. 208.

42. *The Gladstone Diaries*, ed. Matthew, vol. IX, London, 1986, p. 32.

43. *The Times*, 3 April 1875.

44. Findlay, *Moody*, p. 174.

45. *The Times*, 22 June 1875.

46. Ibid., 23 June 1875.

47. Ibid., 21 June 1875.

48. Ibid., 22 June 1875.

49. Ibid., 23 June 1875.

50. Pollock, Moody, p. 145.

51. Ibid., p. 116.

52. Findlay, *Moody*, pp. 173–5.

53. *Annie Besant: An Autobiography*, London, 1893, p. 228.

54. The Knowlton trial is dealt with in Anne Taylor, *Annie Besant: A Biography*, London, 1992, chapters 9 and 10. Bradlaugh and Besant's Free Thought Publishing Company published a verbatim account of the trial in *The Queen v. Charles Bradlaugh and Annie Besant*, 1877. The quotation from the *Lancet* is from Taylor, p. 118.

55. Taylor, *Annie Besant*, p. 115.

56. Annie Besant claimed that the reports of the meeting were inaccurate, as

shown by the attendance being given as 600 whereas 1148 people had paid for admission. *Reynolds's Newspaper*, which had made its view of the trial clear by heading its reports 'The Persecution of Mr Bradlaugh and Mrs Besant', also quoted the 600 figure.

57. *The Times*, 23 July 1875 and Lord George Hamilton, *Parliamentary Reminiscences and Reflections*, London, 1916, p. 96.
58. Walter L Arnstein, *The Bradlaugh Case*, London, 1965, p. 31.
59. *The Times*, 23 June 1880.
60. *Besant: Autobiography*, pp. 256–7.
61. *The Times*, 4 August 1881, and *Besant: Autobiography*, p. 267–8.
62. *Punch*, vol. 81, p. 172.
63. For example, *Besant: Autobiography*, p. 269.
64. Arnstein, *Bradlaugh*, p. 157.
65. This account relies on Glen Petrie, *A Singular Iniquity – The Campaigns of Josephine Butler*, 1971, and Jane Jordan, *Josephine Butler*, London, 2001. Jordan, p. 110 for 'worse than the prostitutes'.
66. *Pall Mall Gazette*, 25 May 1870.
67. Petrie, *Singular Iniquity*, p. 117.
68. Ibid., p. 106.
69. *Saturday Review*, 17 August 1872.
70. Petrie, *Singular Iniquity*, pp. 16–7.
71. Ibid., p. 154.
72. Frederic Whyte, *The Life of W T Stead*, London, 1925, vol. I, p. 161. Whyte relies heavily on Stead's papers.
73. *Pall Mall Gazette*, 4 July 1885.
74. Ibid., 6 and 8 July 1885.
75. Ibid., 6 July 1885.
76. The four articles of 'The Maiden Tribute' were published separately with minor alterations. Unless otherwise stated, quotations are from this separate publication.
77. *Pall Mall Gazette*, 8 July 1885.
78. Ibid., 9 July 1885.
79. Quoted in *Pall Mall Gazette*, 17 July 1885.
80. Ibid., 9 July 1885.
81. Quoted in *Pall Mall Gazette*, 9 November 1885.
82. Published as a *Pall Mall Gazette* Special, with the subheading 'Tory Terrorism in 1887'.
83. Pamela J Walker, *Pulling the Devil's Kingdom Down: The Salvation Army in Victorian Britain*, Berkeley, Los Angeles, London, 2001, p. 104. Walker lays great stress on the sensational aspects of the Salvation Army.
84. Walker, *Devil's Kingdom*, pp. 196–7.

85. Ibid., p. 133.
86. Ibid., p. 140.
87. Ibid., p. 195.
88. Ibid., p. 195.
89. 'It's All Explained in This Way', Harry Nicholls and Hugh Clendon, 1882(?).
90. 'Why Not?', Edward Righton, 1886.
91. 'The One We Loved So Well', Charles Williams, (1885?).
92. Walker, *Devil's Kingdom*, p. 191.
93. Roy Hattersley, *Blood and Fire. William and Catherine Booth and Their Salvation Army*, London, 1999, p. 5.

4: SEX SCANDALS

1. Reported in *Reynolds's Newspaper*, 5 June 1870.
2. *Pall Mall Gazette*, 13 May 1870.
3. During these Bow Street proceedings, the term 'drag' was first heard outside homosexual circles. 'My campish undertakings' was also used.
4. *Pall Mall Gazette*, 16 May 1870.
5. Ibid., 20 May 1870.
6. Ibid., 30 May 1870.
7. *Reynolds's Newspaper*, 29 May 1870.
8. Ibid., 5 June 1870.
9. *The Times*, 7 May 1870; quoted in William A Cohen, *Sex Scandal: The Private Parts of Victorian Fiction*, Durham, NC, 1996, p. 92. The case is the subject of chapter 3.
10. *Daily Telegraph*, 30 May 1870.
11. *Pall Mall Gazette*, 3 June 1870.
12. *Reynolds's Newspaper*, 21 May 1871.
13. Quoted in Cohen, *Sex Scandals*, p. 84.
14. The full trial lasted for six days from 9 May 1871.
15. 'The North American Review', November 1889, quoted in H C G Matthews (ed.) *Gladstone Diaries*, vol. XII, London, 1994, p. 240.
16. Allen Horstman, *Victorian Divorce*, 1985, pp. 85–6.
17. John Coleman, *Charles Reade As I Knew Him*, London, 1904, pp. 263–4.
18. *Vanity Fair*, 23 December 1871.
19. *The Times*, 21 January 1865.
20. Ibid., 17 December 1864.
21. Ibid., 22 December 1864.
22. Ibid., 20 January 1865.

23. See chapter 3 in Dorothy Anderson, *Baker Pasha Misconduct and Mischance*, London, 1999.
24. *The Times*, 3 August 1875.
25. *Daily Telegraph*, 12 December 1861.
26. *The Times*, 3 August 1875.
27. Letter to *Daily Telegraph*, reprinted in *Readiana*, new edition, undated, p. 263.
28. *The Times*, 3 August 1875.
29. 'In the Days of Auld Lang Syne', Tom Bass, 1885.
30. *Referee*, 20 January 1878.
31. *The Career of Colonel Baker*, London, 1875, price 2d.
32. *Pall Mall Gazette*, 8 August 1885.
33. Ibid., 13 February 1886.
34. Ibid.
35. Ibid., 16 February 1886.
36. Ibid, 22 February 1886.
37. Ibid., 22 February 1886.
38. Anon., *A Complete History of the Crawford Divorce Case (Illustrated)*, London, 1886, price 1d, pp. 5–6.
39. 'Charlie Dilke', Fred Gilbert, London, 1886.
40. Jasper Ridley, *Lord Palmerston*, London, 1970, p. 532.
41. *Pall Mall Gazette*, 21 December 1886; quoted in Raymond L Schults, *Crusader in Babylon. W T Stead and The Pall Mall Gazette*, Lincoln, Nebraska, 1972, p. 200.
42. 'That is What the Country Wants to Know', F V St Clair and Elsie Phillips, 1887.
43. The quotations from the *Pall Mall Gazette* of 2, 3 and 14 December 1886 are taken from Schults, *Crusader in Babylon*, pp. 198–9.
44. Details of the case are taken from G H Fleming, *Victorian 'Sex Goddess', Lady Colin Campbell*, London, 1989.
45. 'That's What the Country Wants to Know', F V St Clair and Elsie Phillis, 1887.
46. *Reynolds's Newspaper*, 7 July 1878.
47. Ibid., 5 December 1886.
48. Fleming, *Victorian 'Sex Goddess'*, pp. 1–2.
49. *The Times*, 17 November 1890.
50. 'Now What Will Become of Poor Old Ireland or Charlie Parlie', Arthur West, 1890.
51. *The Times*, 18 November 1890.
52. F S L Lyons, *Charles Stewart Parnell*, London, 1977, pp. 486 and 487.
53. Frank Callanan, *T M Healy*, Cork, 1996, p. 90.

54. H Montgomery Hyde, *The Other Love*, London, 1970, p. 132.

55. *North London Press*, 28 September 1889.

56. Ibid.

57. Lewis Chester, David Leitch and Colin Simpson, *The Cleveland Street Affair*, London, 1977, p. 95.

58. Ibid.

59. Quoted in H. Montgomery Hyde, *The Cleveland Street Scandal*, London, 1976, p. 160.

60. Ibid., pp. 160–1.

61. Ibid., p. 217.

62. The debate from *The Times*, 1 March 1890.

63. Andrew Roberts, *Salisbury, Victorian Titan*, London, 1999, pp. 544–6.

64. *North London Press*, 16 November 1889, quoted in Hyde, *The Cleveland Street Scandal*, p. 106.

65. Theo Aronson, *Prince Eddy and the Homosexual Underworld*, London, 1993, pp. 162–3.

66. Ibid.

67. Notably Chester, Leitch and Simpson, *The Cleveland Street Affair*.

68. Hyde, *The Cleveland Street Scandal*, p. 240.

69. Biographies where these facts can be found include Hesketh Pearson, *The Life of Oscar Wilde*, 1946, and Richard Ellmann, *Oscar Wilde*, London, 1987.

70. *Illustrated Police Budget*, 13 April 1895.

71. *Daily Telegraph*, 27 May 1895.

72. Hyde, *The Other Love*, London, 1970, p. 150.

73. *Illustrated Police Budget*, 27 April 1895.

74. Hesketh Pearson, *Oscar Wilde*, p. 283–4.

75. *The Times*, 4 April 1895.

76. The quotations are taken from the penny account, 'Reprinted verbatim from *Reynolds's Newspaper*'.

77. *Illustrated Police Budget*, supplement, 13 April 1895.

78. *Illustrated Police Budget*, 20 April 1895.

79. Ibid., 27 April 1895.

5: MURDER

1. Henry Mayhew, *London Labour and The London Poor*, vol. 1, London, 1864, p. 237.

2. The Lord William Russell murder is one of the Yseult Bridges, *Two Studies in Crime*, 1959. Many details are taken from there.

3. *Sunday Times*, 10 May 1840.

4. Ibid., 12 June 1840.

5. *Benjamin Disraeli Letters*, M G Wiebe, J B Conaches, John Matthews and Mary S Millar (eds), vol. III, Toronto, 1987, p. 279.

6. *Daily News*, 28 February 1846.

7. Serjeant Ballantine, *Some Experiences of a Barrister's Life*, London, 1882, p. 73.

8. See for example Robert L Patten, *George Cruikshank's Life, Times and Art*, London, 1996, vol. 2, p. 127.

9. W M Thackeray, 'Going to See A Man Hanged' in *Fraser's Magazine*, August 1840.

10. *Daily News*, 28 February 1846.

11. *Observer*, 6 March 1843.

12. *Illustrated London News*, 11 March 1843.

13. Ballantine, *Experiences*, p 196.

14. See Albert Borowitz, *The Bermondsey Horror*, London, 1989.

15. Ballantine, *Experiences*, p. 186.

16. *The Times*, 14 November 1849.

17. See Judith Knelman, *Twisting in the Wind*, Toronto, 1998, p. 201–2.

18. *The Times*, 29 October 1849.

19. Ibid., 14 November 1849.

20. Knelman, *Twisting*, p. 230.

21. *Morning Chronicle*, 14 November 1849.

22. Knelman, *Twisting*, p. 267.

23. The American title of Borowitz's *The Bermondsey Horror*, is *The Woman Who Murdered Black Satin*, but his chapter 18 shows that the rumour was untrue.

24. Knelman, *Twisting*, p. 192.

25. *The Times*, 14 November 1849, and in Graham Storey and K J Fielding (eds), *The Pilgrim Edition of the Letters of Charles Dickens*, vol. 5, Oxford, 1981, pp. 644–5.

26. *Household Words*, 27 April 1850, 27 July 1850, 14 June 1856.

27. 'Lying Awake', in *Household Words*, 30 October 1852.

28. Wilkie Collins, *The Woman in White*, Second Epoch, Chapter 2; M E Braddon, *Lady Audley's Secret*, chapter 18.

29. Borowitz, *Bermondsey Horror*, pp. 12–13.
30. Henry Mayhew, *London Labour and the London Poor*, vol. I, London, 1864, p. 308.
31. John Ashton, *Modern Street Ballads*, London, 1888, reprint 1968, pp. 368–70.
32. *Punch*, vol. XVI, no. 393, p. 33.
33. Ibid., vol. XVII, no. 418, p. 14.
34. Ibid., vol. XVII, no. 438, p. 213.
35. *The Annual Register for 1849*, pp. 377–8.
36. The Rush case is summarized in Richard D Altick, *Victorian Studies in Scarlet*, 1972, pp. 135–45.
37. See Graham Storey and K J Fielding (eds), *The Pilgrim Edition of the Letters of Charles Dickens*, Oxford, 1981, vol. 5, pp. 473–4.
38. *Punch*, vol. XVI, no. 406 p. 155.
39. Ibid., vol. XVII, no. 438, p. 214.
40. Mayhew, *London Labour*, vol. I, p. 249.
41. Ibid., p. 236.
42. Ibid., p. 302–3.
43. Ibid., p. 308.
44. *Household Words*, 9 November 1850, pp. 155–7.
45. Ibid., 13 December 1851, pp. 277–81.
46. The Evanion Collection in the British Library, item 1354.
47. *The Times*, 8 August 1889.
48. Richard D Altick, *Victorian Studies in Scarlet*, London, 1970, p. 152.
49. George Fletcher, *The Life and Career of Dr William Palmer of Rugeley*, London, 1925, p. 18.
50. Anon., 'Illustrated Life and Career of William Palmer of Rugeley', 1856, p. 9.
51. The facts of the Palmer case are in Fletcher, *William Palmer*, and George H Knott (ed.), *The Trial of William Palmer*, London, 1912. See also Altick, *Victorian Studies in Scarlet*, pp. 146–60.
52. *The Times*, 28 May 1856.
53. *Illustrated London News*, 17 May 1856.
54. Ibid., 21 June 1856.
55. H C G Matthew (ed.), *Gladstone Diaries*, vol. V, Oxford, 1978, p. 136.
56. *Household Words*, 14 June 1856, pp. 505–7.
57. Ashton, *Modern Street Ballads*, p. 372.
58. *The Times*, 16 June 1856.
59. The story is told in F Tennyson Jesse (ed.) *The Trial of Madeleine Smith*, Edinburgh 1927. See also Altick, *Victorian Studies in Scarlet*, pp. 175–90.
60. *Glasgow Herald*, quoted in The Times, 5 August 1857.

61. *North British Mail* and *Ayrshire Express*, quoted in *Reynolds's Newspaper*, 5 July 1857.

62. *Reynolds's Newspaper*, 5 July 1857.

63. *The Times*, 1 July 1857.

64. *Ayrshire Express*, quoted in *Reynolds's Newspaper*, 12 July 1857.

65. *The Times*, 2 July 1857.

66. Letters not read out in court have been published since, for example in Peter Hunt, *the Madeleine Smith Affair*, London, 1950, but I have selected only from letters given in evidence and published by the daily press on 6 July 1857 and by the weeklies on the 12 July 1857.

67. *Caledonian Mercury*, quoted in *Reynolds's Newspaper*, 5 July 1857.

68. *North British Mail*, quoted in *Reynolds's Newspaper*, 5 July 1857.

69. Quoted in Altick, *Victorian Studies in Scarlet*, p. 188.

70. Ibid., p. 189.

71. *Illustrated London News*, 5 August 1876.

72. The details are from Yseult Bridges, *How Charles Bravo Died*, London, 1956, and Jane Ruddick, *Death at the Priory*, London, 2001.

73. Quoted in Yseult Bridges, *How Charles Bravo Died*, London, 1957, p. 239.

74. *Illustrated London News*, 5 August 1876.

75. Bridges, *Bravo*, p. 248.

76. *Medical Times and Gazette*, 19 August 1876.

77. See Bridges, *How Charles Bravo Died*, Part IV, 'The Solution', pp. 287–305.

78. Ruddick, *Death at The Priory*, pp. 99–177.

79. Mary Hartman, *Victorian Murderesses*, London, 1976.

80. Quoted in ibid., p. 216.

81. *Reynolds's Newspaper*, 11 August 1889.

82. Many details have been taken from Bernard Ryan, *The Poisoned Life of Mrs Maybrick*, London, 1977.

83. *Liverpool Echo*, 3 August 1889

84. *The Times*, 8 August 1889.

85. *Liverpool Echo*, 5 August 1889

86. *The Times*, 8 August 1889.

87. Quoted in Ryan, *Maybrick*, p. 210

88. Quoted in *Reynolds's Newspaper*, 18 August 1889

89. *Reynolds's Newspaper*, 18 August 1889.

90. The main source is *The Times*' report of the trial, 5 February 1879.

91. *Era*, 2 February 1879.

92. Undated catalogue, 'The Grand Historical Galleries Museum and Wax Work, South Bridge Edinburgh', p. 24; author's collection.

93. *Era*, 23 February 1879.
94. I have relied heavily on Stewart P Evans and Keith Skinner (eds), *The Complete Jack the Ripper Source Book*, London, 2000.
95. The complete text of all the Ripper messages is quoted in ibid., chapter 9.
96. Ibid., chapter 30.
97. Ibid., chapter 6.
98. *Blackwood's*, March 1910
99. *Jewish Chronicle*, 4 and 11 March 1910.
100. *Star*, 1 September 1888.
101. T P O'Connor, *Memoirs of an Old Parliamentarian*, London, 1929, vol. 2, p. 257.
102. *New York World*, 18 November 1888.
103. *Referee*, 9 March 1890.

6: THE 'SENSATION NOVEL'

1. Collins, *No Name* Sc. 4, Chpater 13. So many editions of sensation novels exist that chapter references only are given.
2. *Quarterly Review* vol. 113, no. 226, pp. 482–514.
3. From Mrs Oliphant, 'Sensation Novels' in *Blackwood's* Edinburgh Magazine, May 1862, vol. XCI, no. DLIX, pp. 564–84.
4. Sally Mitchell, introduction to *East Lynne*, Rutgers University Press, 1984, p. xii.
5. 'Lucretia or a Heroine of the Nineteenth Century'; quoted in *Spectator*, 8 August 1868, which refutes this view.
6. *Quarterly Review*, vol. 113, no. 226, pp. 505–6.
7. M E Braddon, *The Doctor's Wife*, vol. 1, chapter 2.
8. Graham Storey and K J Fielding (eds), *The Pilgrim Edition of the Letters of Charles Dickens*, vol. 5, Oxford, 1981, pp. 603–4.
9. Robert Lee Wolff, *Sensational Victorian The Life and Fiction of Mary Elizabeth Braddon*, London, 1979, p. 81.
10. G W M Reynolds, *The Mysteries of the Court of London*, First Series, chapter XXVII, p. 92.
11. *The Mysteries of the Court of London*. Postscript.
12. G W M Reynolds, *The Mysteries of London*, Second Series, chapters 175 and 204.
13. Ibid., Second Series, vol. 2, chapter IX.
14. Ibid., chapter XXXVIII.
15. G W M Reynolds, *Rosa Lambert*, chapter XXXV.
16. *Reynolds's Newspaper*, 6 November 1853.

17. Lynda Nead, *Victorian Babylon*, Newhaven and London, 2000, p. 176.

18. Reynolds, *The Mysteries of the Court*, First Series, chapter IX.

19. Ibid., chapter XIX.

20. Surprisingly, the link with Mrs Braddon's bigamy theme of three years later has scarcely been noticed.

21. Reynolds, The Mysteries of the Court, First Series, chapter XXXV.

22. M E Braddon, *Aurora Floyd*, chapter 5.

23. 'Lucretia or a Heroine of the Nineteenth Century' quoted in Robert Lee Wolff, *Sensational Victorian*, pp. 197 and 219.

24. Jane W Stedman, *Gilbert Before Sullivan. Six Comic Plays by W S Gilbert*, London, 1967, p. 131.

25. Kenneth Robinson, *Wilkie Collins: a Biography*, New York and London, 1952, p. 143.

26. Quoted in Norman Page (ed.), *Wilkie Collins: The Critical Heritage*, London, 1974, p. 13.

27. 'Sensation Novels' in *Blackwood's Edinburgh Magazine*, May 1862, vol. XCI, no. DLIX, pp. 564–84.

28. Page, *Wilkie Collins*, 1974, p. 122.

29. Wilkie Collins, *The Moonstone*, First Period, chapter 23.

30. See John Sutherland, *Victorian Fiction – Writers, Publishers, Readers*, London, 1995, p. 32 ff.

31. Page, *Wilkie Collins*, p. 97.

32. Once in chapter 20 and twice in chapter 25.

33. Braddon, *Lady Audley's Secret*, chapter 7.

34. Stedman, *Gilbert Before Sullivan*, p. 132. *Lady Audley* was thought worthy of satire as late as 1871 when Gilbert's playlet *A Sensation Novel* was first produced.

35. Details of Lytton's extraordinary marriage are in Sutherland, *Victorian Fiction*, p. 71 ff.

36. M E Braddon, *Aurora Floyd*, chapter 9.

37. Ibid., chapter 4.

38. *Blackwood's Edinburgh Magazine*, September 1867, vol. CII, no. DCXXIII, pp. 257–80.

39. *The Times*, 18 November 1862.

40. Adeline Sergeant, 'Mrs Henry Wood', in *Women Novelists of Queen Victoria's Reign*, London 1897, p. 176.

41. Charles H Wood, *Memorials of Mrs Henry Wood*, London, 1894, p. 245.

42. Mrs Henry Wood, *East Lynne*, Part Two, chapter 2.

43. Ibid., chapter 10.

44. See note 24.

45. *Lady Audley's Secret*, chapter 35.

46. Elaine Showalter, *A Literature of Their Own*, Princeton, 1977, p. 167.
47. See *Era*, 8 July 1877.
48. Wilkie Collins, *No Name*, chapter 13.
49. 'Sensation Novels' in *Quarterly Review*, vol. 113, no. 226, p. 496.
50. Collins, *No Name*, Between the Scenes I.
51. Wilkie Collins, *Armadale*, Book Four, chapter 14.
52. Ibid., Book Three, chapter 1.
53. John Sutherland, introduction to *Armadale*, London, 1995, p. xvii.
54. *Athenaeum*, 2 June 1866.
55. Quoted in Robinson, *Wilkie Collins: A Biography*, p. 195.
56. Braddon, *Lady Audley's Secret*, chapter 25.
57. Ibid., chapter 30.
58. Braddon, *Aurora Floyd*, chapter 1.
59. Ibid., chapter 2.
60. Wood, *East Lynne*, Part One, chapter 13.
61. Collins, *The Woman in White*, Third Epoch, chapter II.
62. Charles Reade, *Hard Cash*, chapter 36.
63. Ibid., chapter 38.
64. Ibid., chapter 37.
65. Ibid., chapter 38.
66. Ibid., chapter 43.
67. Ibid.
68. Ibid., preface to second edition.
69. K J Fielding (ed.) *The Speeches of Charles Dickens*, London, 1960, p. 235.
70. For Conolly and his relations with the Dickens circle, see Sutherland, *Victorian Fiction*, pp. 71 ff.
71. Charles Reade and Dion Bonacault, *Foul Play*, chapter 48.
72. William Tinsley, *Random Recollections of an Old Publisher*, quoted in Robinson, *Wilkie Collins: A Biography*, p. 216.
73. Sutherland, Introduction to *Armadale*, p. xx.
74. Collins, *The Moonstone*, second period, third narrative, chapter 3.
75. Ibid., first period, chapter 21.
76. *The Pilgrim Edition of the Letters of Charles Dickens*, vol. 9, ed. Graham Storey, et al, Oxford, 1997, pp. 381 and 383.
77. See Elizabeth Rose Gruner, 'Family Secrets: The Moonstone', in Lyn Pykett (ed.), *Wilkie Collins*, 1998.
78. Wilkie Collins, *The Law and the Lady*, chapter 50.
79. Braddon, *The Doctor's Wife*, vol. 3, chapter 2.

7: THE 'SENSATION DRAMA'

1. *The Times*, 13 March 1862 and 11 November 1861.
2. Ibid.
3. Playbill for the Royal Olympic Theatre, 27 September 1852; author's collection.
4. Wayne Burns, *Charles Reade: A Study in Victorian Authorship*, London, 1961, p. 131.
5. Richard D Altick, *The English Common Reader*, 1957, p. 301; Eric Quayle, *The Collectors' Book of Books*, London, 1971, p. 30; and Robert L Patten, *George Cruikshank's Life, Times and Art*, London, 1996, vol. 2, p. 322.
6. *Era*, 2 January 1853.
7. *Era*, 24 October 1852.
8. *Sunday Times*, 21 November 1852.
9. *Era*, 28 November and 19 December 1852.
10. *Era*, 5 December 1852.
11. *Sunday Times*, 7 November 1852.
12. *Era*, 31 October 1852 and 6 February 1853.
13. Gerald Boardman (ed.), *The Oxford Companion to the American Theatre*, Oxford, 1984, p. 684.
14. *The Times*, 20 March 1863.
15. J P Burnett, *Jo*, 1876, which, as the name indicates, centres on the little crossing sweeper.
16. *The Times*, 8 November 1860.
17. *Era*, 1 March 1863.
18. *Illustrated Sporting and Dramatic News*, 26 May 1877.
19. Surprisingly, the link with Mary Braddon's bigamy theme has scarcely been noticed
20. Henry Morley, *Journal of a London Playgoer*, London, 1866, p. 258.
21. *The Times*, 11 September 1860.
22. Ibid., 24 September 1861.
23. Ibid., 11 November 1861.
24. Ibid., 29 April 1877.
25. George Rowell, *Queen Victoria Goes To the Theatre*, London, 1978, p. 79.
26. *The Times*, 24 June 1862.
27. *The Times*, 14 March 1862.
28. Playbill reproduced in Richard Fawkes, *Dion Boucicault*, p. 129.
29. *The Times*, 12 February 1868.
30. *The Times*, 27 May 1877.

31. *The Times*, 3 August 1864.
32. *Era*, 7 November 1864
33. There is a detailed explanation of how this scene worked in A Nicholas Vardac, *Stage to Screen*, London, 1968, pp. 25 ff.
34. Fawkes, *Boucicault*, 1979, pp. 158 and 170. The complete text of the song is in, David Kruse (ed.), *The Dolmen Press Boucicault*, London, 1964, pp. 1711–12.
35. *The Times*, 17 September 1866.
36. Ibid., 8 October 1866.
37. Ibid., 17 August 1868.
38. Augustin Daly, *Under the Gaslight*, contained a railway rescue scene, and Daly successfully sued Boucicault when he staged *After Dark* in America. However, the history of the famous stage effect is complicated. See M Willson Disher, *Melodrama Plots that Thrilled*, London, 1954, pp. 12–17 and Nicholas Daly, 'Blood on the Tracks – Sensation Drama, the Railway and the Dark Face of Modernity', in *Victorian Studies*, vol. 42, no. 1.
39. *The Times*, 14 September 1868.
40. Fawkes, *Boucicault*, p. 176.
41. *Era*, 30 September 1877.
42. Ibid., 7 October 1877.
43. See note 17.
44. See Burns, *Charles Reade*, p. 132.
45. Ibid., p. 170.
46. See Clement Scott, *The Drama of Yesterday and Today*, London, 1899, pp. 273–5; Erroll Sherson, *London's Lost Theatres of the Nineteenth Century*, London, 1925, p. 357 and John Hollingshead, *My Lifetime*, London, 1895, vol. 1, p. 167.
47. *The Times*, 5 October 1865.
48. Morley, *Journal*, p. 380.
49. *The Times*, 1 June 1868.
50. *Era*, 8 April 1877.
51. Ibid., 23 September 1877.
52. *The Times*, 11 December 1865.
53. *Era*, 25 November 1877.
54. *Era*, 8 June 1879; Allan Stuart Jackson, *The Standard Theatre of Victorian England*, 1993, p. 245 ff, Sherson, *Lost Theatres*, pp. 167–8.
55. 'You Can Go Nap on That', T L Clay, Frank Green and Alfred Lee.
56. *Saturday Review*, 1 November 1879.
57. *The Times*, 18 February 1864.
58. Ibid., 27 October 1864.
59. *Era*, 7 October 1877.

60. Jackson, *Standard Theatre*, pp. 260–2.

61. Ibid., p. 263.

62. *Era*, 11 October 1897.

63. Text from the Lord Chamberlain's copy in the British Library.

64. Disher, *Melodrama Plots*, p. 92.

65. Text from the Lord Chamberlain's copy in the British Library.

66. G A Sala, *Living London*, London, 1883, quoted in Michael Booth, *English Melodrama*, 1965, p. 172.

67. *The Times*, 17 September 1894.

68. Ibid., 17 September 1897.

69. *Referee*, 18 September 1898.

70. Text from the Lord Chamberlain's copy in the British Library.

71. *Era*, 20 September 1900, and Booth, *English Melodrama*, p. 175.

8: STARS OF ENTERTAINMENT

1. See *The Life of P T Barnum Showing his Early History as Clerk, Merchant and Editor and his later Career as a Showman, written by Himself*, London, n.d., chapter 10.

2. Ibid., chapter 10.

3. *Era*, 25 February 1844.

4. *Bell's Life in London*, 25 February 1844.

5. *Era*, 25 February 1844.

6. *Bell's Life in London*, 3 March 1844.

7. *Era*, 25 February 1844.

8. Ibid., 25 February 1844.

9. Ibid., 14 April 1844.

10. *Bell's Life in London*, 7 April 1844.

11. *Barnum*, p. 210.

12. *Bell's Life in London*, 16 March 1846.

13. The negotiations with the two theatres are described in Joan Bulman, *Jenny Lind*, London, 1956, chapter 7 and 8.

14. *Era*, 2 May 1847.

15. Ibid., 9 May 1847.

16. *The Times*, 5 May 1847.

17. *Era*, 9 May 1847.

18. Ibid., 16 May 1847.

19. Ibid., 30 May 1847.

20. Ibid., 7 May 1848.

21. Arthur Hedley (ed.), *Selected Correspondence of Fryderyk Chopin*, London, 1962, p. 315.

22. *Era*, 7 May 1848.
23. Cecil Woodham-Smith, *Queen Victoria Her Life and Times 1819–61*, London, 1975, p. 370.
24. J W Robinson (ed.), *Theatrical Street Ballads*, London, 1971, pp. 80–1.
25. *Era*, 7 May 1848.
26. Ibid., 20 June 1847.
27. J C Trewin (ed.), *The Journals of William Charles Macready*, London, 1967, p. 227.
28. Charles Kent, *Charles Dickens as a Reader*, London, 1872, pp. 19–20.
29. Ibid., p. 51.
30. Letter of 16 March 1862, *The Pilgrim Edition of the Letters of Charles Dickens*, vol. 10, ed. Graham Storey, Oxford, 1998, p. 55.
31. Ibid., pp. 7–8.
32. Quoted in Edgar Johnson, *Charles Dickens His Tragedy and His Triumph*, vol. 2, London, 1953, p. 1009.
33. Quoted in K J Fielding (ed.), *The Speeches of Charles Dickens*, London, 1960, p. 412.
34. Kent, *Dickens as a Reader*, p. 269.
35. *Speeches of Charles Dickens*, p. 413.
36. George Dolby, *Charles Dickens As I Knew Him*, London, 1887, p. 450.
37. *Era*, 19 May 1861.
38. Ibid., 26 May 1861.
39. 'The Flying Trapeze', George Leybourne and Alfred Lee.
40. *Era*, 9 June 1861.
41. *All The Year Round*, 4 May 1861.
42. *Era*, 16 June 1861.
43. Ibid., 4 August 1861.
44. Ibid., 21 July 1861.
45. Ibid., 9 June 1861.
46. Ibid., 7 July 1861.
47. Ibid., 17 November 1861.
48. T Edgar Pemberton, *A Memoir of Edward Askew Sothern*, London, 1890, p. 31.
49. Ibid., p. 43.
50. Programme dated 4 November 1867; author's collection.
51. Bernard Falk, *The Naked Lady*, London, 1934, p. 85.
52. Ibid., p. 86.
53. Ibid., pp. 94–5.
54. Ibid., p. 90.
55. David Mayer (ed.), *Henry Irving and The Bells*, London, 1980, p. 101.
56. Ibid., p. 103.

57. Edward Gordon Craig, *Henry Irving*, London, 1930, p. 60.

58. Mayer, *Irving and The Bells*, p. 105.

59. *Era*, 26 November 1871.

60. *Vanity Fair*, 18 March, 1882.

61. Laurence Irving, *Henry Irving: The Actor and His World*, London, 1951, p. 193.

62. *Era*, 1 November 1874.

63. Clement Scott, *The Drama of Yesterday and Today*, London, 1899, vol. 2, p. 62.

64. Margaret Smith (ed.), *The Letters of Charlotte Bronte*, London, vol. 2, p. 717.

65. George Rowell, *Queen Victoria Goes to the Theatre*, London, 1978, p. 43.

66. Mrs Arthur Kennard, *Rachel*, 1885, p. 70.

67. Scott, *Drama*, vol. 2, p. 445.

68. *Vanity Fair*, 25 June 1881.

69. Bernard Shaw, *Dramatic Opinions and Essays*, London, 1909, Volume 2, p. 293.

70. Rupert Hart-Davis (ed.), *The Letters of Oscar Wilde*, p. 695.

71. Arthur Hedley (ed.), *Selected Correspondence of Fryderyk Chopin*, London, 1962, p. 320.

72. Alan Walker, *Franz Liszt*, vol. 3, London, 1997, p. 486.

73. Ibid., p. 484.

74. Ibid., p. 488.

75. Ibid., p. 494.

76. Victor Weybright and Henry Sell, *Buffalo Bill and the Wild West*, London, 1956, p. 150.

77. *Era*, 14 May 1887.

78. *The Times*, 22 June 1887.

79. Weybright and Sell, *Buffalo Bill*, pp. 151–2.

80. W P Jolly, *Jumbo*, London, 1976.

81. 'Why Part With Jumbo (The Pet of the Zoo)?', G H Macdermott and E J Symons.

82. This account is based on *The Times*, 12 November 1889; and A H Saxon, *P T Barnum: The Legend and the Man*, London, 1989, especially pp. 319–20.

83. Details of 'Nero . . .' from the booklet sold at the show; author's collection.

AFTERWORD

1. Leonard Parsons, *H M Walbrook, A Playgoer's Wanderings*, London, 1926, pp. 53–4. The two murders were committed in September, rather than August as reported by Walbrook.

INDEX